FIRE FORCE

ATSUSHI
OHKUBO

19

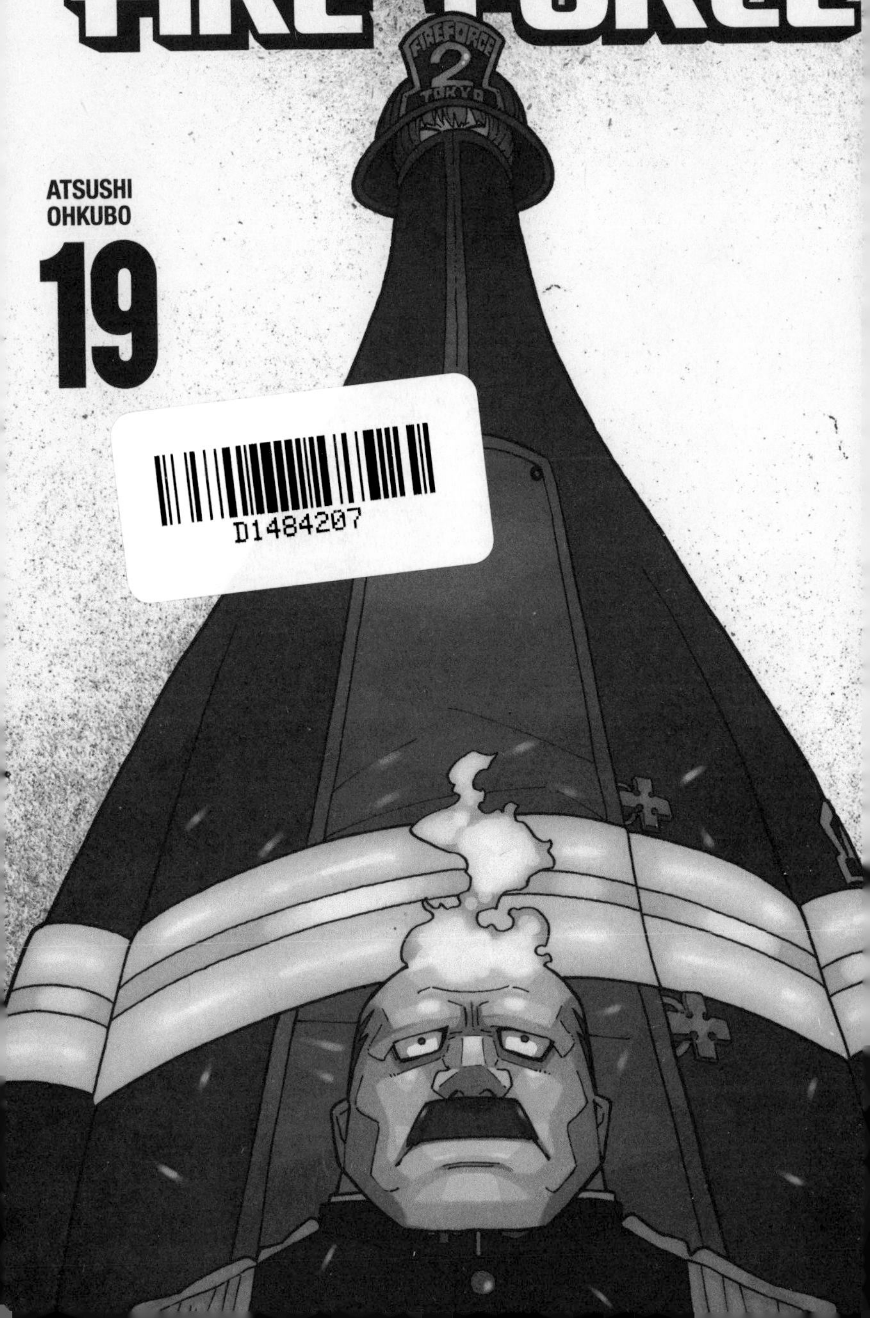
FIREFORCE
2
TOKYO

world
is
ching...

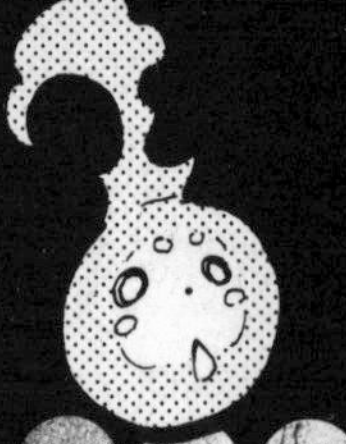

VOL. 19

ATSUSHI OHKUBO

The nether approa

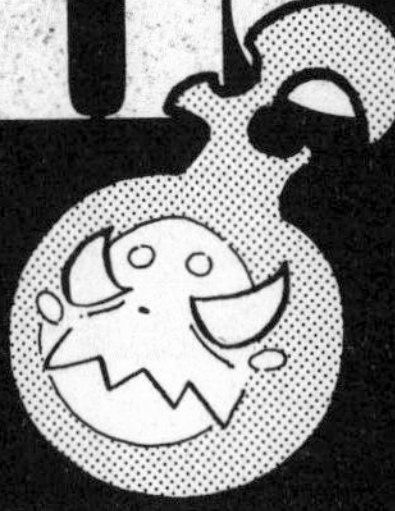

FIRE FORCE

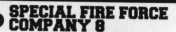

SPECIAL FIRE FORCE COMPANY 8

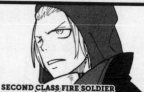

CAPTAIN (NON-POWERED)
AKITARU ŌBI

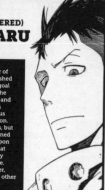

The caring leader of the newly established Company 8. His goal is to investigate the other companies and uncover the truth about spontaneous human combustion. He has no powers, but uses his finely honed muscles as a weapon in a battle style that makes him worthy of the Captain title. A man of character, respected even in other companies.

SECOND CLASS FIRE SOLDIER (THIRD GENERATION PYROKINETIC)
ARTHUR BOYLE

Trained at the academy with Shinra. He follows his own personal code of chivalry as the self-proclaimed Knight King. He may be a blockhead who's bad at mental exercises, but the ladies love him. He creates a fire sword with a blade that can cut through most anything. He's a weirdo who grows stronger the more delusional he gets.

WATCHES OUT FOR

TRUSTS

IDIOT!!

WATCHES OUT FOR

TRUSTS

STRONG BOND

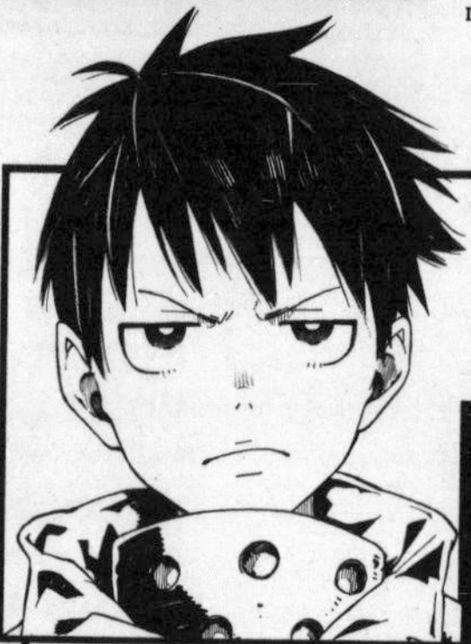

SECOND CLASS FIRE SOLDIER (THIRD GENERATION PYROKINETIC)
SHINRA KUSAKABE

The bizarre smile that shows on his face when he gets nervous has earned him the derisive nickname of "devil," but he dreams of becoming a hero who saves people from spontaneous combustion! His weapon is a fiery kick. He wields a special flame called the Adolla Burst. His long-lost little brother Shō was kidnapped by the Evangelist and is now the commander of the Knights of the Ashen Flame.

A NICE GIRL

LOOKS AWESOME ON THE JOB

A TOUGH BUT WEIRD LADY

HANG IN THERE, ROOKIE!

TERRIFIED

STRICT DISCIPLINARIAN

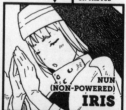

NUN (NON-POWERED)
IRIS

A sister of the Holy Sol Temple, her prayers are an indispensable part of extinguishing Infernals. Personality-wise, she is nothing short of angelic. Her boobs are big. Very big. She demonstrated incredible resilience in facing the Infernal hordes. She is like Company 8's sunflower. Except she's an iris.

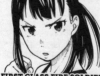

FIRST CLASS FIRE SOLDIER (SECOND GENERATION PYROKINETIC)
MAKI OZE

A former member of the military, she is an excellent fighter who controls fire. She's a cool lady, but is mad about love stories, and her beauty is overshadowed by her "head full of flowers and wedding bells." She's friendly, but goes berserk when anyone comments on her muscles. Under her father General Oze's orders, she was forced to immediately transfer back to the Tokyo Imperial Army as a member of its Secretarial Division.

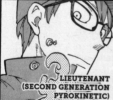

LIEUTENANT (SECOND GENERATION PYROKINETIC)
TAKEHISA HINAWA

A dry, unemotional ex-military man, whose stern discipline is feared among the new recruits. He helped Ōbi to found Company 8. He never allows the soldiers to play with fire. The gun he uses is a cherished memento from his friend who became an Infernal.

THE GIRLS' CLUB

RESPECTS

THE OZE FAMILY

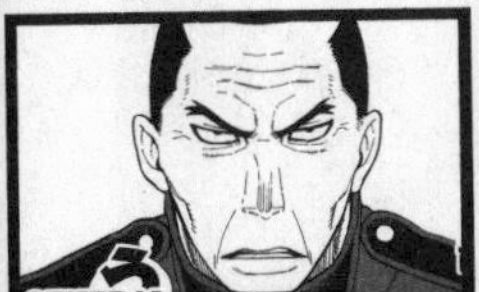

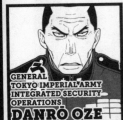

GENERAL
TOKYO IMPERIAL ARMY
INTEGRATED SECURITY
OPERATIONS
DANRŌ OZE

Maki's father. They call him "the Scowling Guardian of the Empire," but he turns to mush when his daughter is around.

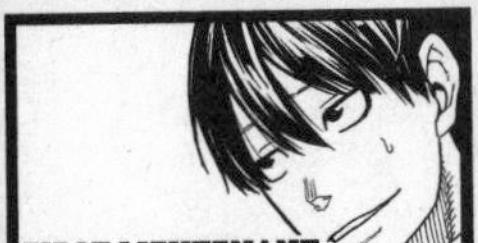

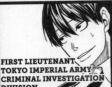

FIRST LIEUTENANT
TOKYO IMPERIAL ARMY
CRIMINAL INVESTIGATION
DIVISION
TAKIGI OZE

Maki's older brother. Talks baby talk when with his girlfriend. Is hostile towards Hinawa, who recruited Maki to the Firce Force.

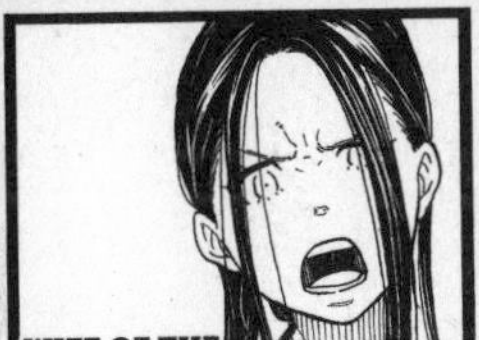

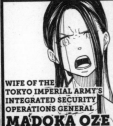

WIFE OF THE
TOKYO IMPERIAL ARMY'S
INTEGRATED SECURITY
OPERATIONS GENERAL
MADOKA OZE

Maki's mother. The strongest member of the family.

FOLLOWERS OF THE EVANGELIST

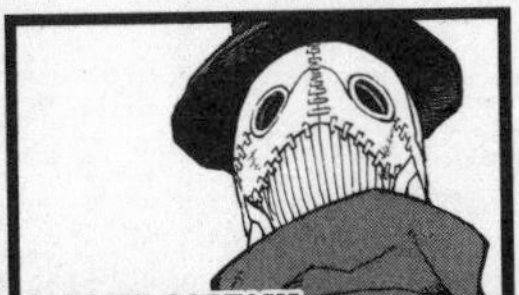

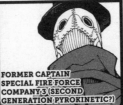

FORMER CAPTAIN
SPECIAL FIRE FORCE
COMPANY 3 (SECOND
GENERATION PYROKINETIC?)
DR. GIOVANNI

A traitor who started working for the Evangelist despite being a captain in the Special Fire Force. Is performing experiments using bugs to create artificial Infernals.

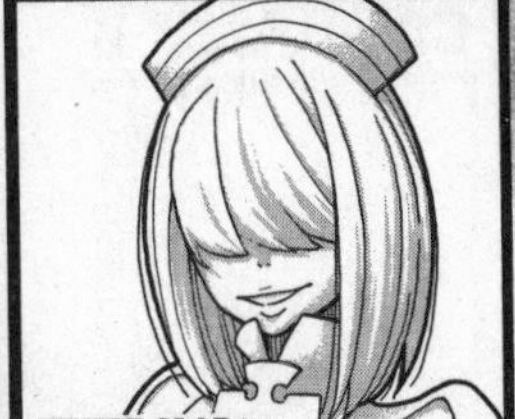

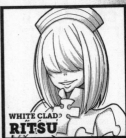

WHITE CLAD
RITSU

Guardian Maid of the Fifth Pillar Inca. Has the power to animate the dead and create the giant Great Fiery Infernal. Commands the Knights of the Purple Haze.

SPECIAL FIRE FORCE COMPANY 2

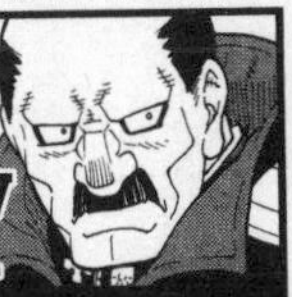

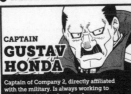

CAPTAIN
GUSTAV HONDA

Captain of Company 2, directly affiliated with the military. Is always working to strengthen his head and neck.

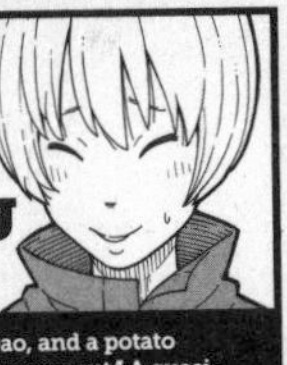

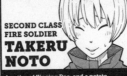

SECOND CLASS
FIRE SOLDIER
TAKERU NOTO

A native of Xinqing Dao, and a potato farmer nicknamed "Juggernaut." A quasi-immortal character who keeps himself alive by bundling up in his turnout gear. Sacrificed himself to protect his beloved Tamaki.

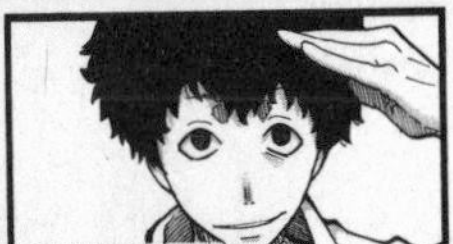

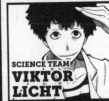

SCIENCE TEAM
VIKTOR LICHT

A suspicious genius deployed from Haijima Industries to fill the vacancy in Company 8's science department. He also analyzes fire scenes. Has confessed to being a Haijima spy.

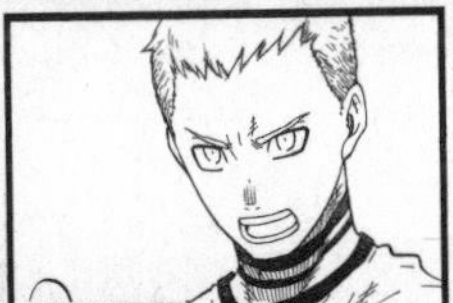

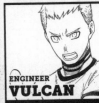

ENGINEER
VULCAN

The greatest engineer of the day, renowned as the God of Fire and the Forge. The weapons he created have increased Company 8's powers immensely.

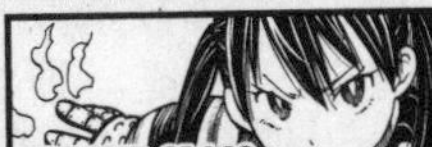

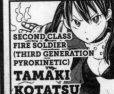

SECOND CLASS
FIRE SOLDIER
(THIRD GENERATION
PYROKINETIC)
TAMAKI KOTATSU

A rookie from Company 1 currently in Company 8's care. Although she has a "Lucky Lecher Lure" condition, she nevertheless has a pure heart. Is surprisingly popular with the guys.

SUMMARY

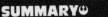

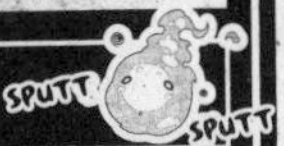
SPUTT
SPUTT

While investigating reports of a strange smell in the Nether, Maki's brother Detective Takigi is badly injured when he discovers an experimental facility belonging to the Evangelist. Danrō, head of the Oze family and general of the Imperial Army, is concerned by the disturbing actions of the Evangelist's cult and so orders the military's Fire Force company, Company 2, to investigate the Nether. They request aid from Company 8. Meanwhile, Maki is ordered to return to the military, where she becomes a part of the Secretarial Division. Company 8 and Company 2 begin their joint investigation of the Nether, but they are met by an ambush of Infernals and Knights of the Purple Haze, placing both companies in danger of annihilation...

FIRE FORCE 19
CONTENTS

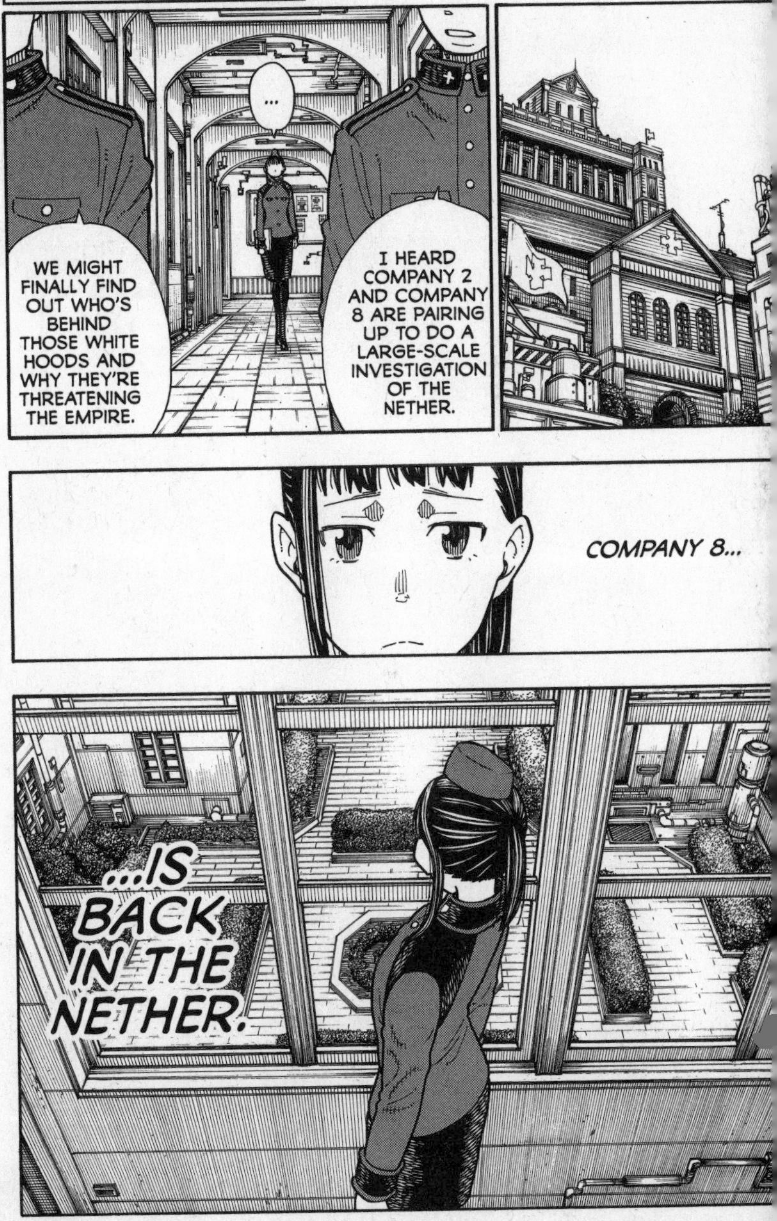
...
I HEARD COMPANY 2 AND COMPANY 8 ARE PAIRING UP TO DO A LARGE-SCALE INVESTIGATION OF THE NETHER.
WE MIGHT FINALLY FIND OUT WHO'S BEHIND THOSE WHITE HOODS AND WHY THEY'RE THREATENING THE EMPIRE.
COMPANY 8...
...IS BACK IN THE NETHER.

HUMAN AND BUG POWERS COMBINED

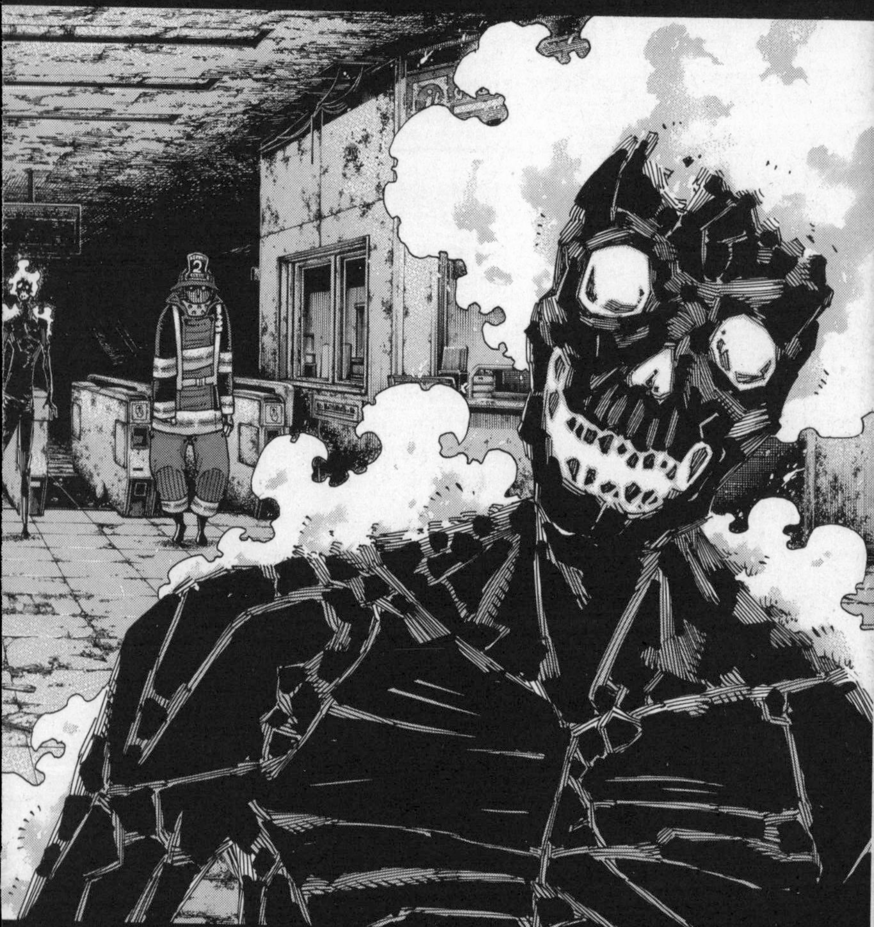

CHAPTER CLX:

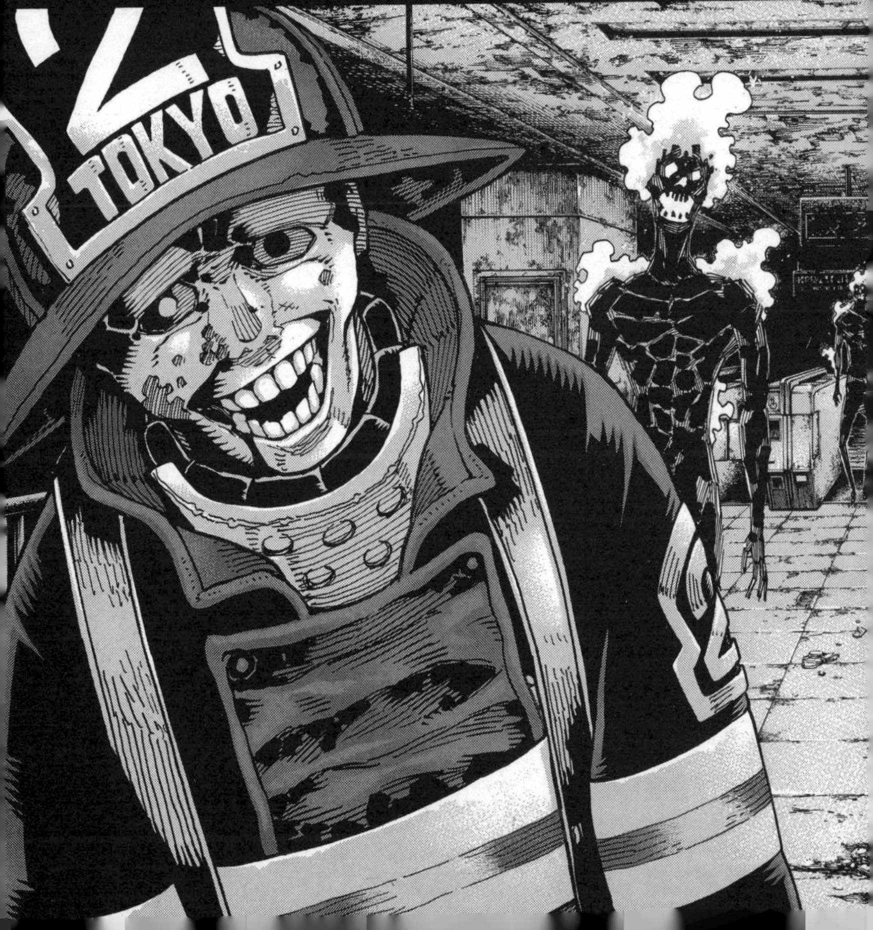
TOKYO

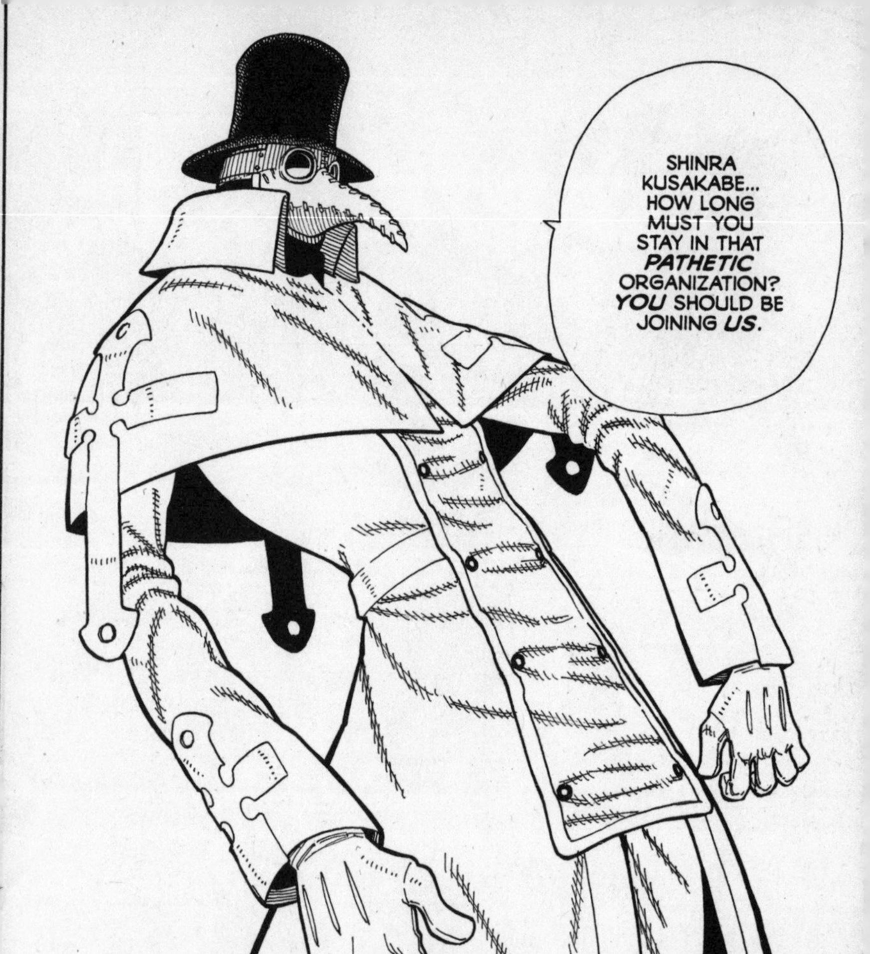
SHINRA KUSAKABE... HOW LONG MUST YOU STAY IN THAT *PATHETIC* ORGANIZATION? *YOU* SHOULD BE JOINING *US*.
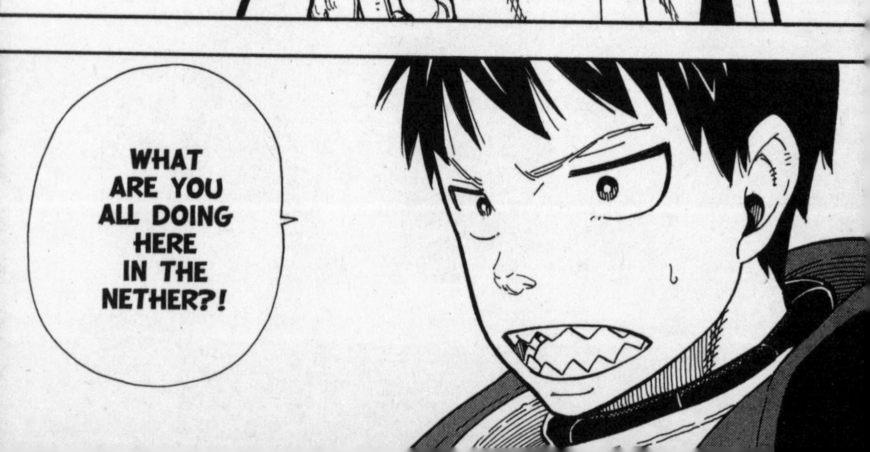
WHAT ARE YOU ALL DOING HERE IN THE NETHER?!

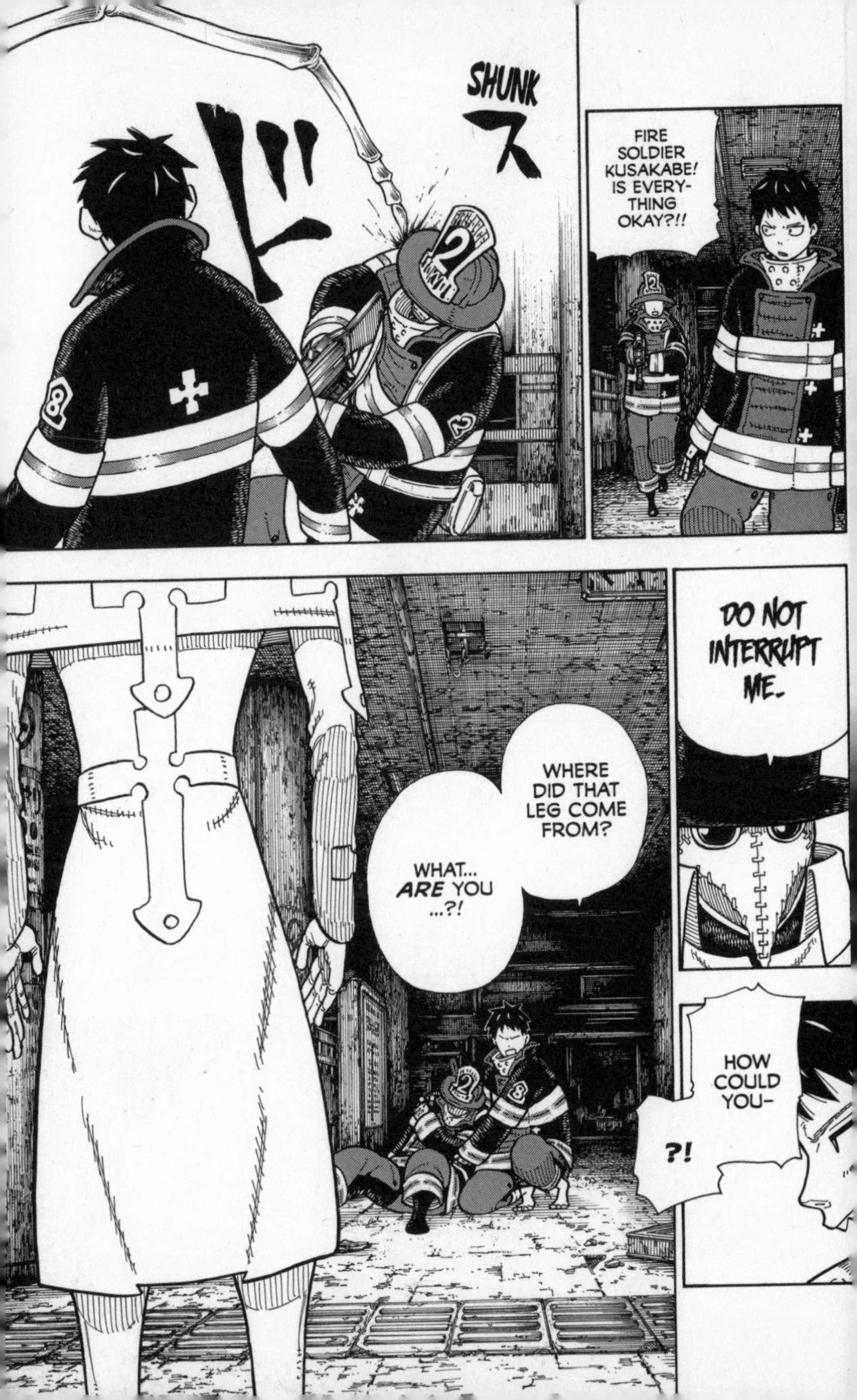
FIRE SOLDIER KUSAKABE! IS EVERY-THING OKAY?!!
SHUNK
ド
ス
DO NOT INTERRUPT ME.
HOW COULD YOU-
?!
WHERE DID THAT LEG COME FROM?
WHAT... **ARE** YOU ...?!

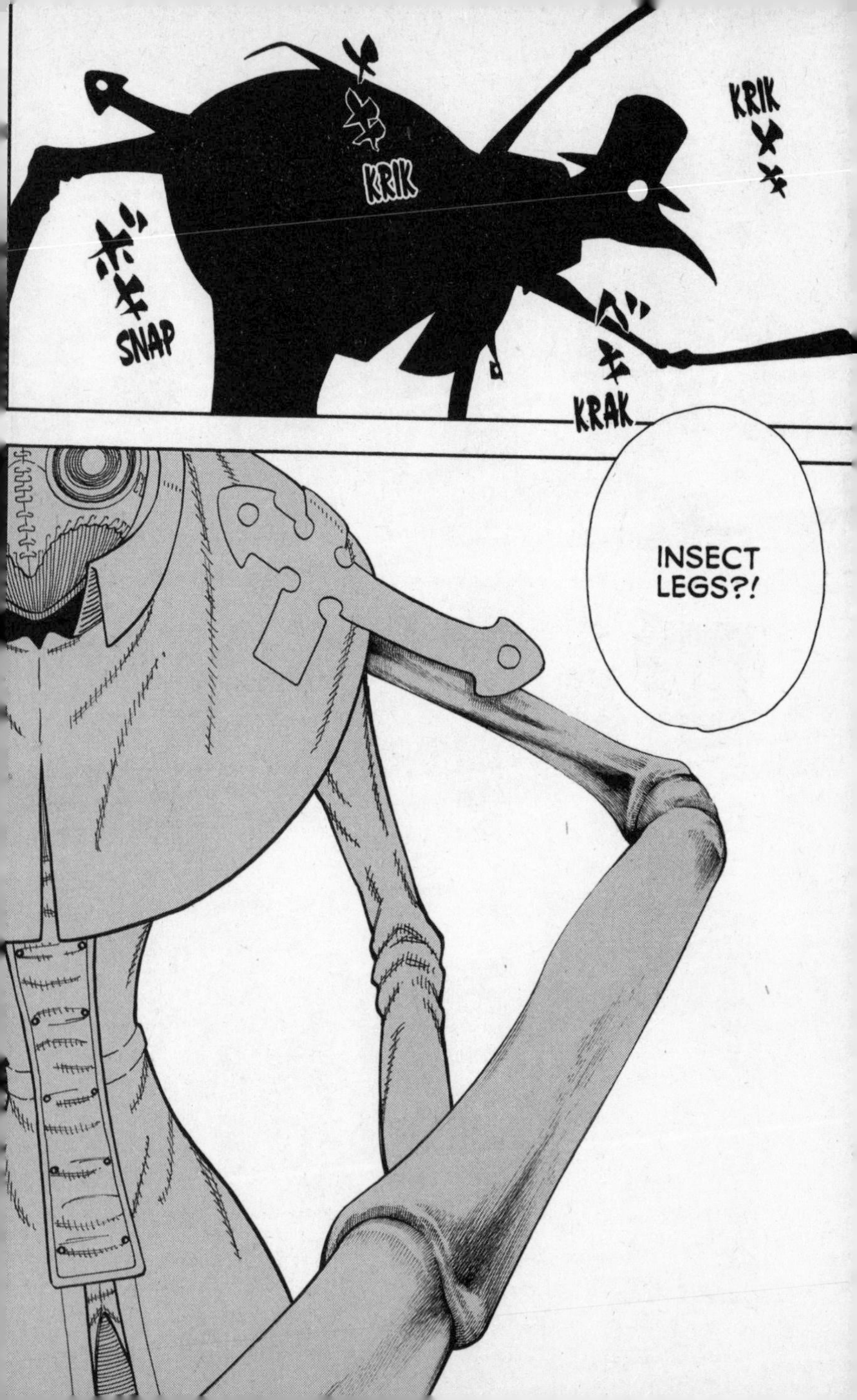
KRIK
KRIK
ベキ
KRAK
ボキ
SNAP
INSECT LEGS?!

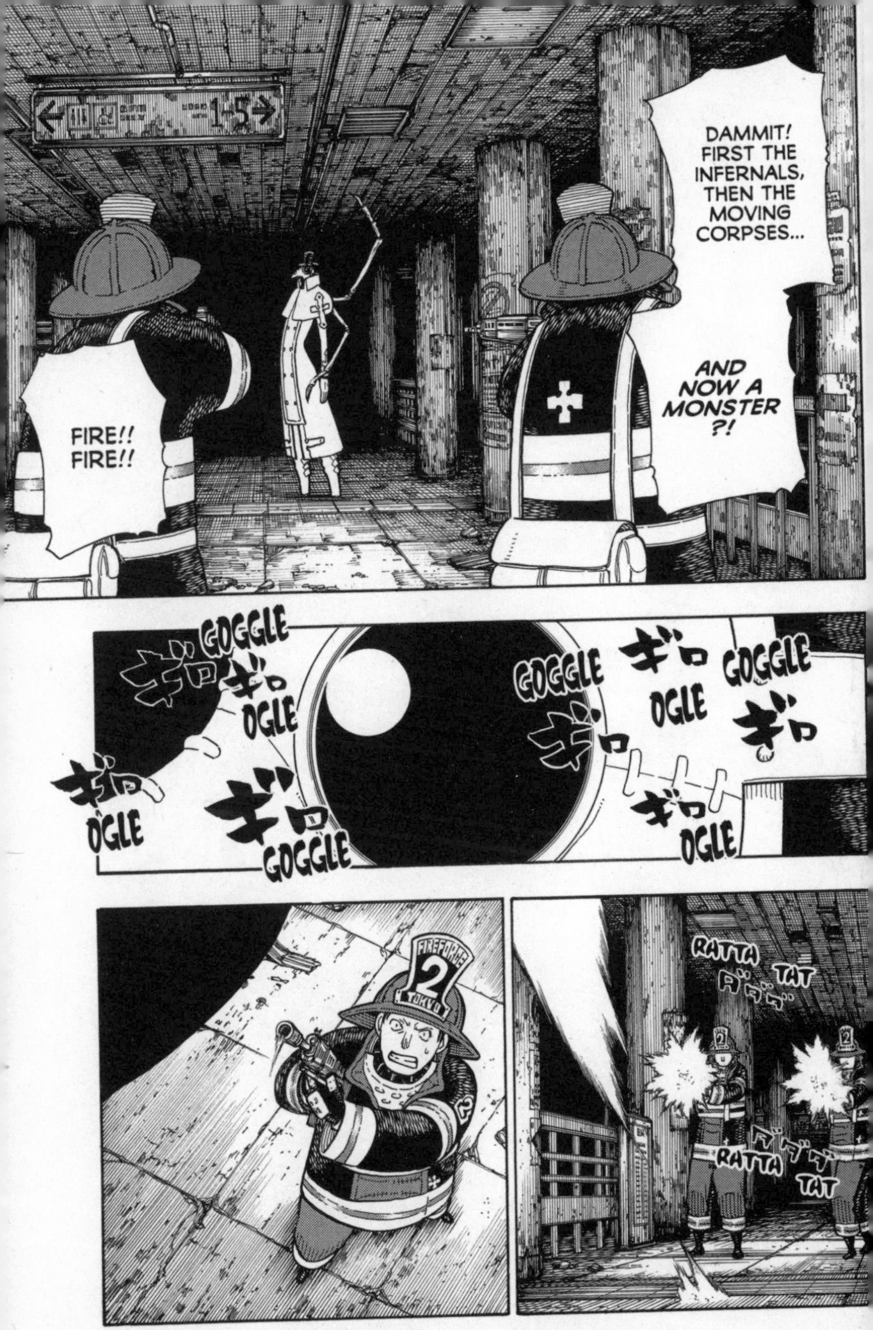
DAMMIT! FIRST THE INFERNALS, THEN THE MOVING CORPSES...
AND NOW A MONSTER?!
FIRE!! FIRE!!
GOGGLE ギロ
ギロ OGLE
GOGGLE ギロ
ギロ OGLE
ギロ OGLE
ギロ GOGGLE
GOGGLE ギロ
ギロ OGLE
ギロ OGLE
RATTA TAT ダダダ
ダダダ RATTA TAT

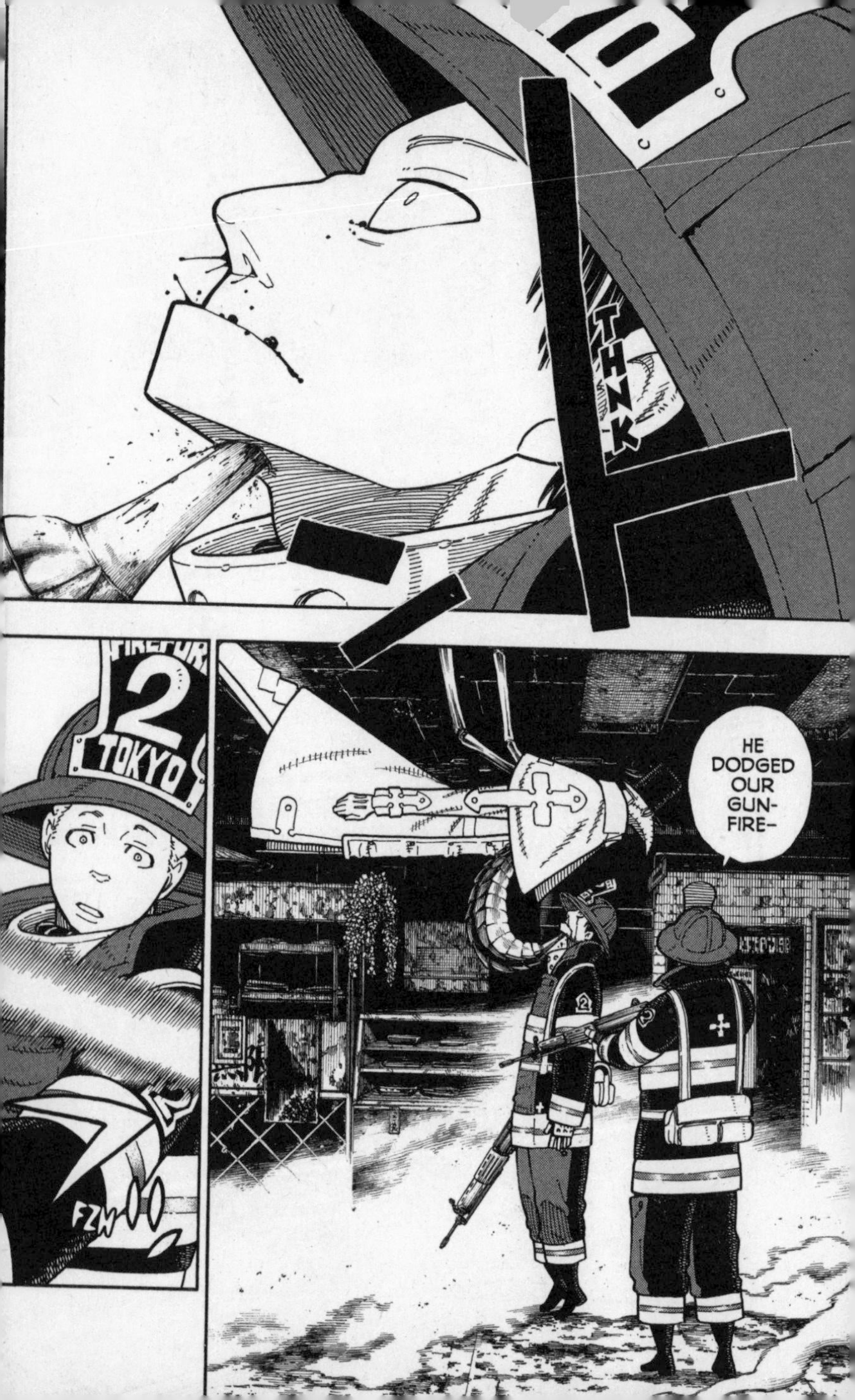
THNK
HE DODGED OUR GUN-FIRE–
2
TOKYO
FZW

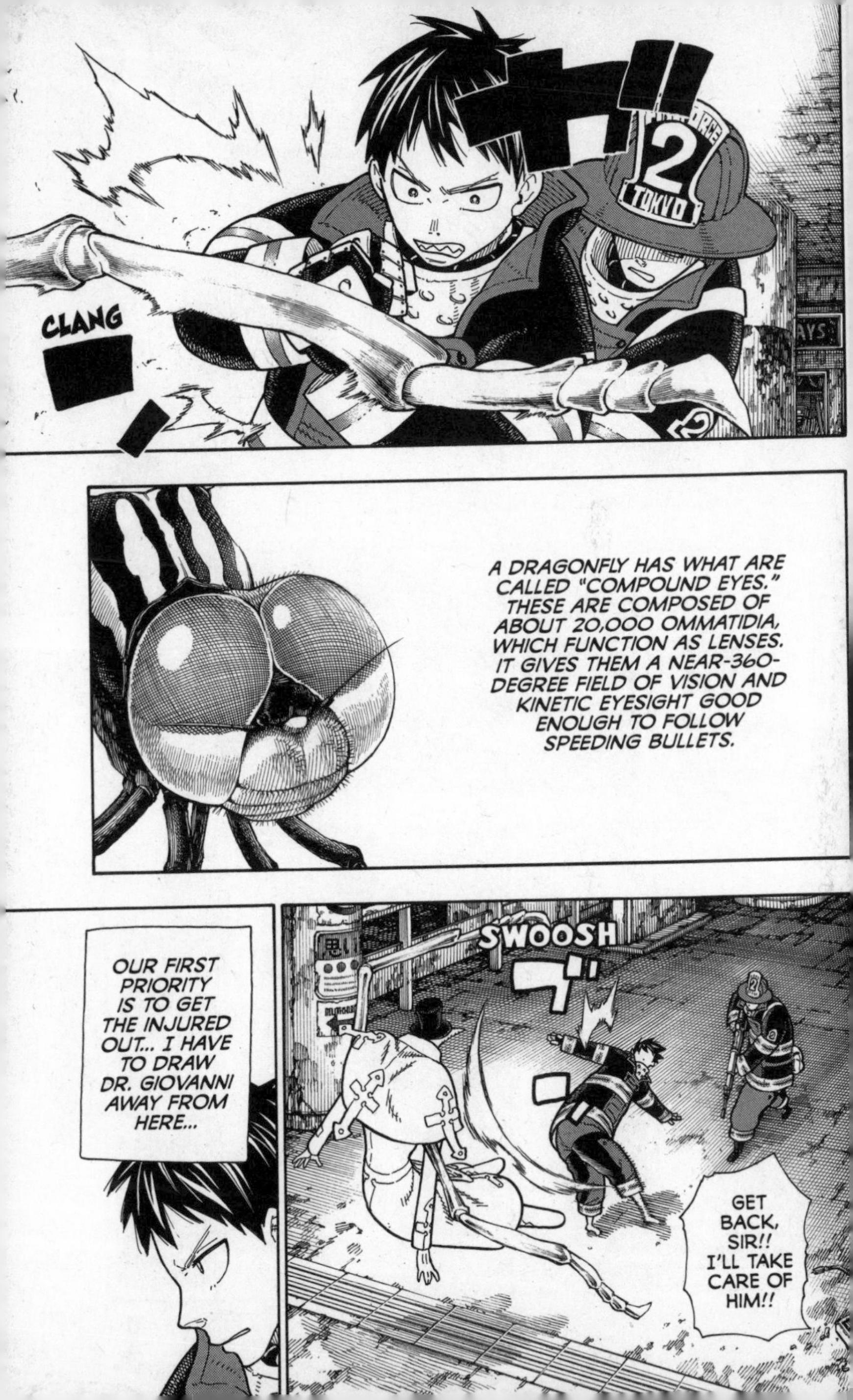
CLANG
A DRAGONFLY HAS WHAT ARE CALLED "COMPOUND EYES." THESE ARE COMPOSED OF ABOUT 20,000 OMMATIDIA, WHICH FUNCTION AS LENSES. IT GIVES THEM A NEAR-360-DEGREE FIELD OF VISION AND KINETIC EYESIGHT GOOD ENOUGH TO FOLLOW SPEEDING BULLETS.
SWOOSH
GET BACK, SIR!! I'LL TAKE CARE OF HIM!!
OUR FIRST PRIORITY IS TO GET THE INJURED OUT... I HAVE TO DRAW DR. GIOVANNI AWAY FROM HERE...

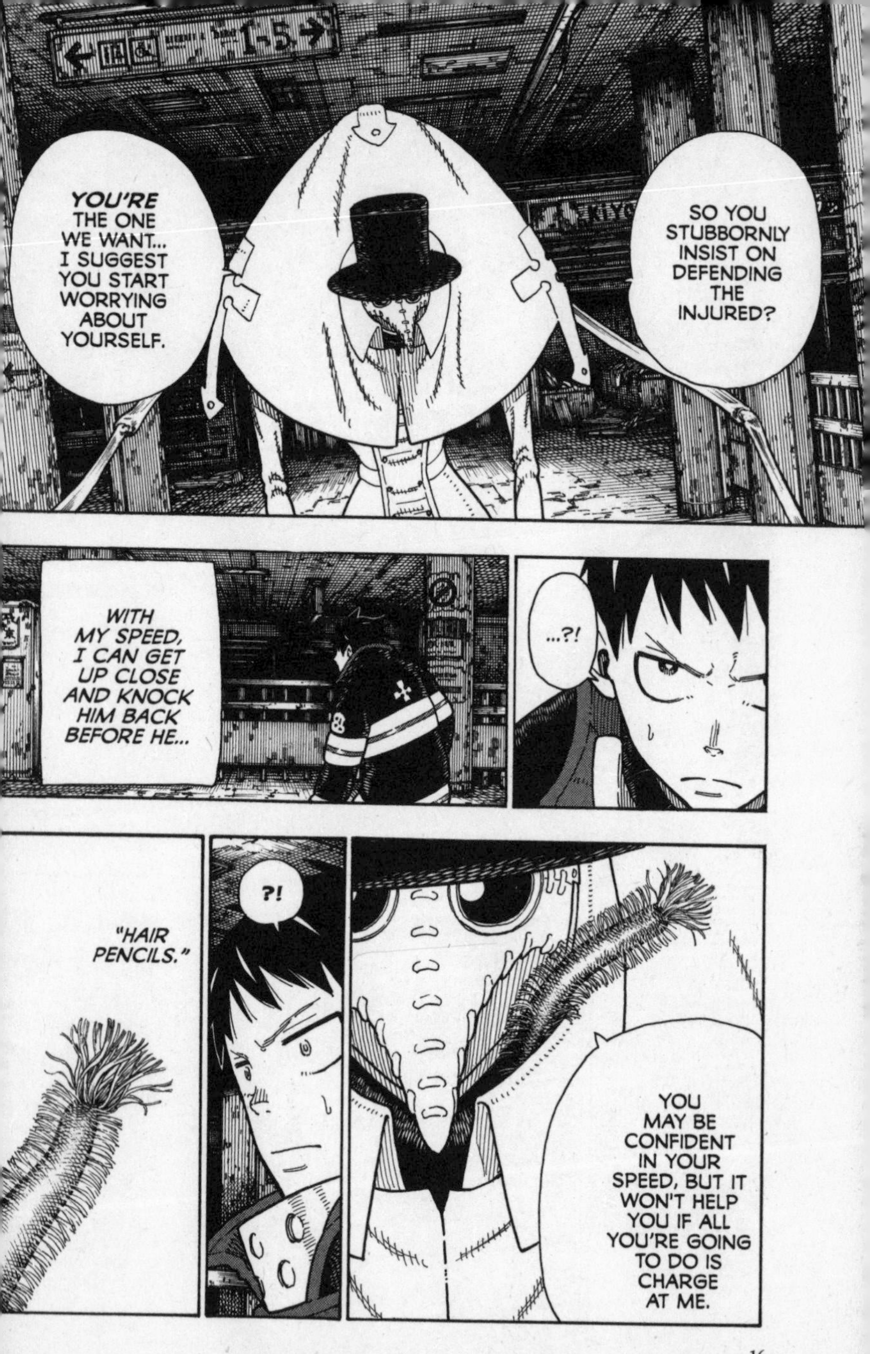
SO YOU STUBBORNLY INSIST ON DEFENDING THE INJURED?
YOU'RE THE ONE WE WANT... I SUGGEST YOU START WORRYING ABOUT YOURSELF.
...?!
WITH MY SPEED, I CAN GET UP CLOSE AND KNOCK HIM BACK BEFORE HE...
YOU MAY BE CONFIDENT IN YOUR SPEED, BUT IT WON'T HELP YOU IF ALL YOU'RE GOING TO DO IS CHARGE AT ME.
?!
"HAIR PENCILS."

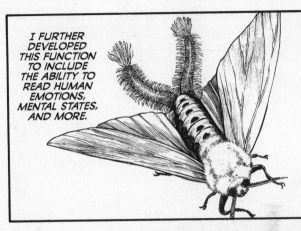

PHEROMONE-REGULATING STRUCTURES FOUND IN MALE MOTHS. THESE RELEASE AND DETECT PHEROMONES.
I FURTHER DEVELOPED THIS FUNCTION TO INCLUDE THE ABILITY TO READ HUMAN EMOTIONS, MENTAL STATES, AND MORE.
I *KNOW* EVERYTHING ABOUT YOU. LET'S JUST SAY...I PUT A "BUG" IN MY EAR.
WHAT THE...
BUGS ...?
WHY DO YOU KEEP GOING ON ABOUT *BUGS?*
SURELY YOU'VE HEARD THE THEORY THAT INSECTS ARE EXTRATERRESTRIAL LIFEFORMS. THEY FLEW TO EARTH IN EGGS ATTACHED TO METEORITES.
AS THE THEORY SUGGESTS... *BUGS ARE NOT OF THIS WORLD.*

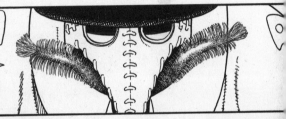

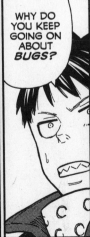

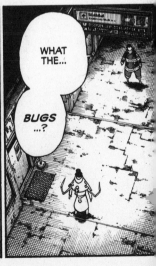

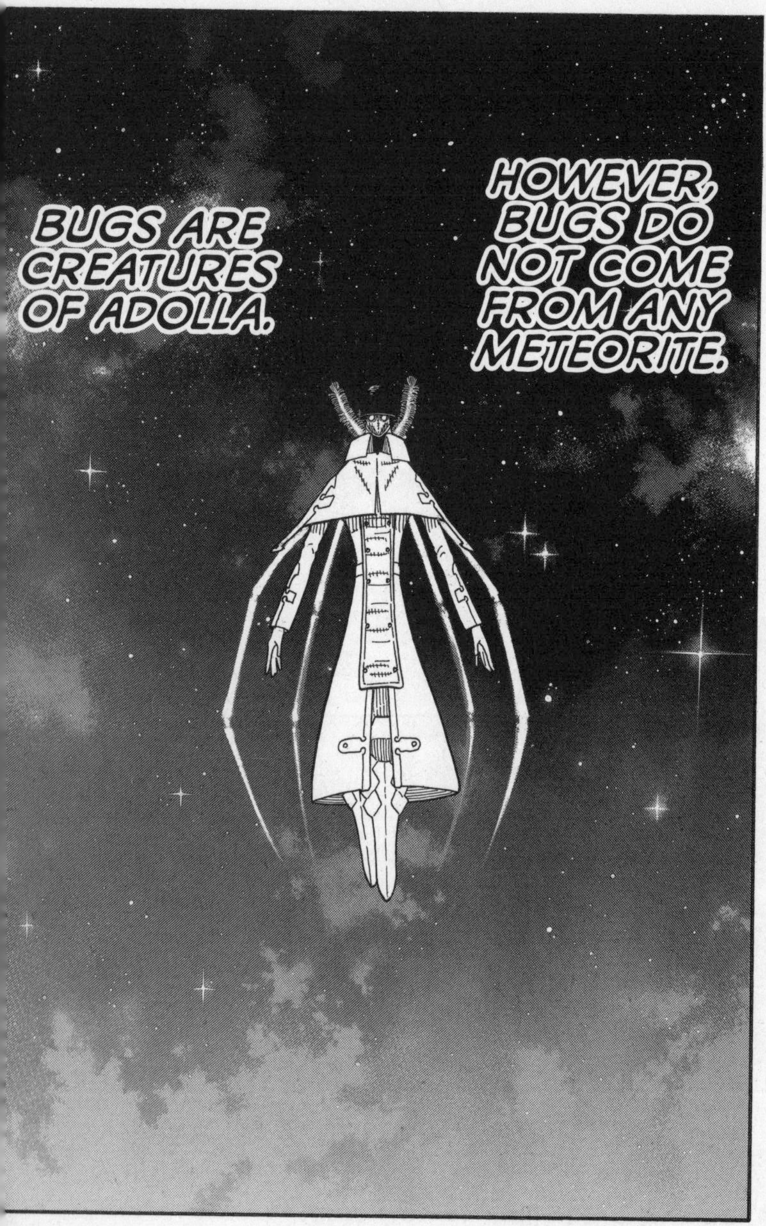
HOWEVER, BUGS DO NOT COME FROM ANY METEORITE.
BUGS ARE CREATURES OF ADOLLA.

I HAVE BEEN TESTING MY HYPOTHESIS THAT FUSING A HUMAN BEING WITH THE BUGS OF ADOLLA WILL BRING SAID HUMAN CLOSER TO ADOLLA.

AND THOSE EXTRA LEGS... DON'T TELL ME YOU'VE BEEN USING *YOURSELF* AS A GUINEA PIG TO TEST HUMAN COMPATIBILITY WITH BUGS AND ADOLLA!

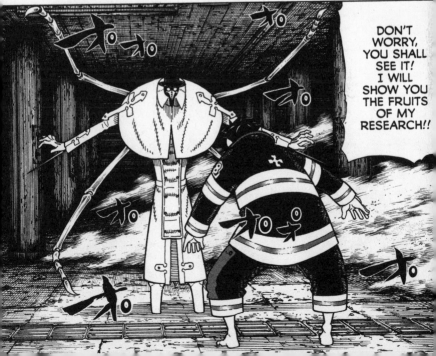

DON'T WORRY, YOU SHALL SEE IT! I WILL SHOW YOU THE FRUITS OF MY RESEARCH!!

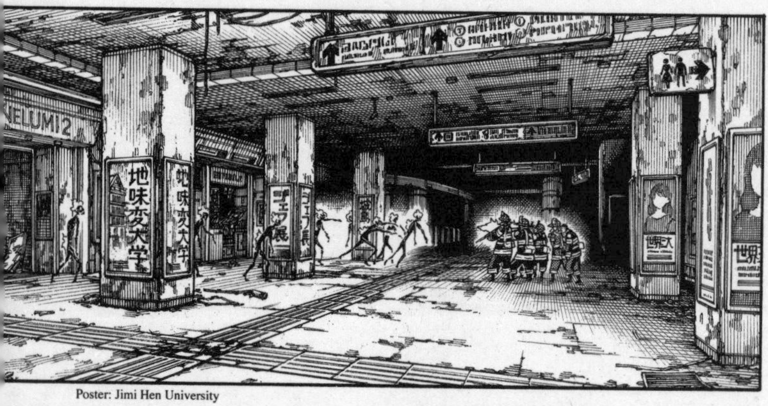
地味変大学

Poster: Jimi Hen University

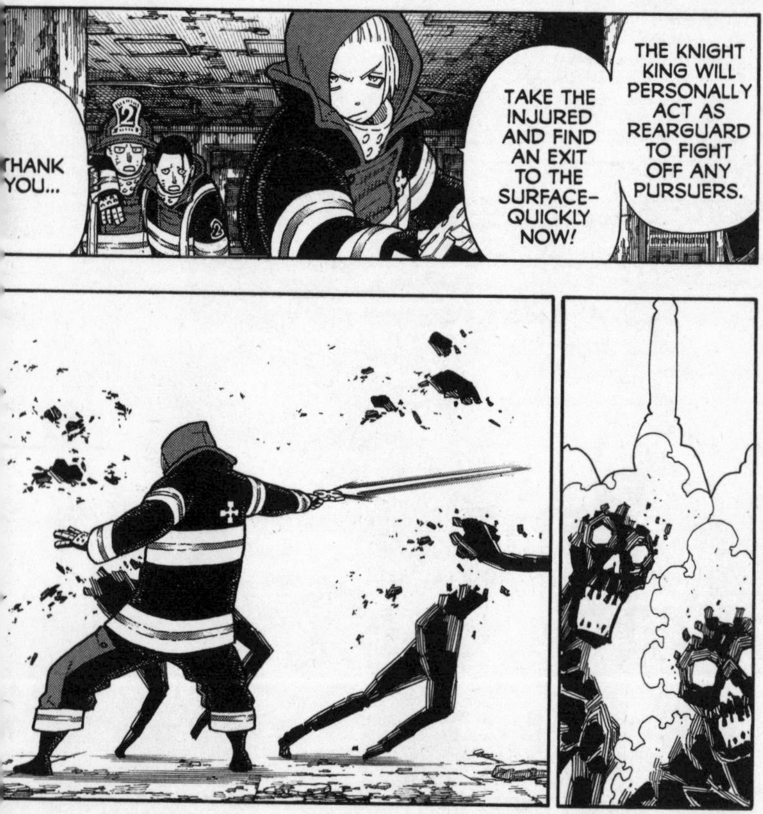
THE KNIGHT KING WILL PERSONALLY ACT AS REARGUARD TO FIGHT OFF ANY PURSUERS.
TAKE THE INJURED AND FIND AN EXIT TO THE SURFACE-QUICKLY NOW!
THANK YOU...

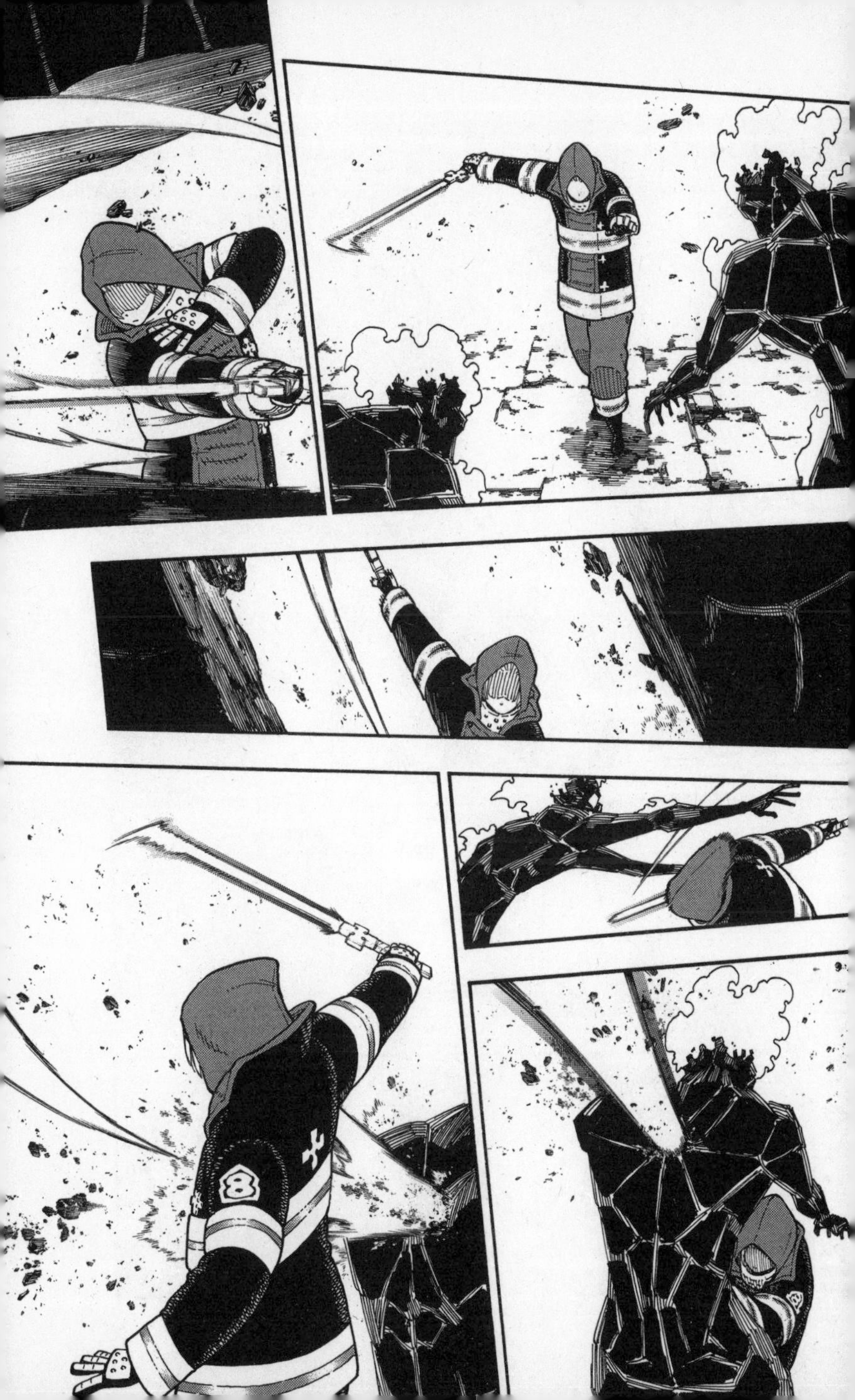

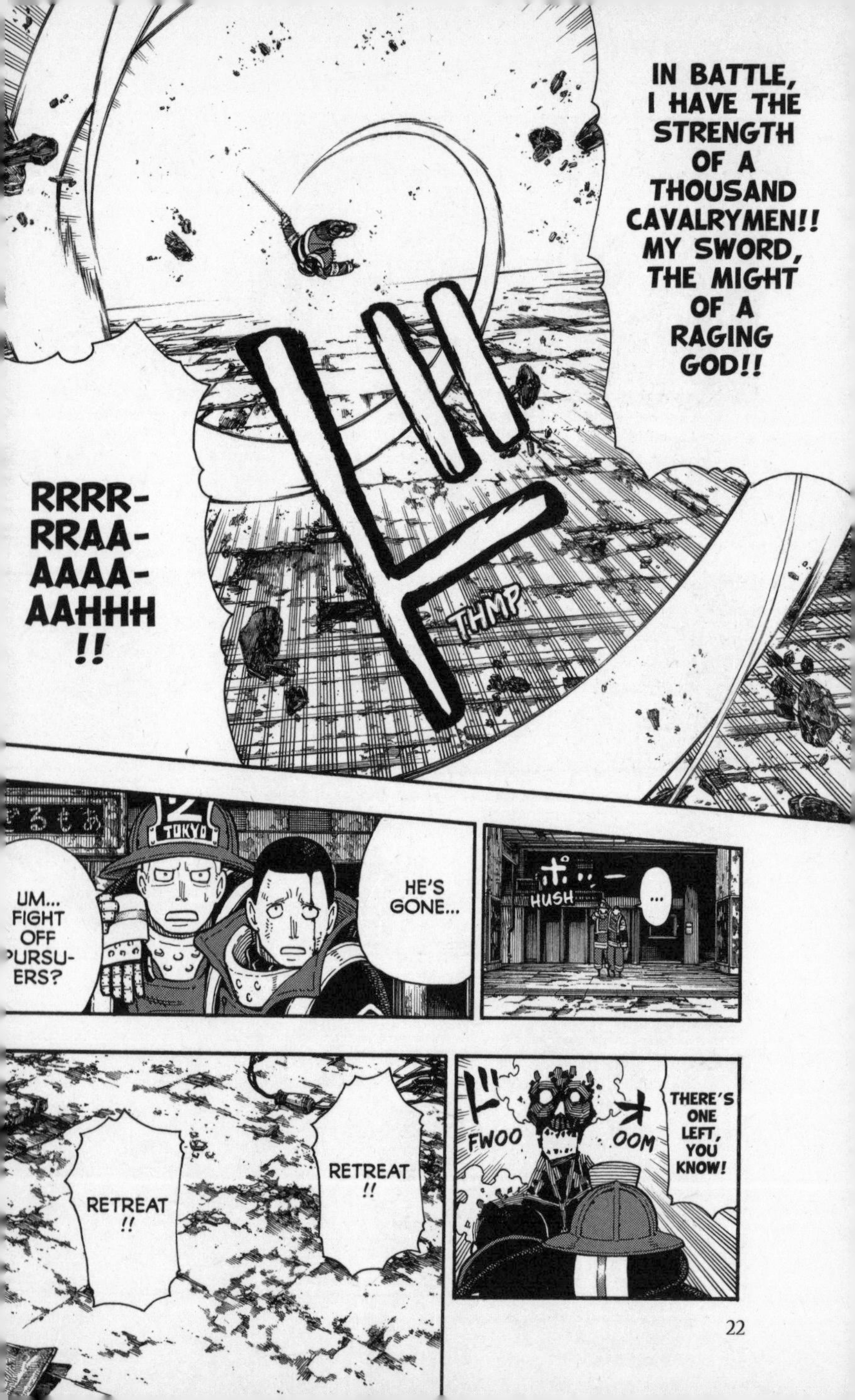

IN BATTLE, I HAVE THE STRENGTH OF A THOUSAND CAVALRYMEN!! MY SWORD, THE MIGHT OF A RAGING GOD!!
RRRR-RRAA-AAAA-AAHHH!!
THMP
HUSH
...
HE'S GONE...
UM... FIGHT OFF PURSU-ERS?
FWOOOOM
THERE'S ONE LEFT, YOU KNOW!
RETREAT!!
RETREAT!!

Top Sign: Tickets
Bottom signs (L, R): Security Cameras in Use, Platform

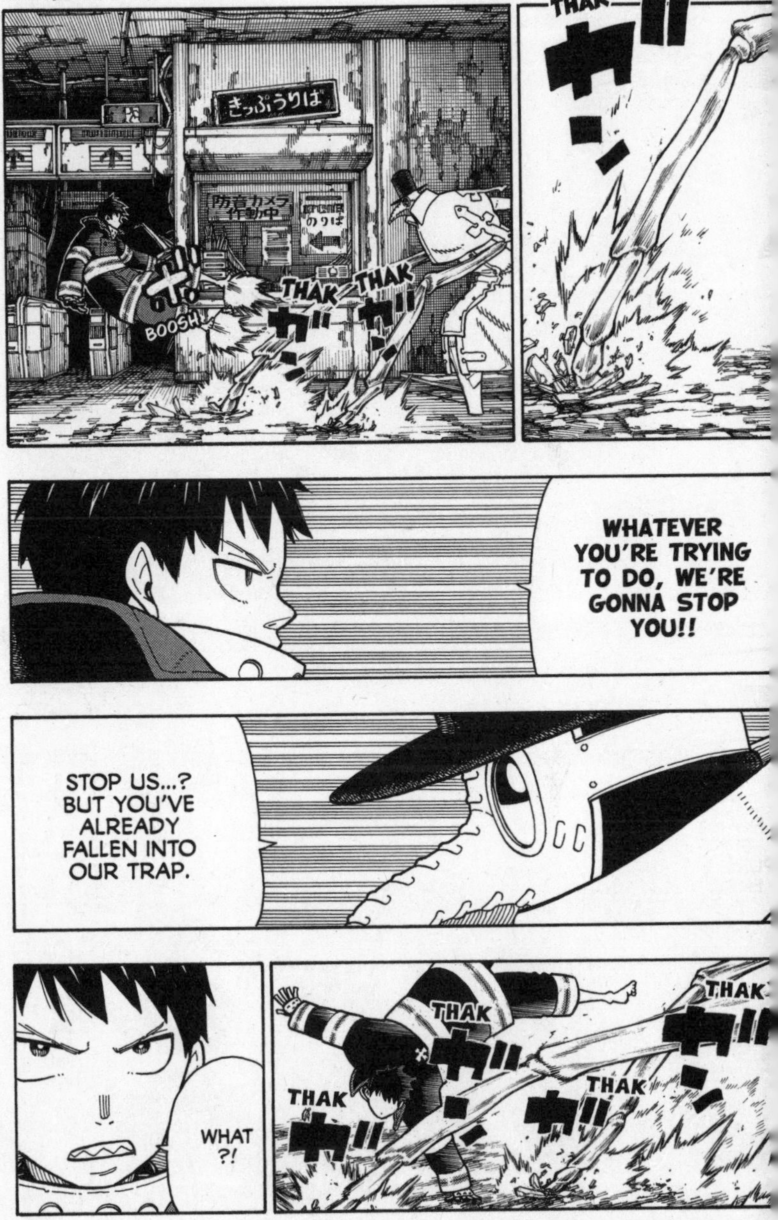
THAK
きっぷうりば
THAK
THAK
BOOSH
WHATEVER YOU'RE TRYING TO DO, WE'RE GONNA STOP YOU!!
STOP US...? BUT YOU'VE ALREADY FALLEN INTO OUR TRAP.
THAK
THAK
THAK
THAK
WHAT ?!

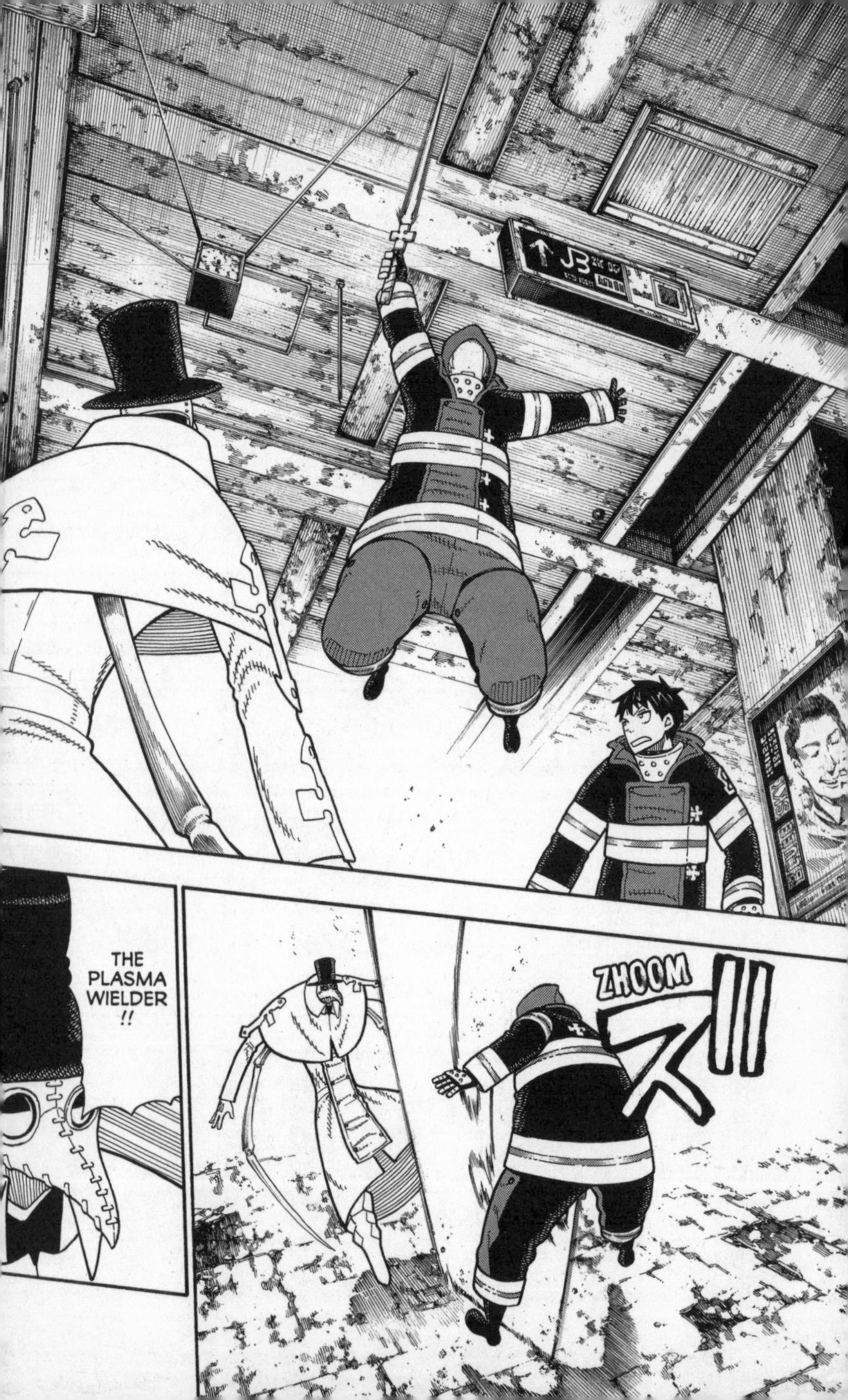
ZHOOM
THE PLASMA WIELDER !!

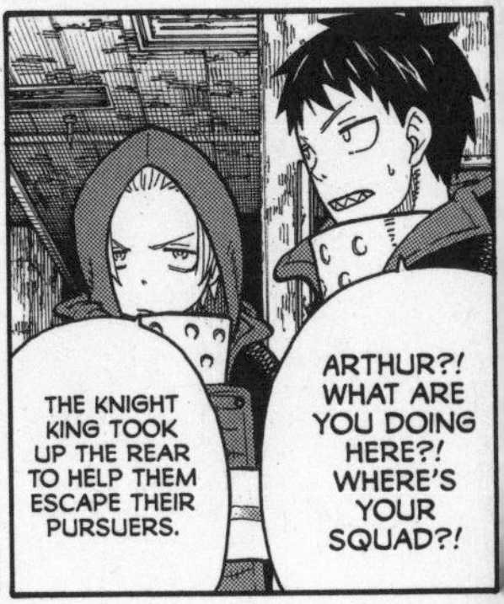
ARTHUR?! WHAT ARE YOU DOING HERE?! WHERE'S YOUR SQUAD?!
THE KNIGHT KING TOOK UP THE REAR TO HELP THEM ESCAPE THEIR PURSUERS.

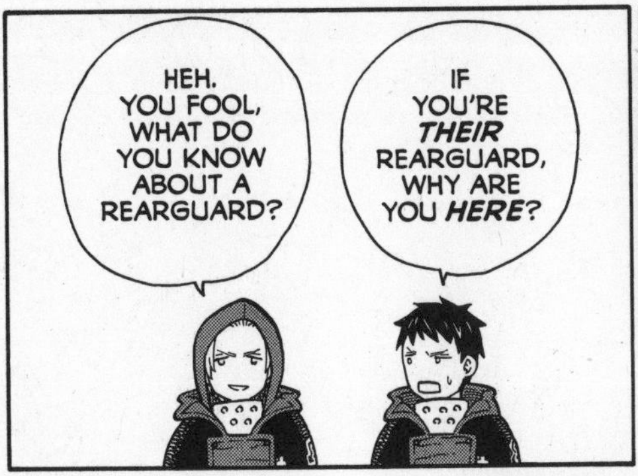
IF YOU'RE *THEIR* REARGUARD, WHY ARE YOU *HERE*?
HEH. YOU FOOL, WHAT DO YOU KNOW ABOUT A REARGUARD?

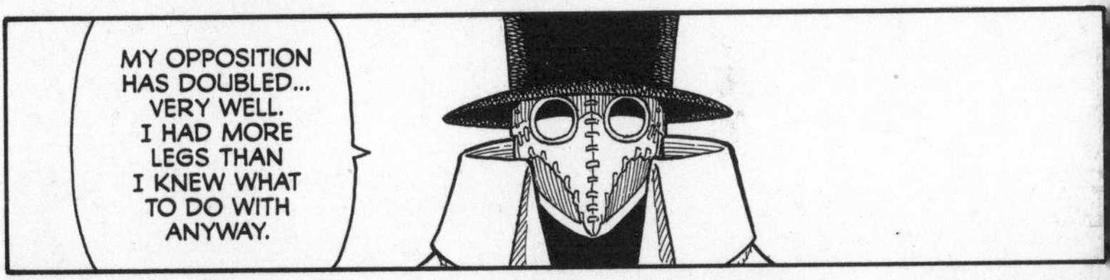
MY OPPOSITION HAS DOUBLED... VERY WELL. I HAD MORE LEGS THAN I KNEW WHAT TO DO WITH ANYWAY.

Poster: Assistants Wanted, Cats and Dogs Welcome

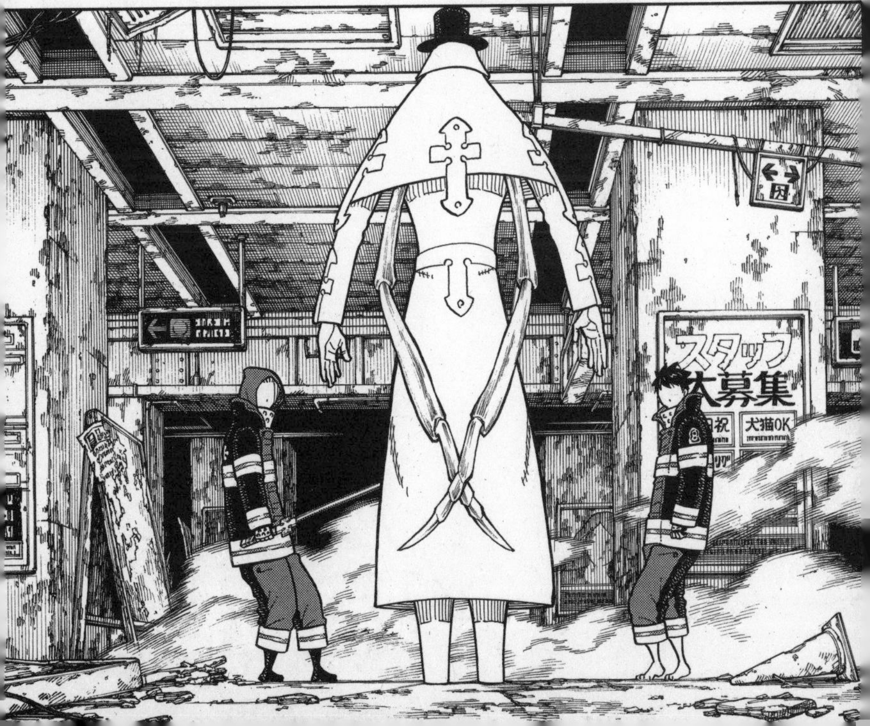
スタッフ大募集
犬猫OK

FIRE FORCE

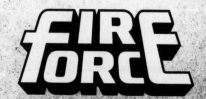

CHAPTER CLXI: STRUGGLES

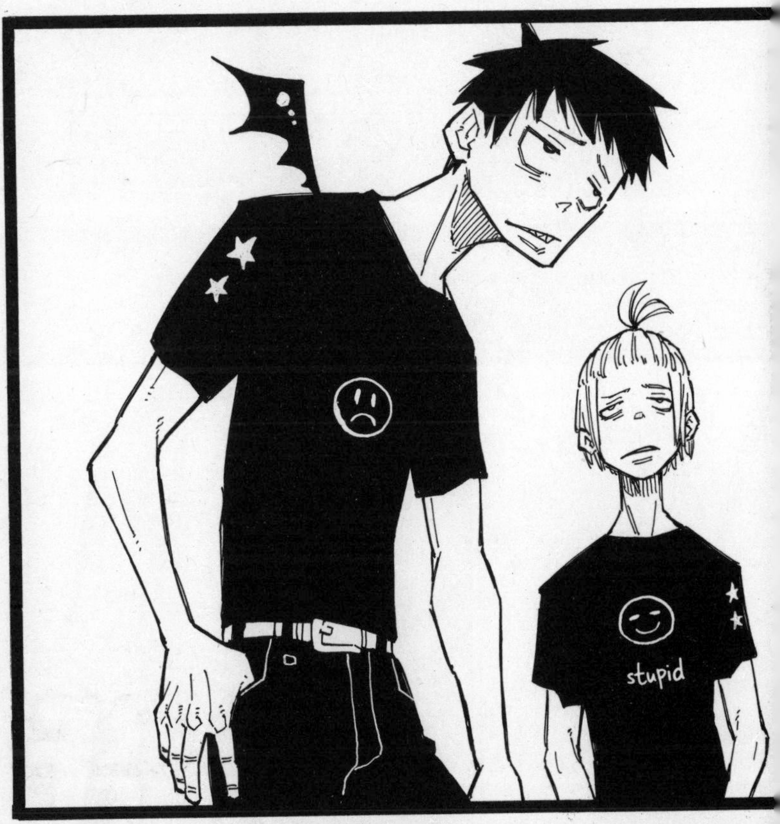
stupid

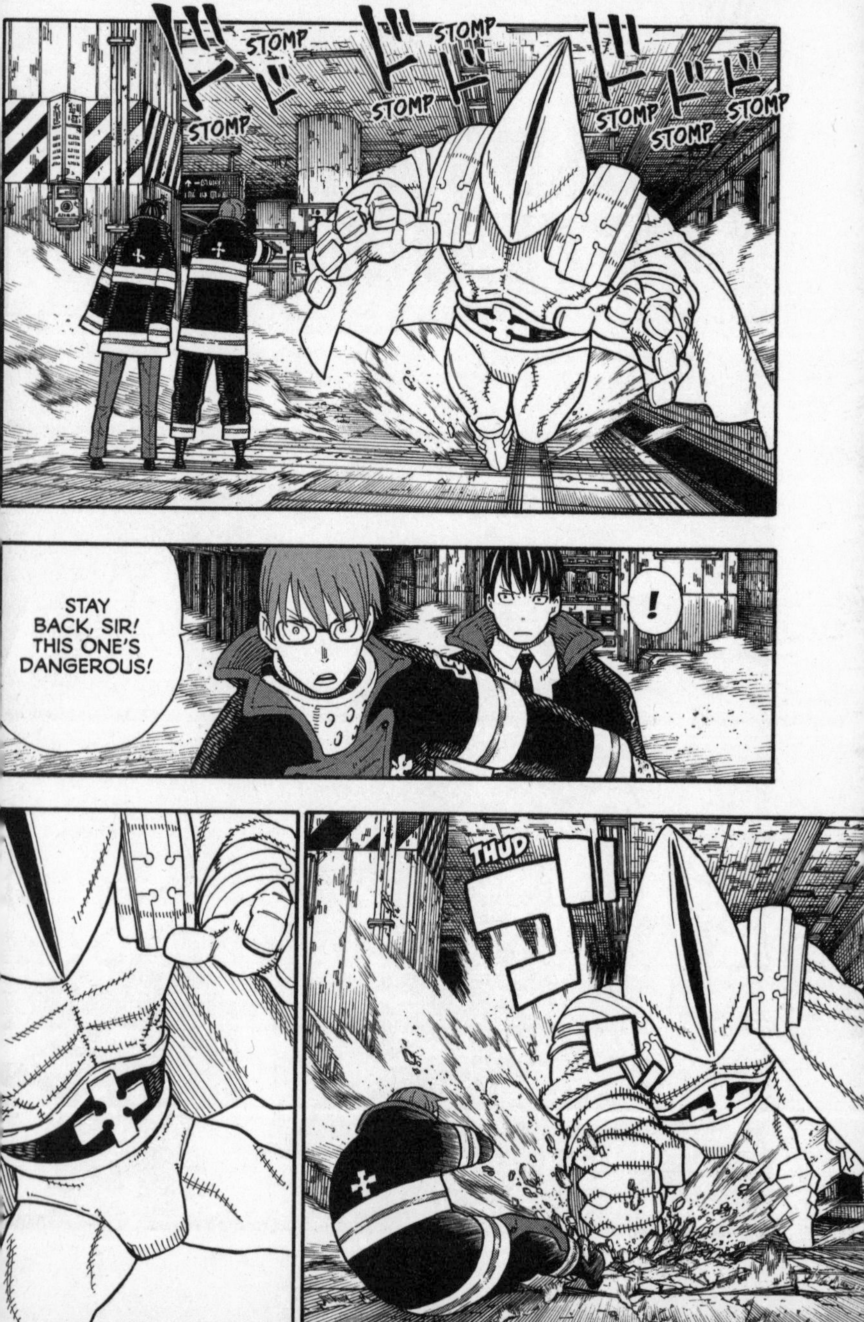
STOMP
STOMP
STOMP
STOMP
STOMP
STOMP
STOMP
STOMP
!
STAY BACK, SIR! THIS ONE'S DANGEROUS!
THUD

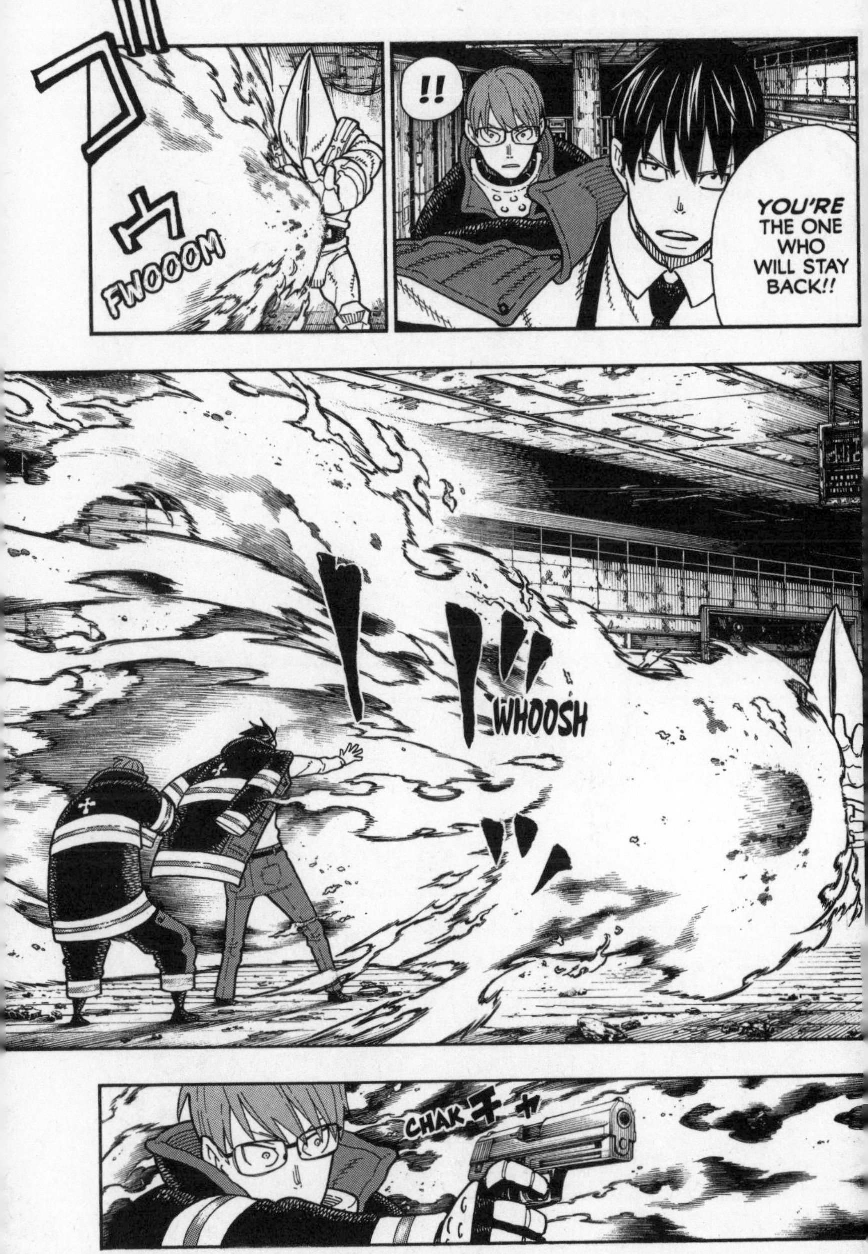
!!
YOU'RE THE ONE WHO WILL STAY BACK!!
FWOOOM
WHOOSH
CHAK チャ

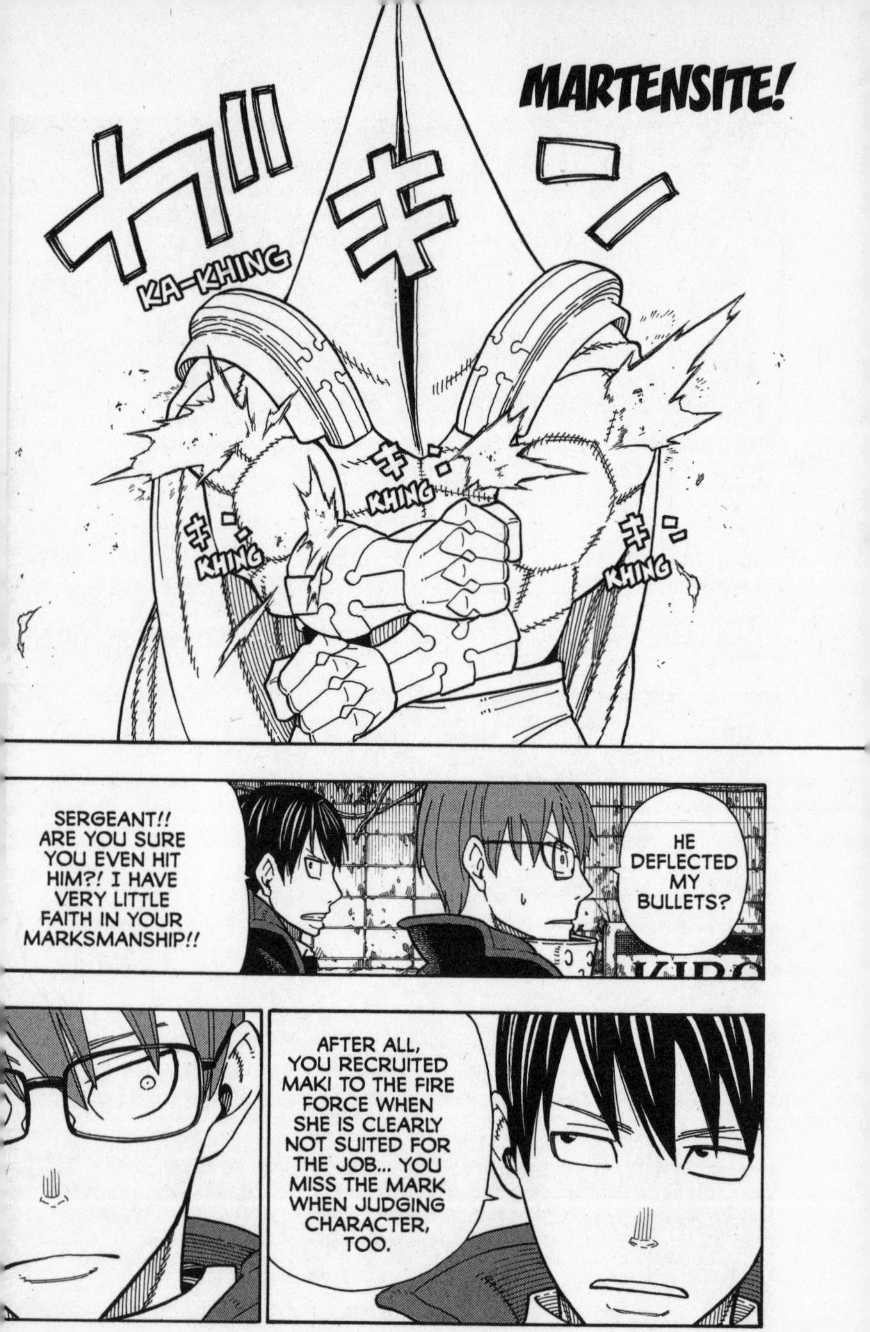
MARTENSITE!
KA-KHING
KHING
KHING
KHING
HE DEFLECTED MY BULLETS?
SERGEANT!! ARE YOU SURE YOU EVEN HIT HIM?! I HAVE VERY LITTLE FAITH IN YOUR MARKSMANSHIP!!
AFTER ALL, YOU RECRUITED MAKI TO THE FIRE FORCE WHEN SHE IS CLEARLY NOT SUITED FOR THE JOB... YOU MISS THE MARK WHEN JUDGING CHARACTER, TOO.

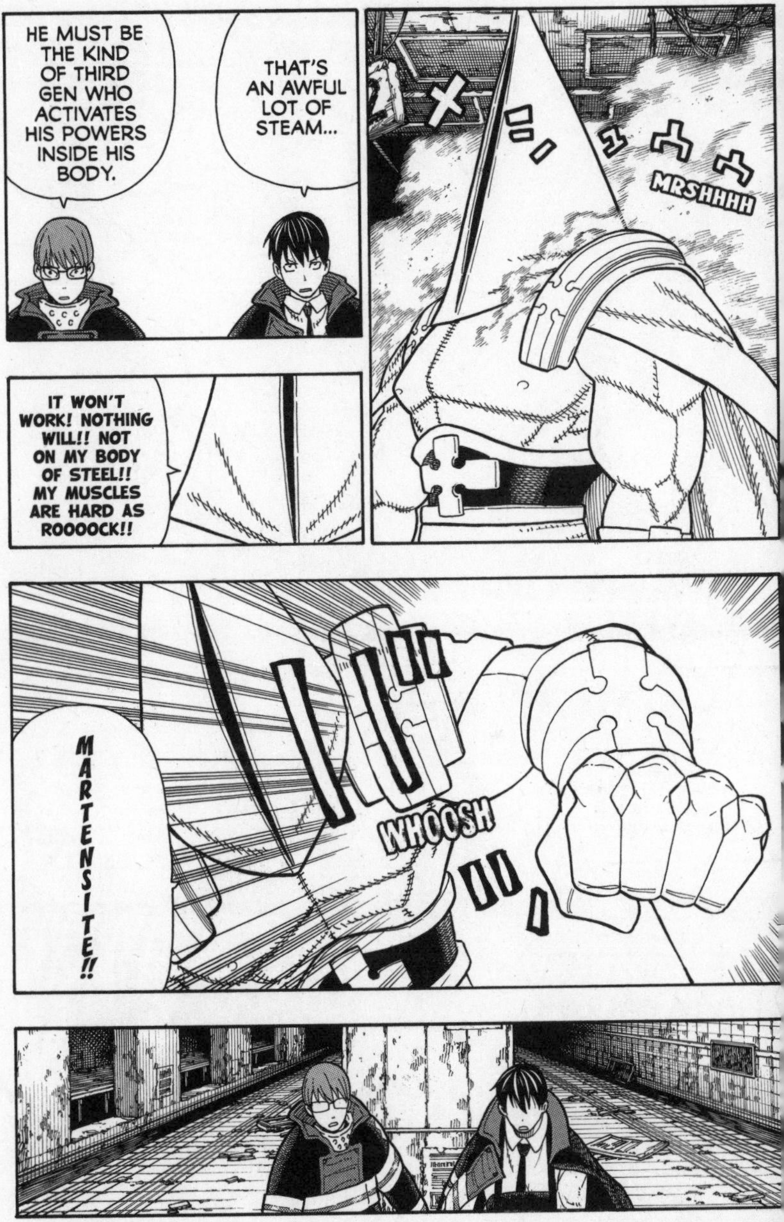
MRSHHHH
THAT'S AN AWFUL LOT OF STEAM...
HE MUST BE THE KIND OF THIRD GEN WHO ACTIVATES HIS POWERS INSIDE HIS BODY.
IT WON'T WORK! NOTHING WILL!! NOT ON MY BODY OF STEEL!! MY MUSCLES ARE HARD AS ROOOOCK!!
WHOOSH
MARTENSITE!!

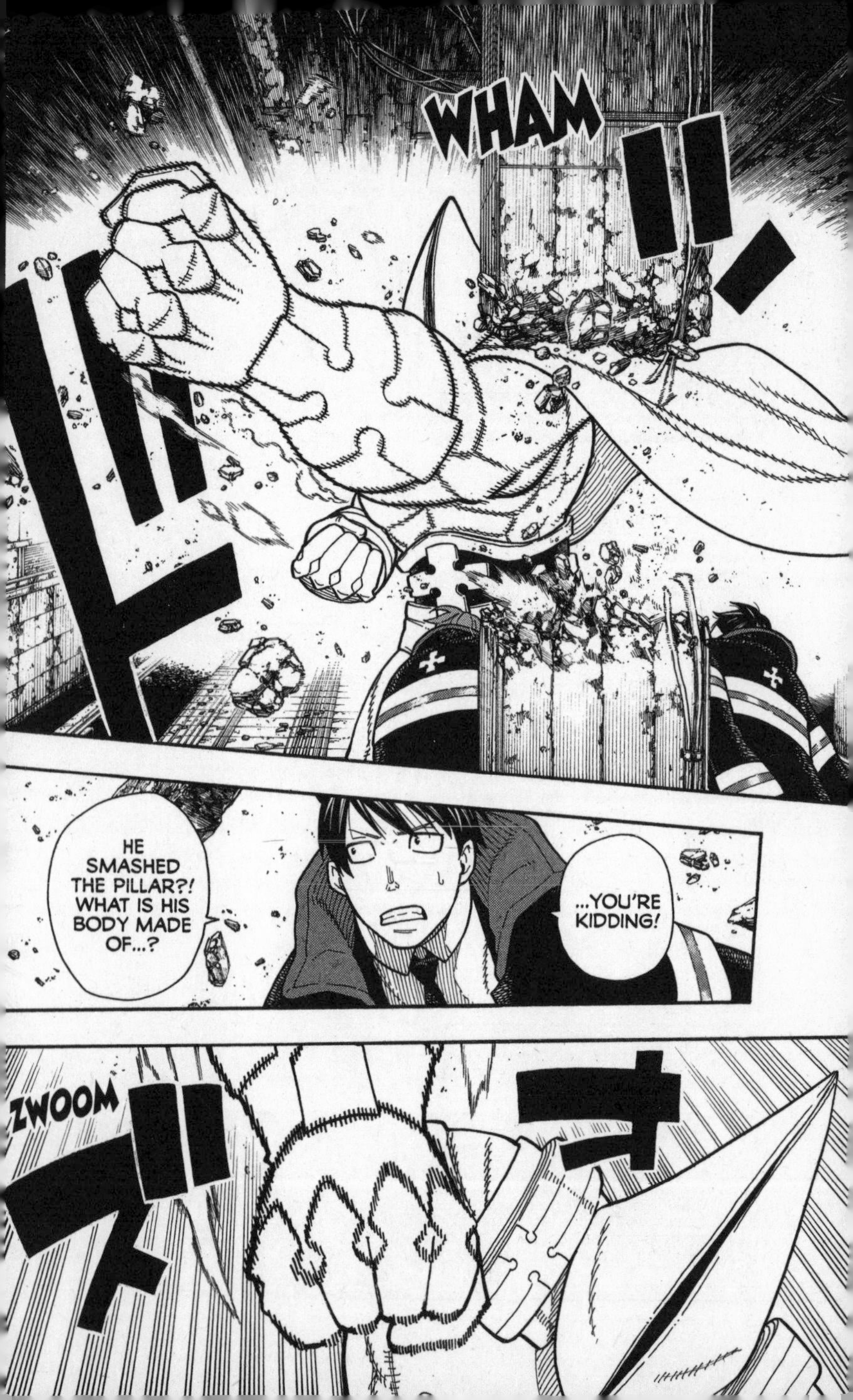
WHAM
...YOU'RE KIDDING!
HE SMASHED THE PILLAR?! WHAT IS HIS BODY MADE OF...?
ZWOOM

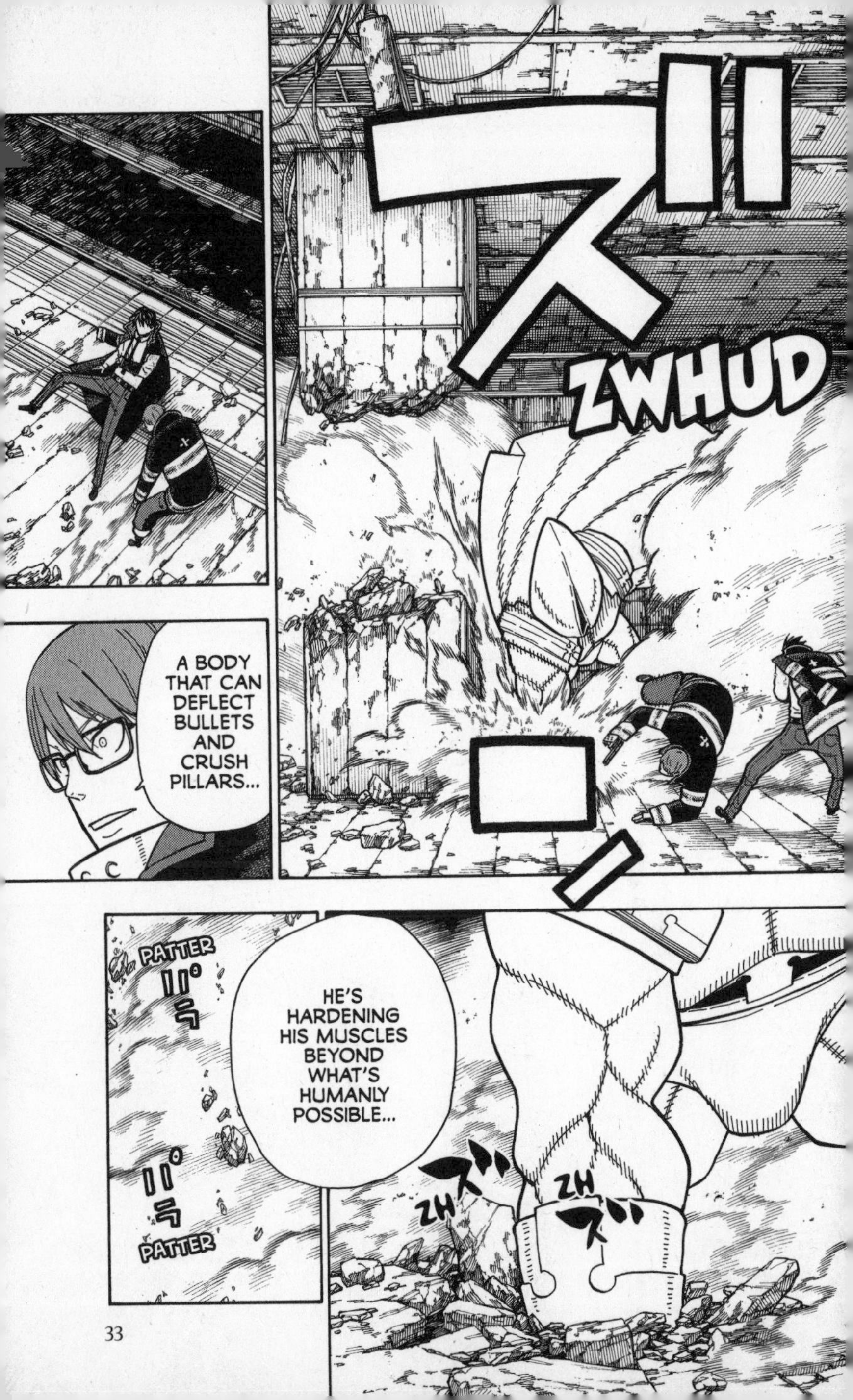
ZWHUD
A BODY THAT CAN DEFLECT BULLETS AND CRUSH PILLARS...
HE'S HARDENING HIS MUSCLES BEYOND WHAT'S HUMANLY POSSIBLE...
ZH
ZH
PATTER
PATTER

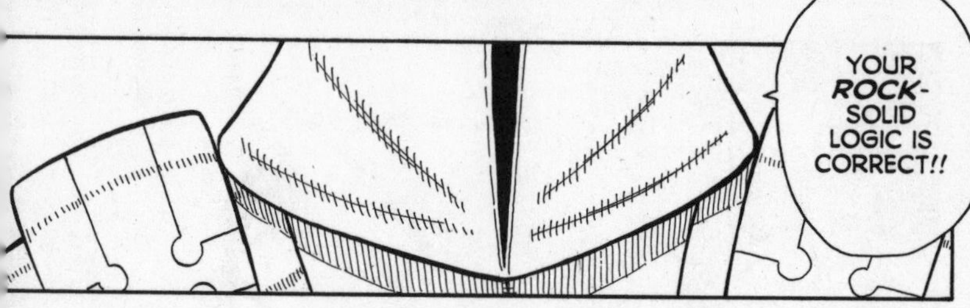
YOUR ROCK-SOLID LOGIC IS CORRECT!!

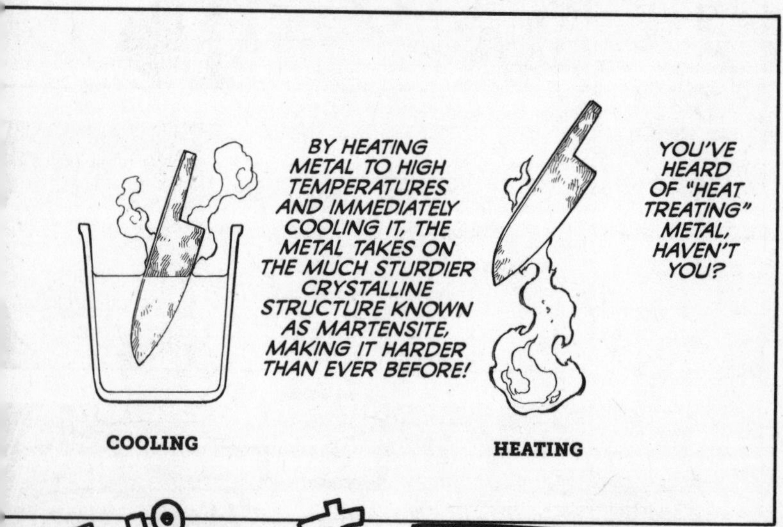
YOU'VE HEARD OF "HEAT TREATING" METAL, HAVEN'T YOU?
BY HEATING METAL TO HIGH TEMPERATURES AND IMMEDIATELY COOLING IT, THE METAL TAKES ON THE MUCH STURDIER CRYSTALLINE STRUCTURE KNOWN AS MARTENSITE, MAKING IT HARDER THAN EVER BEFORE!
HEATING
COOLING

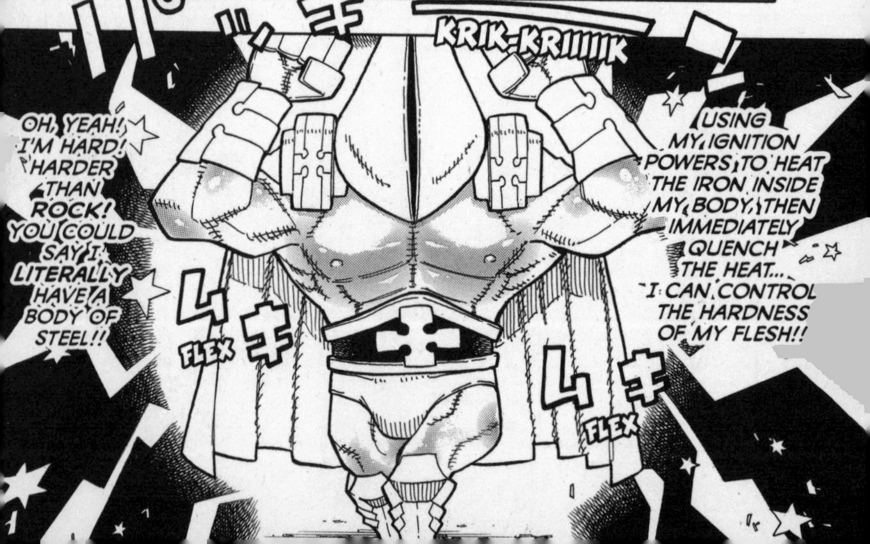
KRIK-KRIIIIIK
USING MY IGNITION POWERS TO HEAT THE IRON INSIDE MY BODY, THEN IMMEDIATELY QUENCH THE HEAT... I CAN CONTROL THE HARDNESS OF MY FLESH!!
OH, YEAH! I'M HARD! HARDER THAN ROCK! YOU COULD SAY I LITERALLY HAVE A BODY OF STEEL!!
FLEX
FLEX

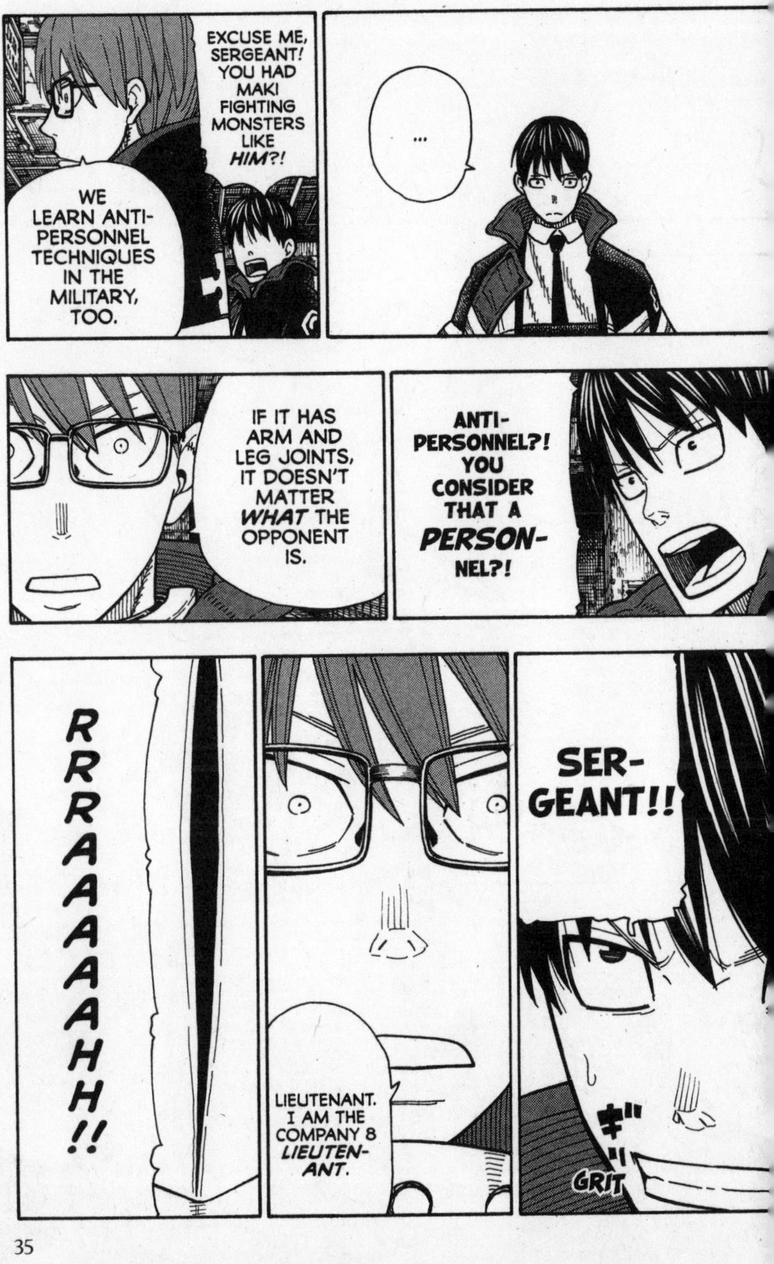
...
EXCUSE ME, SERGEANT! YOU HAD MAKI FIGHTING MONSTERS LIKE *HIM*?!
WE LEARN ANTI-PERSONNEL TECHNIQUES IN THE MILITARY, TOO.
ANTI-PERSONNEL?! YOU CONSIDER THAT A *PERSON*-NEL?!
IF IT HAS ARM AND LEG JOINTS, IT DOESN'T MATTER *WHAT* THE OPPONENT IS.
SER-GEANT!!
GRIT
LIEUTENANT. I AM THE COMPANY 8 *LIEUTEN-ANT*.
RRRAAAAAAHH!!

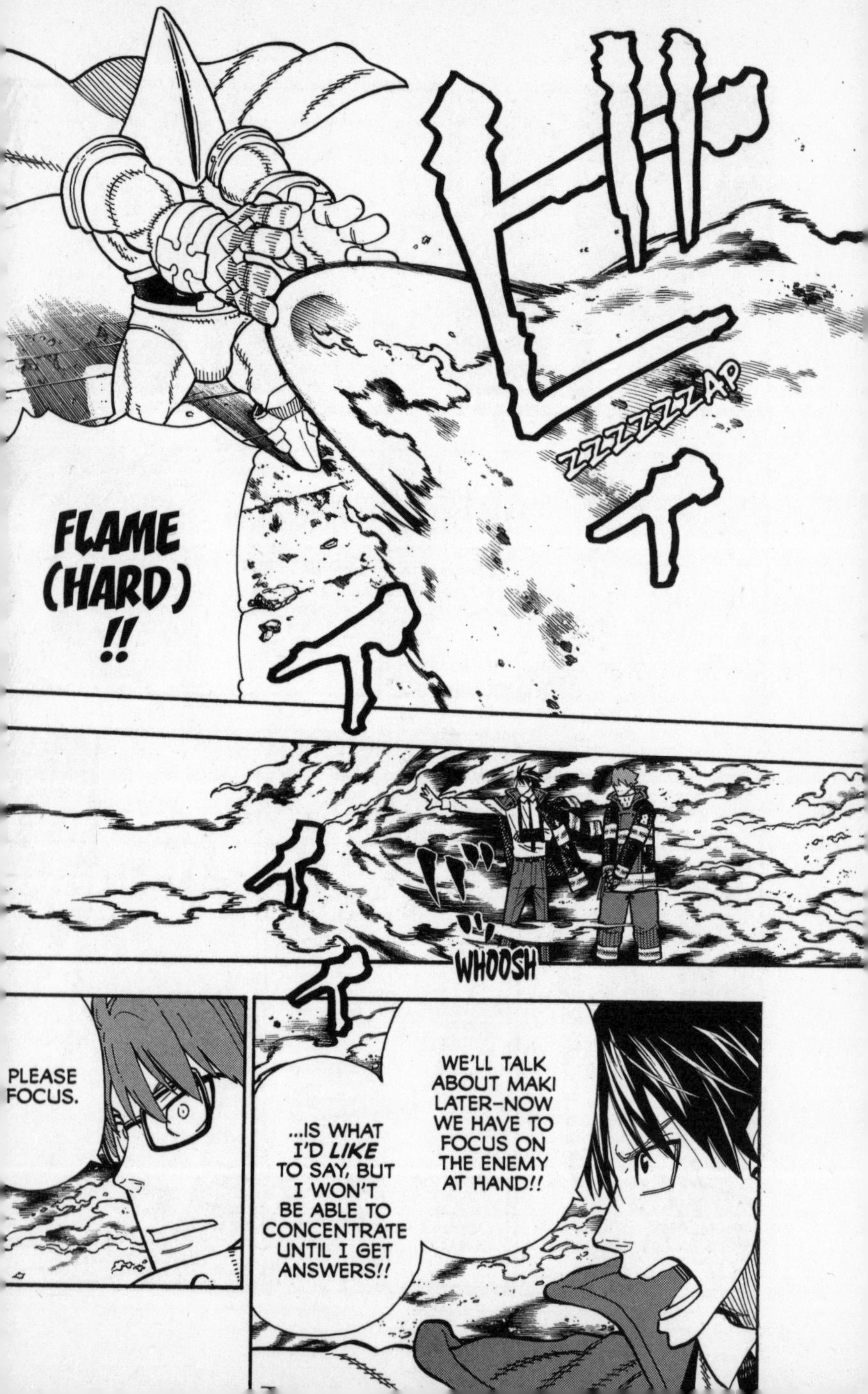
FLAME (HARD)!!
ZZZZZZZZAP
WHOOSH
WE'LL TALK ABOUT MAKI LATER–NOW WE HAVE TO FOCUS ON THE ENEMY AT HAND!!
...IS WHAT I'D *LIKE* TO SAY, BUT I WON'T BE ABLE TO CONCENTRATE UNTIL I GET ANSWERS!!
PLEASE FOCUS.

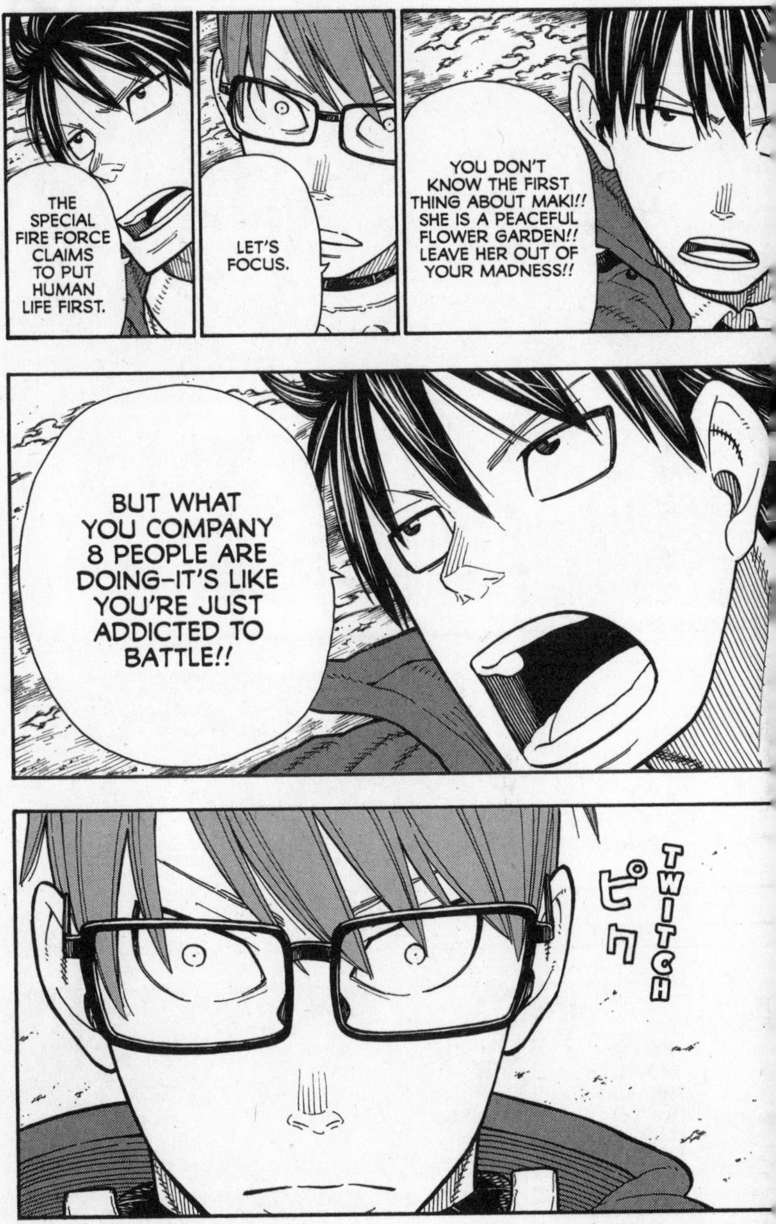
YOU DON'T KNOW THE FIRST THING ABOUT MAKI!! SHE IS A PEACEFUL FLOWER GARDEN!! LEAVE HER OUT OF YOUR MADNESS!!
LET'S FOCUS.
THE SPECIAL FIRE FORCE CLAIMS TO PUT HUMAN LIFE FIRST.
BUT WHAT YOU COMPANY 8 PEOPLE ARE DOING–IT'S LIKE YOU'RE JUST ADDICTED TO BATTLE!!
TWITCH
ピク

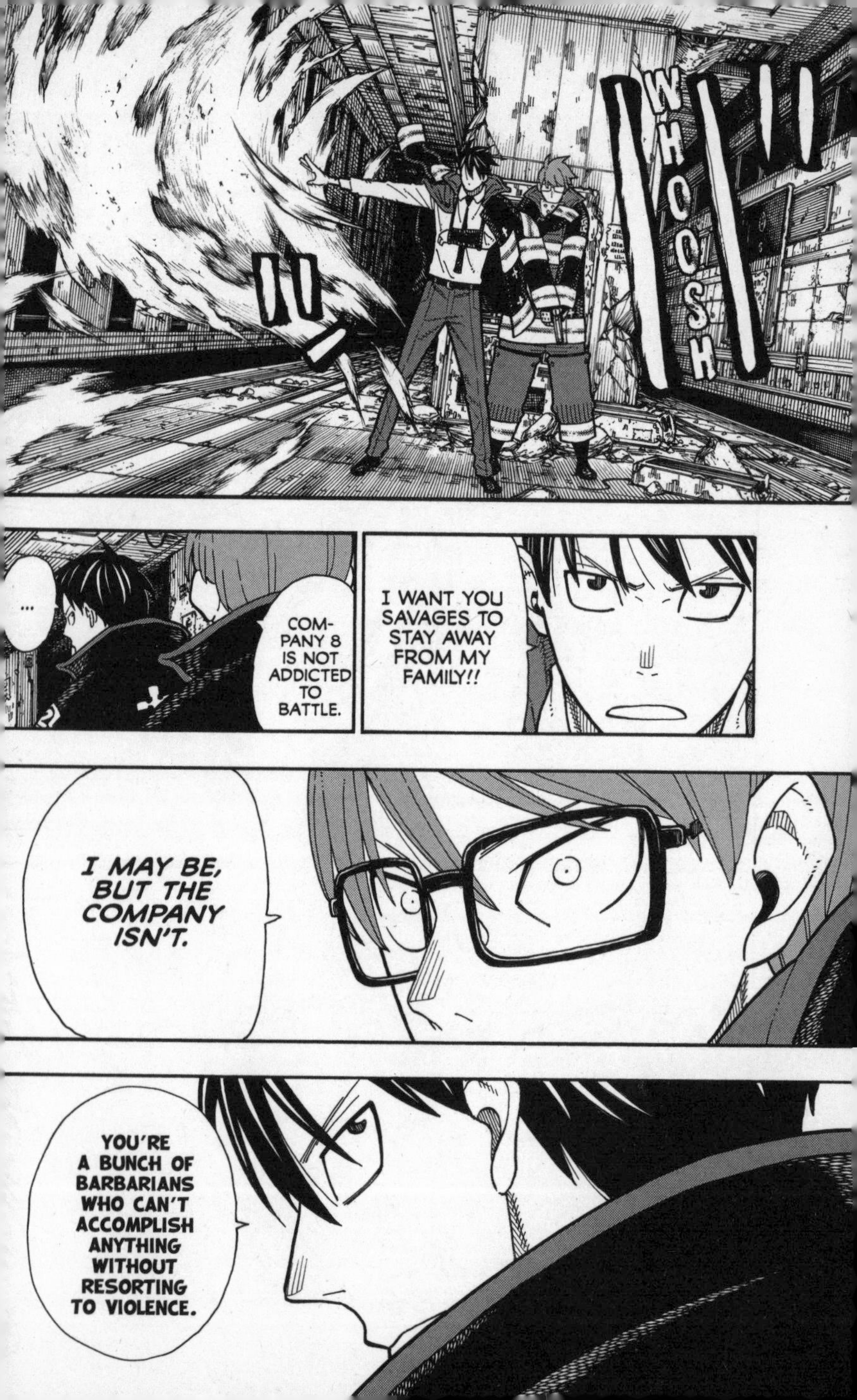
WHOOSH
I WANT YOU SAVAGES TO STAY AWAY FROM MY FAMILY!!
COM-PANY 8 IS NOT ADDICTED TO BATTLE.
...
I MAY BE, BUT THE COMPANY ISN'T.
YOU'RE A BUNCH OF BARBARIANS WHO CAN'T ACCOMPLISH ANYTHING WITHOUT RESORTING TO VIOLENCE.

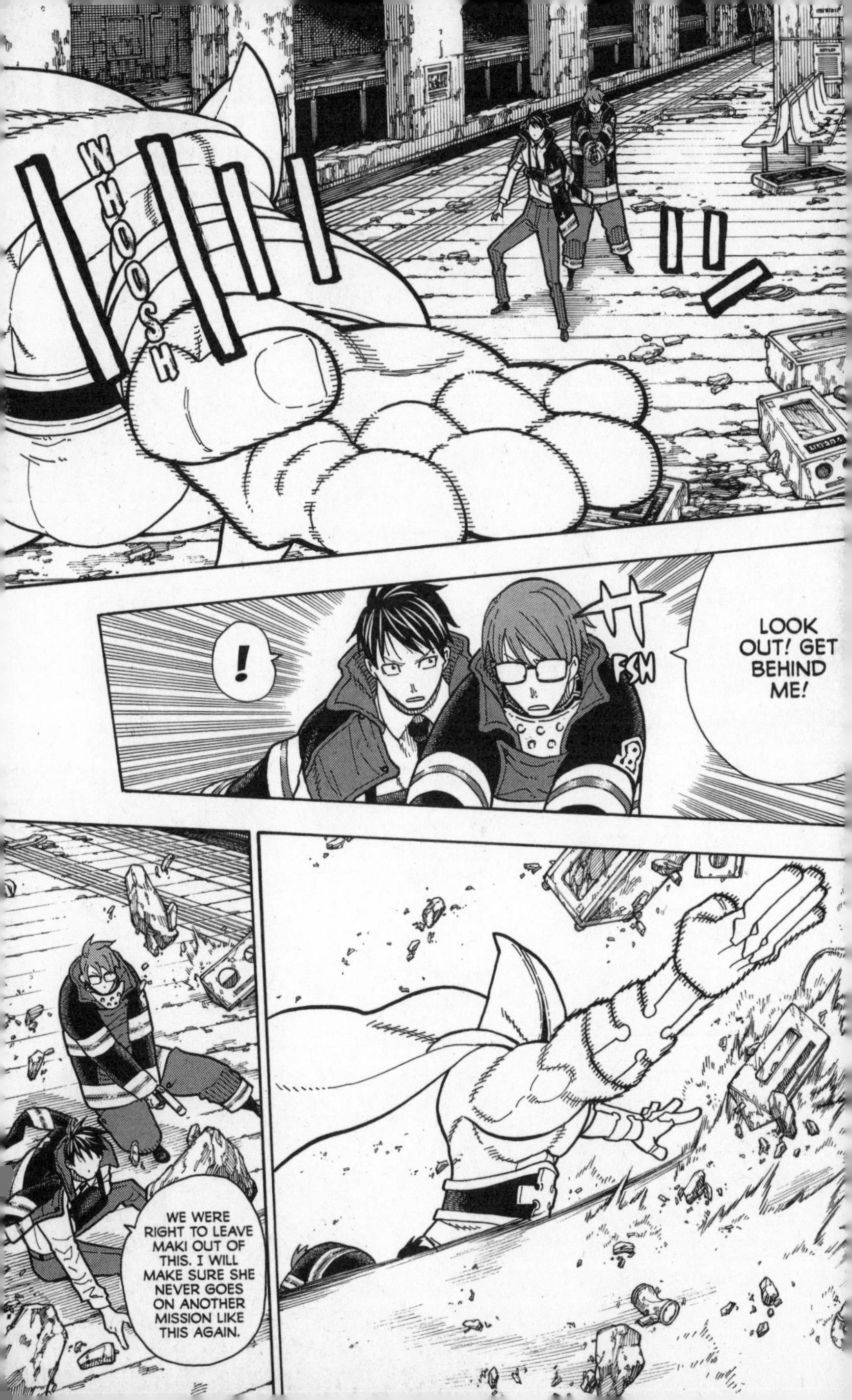
WHOOSH
LOOK OUT! GET BEHIND ME!
FSH
!
WE WERE RIGHT TO LEAVE MAKI OUT OF THIS. I WILL MAKE SURE SHE NEVER GOES ON ANOTHER MISSION LIKE THIS AGAIN.

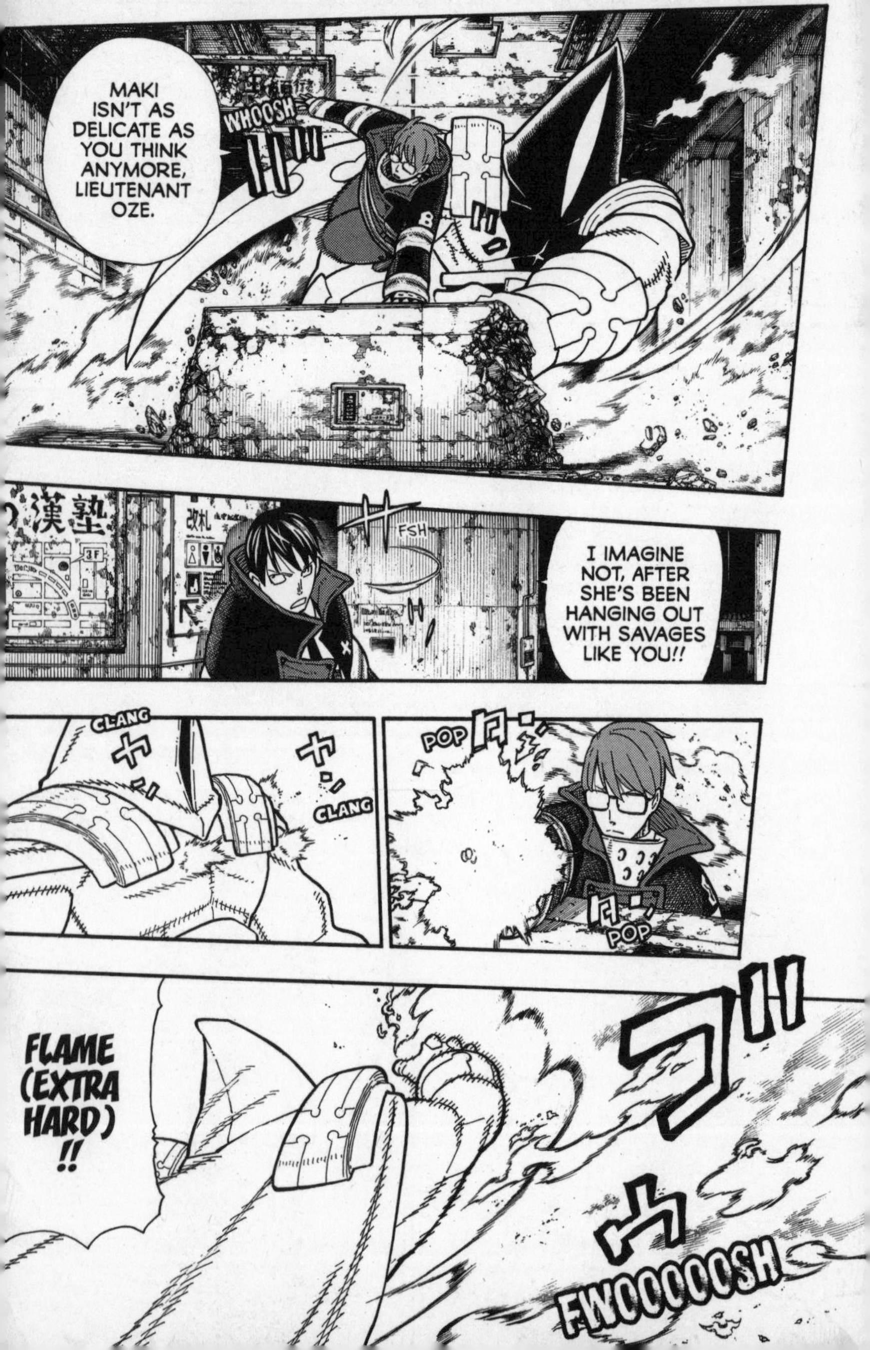
WHOOSH
MAKI ISN'T AS DELICATE AS YOU THINK ANYMORE, LIEUTENANT OZE.
I IMAGINE NOT, AFTER SHE'S BEEN HANGING OUT WITH SAVAGES LIKE YOU!!
FSH
POP
POP
CLANG
CLANG
FLAME (EXTRA HARD) !!
FWOOOOOOSH

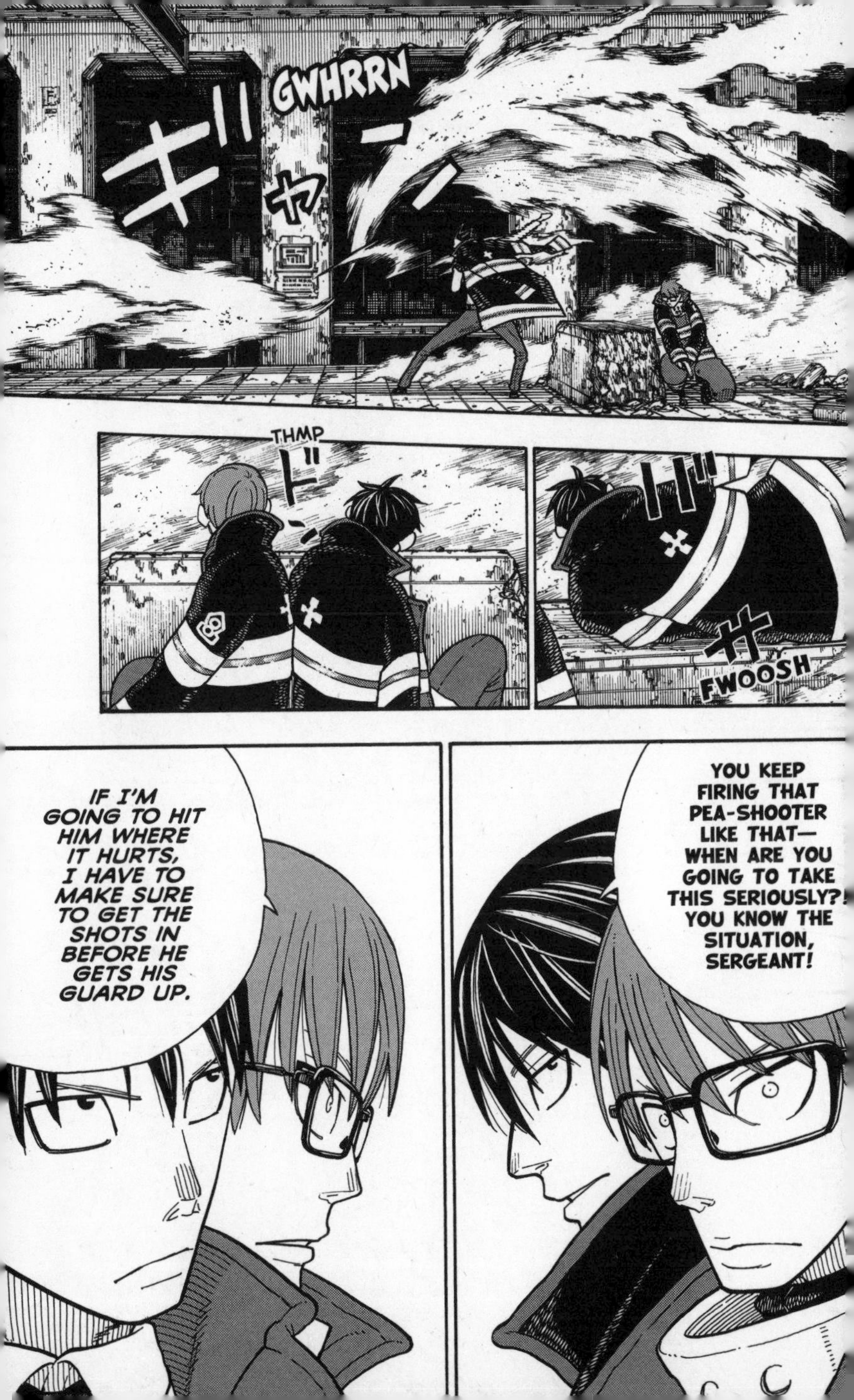
GWHRRN
ギャーー
FWOOSH
THMP
YOU KEEP FIRING THAT PEA-SHOOTER LIKE THAT— WHEN ARE YOU GOING TO TAKE THIS SERIOUSLY?! YOU KNOW THE SITUATION, SERGEANT!
IF I'M GOING TO HIT HIM WHERE IT HURTS, I HAVE TO MAKE SURE TO GET THE SHOTS IN BEFORE HE GETS HIS GUARD UP.

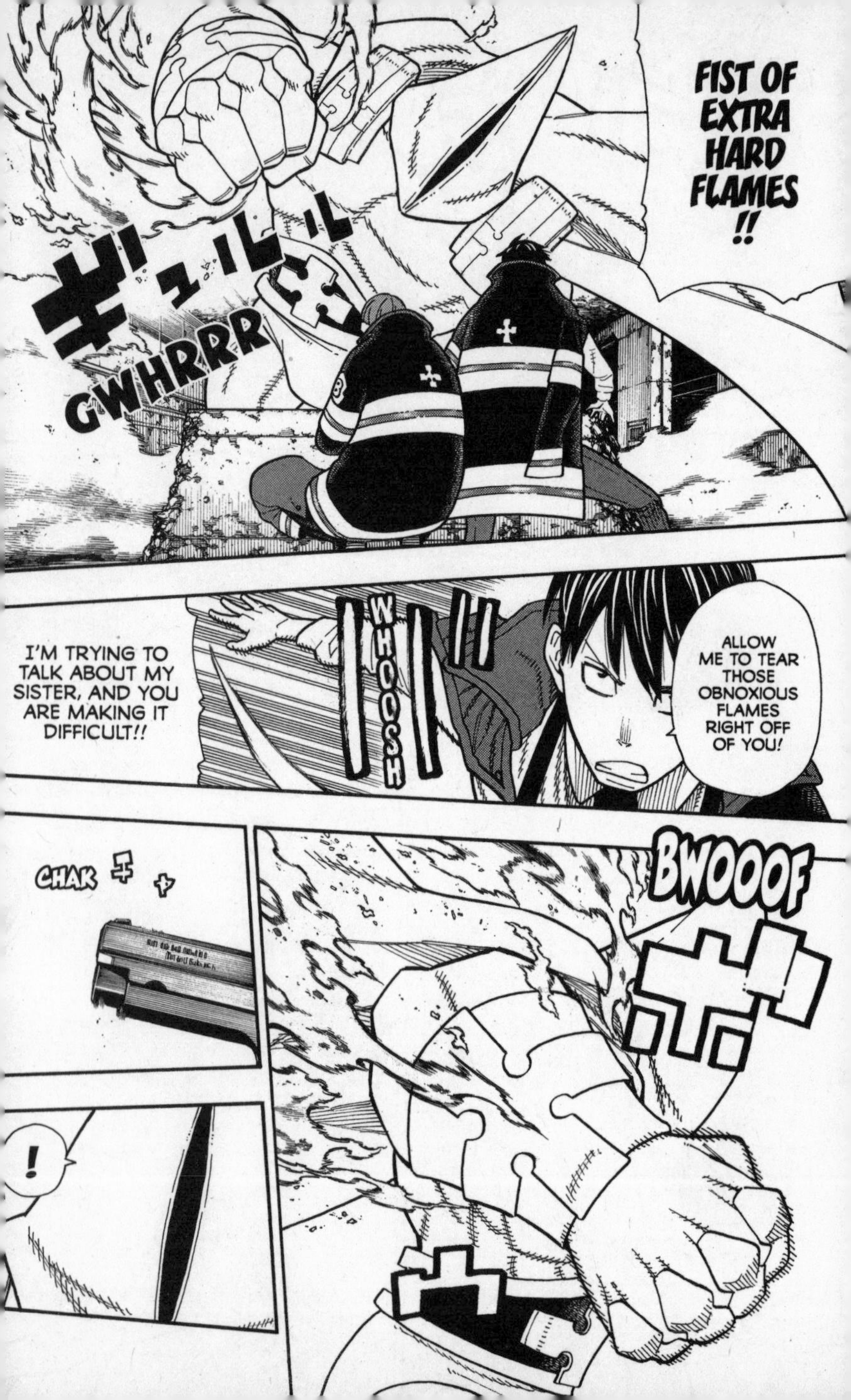
FIST OF EXTRA HARD FLAMES!!
GWHRRR
ALLOW ME TO TEAR THOSE OBNOXIOUS FLAMES RIGHT OFF OF YOU!
WHOOSH
I'M TRYING TO TALK ABOUT MY SISTER, AND YOU ARE MAKING IT DIFFICULT!!
BWOOOF
CHAK
!

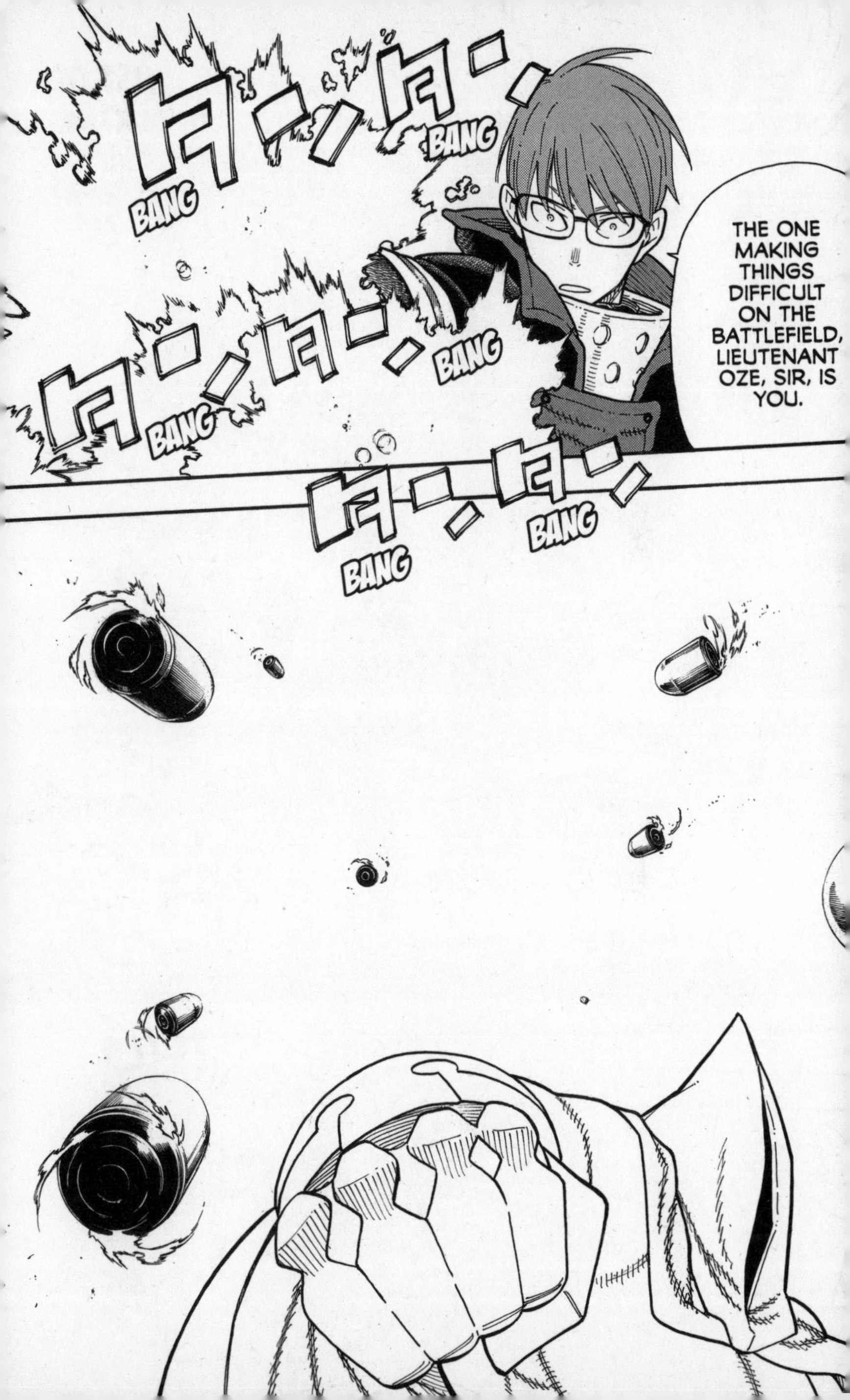
THE ONE MAKING THINGS DIFFICULT ON THE BATTLEFIELD, LIEUTENANT OZE, SIR, IS YOU.
BANG
BANG
BANG
BANG
BANG
BANG

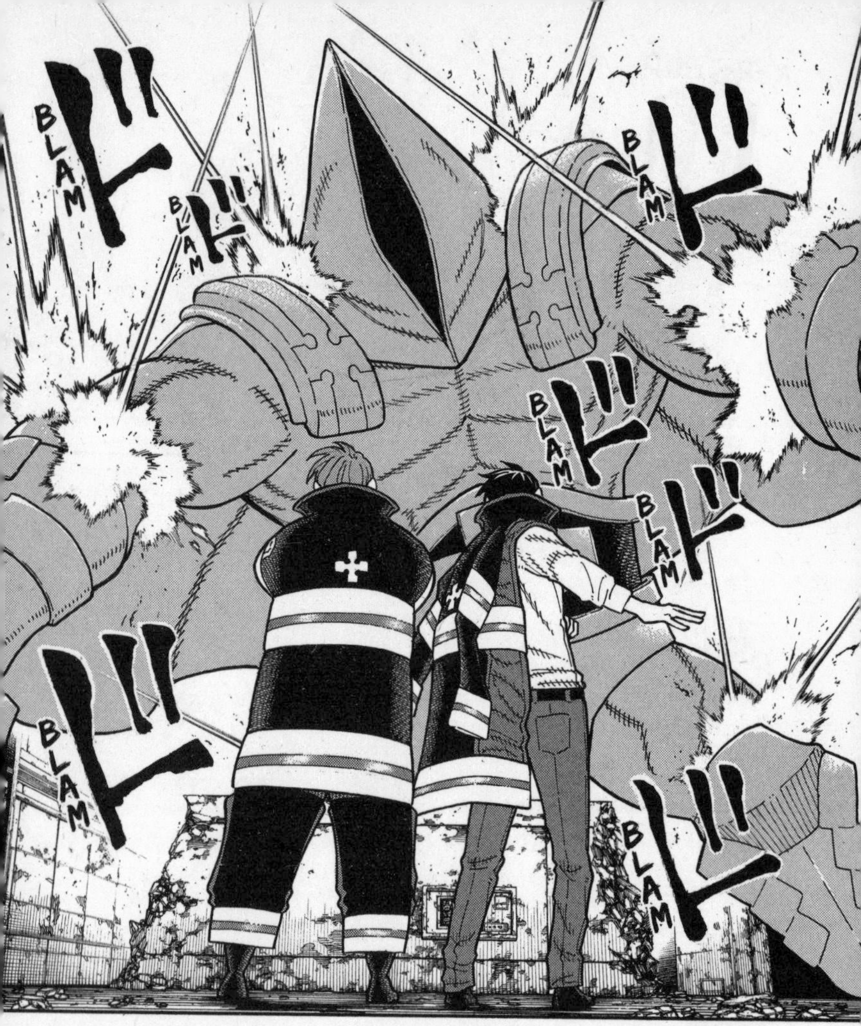
BLAM
BLAM
BLAM
BLAM
BLAM
BLAM
BLAM
BLAM

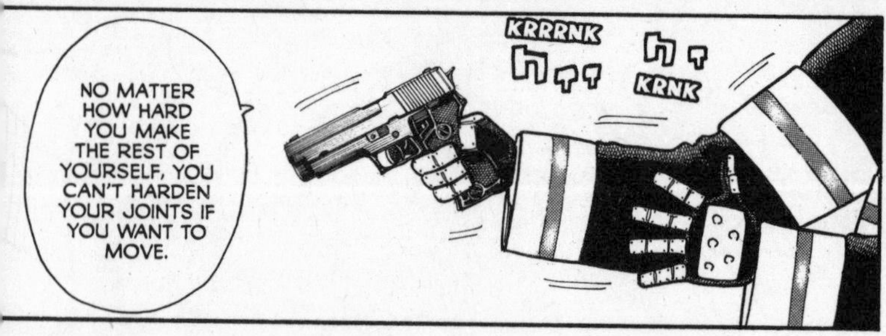
KRRRNK
KRNK
NO MATTER HOW HARD YOU MAKE THE REST OF YOURSELF, YOU CAN'T HARDEN YOUR JOINTS IF YOU WANT TO MOVE.

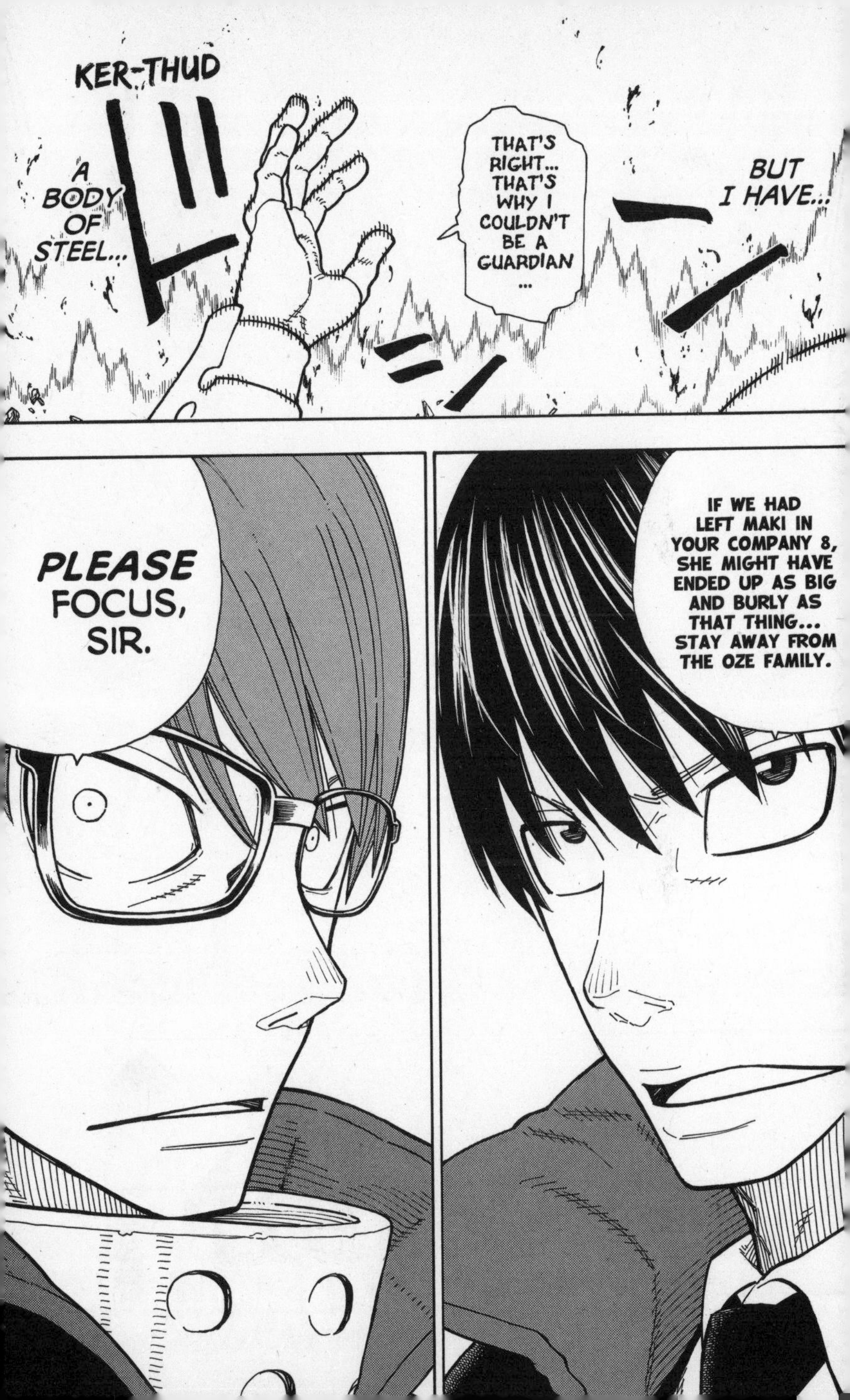
BUT I HAVE...
THAT'S RIGHT... THAT'S WHY I COULDN'T BE A GUARDIAN...
KER-THUD
A BODY OF STEEL...
IF WE HAD LEFT MAKI IN YOUR COMPANY 8, SHE MIGHT HAVE ENDED UP AS BIG AND BURLY AS THAT THING... STAY AWAY FROM THE OZE FAMILY.
PLEASE FOCUS, SIR.

FIRE FORCE

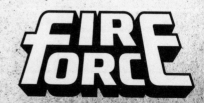

CHAPTER CLXII: HE WHO CARRIES THE WEIGHT

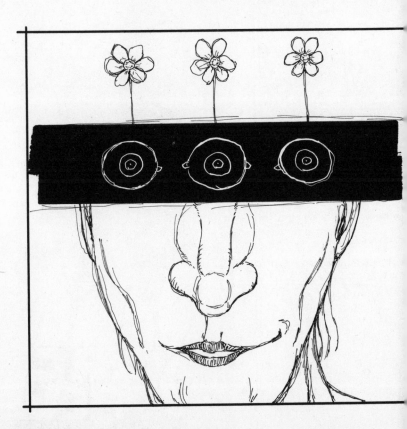

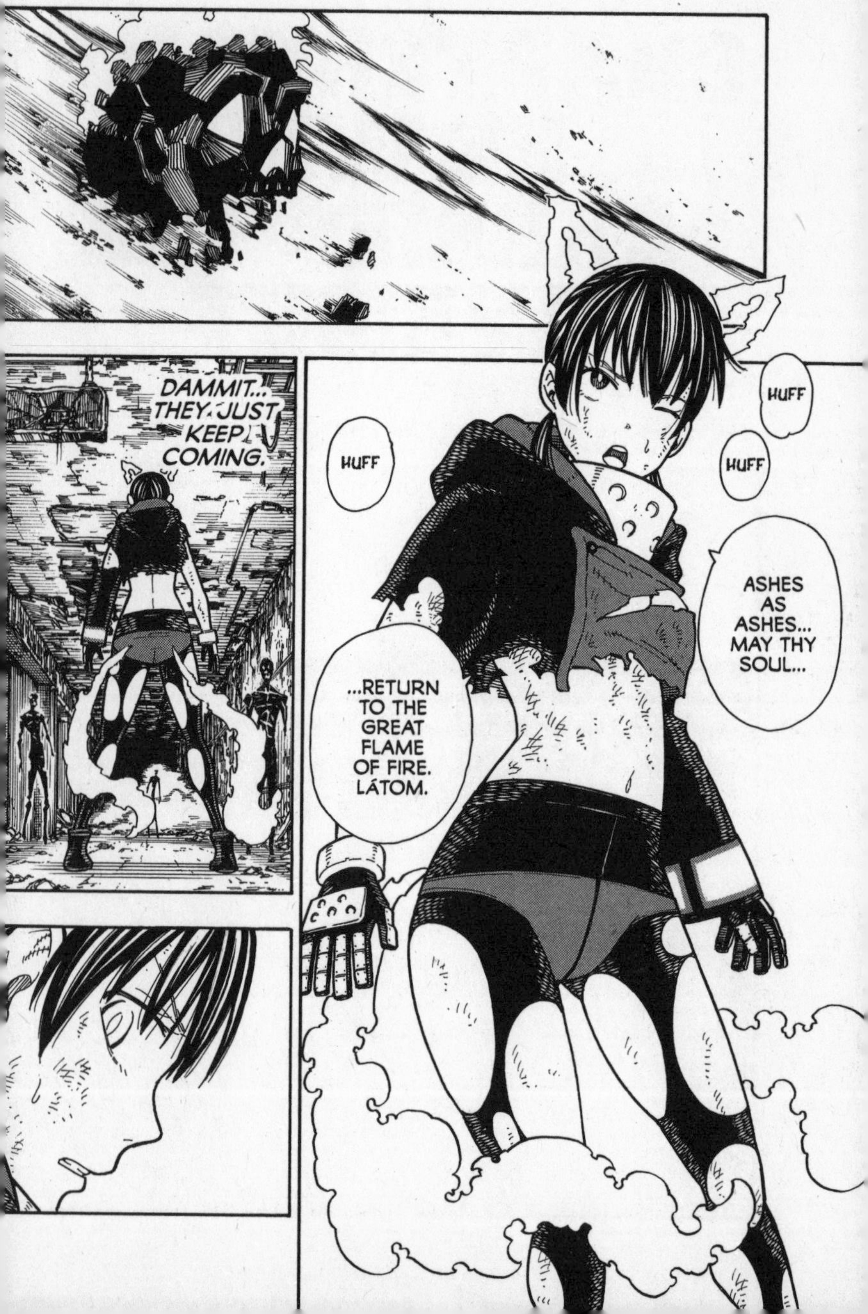
HUFF
HUFF
HUFF
ASHES AS ASHES... MAY THY SOUL...
...RETURN TO THE GREAT FLAME OF FIRE. LÁTOM.
DAMMIT... THEY JUST KEEP COMING.

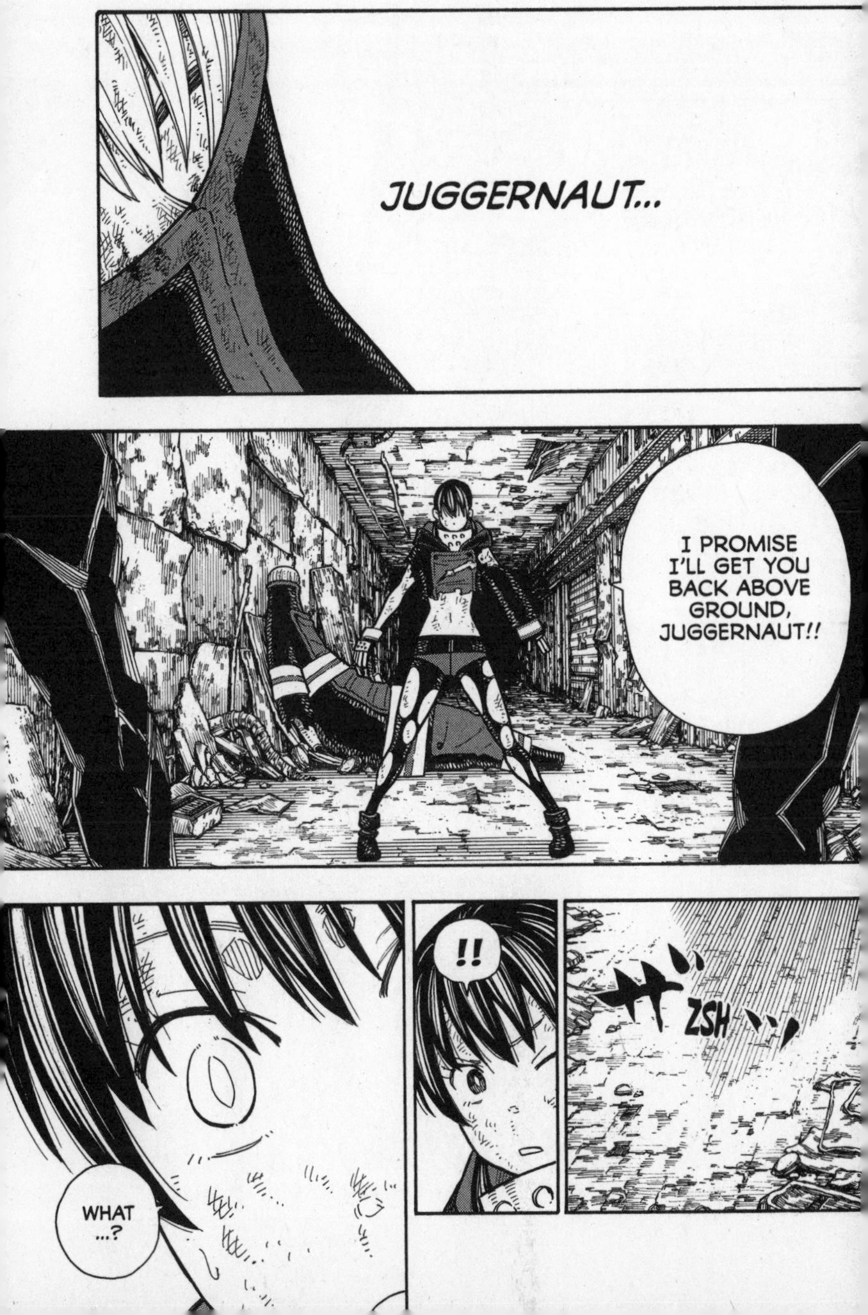
JUGGERNAUT...
I PROMISE I'LL GET YOU BACK ABOVE GROUND, JUGGERNAUT!!
ZSH
!!
WHAT ...?

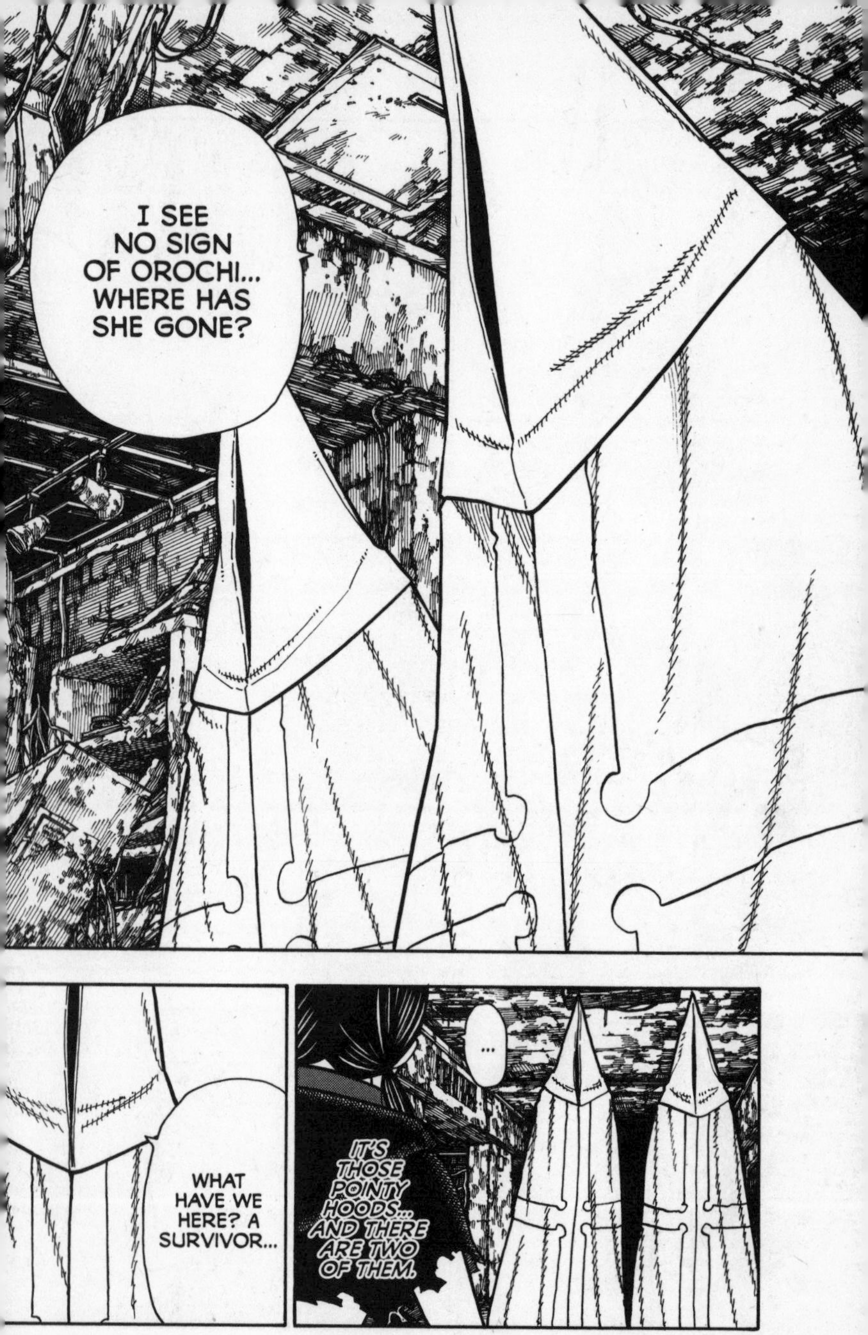
I SEE NO SIGN OF OROCHI... WHERE HAS SHE GONE?
...
IT'S THOSE POINTY HOODS... AND THERE ARE TWO OF THEM.
WHAT HAVE WE HERE? A SURVIVOR...

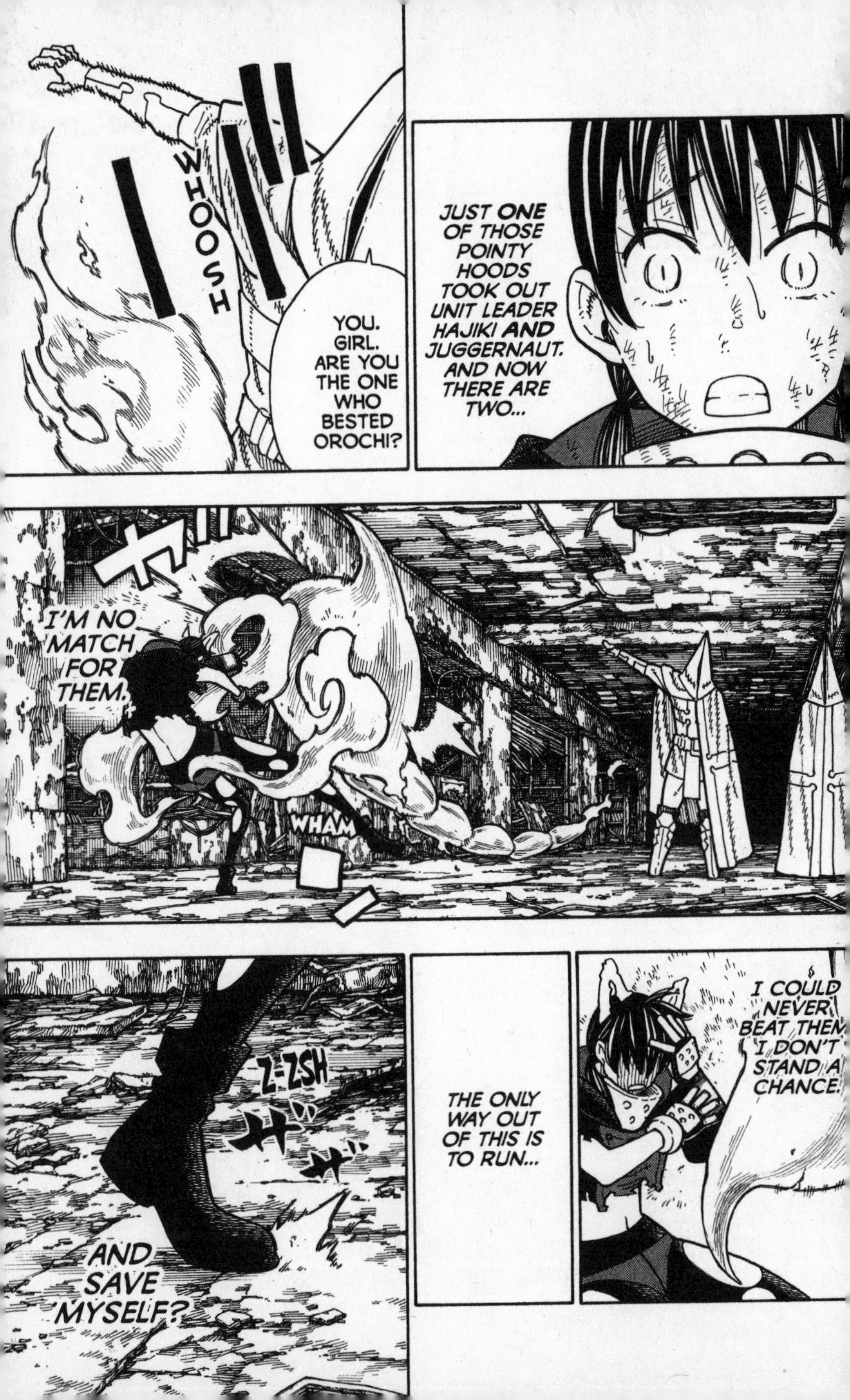
JUST ONE OF THOSE POINTY HOODS TOOK OUT UNIT LEADER HAJIKI AND JUGGERNAUT. AND NOW THERE ARE TWO...
WHOOSH
YOU. GIRL. ARE YOU THE ONE WHO BESTED OROCHI?
I'M NO MATCH FOR THEM.
WHAM
I COULD NEVER BEAT THEM. I DON'T STAND A CHANCE.
THE ONLY WAY OUT OF THIS IS TO RUN...
Z-ZSH
AND SAVE MYSELF?

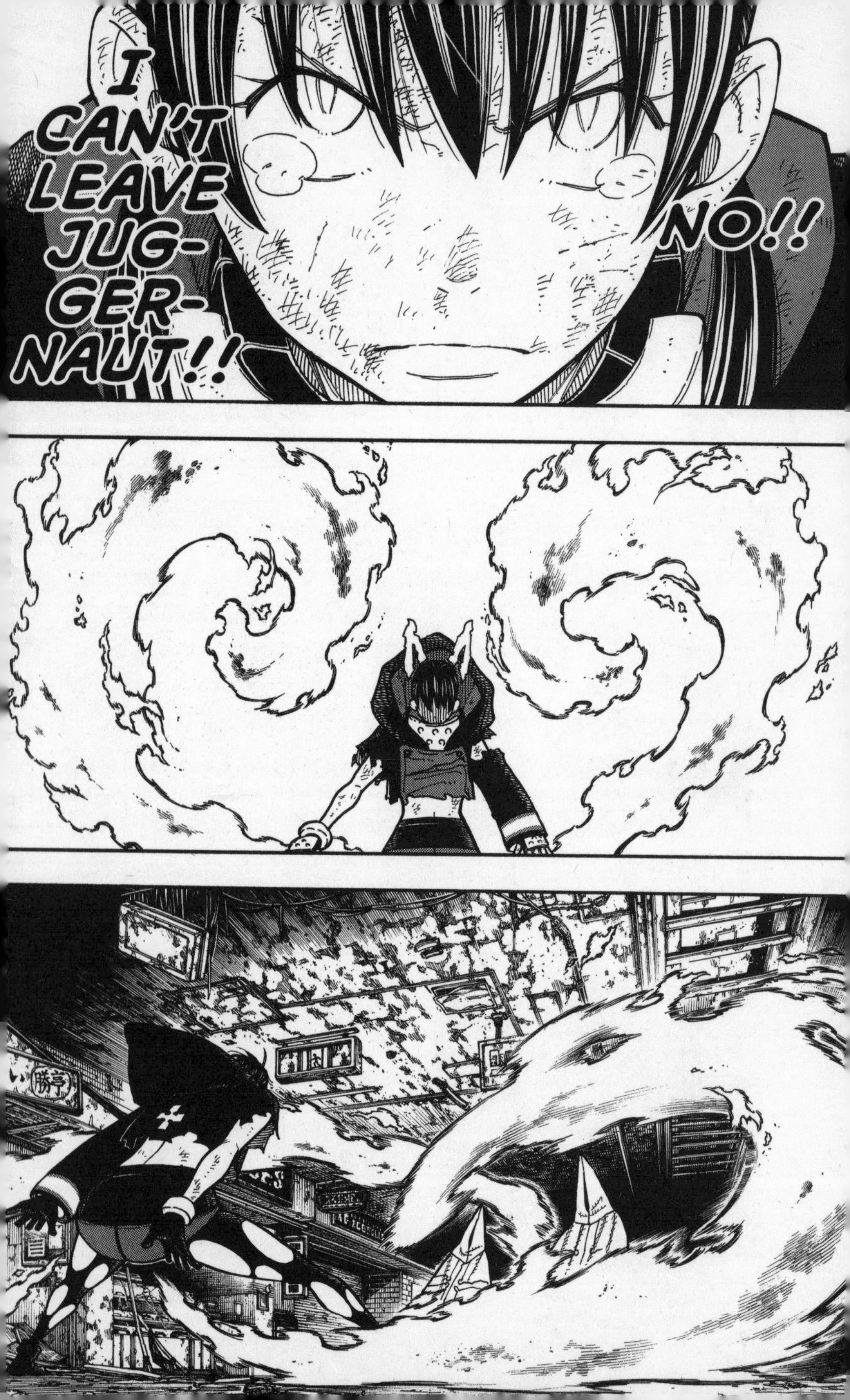
NO!!
I CAN'T LEAVE JUG-GER-NAUT!!

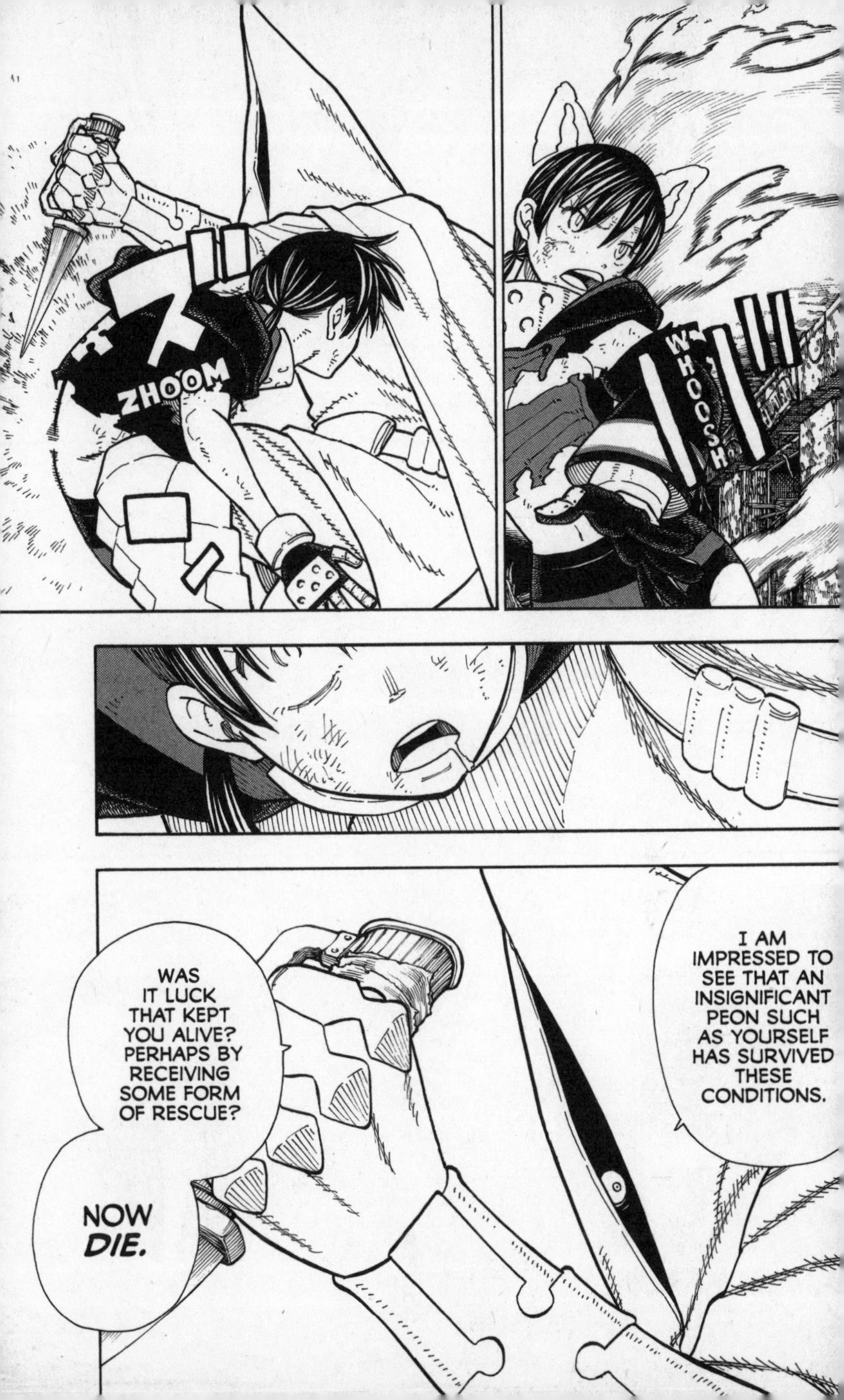
WHOOSH
ZHOOM
I AM IMPRESSED TO SEE THAT AN INSIGNIFICANT PEON SUCH AS YOURSELF HAS SURVIVED THESE CONDITIONS.
WAS IT LUCK THAT KEPT YOU ALIVE? PERHAPS BY RECEIVING SOME FORM OF RESCUE?
NOW *DIE.*

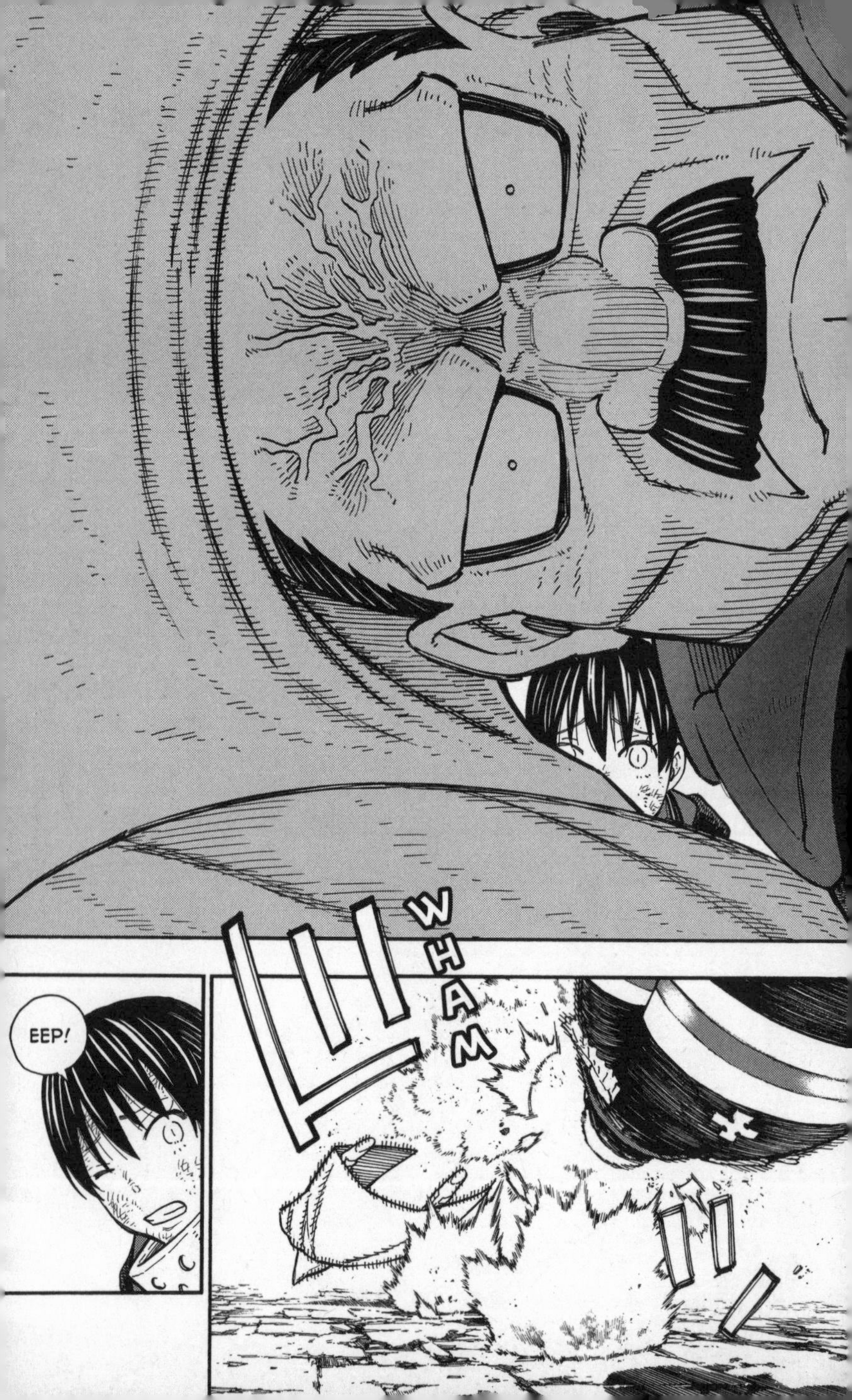
WHAM
EEP!

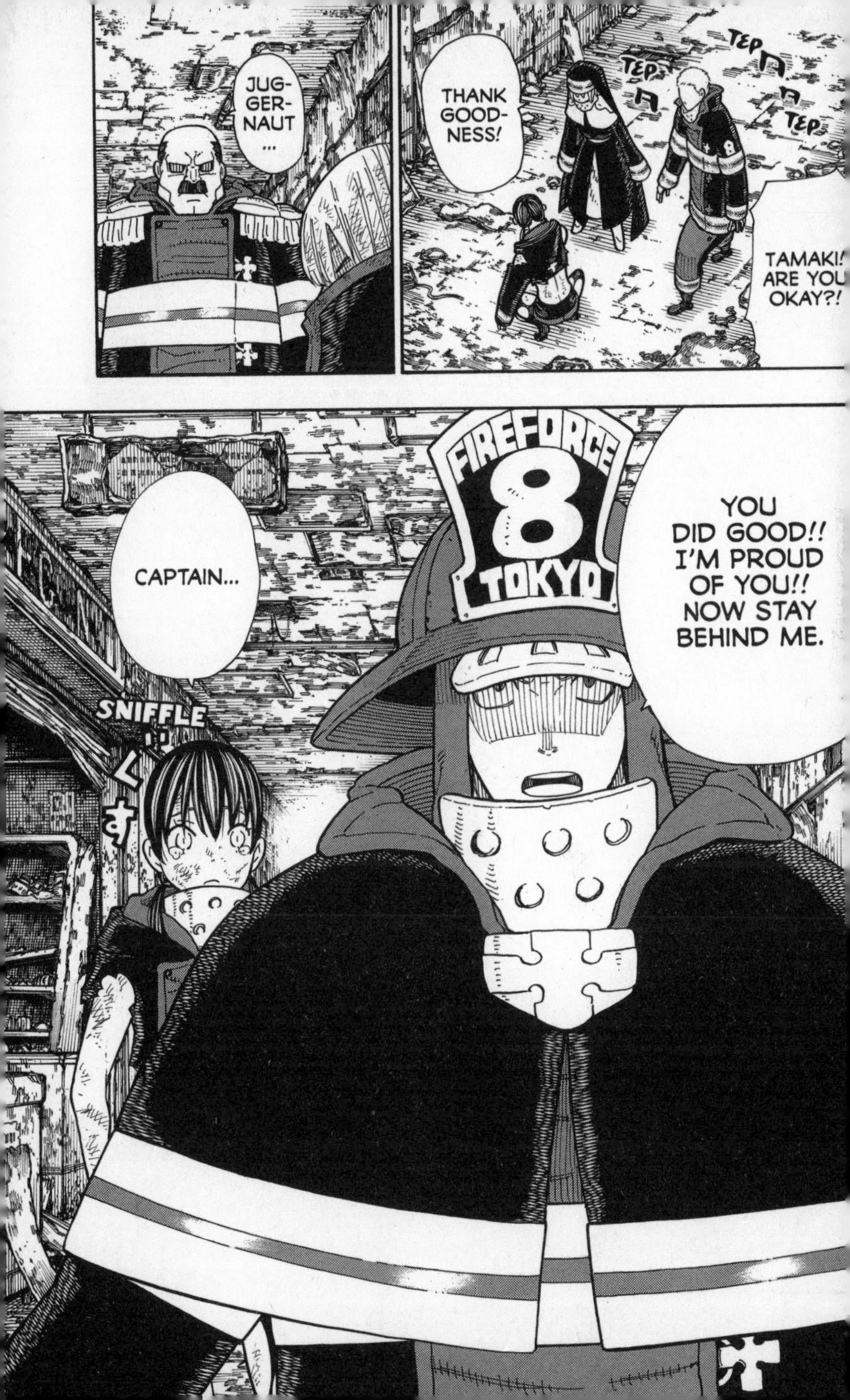
TEP
TEP
TEP
THANK GOODNESS!
TAMAKI! ARE YOU OKAY?!
JUGGERNAUT...
YOU DID GOOD!! I'M PROUD OF YOU!! NOW STAY BEHIND ME.
CAPTAIN...
SNIFFLE
FIREFORCE 8 TOKYO

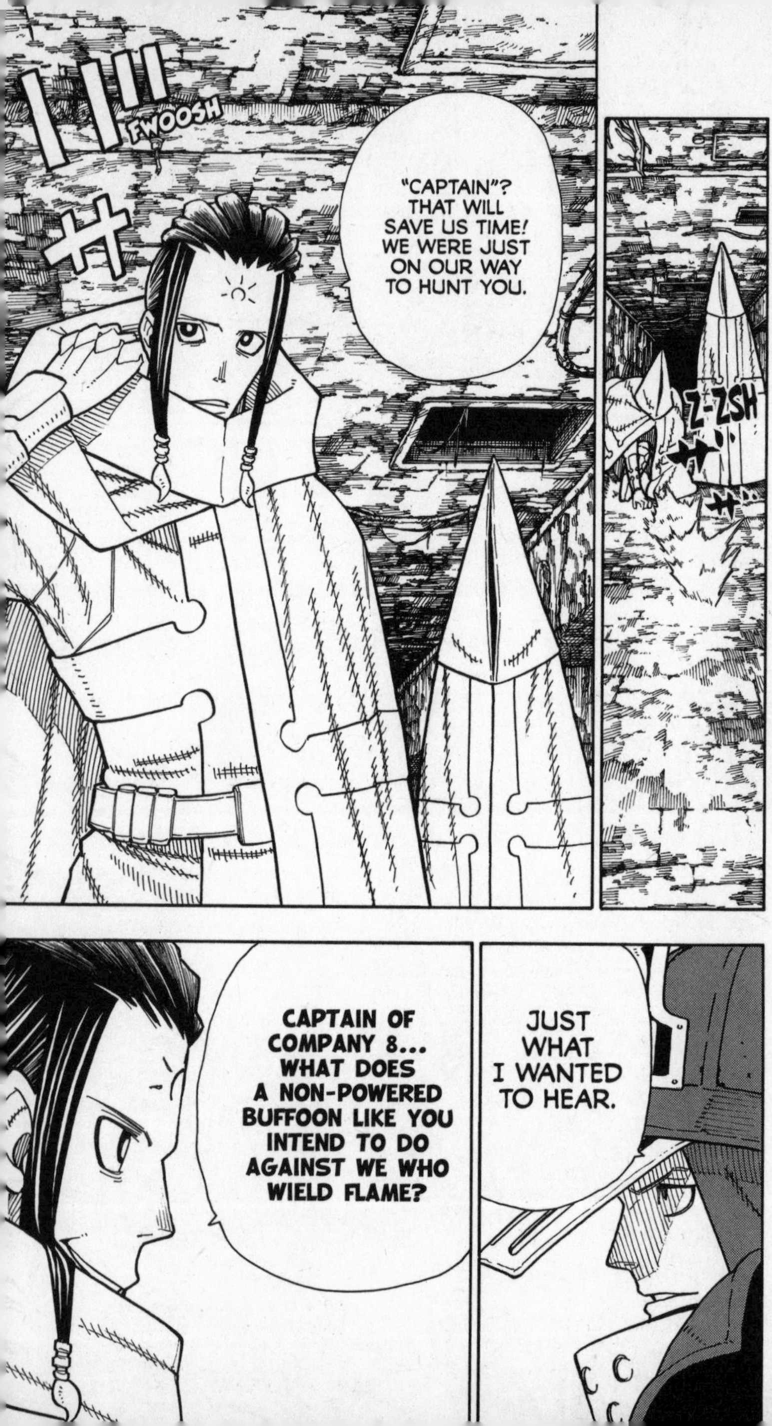
Z-ZSH
"CAPTAIN"? THAT WILL SAVE US TIME! WE WERE JUST ON OUR WAY TO HUNT YOU.
FWOOSH
JUST WHAT I WANTED TO HEAR.
CAPTAIN OF COMPANY 8... WHAT DOES A NON-POWERED BUFFOON LIKE YOU INTEND TO DO AGAINST WE WHO WIELD FLAME?

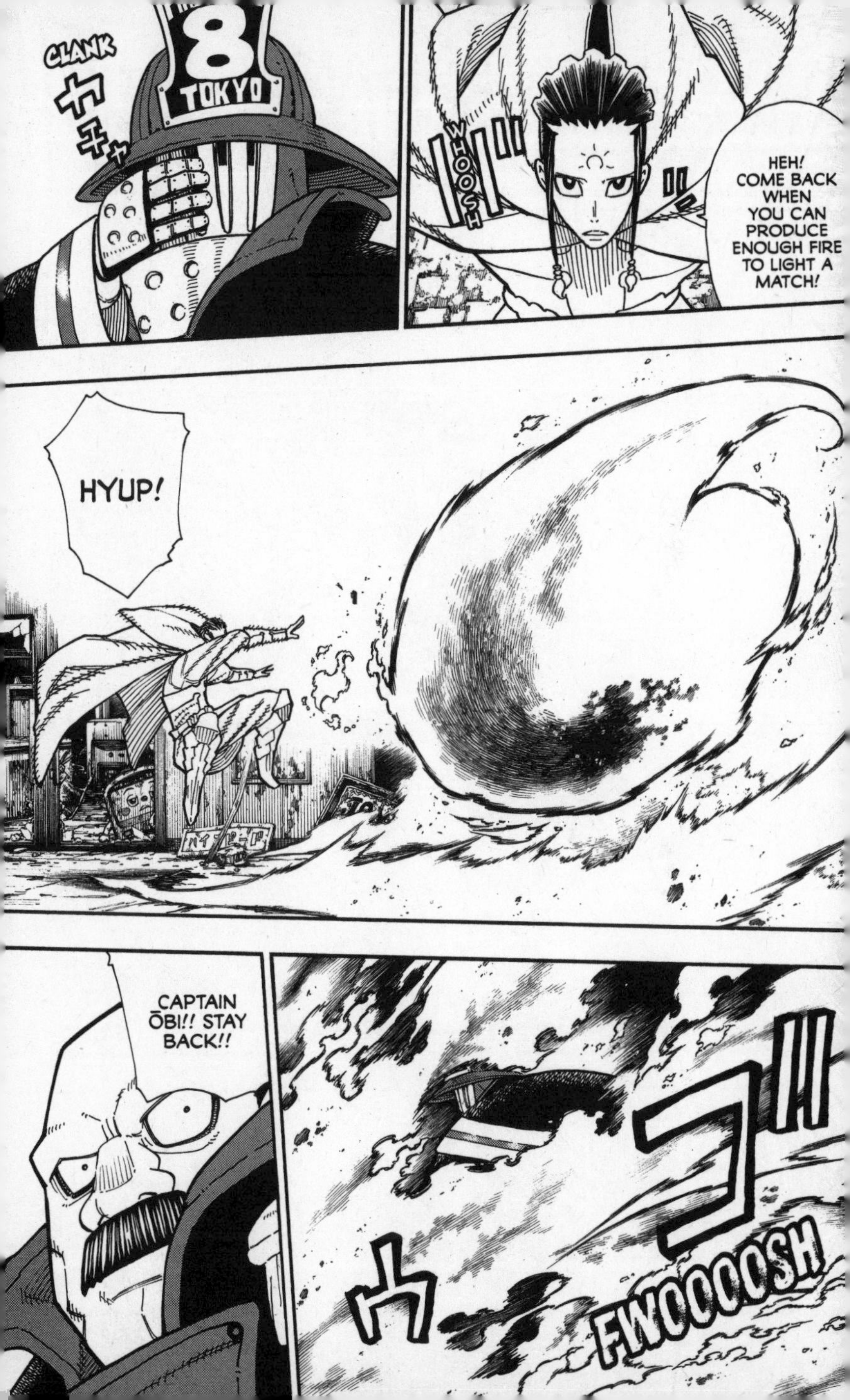
WHOOSH
HEH! COME BACK WHEN YOU CAN PRODUCE ENOUGH FIRE TO LIGHT A MATCH!
CLANK
HYUP!
FWOOOOOSH
CAPTAIN ŌBI!! STAY BACK!!

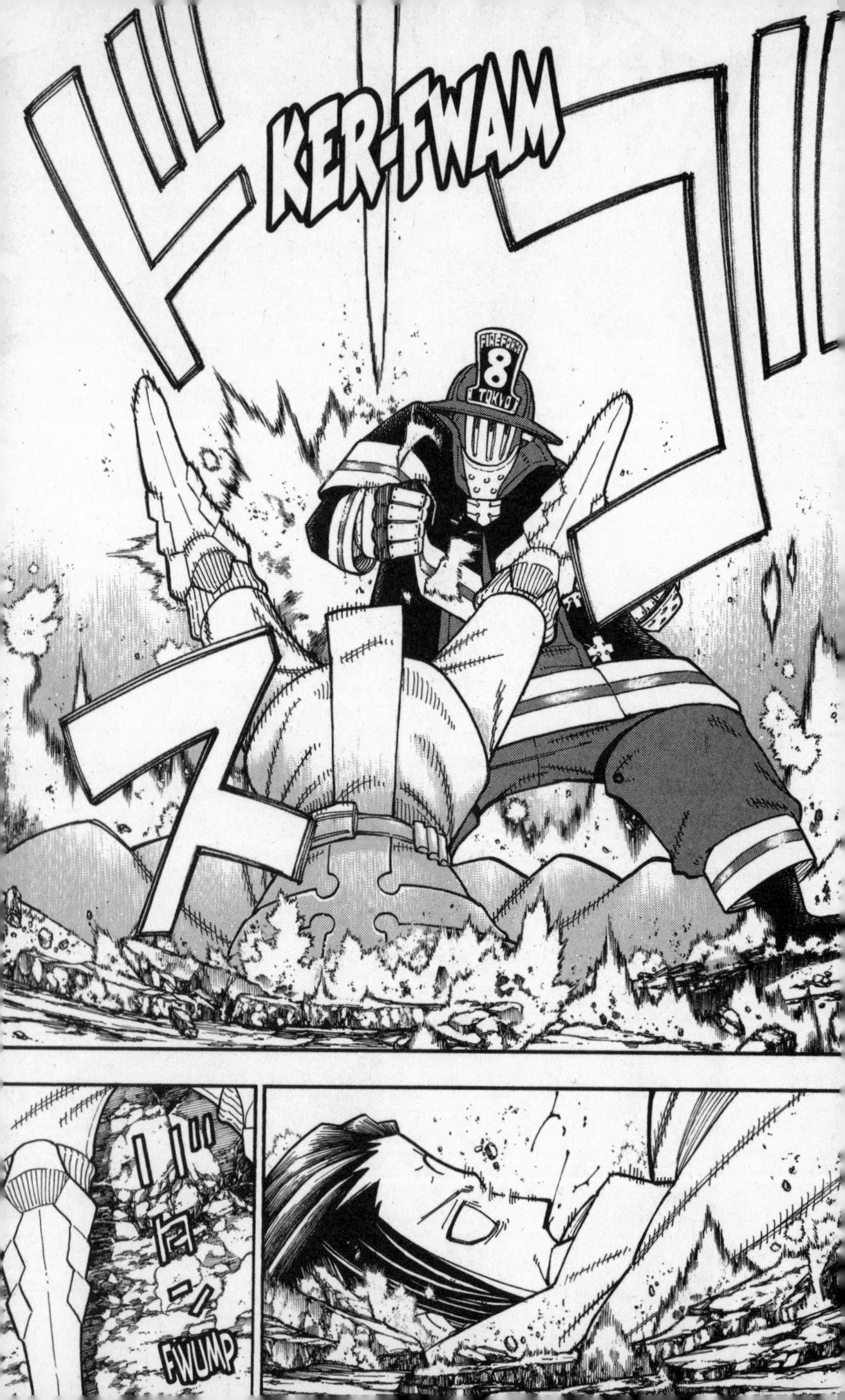
KER-FWAM
FIRE FORCE
8
TOKYO
FWUMP

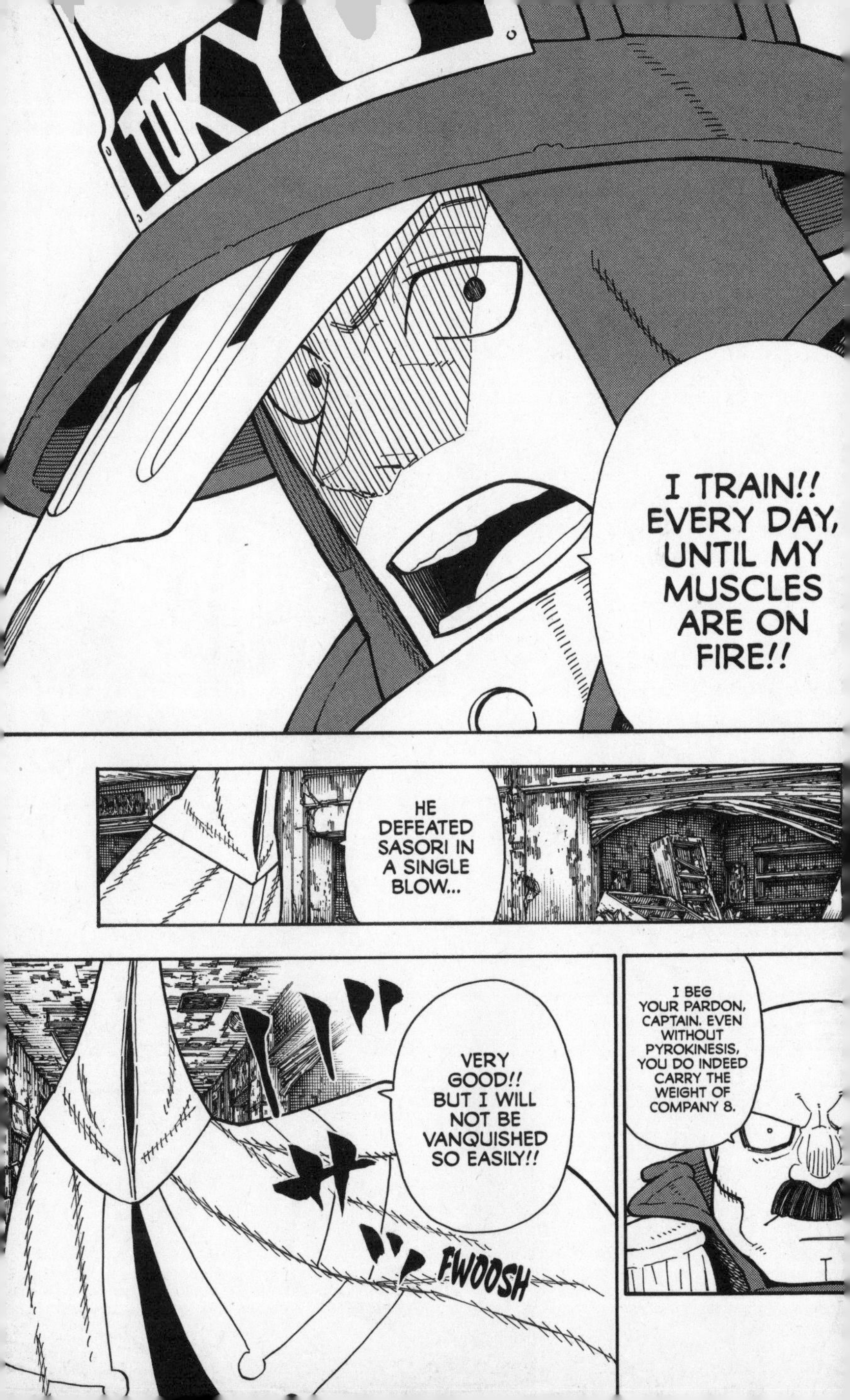
I TRAIN!! EVERY DAY, UNTIL MY MUSCLES ARE ON FIRE!!
HE DEFEATED SASORI IN A SINGLE BLOW...
I BEG YOUR PARDON, CAPTAIN. EVEN WITHOUT PYROKINESIS, YOU DO INDEED CARRY THE WEIGHT OF COMPANY 8.
VERY GOOD!! BUT I WILL NOT BE VANQUISHED SO EASILY!!
FWOOSH

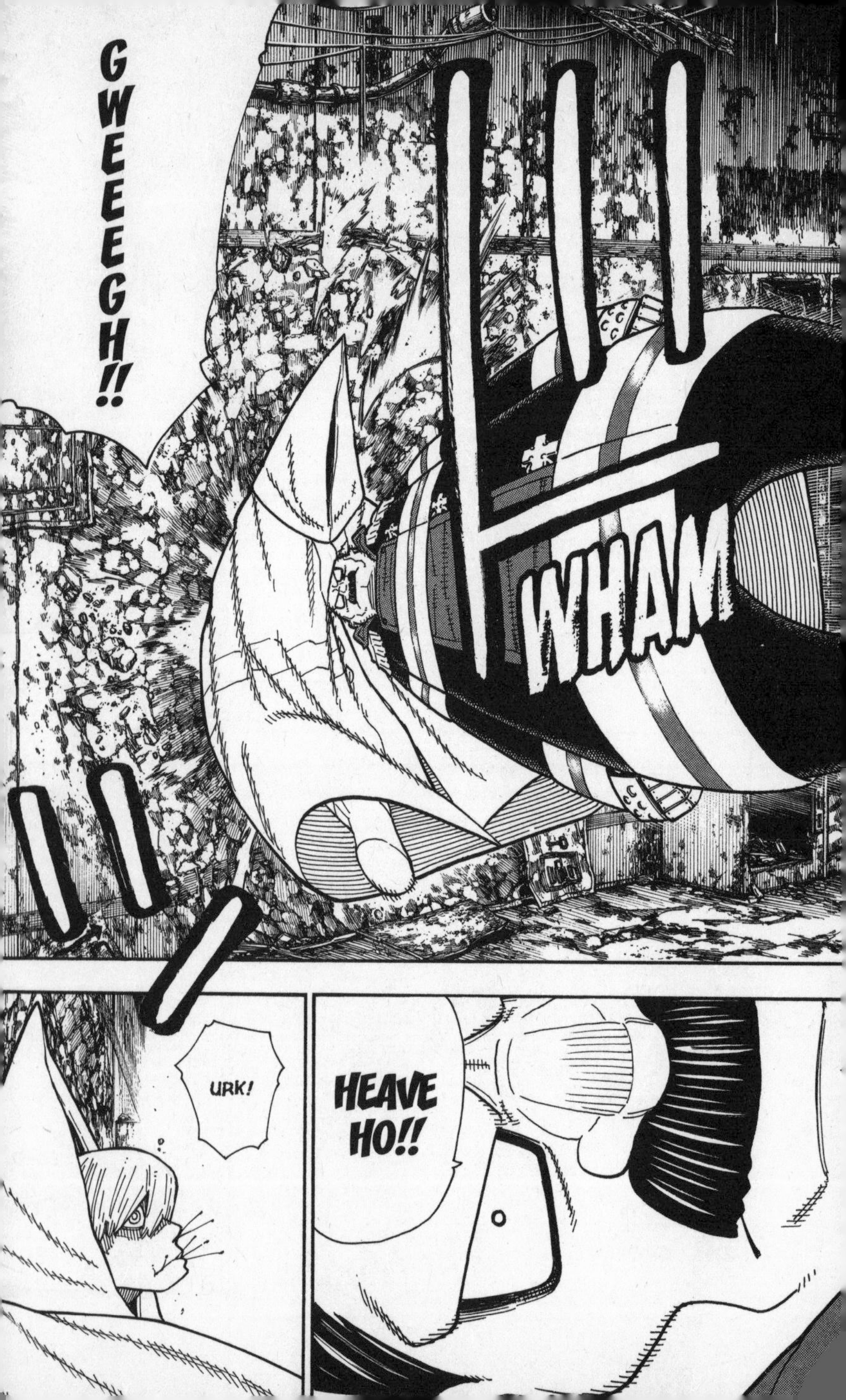
WHAM
GWEEEGH!!
HEAVE HO!!
URK!

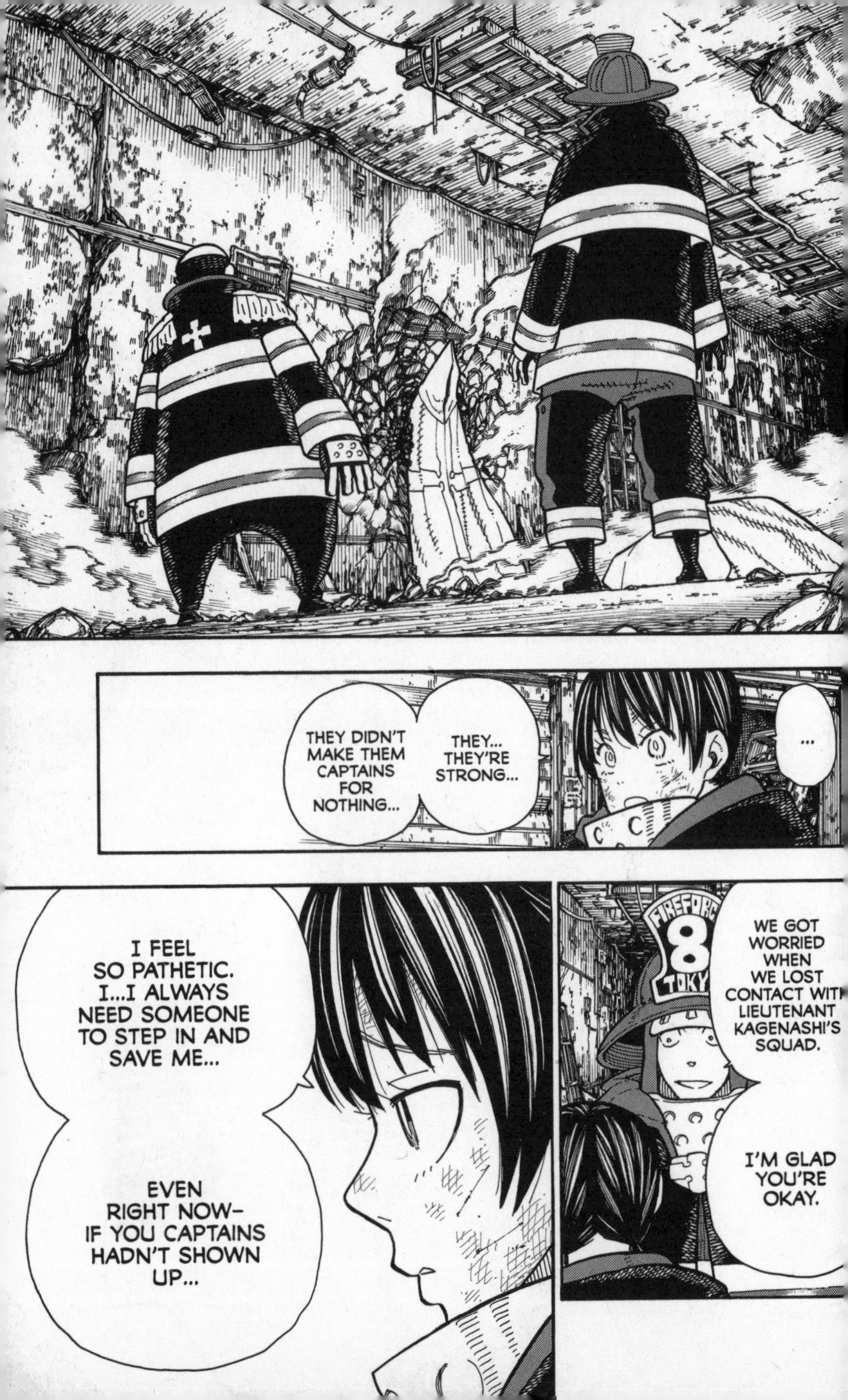
...
THEY... THEY'RE STRONG...
THEY DIDN'T MAKE THEM CAPTAINS FOR NOTHING...
WE GOT WORRIED WHEN WE LOST CONTACT WIT LIEUTENANT KAGENASHI'S SQUAD.
I'M GLAD YOU'RE OKAY.
I FEEL SO PATHETIC. I...I ALWAYS NEED SOMEONE TO STEP IN AND SAVE ME...
EVEN RIGHT NOW– IF YOU CAPTAINS HADN'T SHOWN UP...

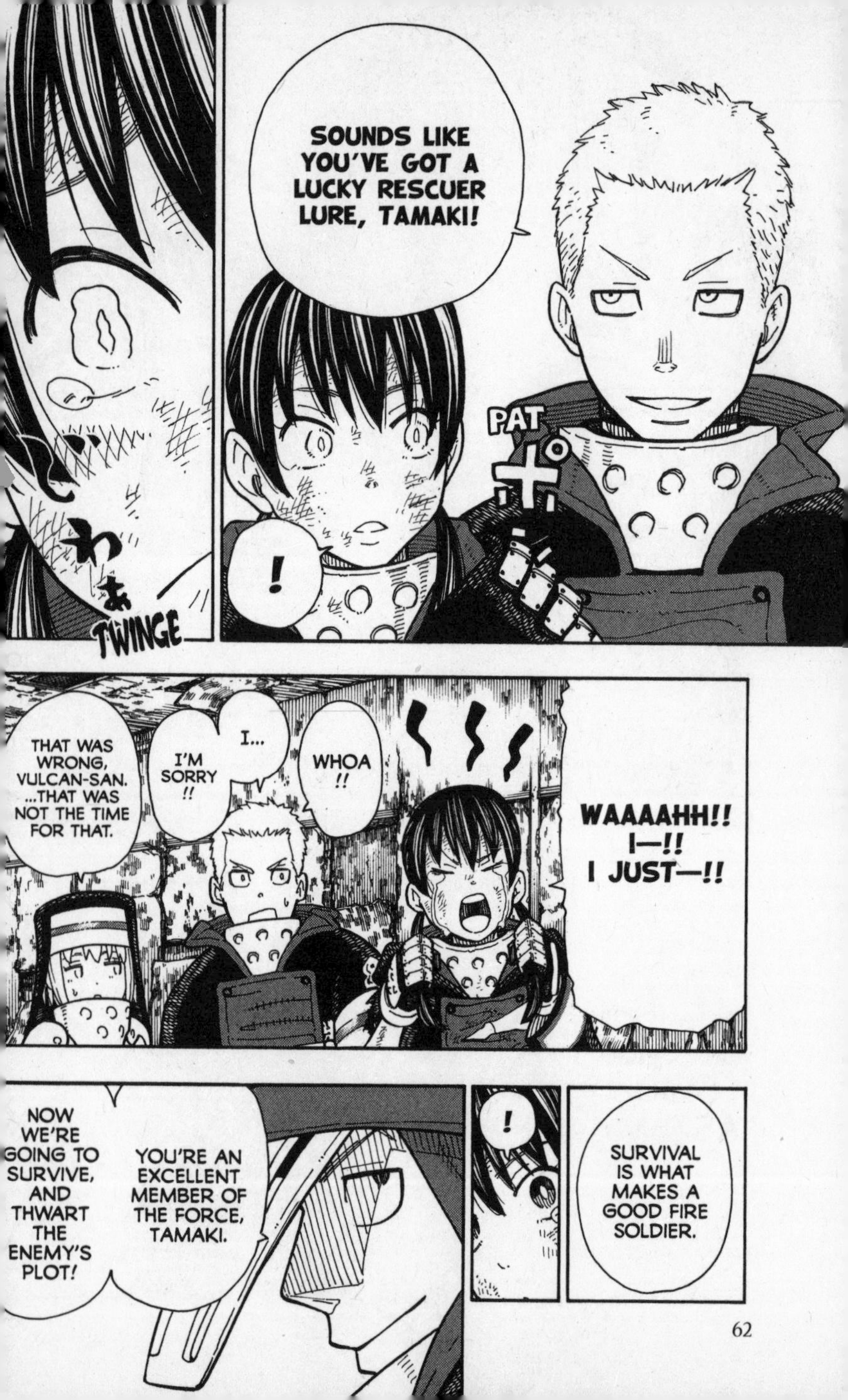
SOUNDS LIKE YOU'VE GOT A LUCKY RESCUER LURE, TAMAKI!
PAT
!
TWINGE
WAAAAHH!! I—!! I JUST—!!
WHOA !!
I...
I'M SORRY !!
THAT WAS WRONG, VULCAN-SAN. ...THAT WAS NOT THE TIME FOR THAT.
SURVIVAL IS WHAT MAKES A GOOD FIRE SOLDIER.
!
YOU'RE AN EXCELLENT MEMBER OF THE FORCE, TAMAKI.
NOW WE'RE GOING TO SURVIVE, AND THWART THE ENEMY'S PLOT!

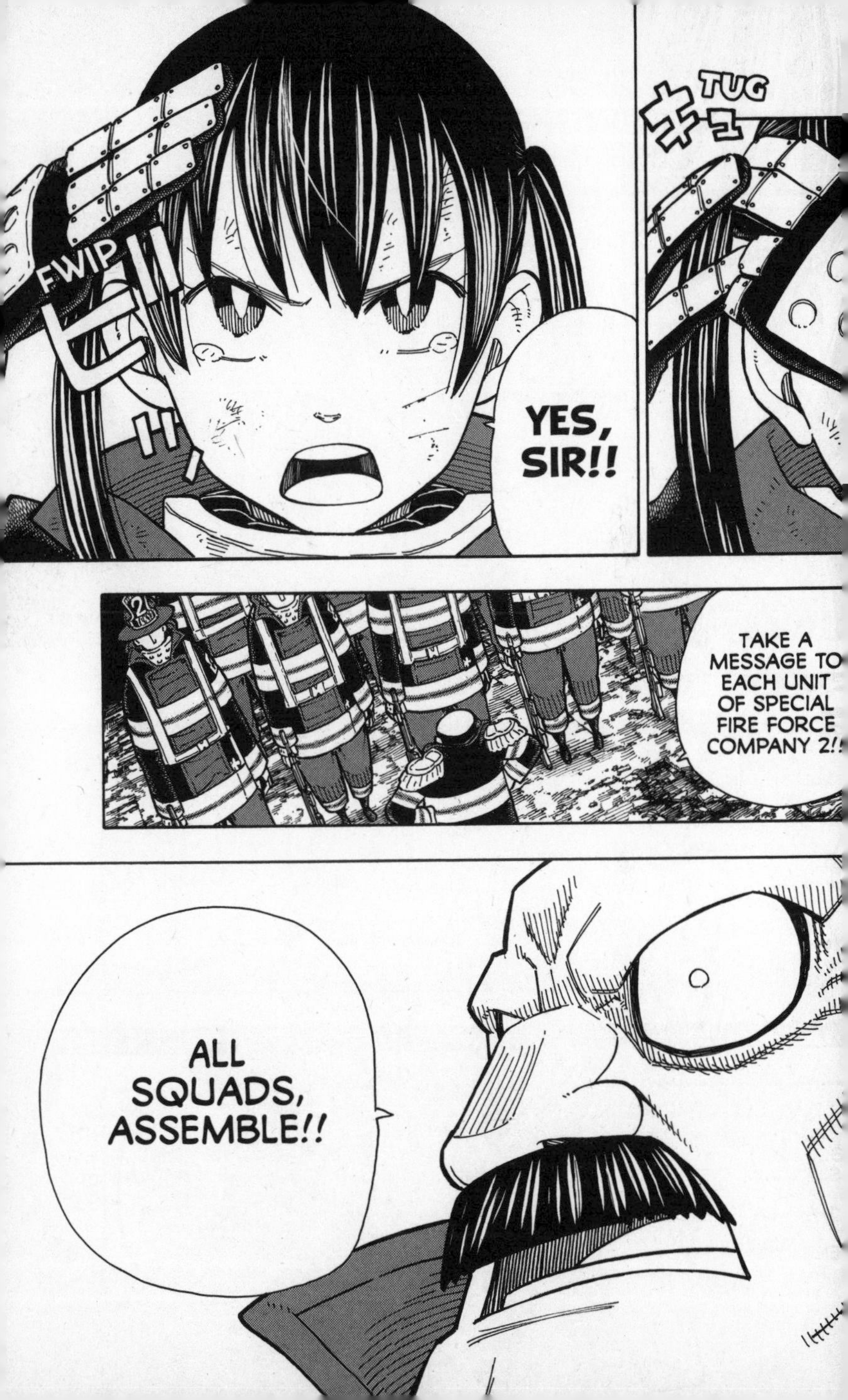
キュ
TUG
ビッ
FWIP
YES, SIR!!
TAKE A MESSAGE TO EACH UNIT OF SPECIAL FIRE FORCE COMPANY 2!!
ALL SQUADS, ASSEMBLE!!

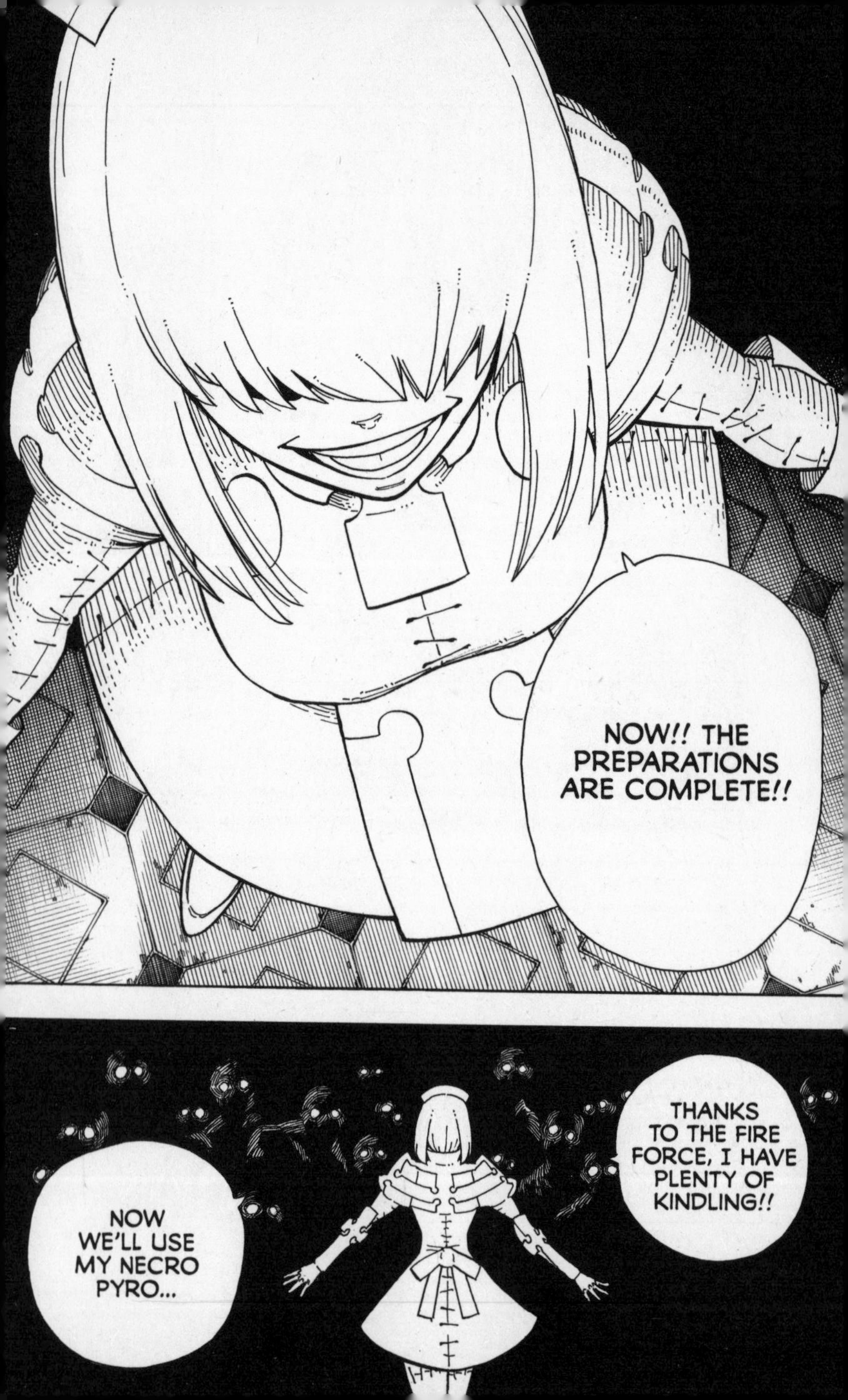
NOW!! THE PREPARATIONS ARE COMPLETE!!
THANKS TO THE FIRE FORCE, I HAVE PLENTY OF KINDLING!!
NOW WE'LL USE MY NECRO PYRO...

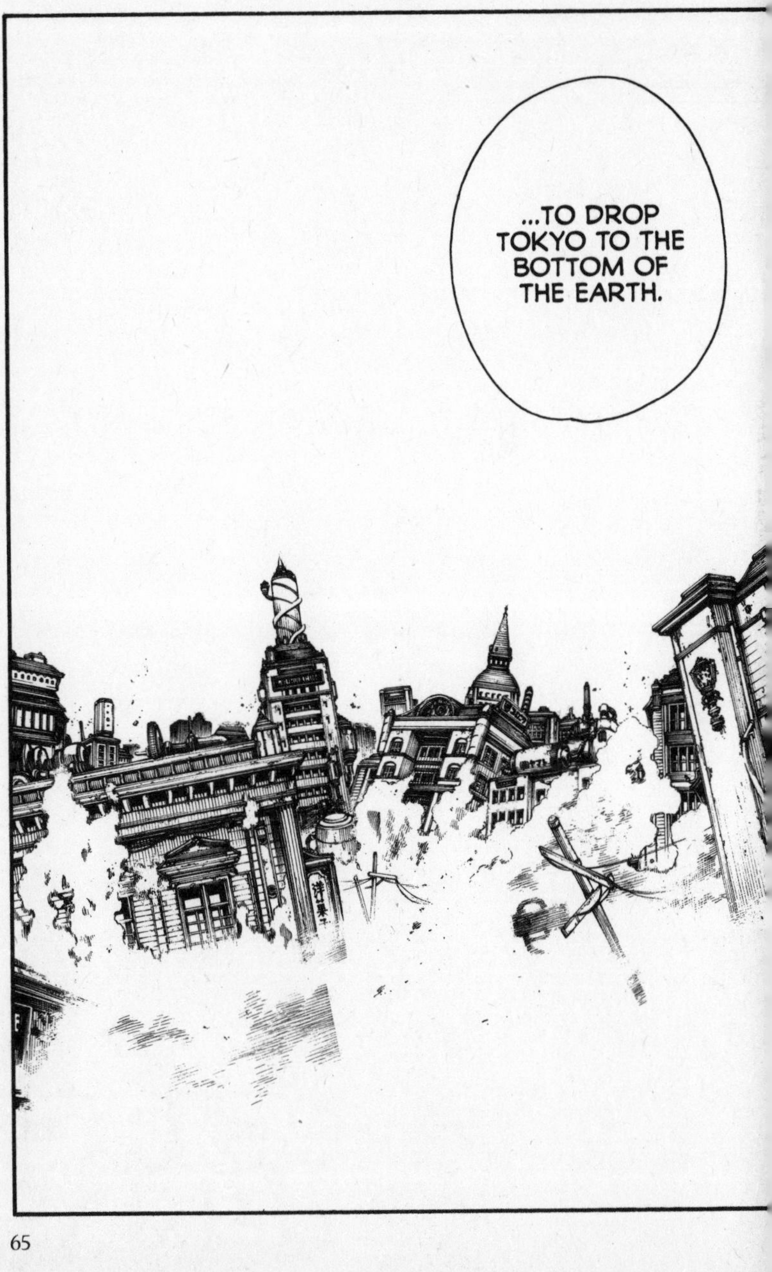
...TO DROP TOKYO TO THE BOTTOM OF THE EARTH.

FIRE FORCE

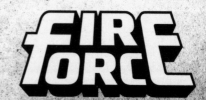

CHAPTER CLXIII: A PLOT FOR EXTINCTION

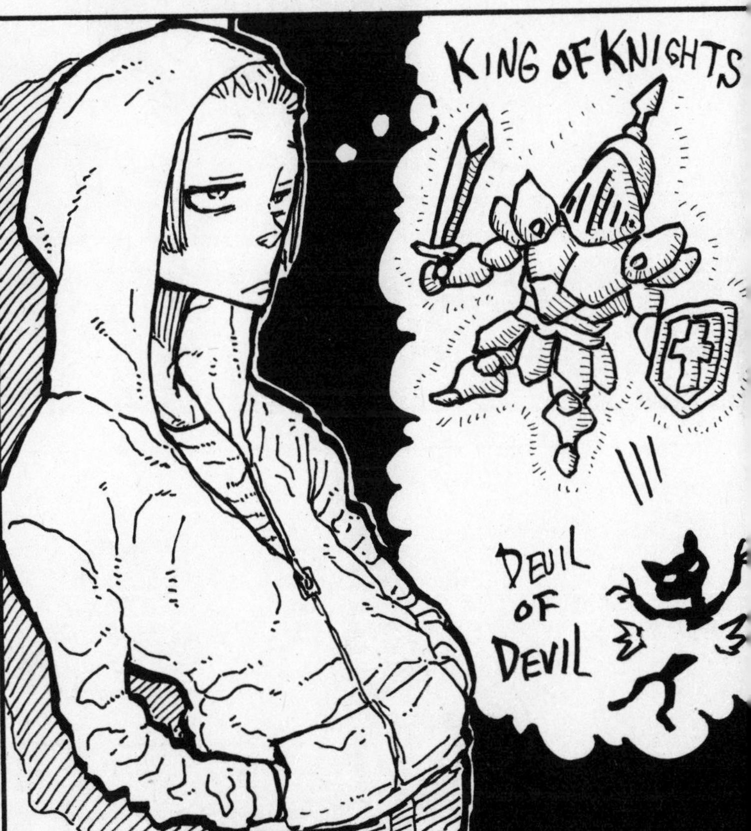
KING OF KNIGHTS
DEVIL OF DEVIL

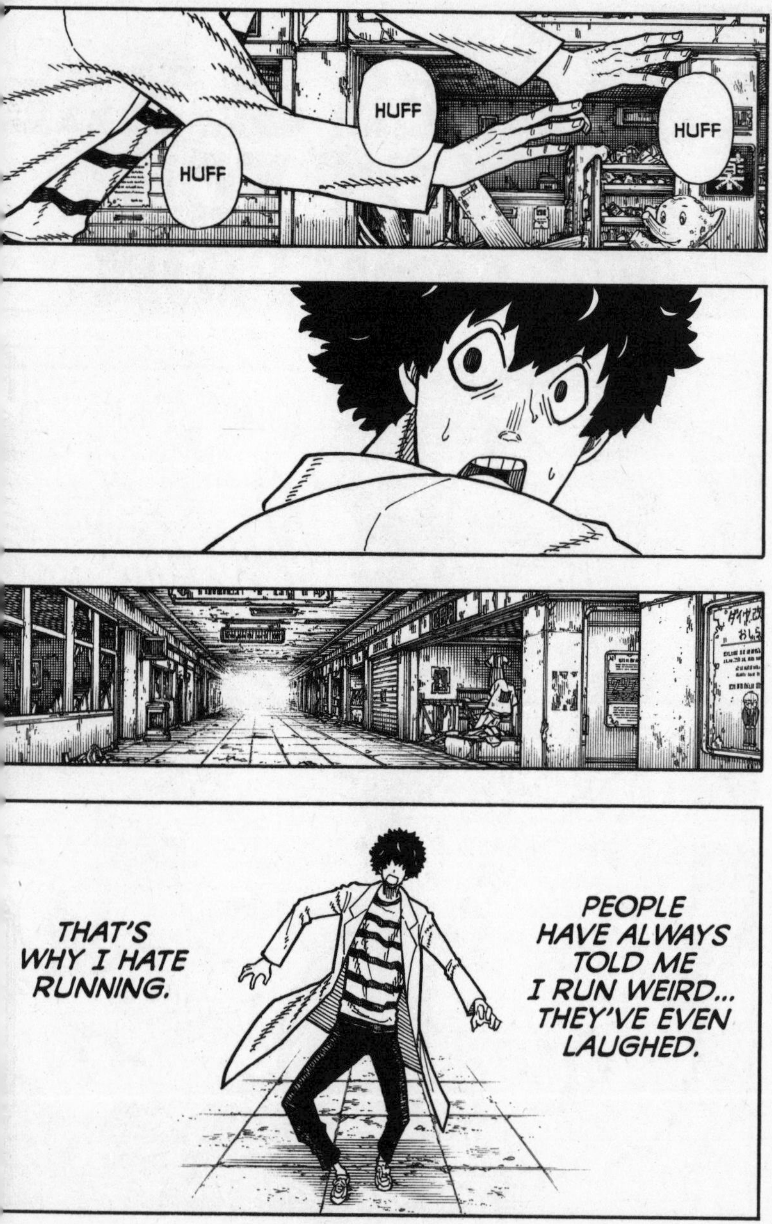
HUFF
HUFF
HUFF
PEOPLE HAVE ALWAYS TOLD ME I RUN WEIRD... THEY'VE EVEN LAUGHED.
THAT'S WHY I HATE RUNNING.

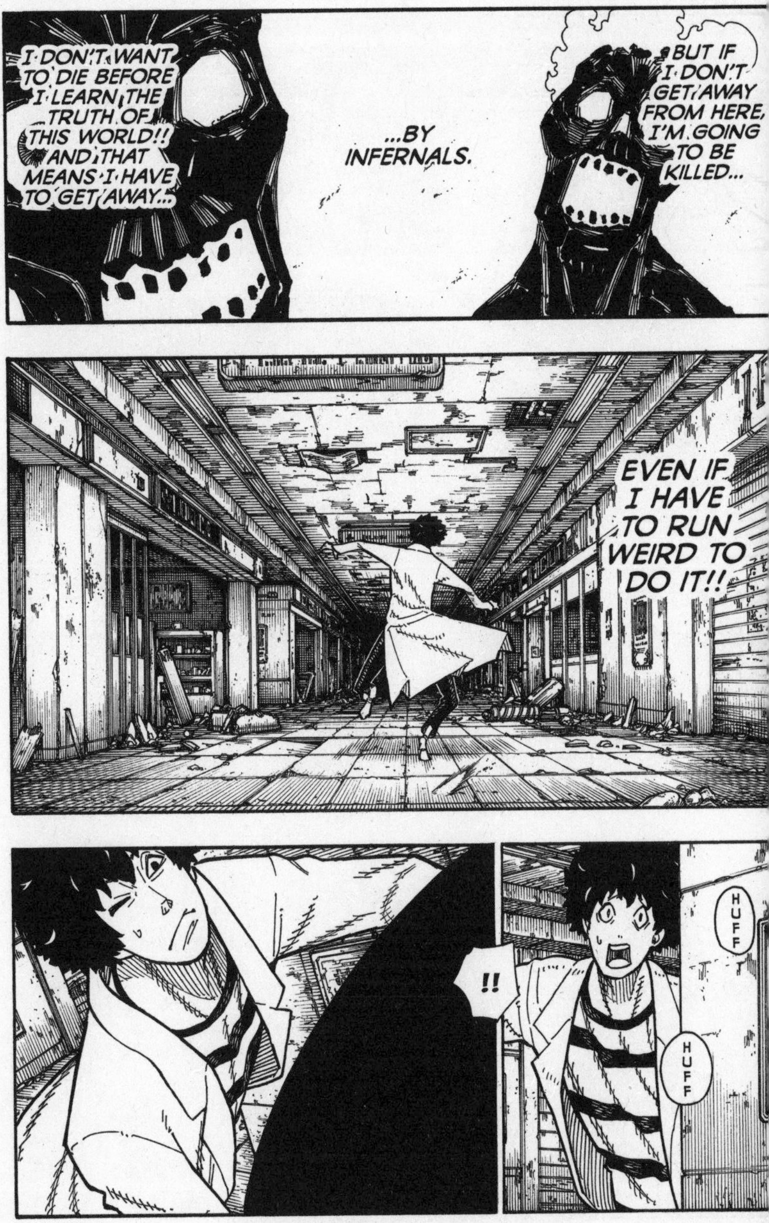
BUT IF I DON'T GET AWAY FROM HERE, I'M GOING TO BE KILLED...
...BY INFERNALS.
I DON'T WANT TO DIE BEFORE I LEARN THE TRUTH OF THIS WORLD!! AND THAT MEANS I HAVE TO GET AWAY...
EVEN IF I HAVE TO RUN WEIRD TO DO IT!!
HUFF
HUFF
!!

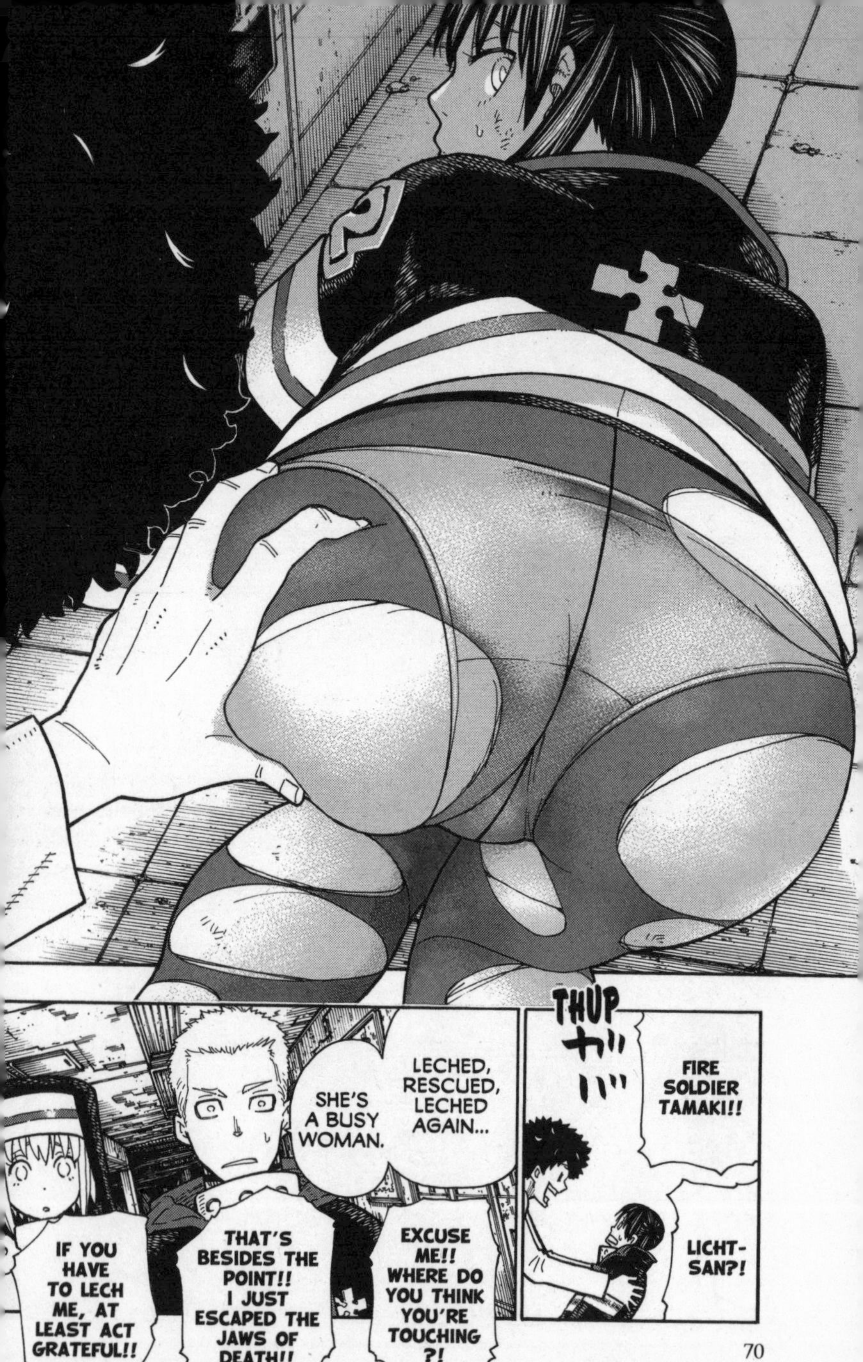
THUP
FIRE SOLDIER TAMAKI!!
LICHT-SAN?!
LECHED, RESCUED, LECHED AGAIN...
SHE'S A BUSY WOMAN.
EXCUSE ME!! WHERE DO YOU THINK YOU'RE TOUCHING?!
THAT'S BESIDES THE POINT!! I JUST ESCAPED THE JAWS OF DEATH!!
IF YOU HAVE TO LECH ME, AT LEAST ACT GRATEFUL!!

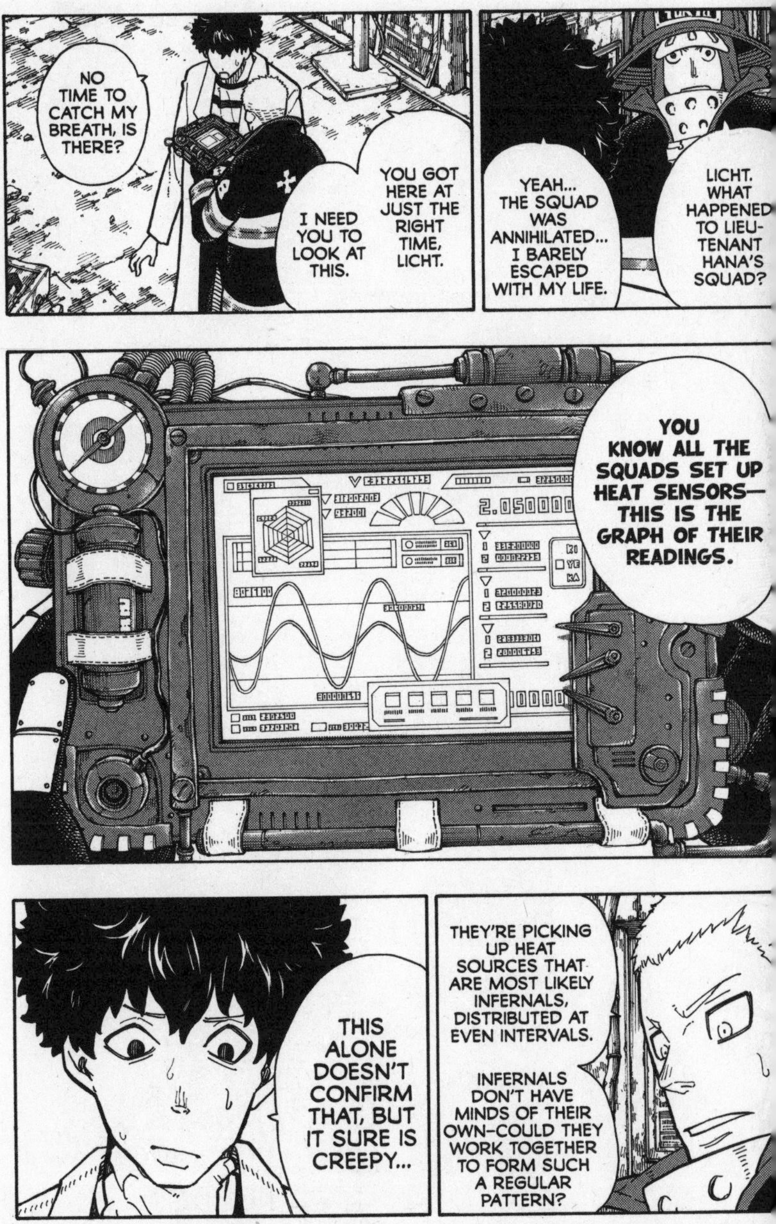
LICHT. WHAT HAPPENED TO LIEU-TENANT HANA'S SQUAD?
YEAH... THE SQUAD WAS ANNIHILATED... I BARELY ESCAPED WITH MY LIFE.
YOU GOT HERE AT JUST THE RIGHT TIME, LICHT.
I NEED YOU TO LOOK AT THIS.
NO TIME TO CATCH MY BREATH, IS THERE?
YOU KNOW ALL THE SQUADS SET UP HEAT SENSORS—THIS IS THE GRAPH OF THEIR READINGS.
THEY'RE PICKING UP HEAT SOURCES THAT ARE MOST LIKELY INFERNALS, DISTRIBUTED AT EVEN INTERVALS.
INFERNALS DON'T HAVE MINDS OF THEIR OWN—COULD THEY WORK TOGETHER TO FORM SUCH A REGULAR PATTERN?
THIS ALONE DOESN'T CONFIRM THAT, BUT IT SURE IS CREEPY...

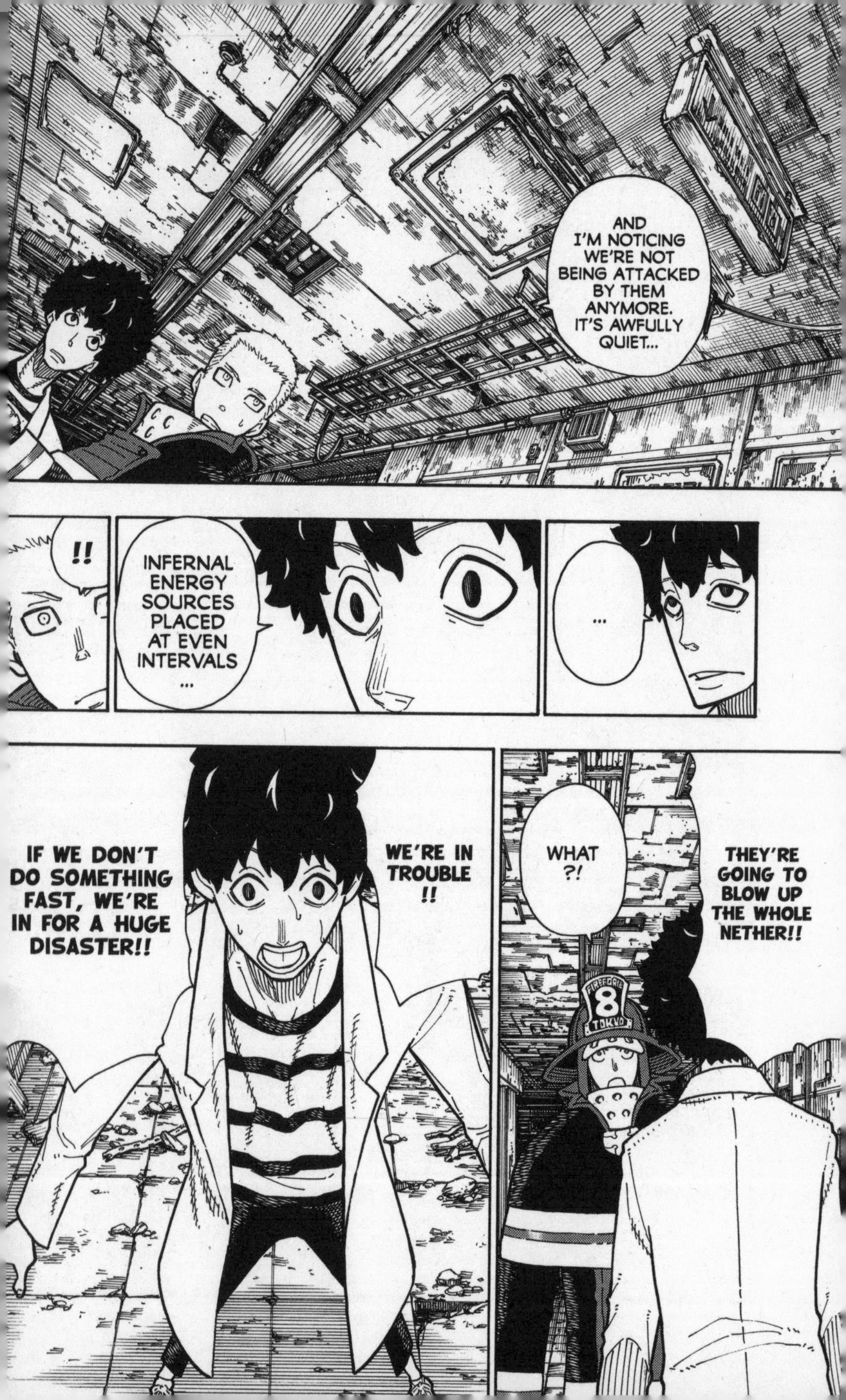
AND I'M NOTICING WE'RE NOT BEING ATTACKED BY THEM ANYMORE. IT'S AWFULLY QUIET...
...
INFERNAL ENERGY SOURCES PLACED AT EVEN INTERVALS ...
!!
THEY'RE GOING TO BLOW UP THE WHOLE NETHER!!
WHAT ?!
WE'RE IN TROUBLE !!
IF WE DON'T DO SOMETHING FAST, WE'RE IN FOR A HUGE DISASTER!!

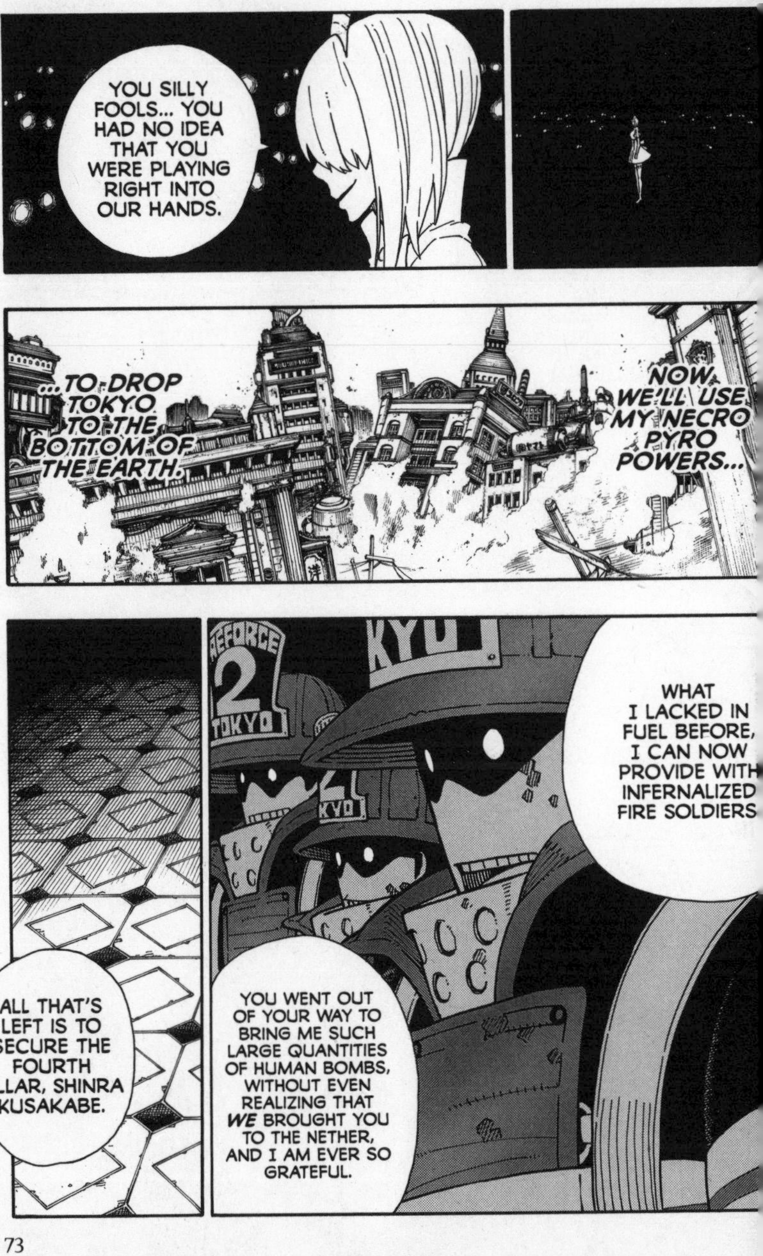
YOU SILLY FOOLS... YOU HAD NO IDEA THAT YOU WERE PLAYING RIGHT INTO OUR HANDS.
NOW WE'LL USE MY NECRO PYRO POWERS...
...TO DROP TOKYO TO THE BOTTOM OF THE EARTH.
WHAT I LACKED IN FUEL BEFORE, I CAN NOW PROVIDE WITH INFERNALIZED FIRE SOLDIERS.
YOU WENT OUT OF YOUR WAY TO BRING ME SUCH LARGE QUANTITIES OF HUMAN BOMBS, WITHOUT EVEN REALIZING THAT *WE* BROUGHT YOU TO THE NETHER, AND I AM EVER SO GRATEFUL.
ALL THAT'S LEFT IS TO SECURE THE FOURTH PILLAR, SHINRA KUSAKABE.

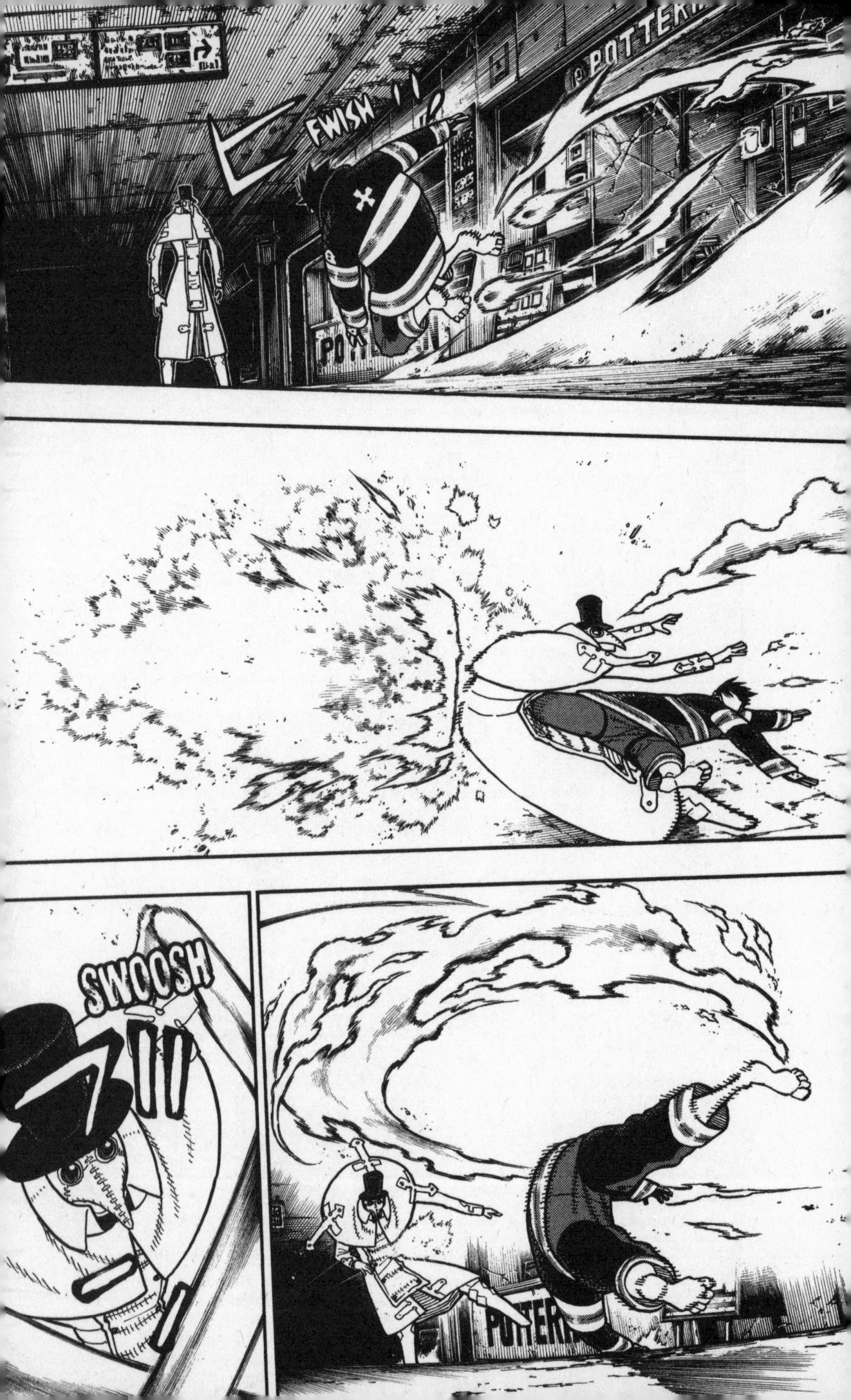
FWISH
SWOOSH

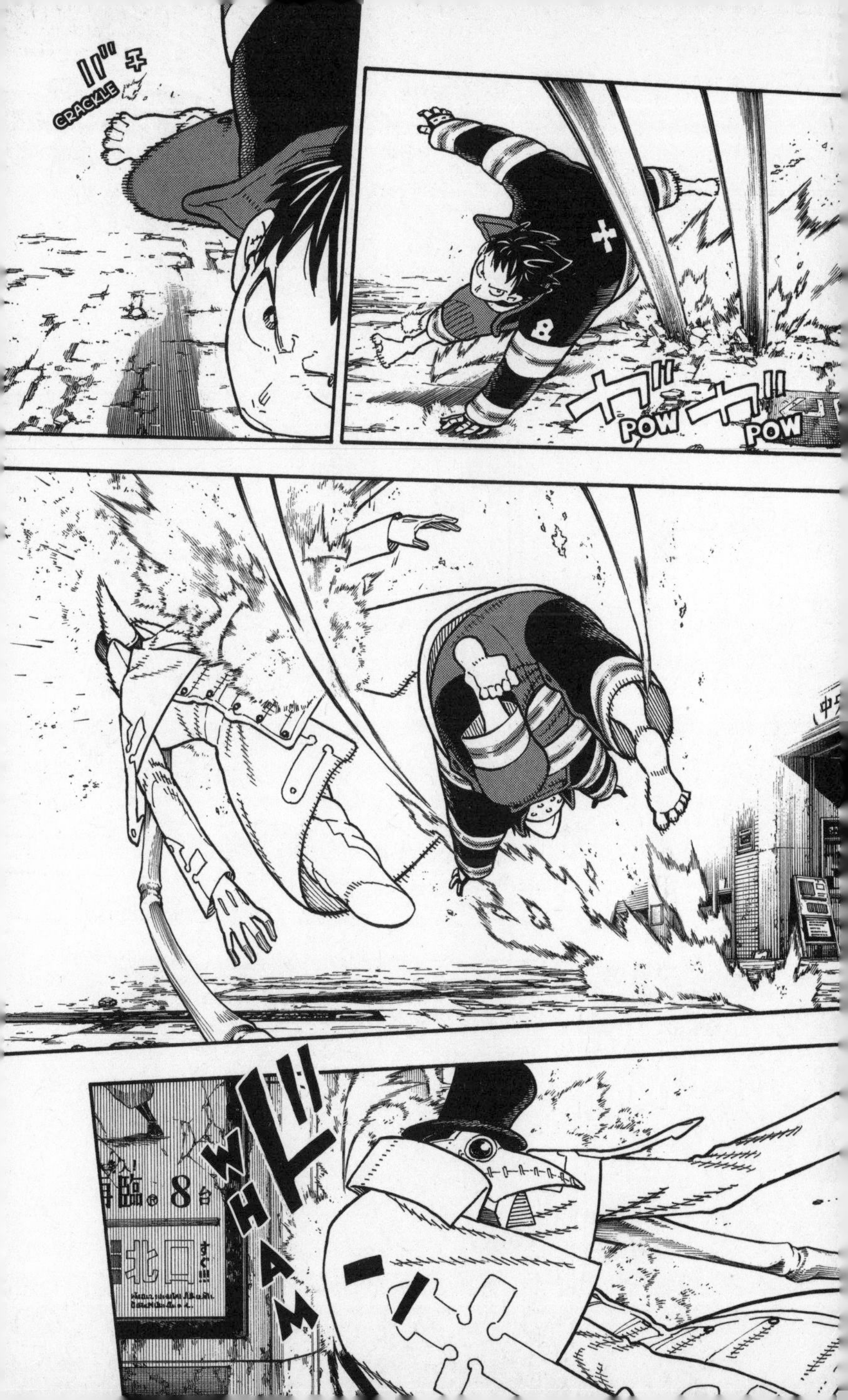
POW
POW
CRACKLE
WHAM

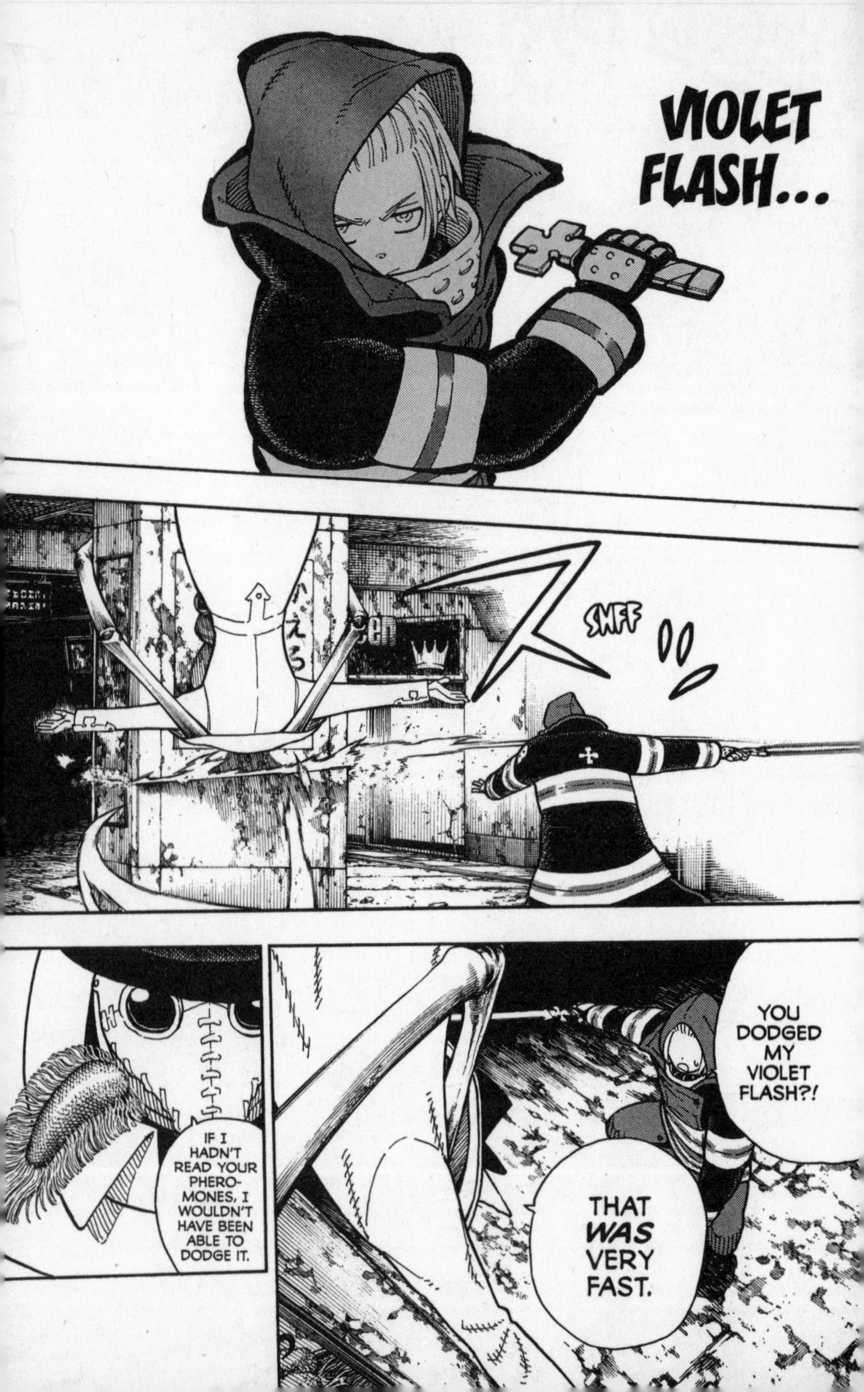
VIOLET FLASH...
SMFF
YOU DODGED MY VIOLET FLASH?!
THAT WAS VERY FAST.
IF I HADN'T READ YOUR PHEROMONES, I WOULDN'T HAVE BEEN ABLE TO DODGE IT.

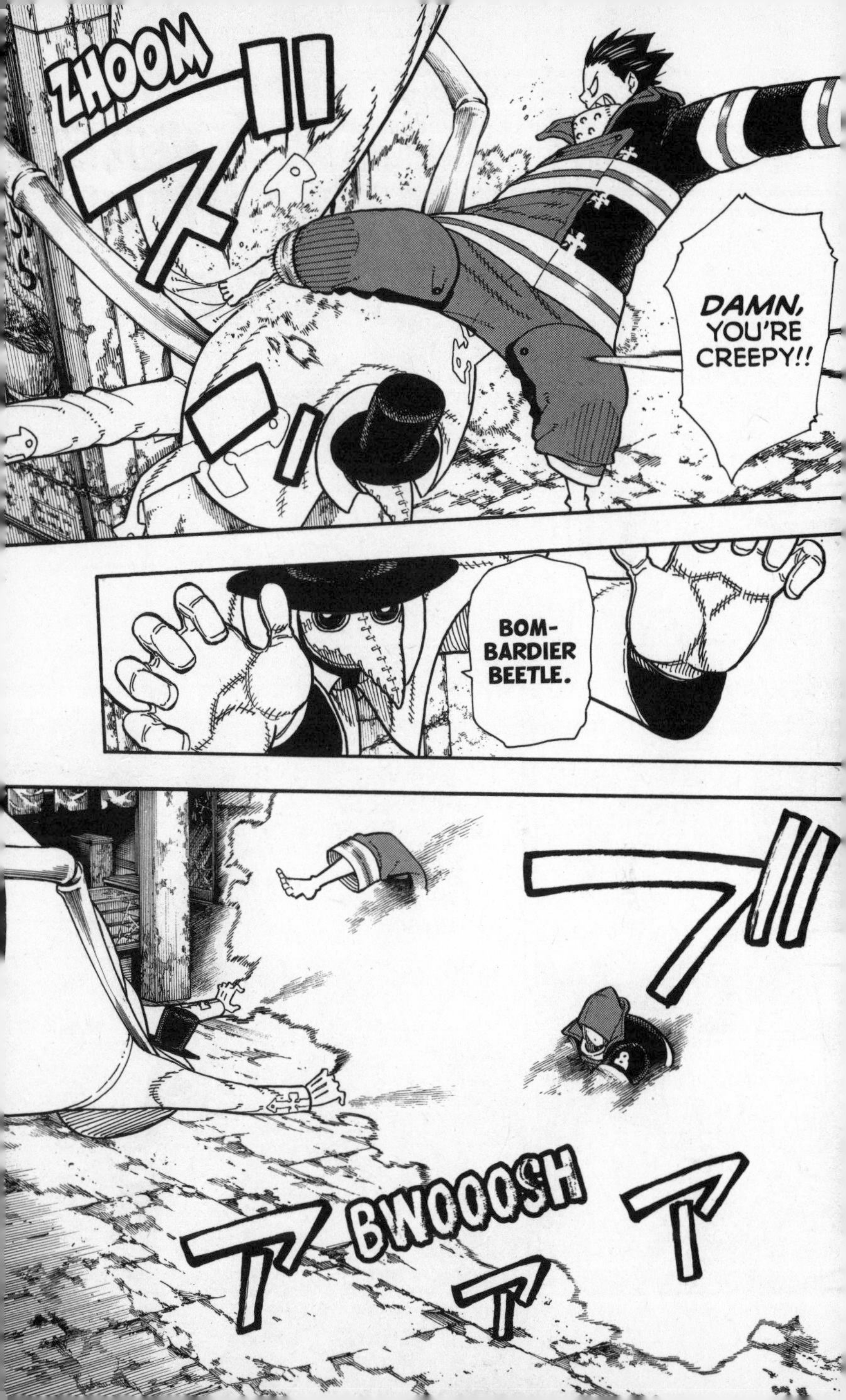
ZHOOM
DAMN, YOU'RE CREEPY!!
BOM-BARDIER BEETLE.
BWOOOSH

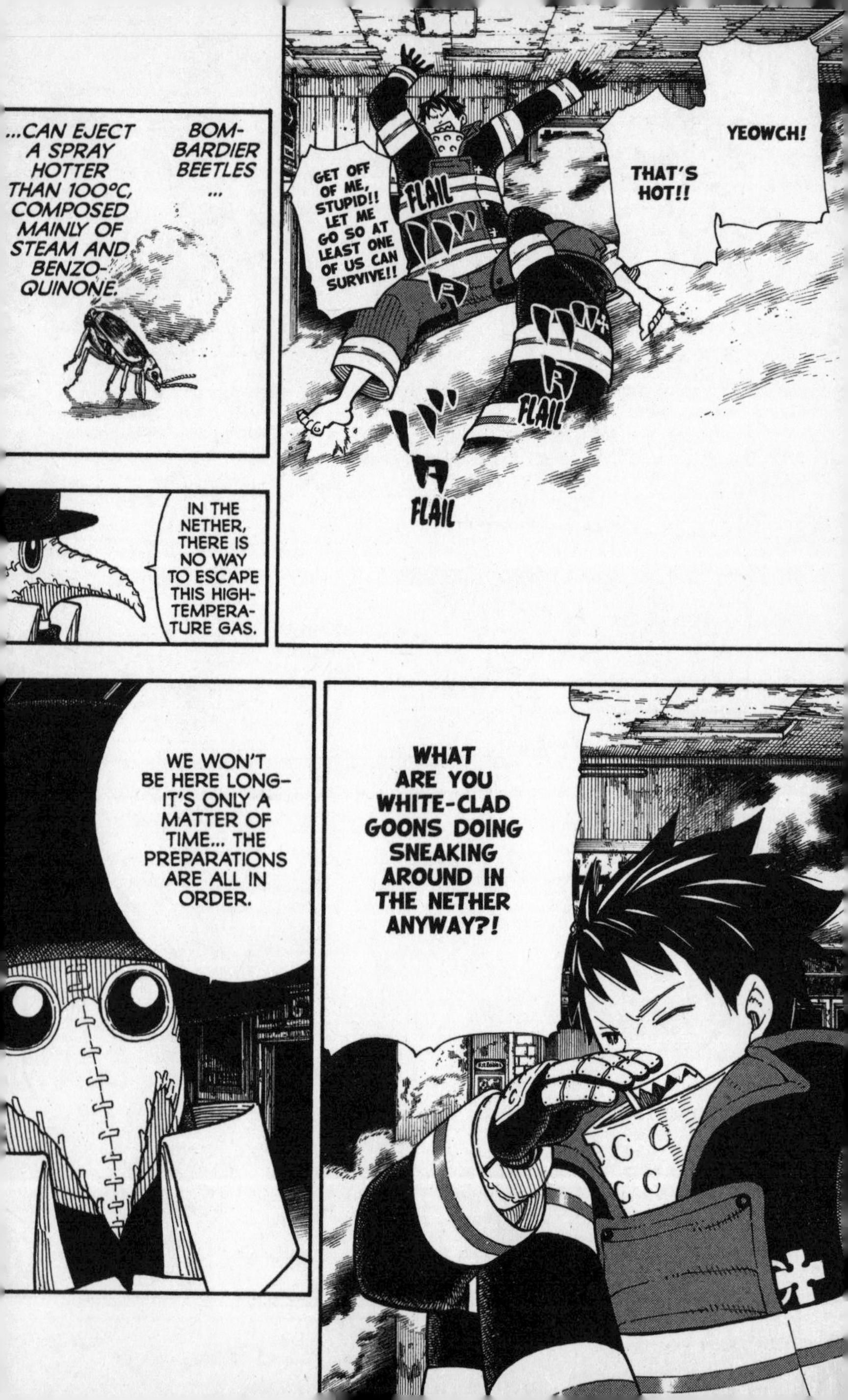
YEOWCH!
THAT'S HOT!!
GET OFF OF ME, STUPID!! LET ME GO SO AT LEAST ONE OF US CAN SURVIVE!!
FLAIL
FLAIL
FLAIL
BOM-BARDIER BEETLES ...
...CAN EJECT A SPRAY HOTTER THAN 100°C, COMPOSED MAINLY OF STEAM AND BENZO-QUINONE.
IN THE NETHER, THERE IS NO WAY TO ESCAPE THIS HIGH-TEMPERA-TURE GAS.
WHAT ARE YOU WHITE-CLAD GOONS DOING SNEAKING AROUND IN THE NETHER ANYWAY?!
WE WON'T BE HERE LONG– IT'S ONLY A MATTER OF TIME... THE PREPARATIONS ARE ALL IN ORDER.

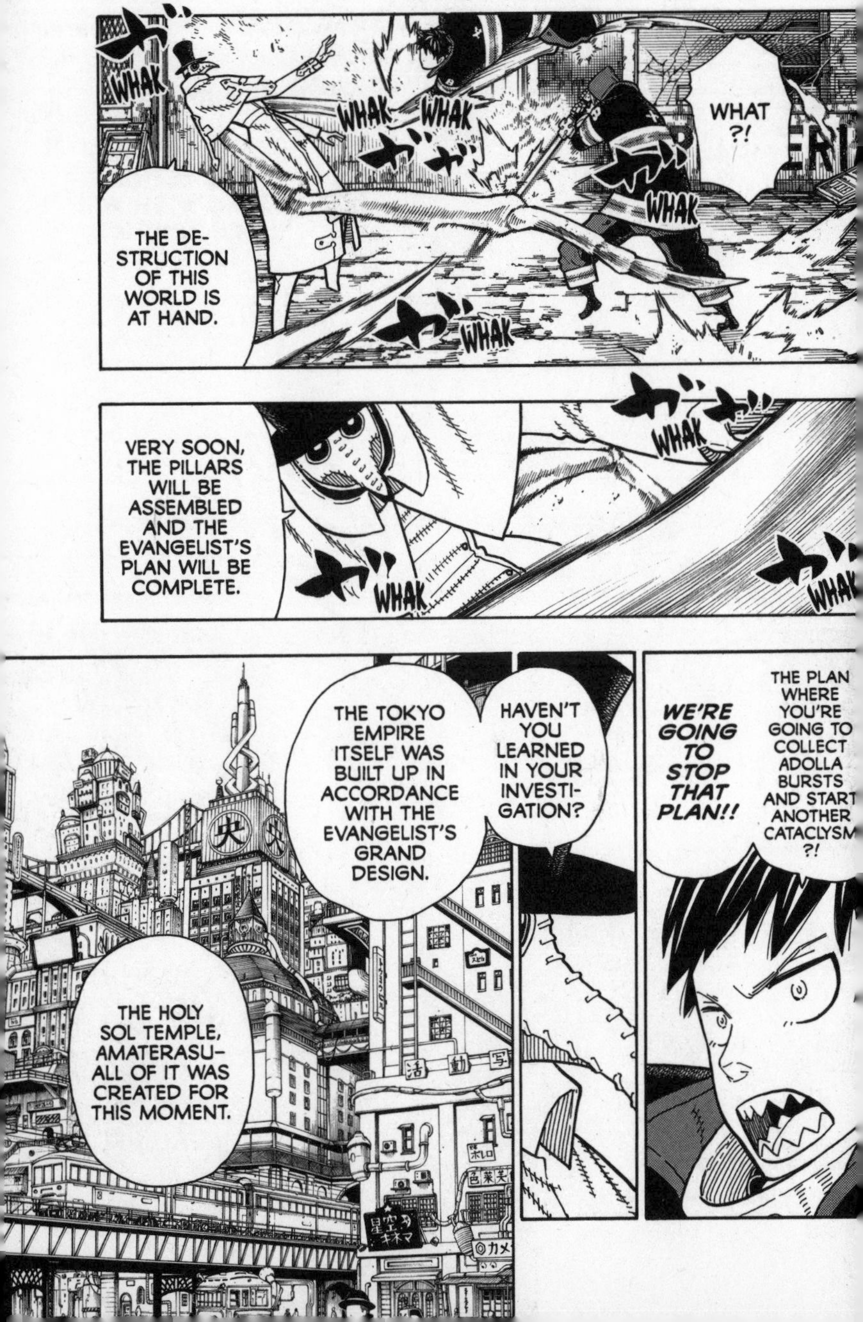
WHAT ?!
WHAK
WHAK
WHAK
WHAK
THE DE-STRUCTION OF THIS WORLD IS AT HAND.
WHAK
WHAK
WHAK
VERY SOON, THE PILLARS WILL BE ASSEMBLED AND THE EVANGELIST'S PLAN WILL BE COMPLETE.
WHAK
THE PLAN WHERE YOU'RE GOING TO COLLECT ADOLLA BURSTS AND START ANOTHER CATACLYSM ?!
WE'RE GOING TO STOP THAT PLAN!!
HAVEN'T YOU LEARNED IN YOUR INVESTI-GATION?
THE TOKYO EMPIRE ITSELF WAS BUILT UP IN ACCORDANCE WITH THE EVANGELIST'S GRAND DESIGN.
THE HOLY SOL TEMPLE, AMATERASU– ALL OF IT WAS CREATED FOR THIS MOMENT.

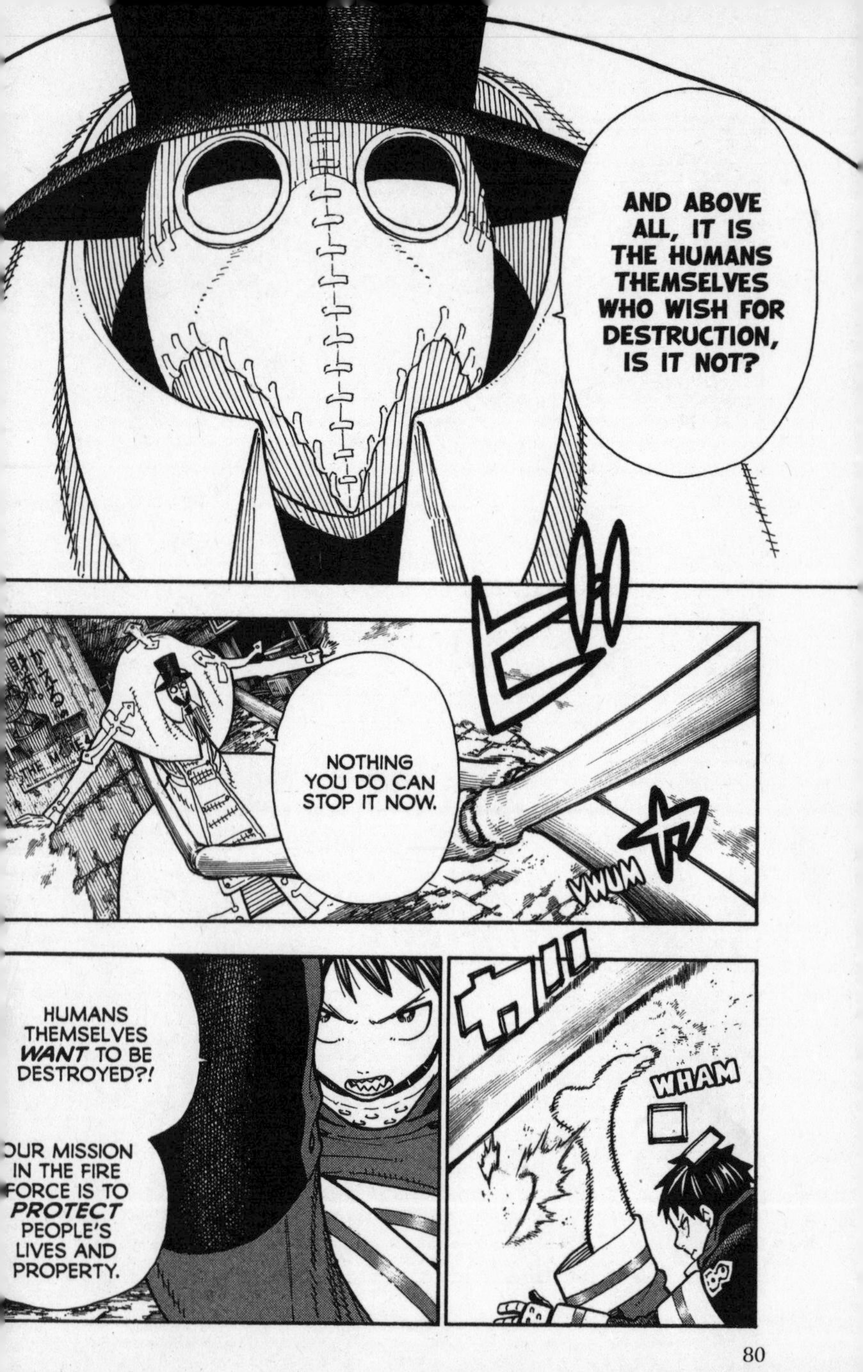
AND ABOVE ALL, IT IS THE HUMANS THEMSELVES WHO WISH FOR DESTRUCTION, IS IT NOT?
NOTHING YOU DO CAN STOP IT NOW.
VWUM
WHAM
HUMANS THEMSELVES *WANT* TO BE DESTROYED?!
OUR MISSION IN THE FIRE FORCE IS TO ***PROTECT*** PEOPLE'S LIVES AND PROPERTY.

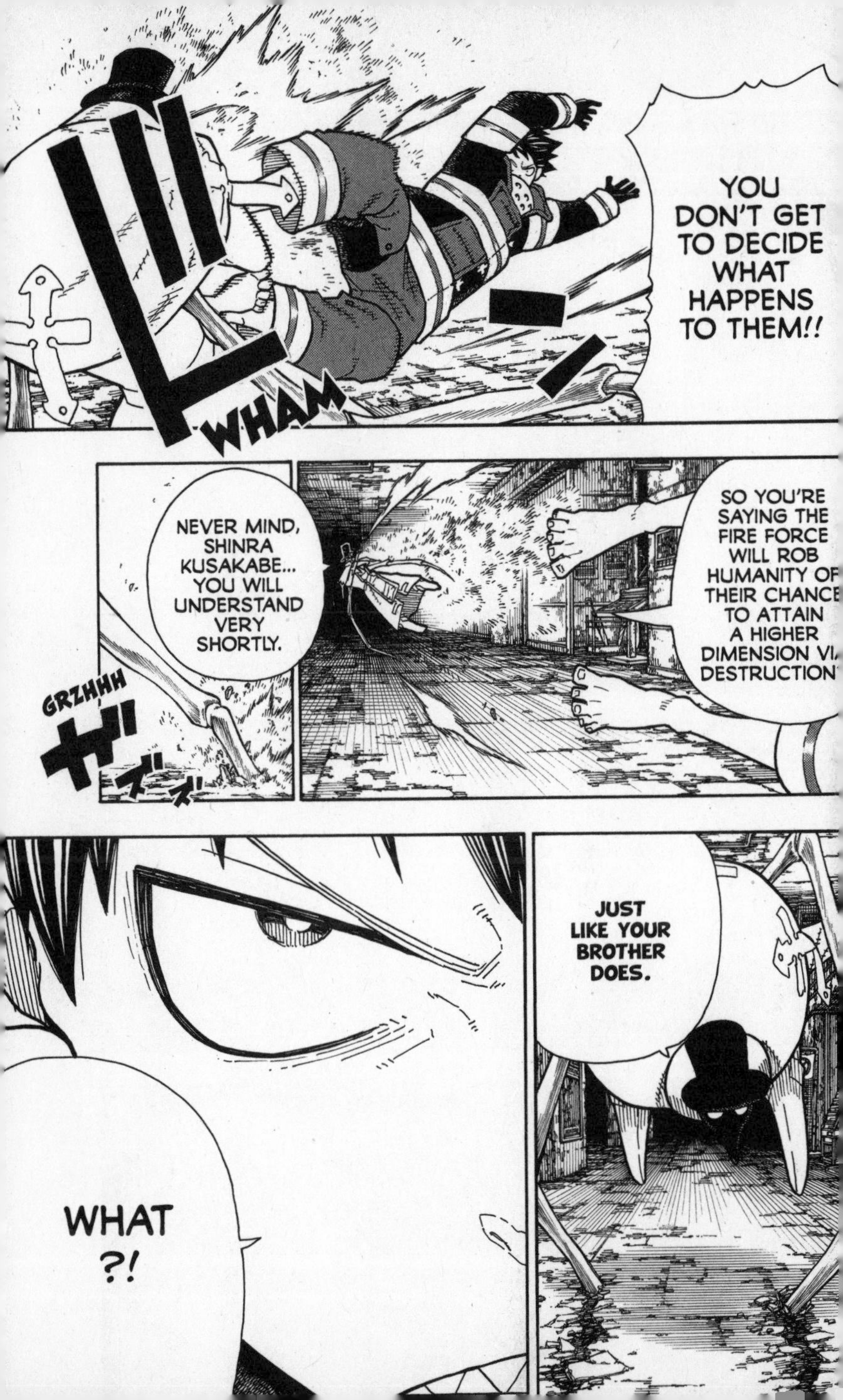
YOU DON'T GET TO DECIDE WHAT HAPPENS TO THEM!!
WHAM
SO YOU'RE SAYING THE FIRE FORCE WILL ROB HUMANITY OF THEIR CHANCE TO ATTAIN A HIGHER DIMENSION VIA DESTRUCTION
NEVER MIND, SHINRA KUSAKABE... YOU WILL UNDERSTAND VERY SHORTLY.
GRZHHH
JUST LIKE YOUR BROTHER DOES.
WHAT ?!

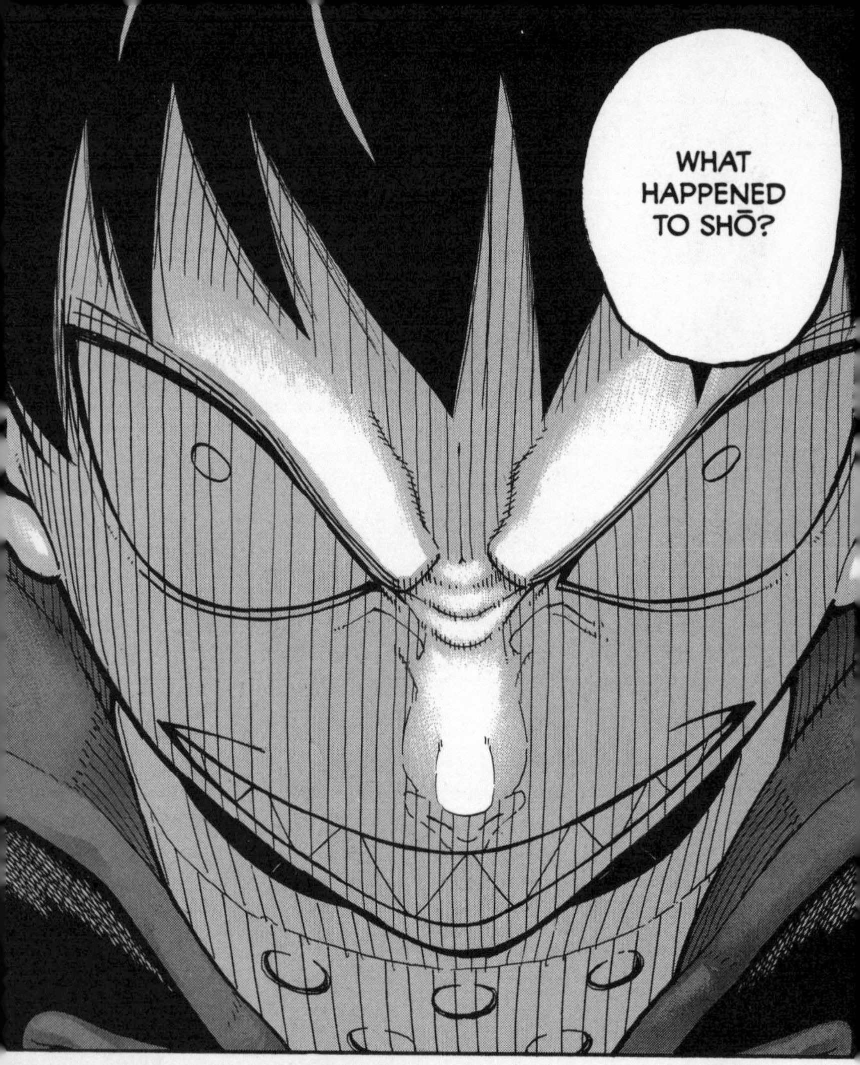
WHAT HAPPENED TO SHŌ?
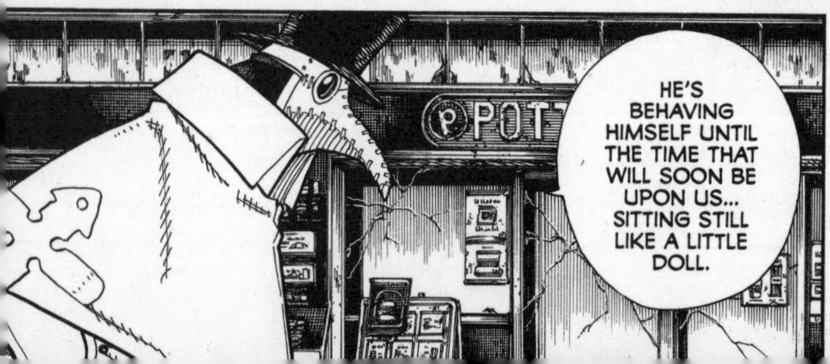
HE'S BEHAVING HIMSELF UNTIL THE TIME THAT WILL SOON BE UPON US... SITTING STILL LIKE A LITTLE DOLL.
POT

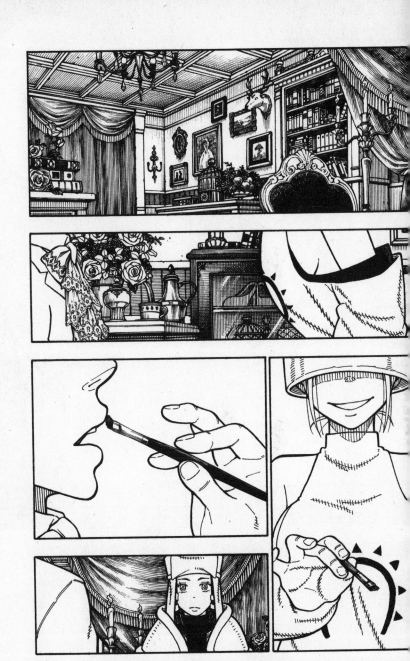

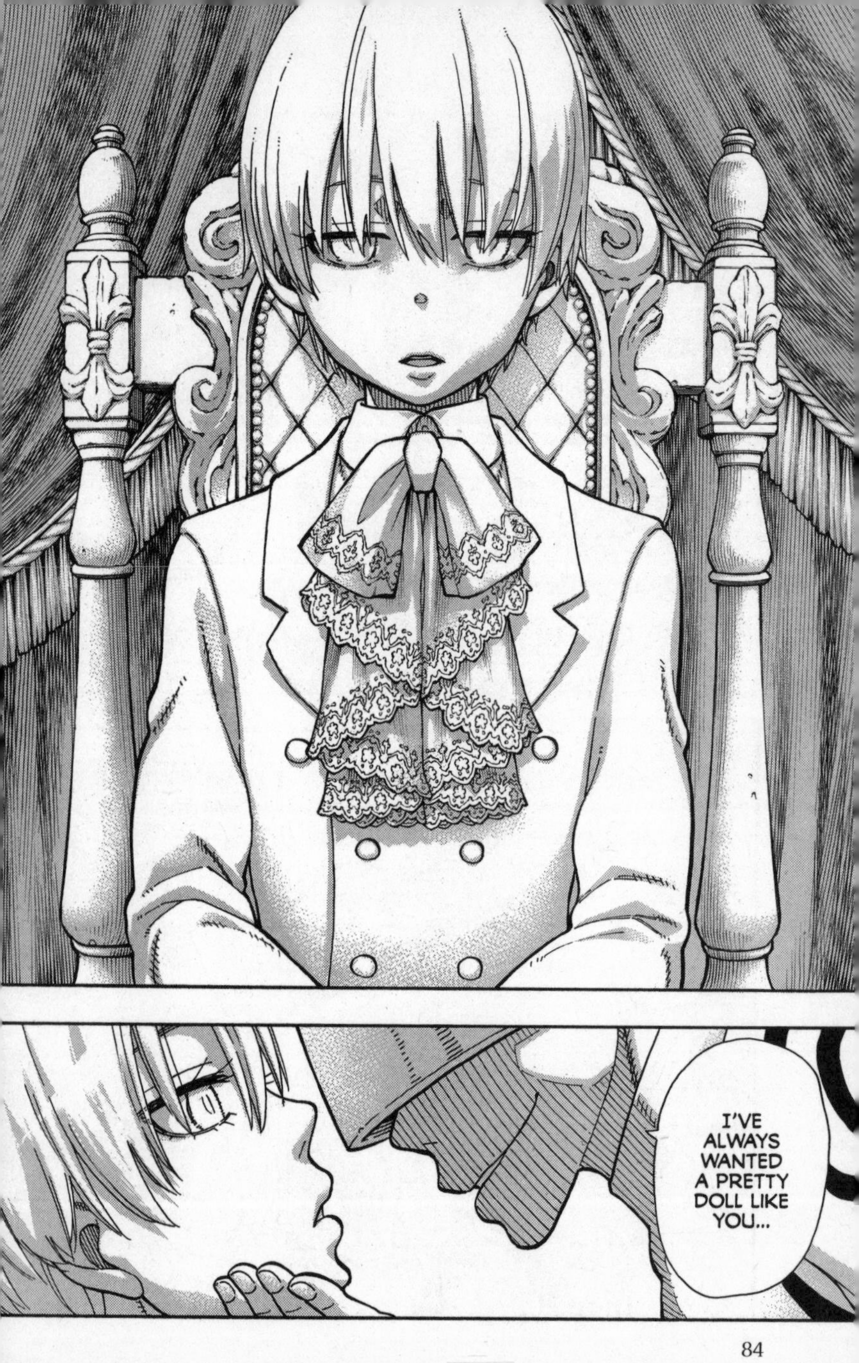
I'VE ALWAYS WANTED A PRETTY DOLL LIKE YOU...

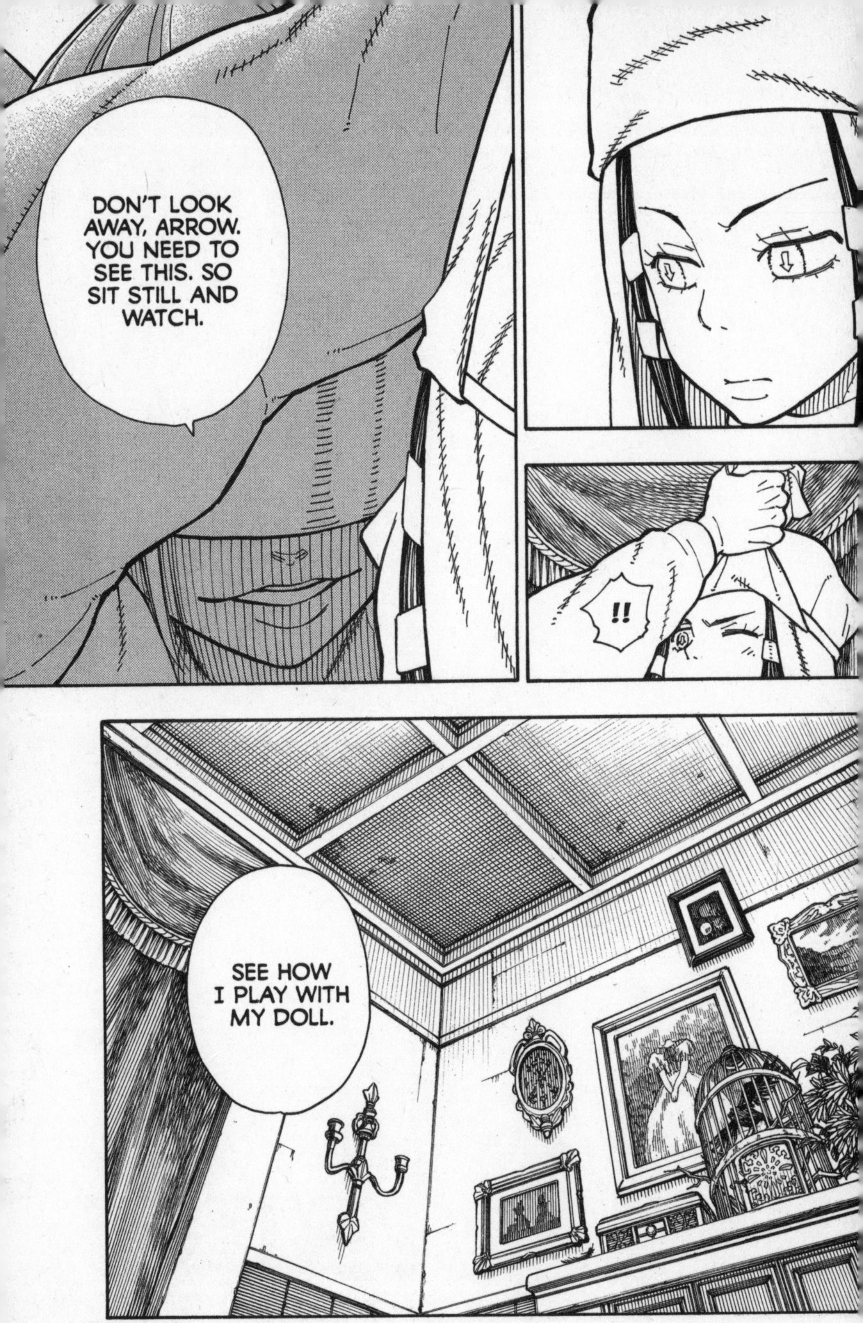
!!
DON'T LOOK AWAY, ARROW. YOU NEED TO SEE THIS. SO SIT STILL AND WATCH.
SEE HOW I PLAY WITH MY DOLL.

FIRE FORCE

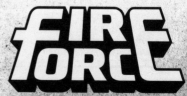

CHAPTER CLXIV: WHEN DUTY CALLS

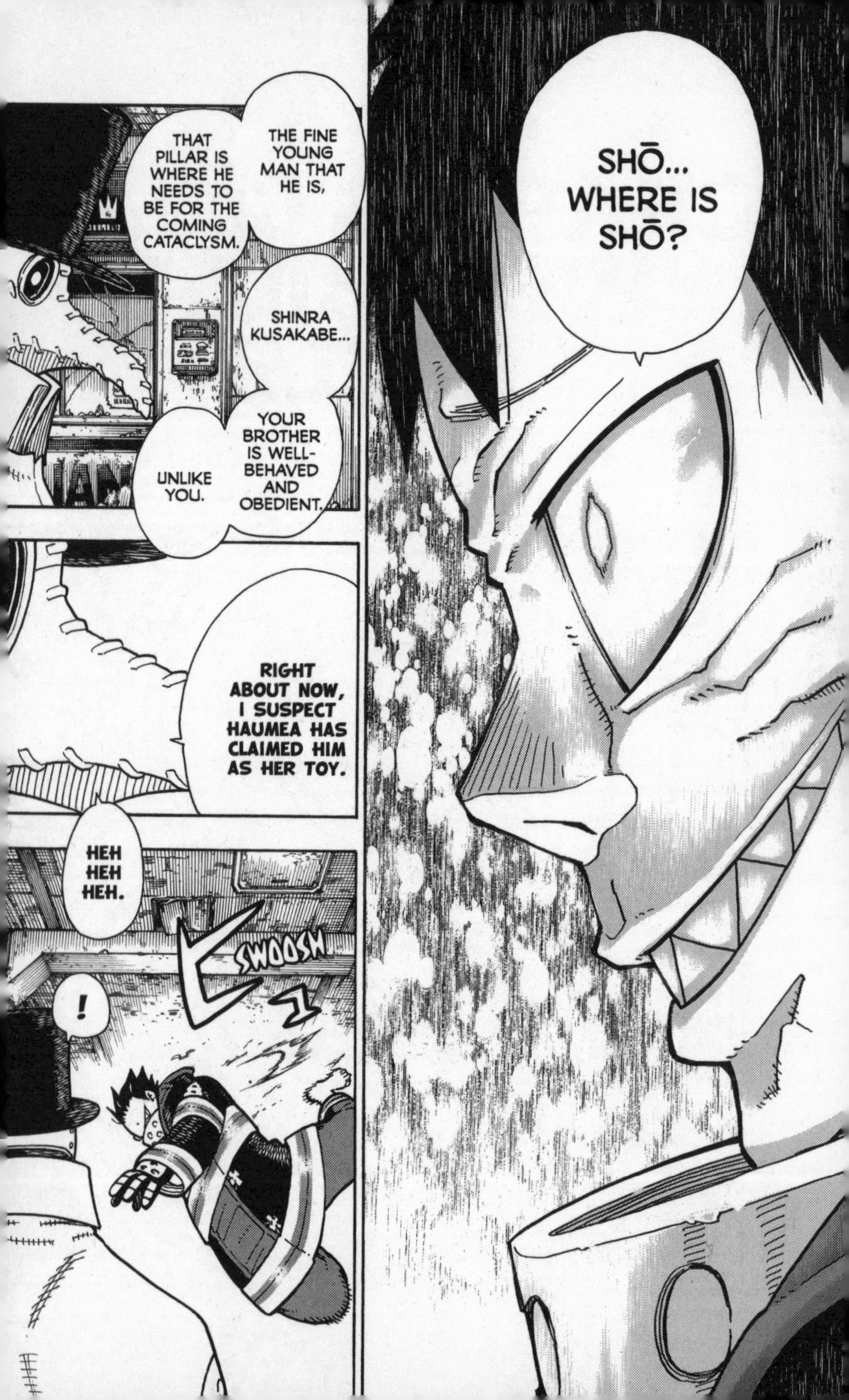
SHŌ... WHERE IS SHŌ?
THE FINE YOUNG MAN THAT HE IS,
THAT PILLAR IS WHERE HE NEEDS TO BE FOR THE COMING CATACLYSM.
SHINRA KUSAKABE...
YOUR BROTHER IS WELL-BEHAVED AND OBEDIENT.
UNLIKE YOU.
RIGHT ABOUT NOW, I SUSPECT HAUMEA HAS CLAIMED HIM AS HER TOY.
HEH HEH HEH.
SWOOSH
!

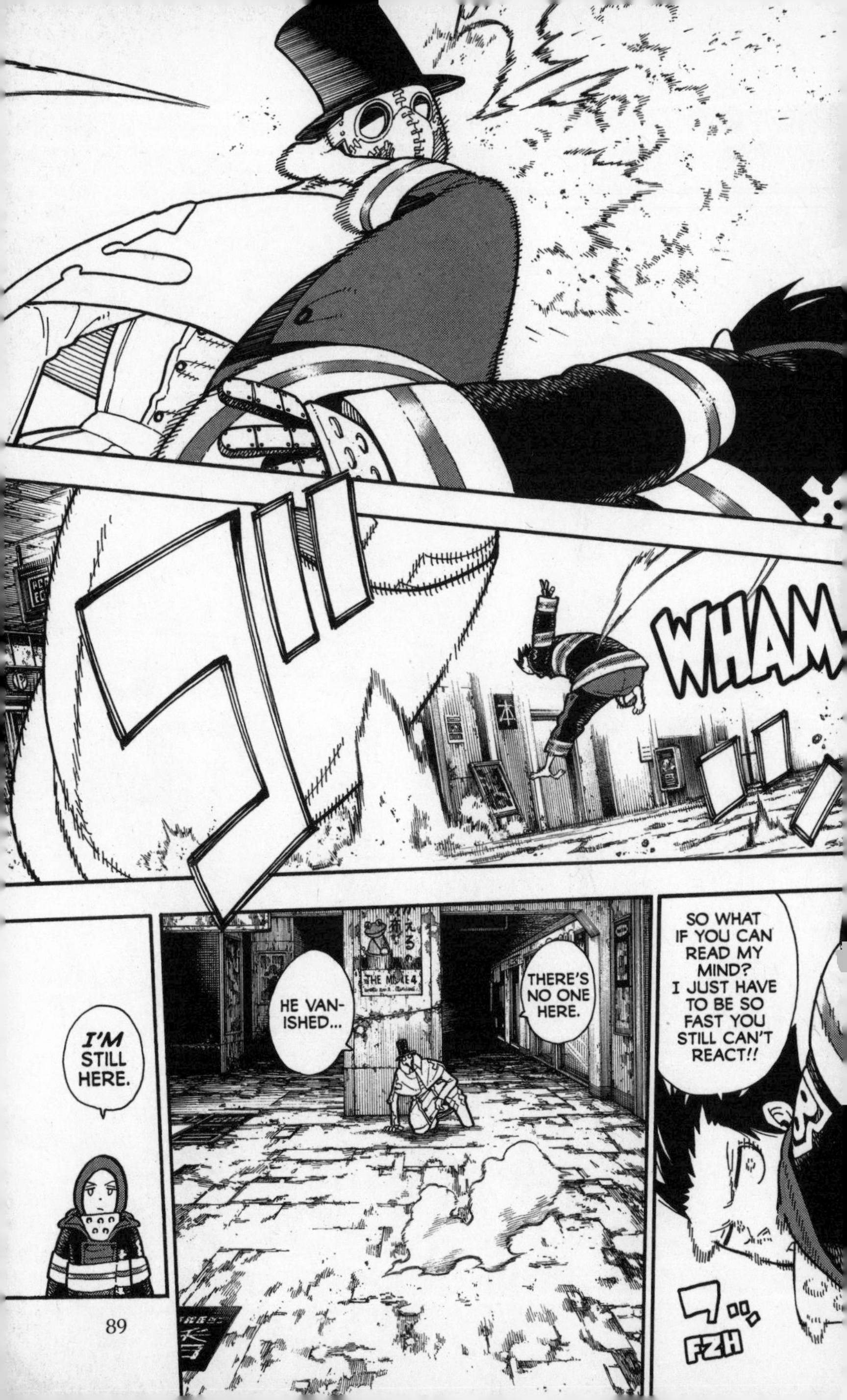
WHAM
SO WHAT IF YOU CAN READ MY MIND? I JUST HAVE TO BE SO FAST YOU STILL CAN'T REACT!!
FZH
THERE'S NO ONE HERE.
HE VAN-ISHED...
I'M STILL HERE.

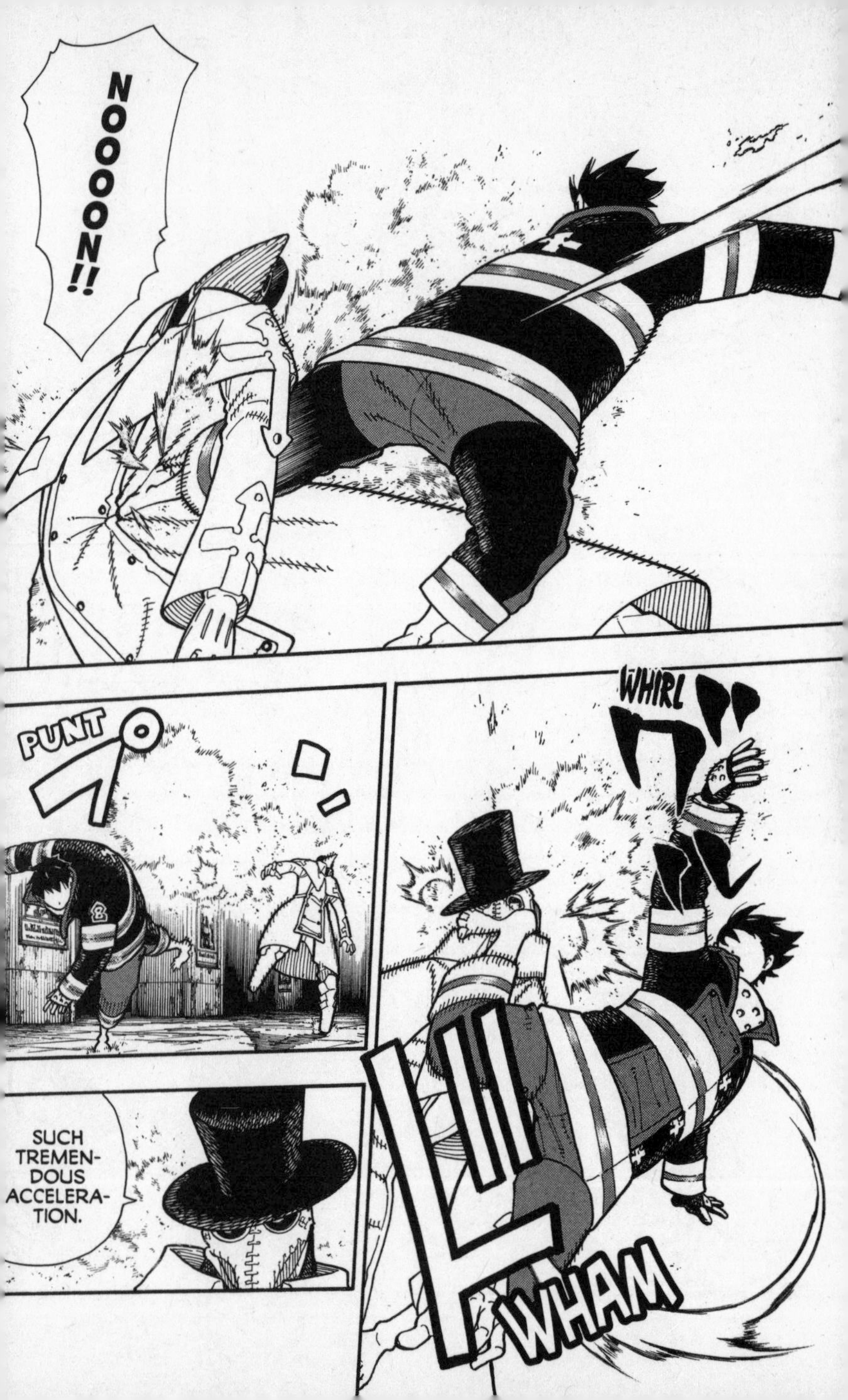
NOOOOON!!
WHIRL
PUNT
WHAM
SUCH TREMEN-DOUS ACCELERA-TION.

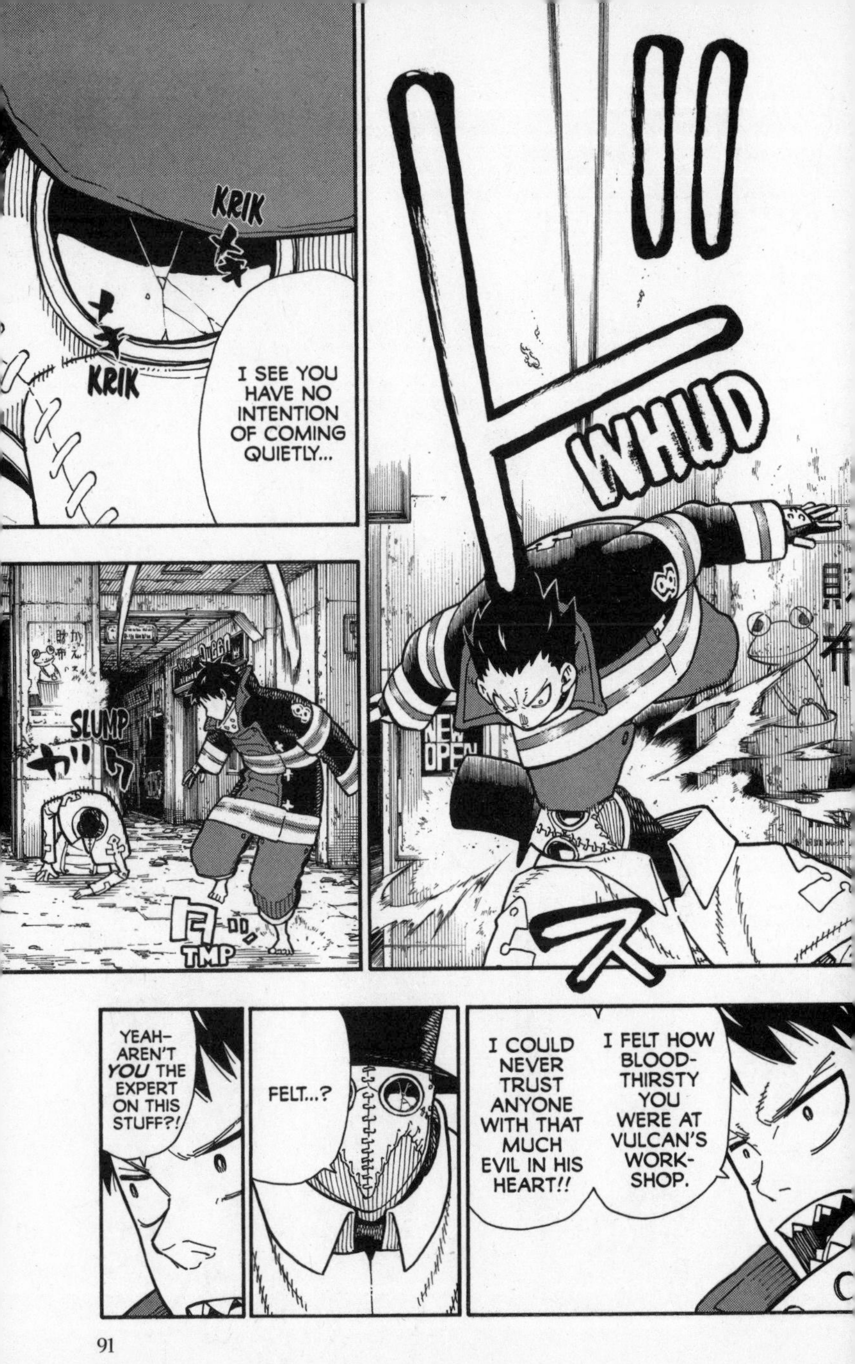
WHUD
KRIK
KRIK
I SEE YOU HAVE NO INTENTION OF COMING QUIETLY...
SLUMP
TMP
I FELT HOW BLOOD-THIRSTY YOU WERE AT VULCAN'S WORK-SHOP.
I COULD NEVER TRUST ANYONE WITH THAT MUCH EVIL IN HIS HEART!!
FELT...?
YEAH-AREN'T *YOU* THE EXPERT ON THIS STUFF?!

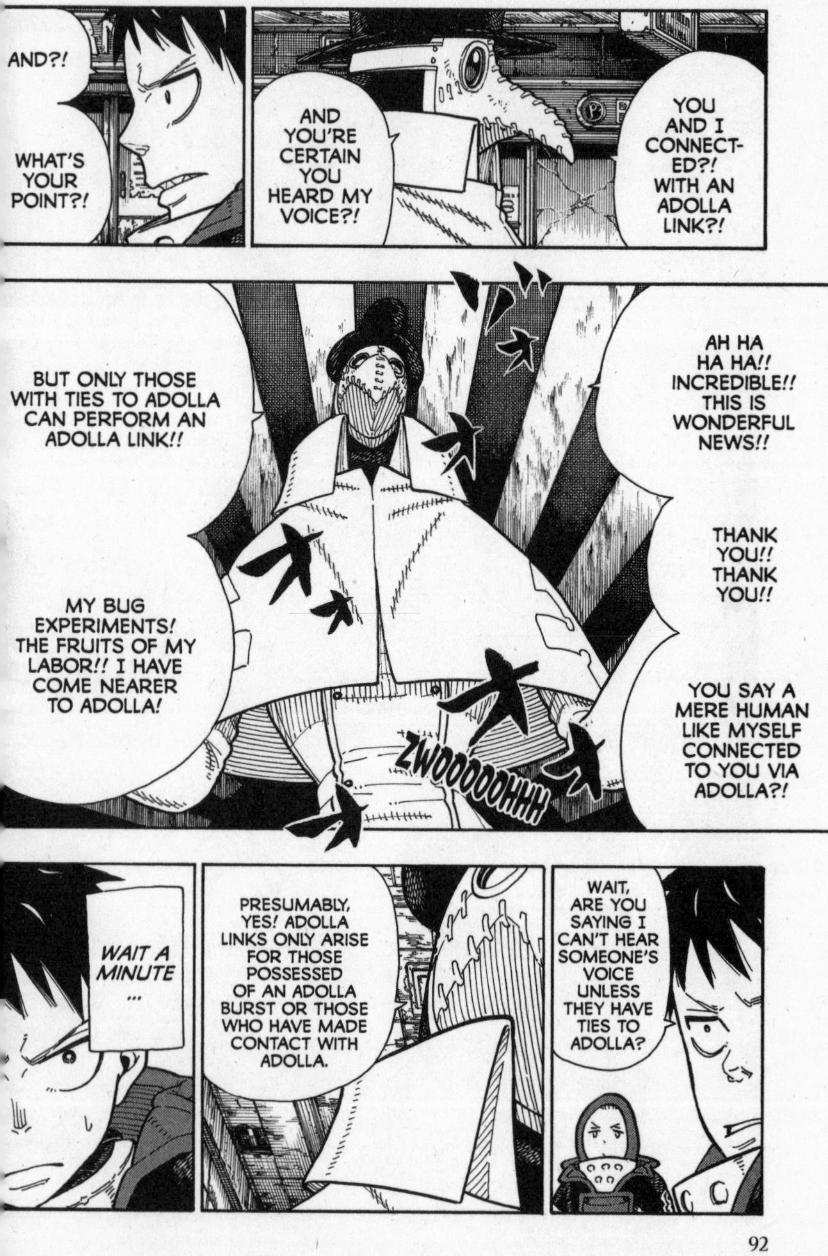
YOU AND I CONNECT-ED?! WITH AN ADOLLA LINK?!
AND YOU'RE CERTAIN YOU HEARD MY VOICE?!
AND?!
WHAT'S YOUR POINT?!
AH HA HA HA!! INCREDIBLE!! THIS IS WONDERFUL NEWS!!
THANK YOU!! THANK YOU!!
YOU SAY A MERE HUMAN LIKE MYSELF CONNECTED TO YOU VIA ADOLLA?!
BUT ONLY THOSE WITH TIES TO ADOLLA CAN PERFORM AN ADOLLA LINK!!
MY BUG EXPERIMENTS! THE FRUITS OF MY LABOR!! I HAVE COME NEARER TO ADOLLA!
ZWOOOOOOHHH
WAIT, ARE YOU SAYING I CAN'T HEAR SOMEONE'S VOICE UNLESS THEY HAVE TIES TO ADOLLA?
PRESUMABLY, YES! ADOLLA LINKS ONLY ARISE FOR THOSE POSSESSED OF AN ADOLLA BURST OR THOSE WHO HAVE MADE CONTACT WITH ADOLLA.
WAIT A MINUTE ...

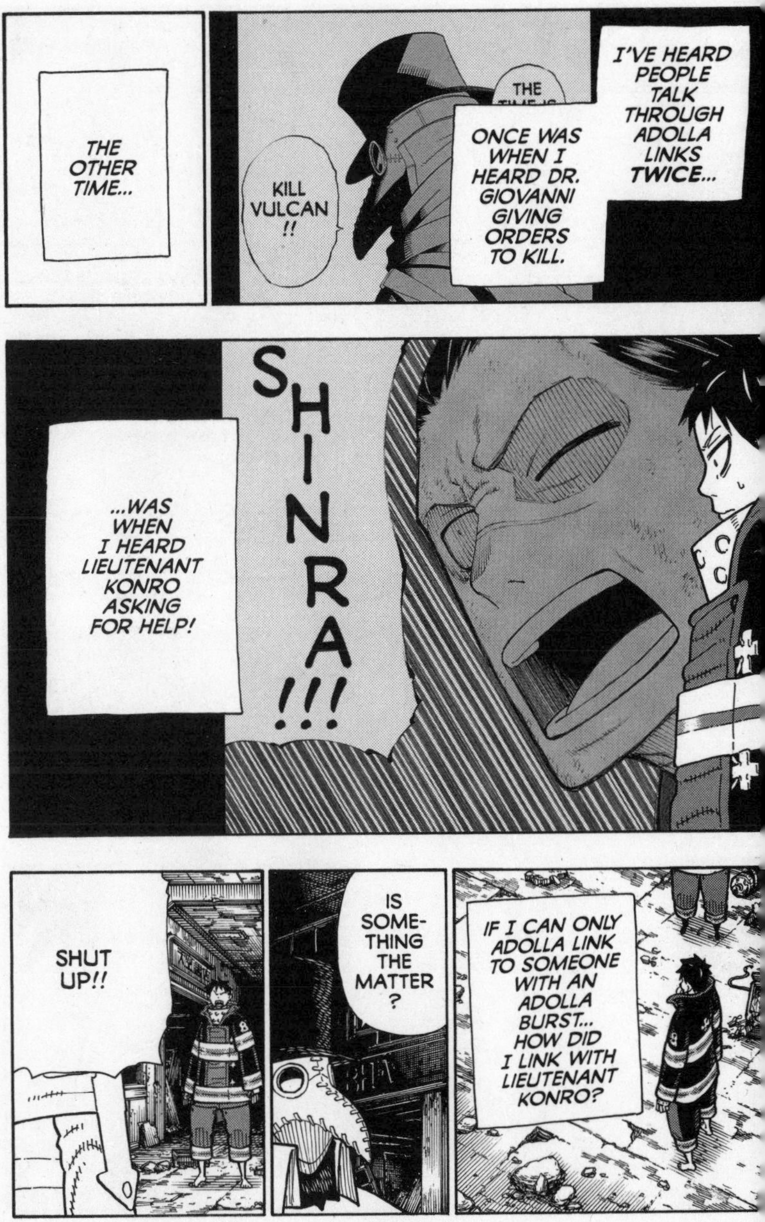
I'VE HEARD PEOPLE TALK THROUGH ADOLLA LINKS TWICE...
THE
ONCE WAS WHEN I HEARD DR. GIOVANNI GIVING ORDERS TO KILL.
KILL VULCAN !!
THE OTHER TIME...
SHINRA!!!
...WAS WHEN I HEARD LIEUTENANT KONRO ASKING FOR HELP!
IF I CAN ONLY ADOLLA LINK TO SOMEONE WITH AN ADOLLA BURST... HOW DID I LINK WITH LIEUTENANT KONRO?
IS SOMETHING THE MATTER?
SHUT UP!!

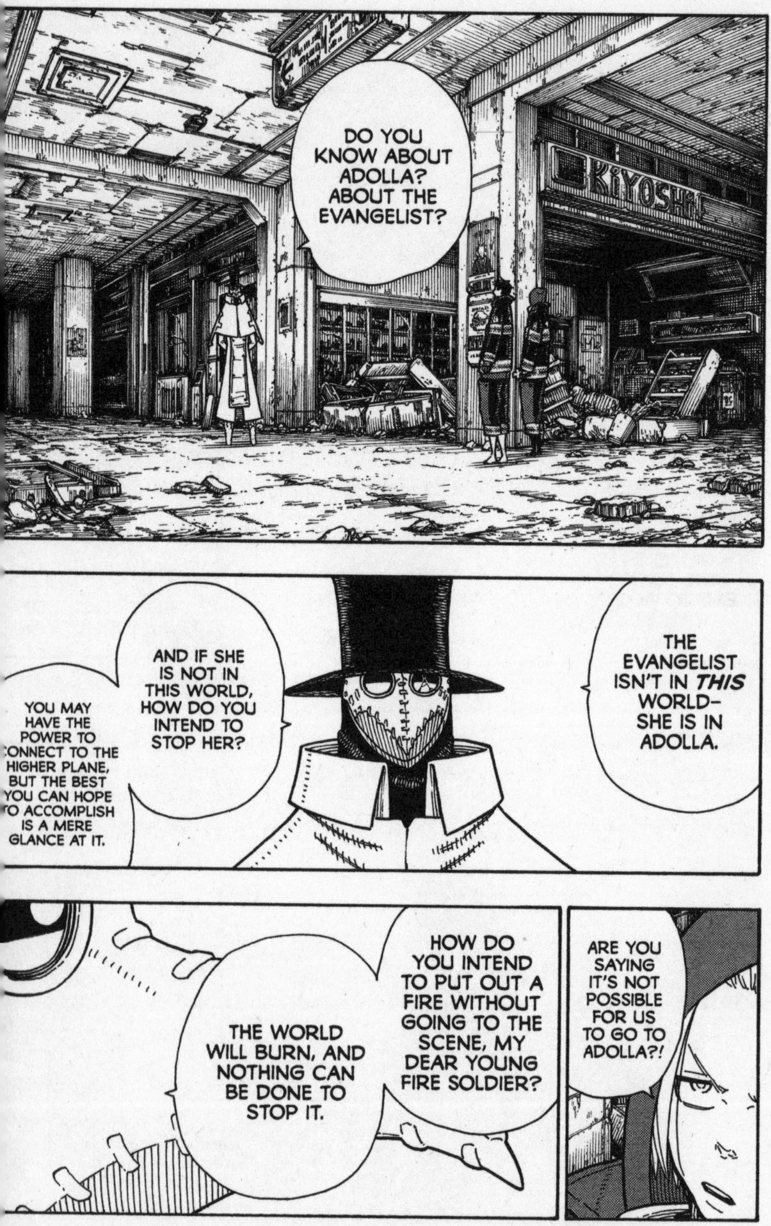
DO YOU KNOW ABOUT ADOLLA? ABOUT THE EVANGELIST?
KIYOSHI
THE EVANGELIST ISN'T IN *THIS* WORLD— SHE IS IN ADOLLA.
AND IF SHE IS NOT IN THIS WORLD, HOW DO YOU INTEND TO STOP HER?
YOU MAY HAVE THE POWER TO ONNECT TO THE HIGHER PLANE, BUT THE BEST YOU CAN HOPE O ACCOMPLISH IS A MERE GLANCE AT IT.
ARE YOU SAYING IT'S NOT POSSIBLE FOR US TO GO TO ADOLLA?!
HOW DO YOU INTEND TO PUT OUT A FIRE WITHOUT GOING TO THE SCENE, MY DEAR YOUNG FIRE SOLDIER?
THE WORLD WILL BURN, AND NOTHING CAN BE DONE TO STOP IT.

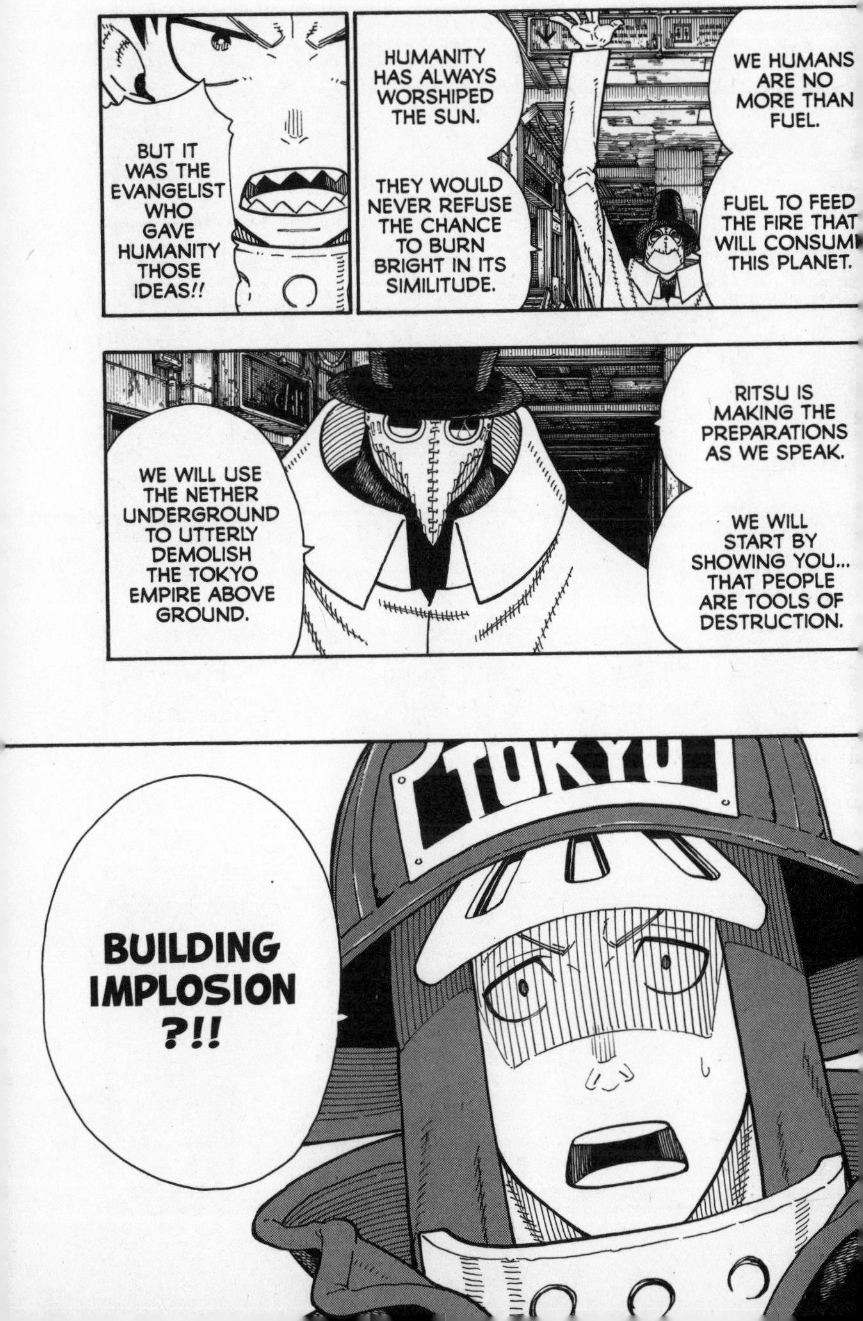
WE HUMANS ARE NO MORE THAN FUEL.
FUEL TO FEED THE FIRE THAT WILL CONSUM THIS PLANET.
HUMANITY HAS ALWAYS WORSHIPED THE SUN.
THEY WOULD NEVER REFUSE THE CHANCE TO BURN BRIGHT IN ITS SIMILITUDE.
BUT IT WAS THE EVANGELIST WHO GAVE HUMANITY THOSE IDEAS!!
RITSU IS MAKING THE PREPARATIONS AS WE SPEAK.
WE WILL USE THE NETHER UNDERGROUND TO UTTERLY DEMOLISH THE TOKYO EMPIRE ABOVE GROUND.
WE WILL START BY SHOWING YOU... THAT PEOPLE ARE TOOLS OF DESTRUCTION.
TOKYO
BUILDING IMPLOSION ?!!

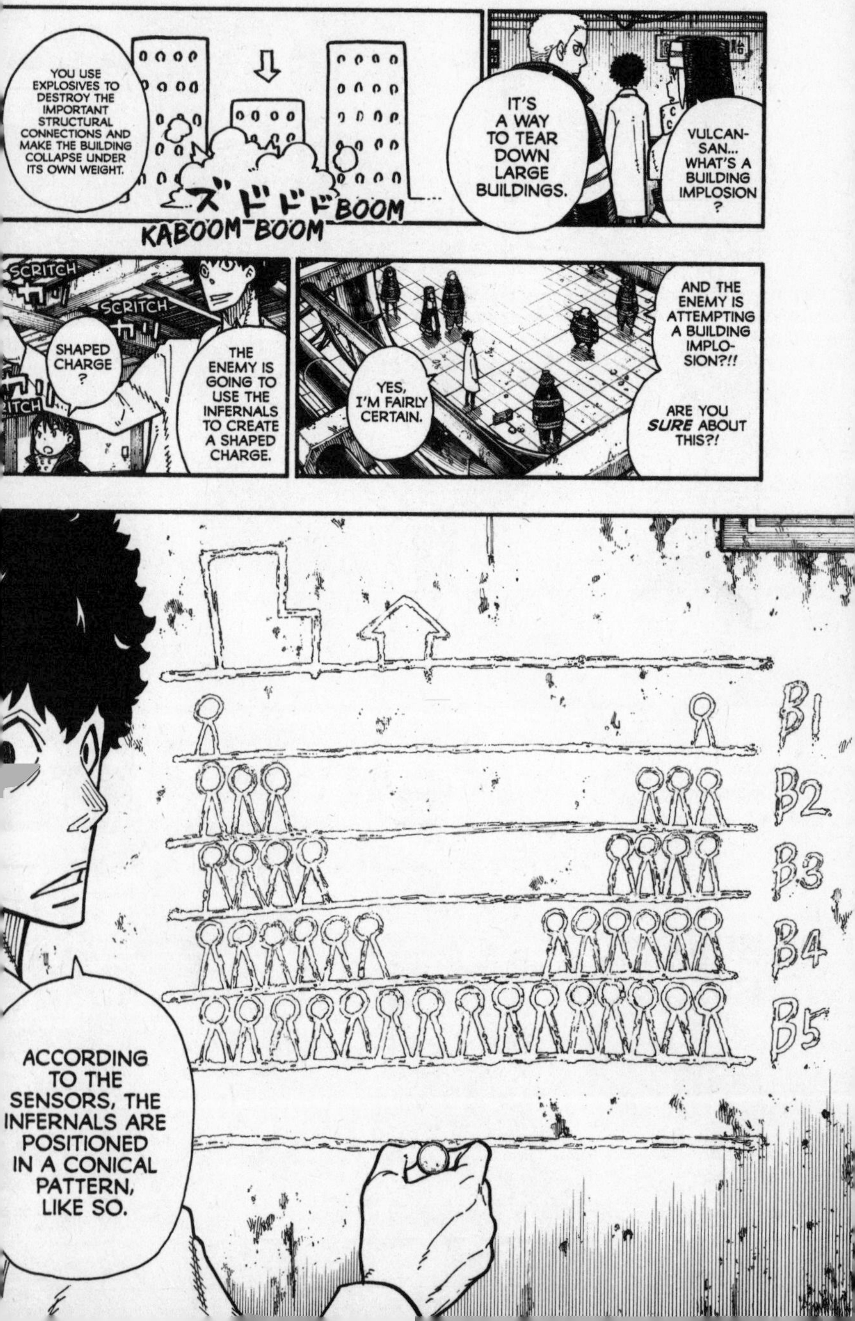
VULCAN-SAN... WHAT'S A BUILDING IMPLOSION?
IT'S A WAY TO TEAR DOWN LARGE BUILDINGS.
YOU USE EXPLOSIVES TO DESTROY THE IMPORTANT STRUCTURAL CONNECTIONS AND MAKE THE BUILDING COLLAPSE UNDER ITS OWN WEIGHT.
ズドドド
KABOOM BOOM BOOM
AND THE ENEMY IS ATTEMPTING A BUILDING IMPLOSION?!!
ARE YOU SURE ABOUT THIS?!
YES, I'M FAIRLY CERTAIN.
THE ENEMY IS GOING TO USE THE INFERNALS TO CREATE A SHAPED CHARGE.
SCRITCH
SCRITCH
SHAPED CHARGE?
B1
B2
B3
B4
B5
ACCORDING TO THE SENSORS, THE INFERNALS ARE POSITIONED IN A CONICAL PATTERN, LIKE SO.

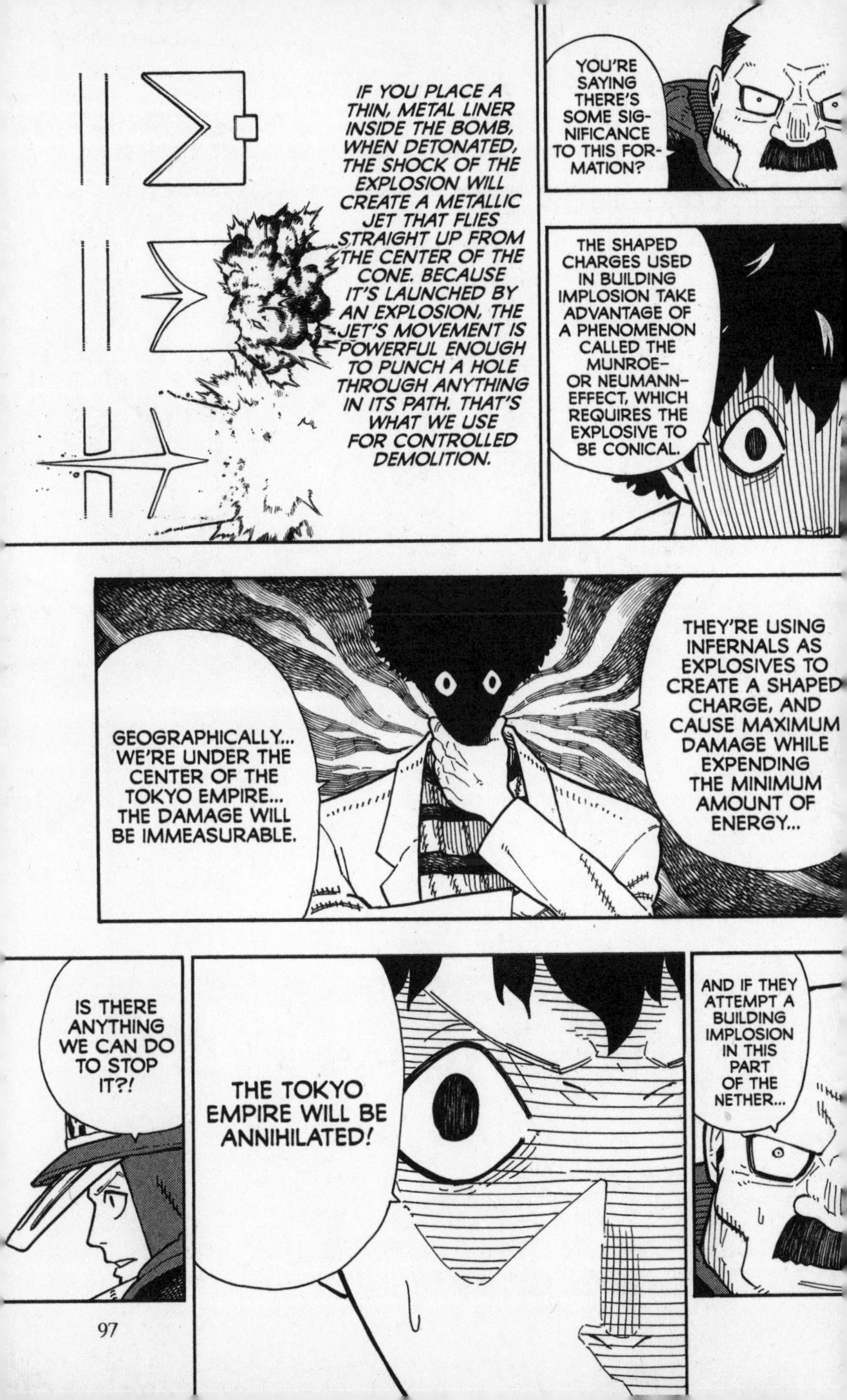
YOU'RE SAYING THERE'S SOME SIGNIFICANCE TO THIS FORMATION?
THE SHAPED CHARGES USED IN BUILDING IMPLOSION TAKE ADVANTAGE OF A PHENOMENON CALLED THE MUNROE- OR NEUMANN-EFFECT, WHICH REQUIRES THE EXPLOSIVE TO BE CONICAL.
IF YOU PLACE A THIN, METAL LINER INSIDE THE BOMB, WHEN DETONATED, THE SHOCK OF THE EXPLOSION WILL CREATE A METALLIC JET THAT FLIES STRAIGHT UP FROM THE CENTER OF THE CONE. BECAUSE IT'S LAUNCHED BY AN EXPLOSION, THE JET'S MOVEMENT IS POWERFUL ENOUGH TO PUNCH A HOLE THROUGH ANYTHING IN ITS PATH. THAT'S WHAT WE USE FOR CONTROLLED DEMOLITION.
THEY'RE USING INFERNALS AS EXPLOSIVES TO CREATE A SHAPED CHARGE, AND CAUSE MAXIMUM DAMAGE WHILE EXPENDING THE MINIMUM AMOUNT OF ENERGY...
GEOGRAPHICALLY... WE'RE UNDER THE CENTER OF THE TOKYO EMPIRE... THE DAMAGE WILL BE IMMEASURABLE.
AND IF THEY ATTEMPT A BUILDING IMPLOSION IN THIS PART OF THE NETHER...
THE TOKYO EMPIRE WILL BE ANNIHILATED!
IS THERE ANYTHING WE CAN DO TO STOP IT?!

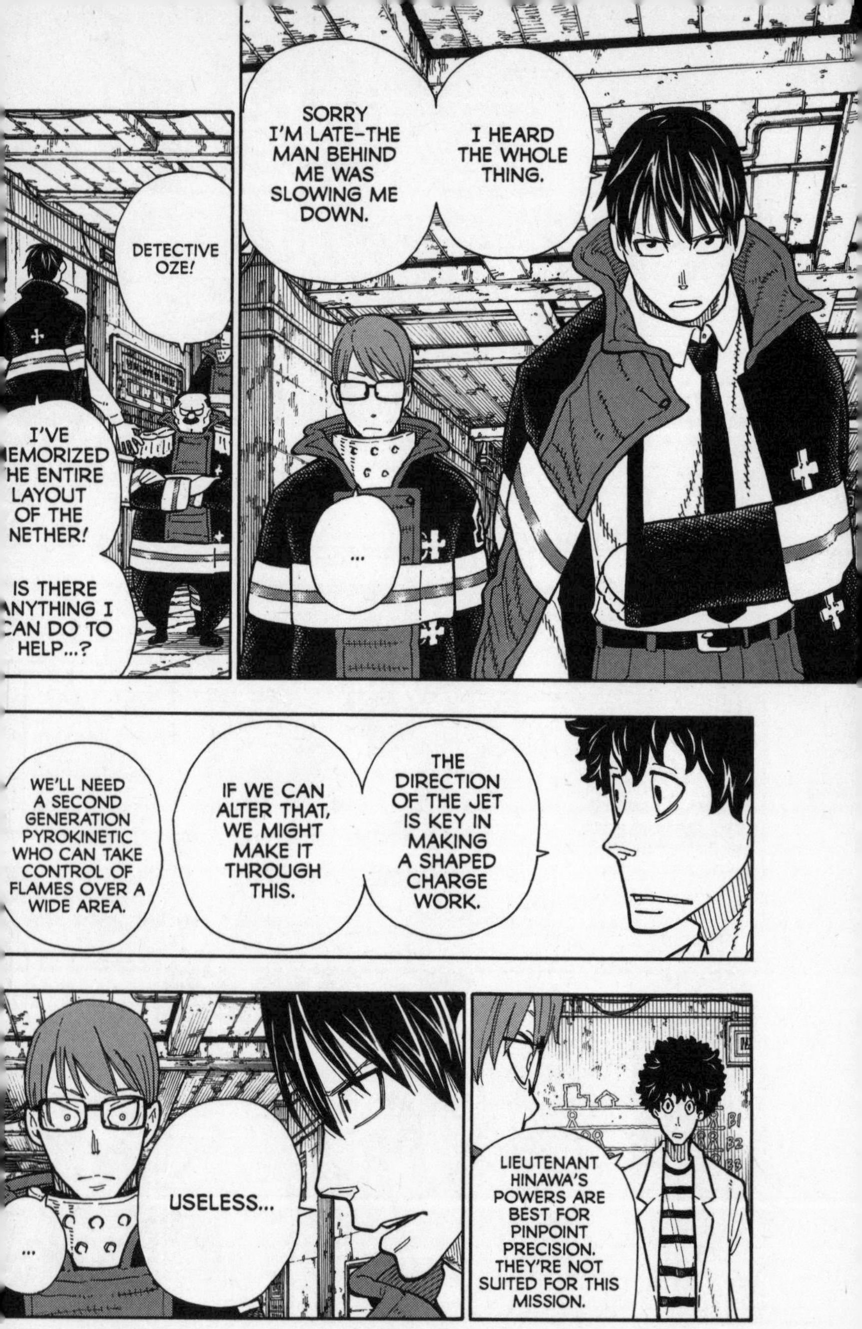
I HEARD THE WHOLE THING.
SORRY I'M LATE—THE MAN BEHIND ME WAS SLOWING ME DOWN.
...
DETECTIVE OZE!
I'VE EMORIZED HE ENTIRE LAYOUT OF THE NETHER!
IS THERE NYTHING I CAN DO TO HELP...?
THE DIRECTION OF THE JET IS KEY IN MAKING A SHAPED CHARGE WORK.
IF WE CAN ALTER THAT, WE MIGHT MAKE IT THROUGH THIS.
WE'LL NEED A SECOND GENERATION PYROKINETIC WHO CAN TAKE CONTROL OF FLAMES OVER A WIDE AREA.
LIEUTENANT HINAWA'S POWERS ARE BEST FOR PINPOINT PRECISION. THEY'RE NOT SUITED FOR THIS MISSION.
USELESS...
...

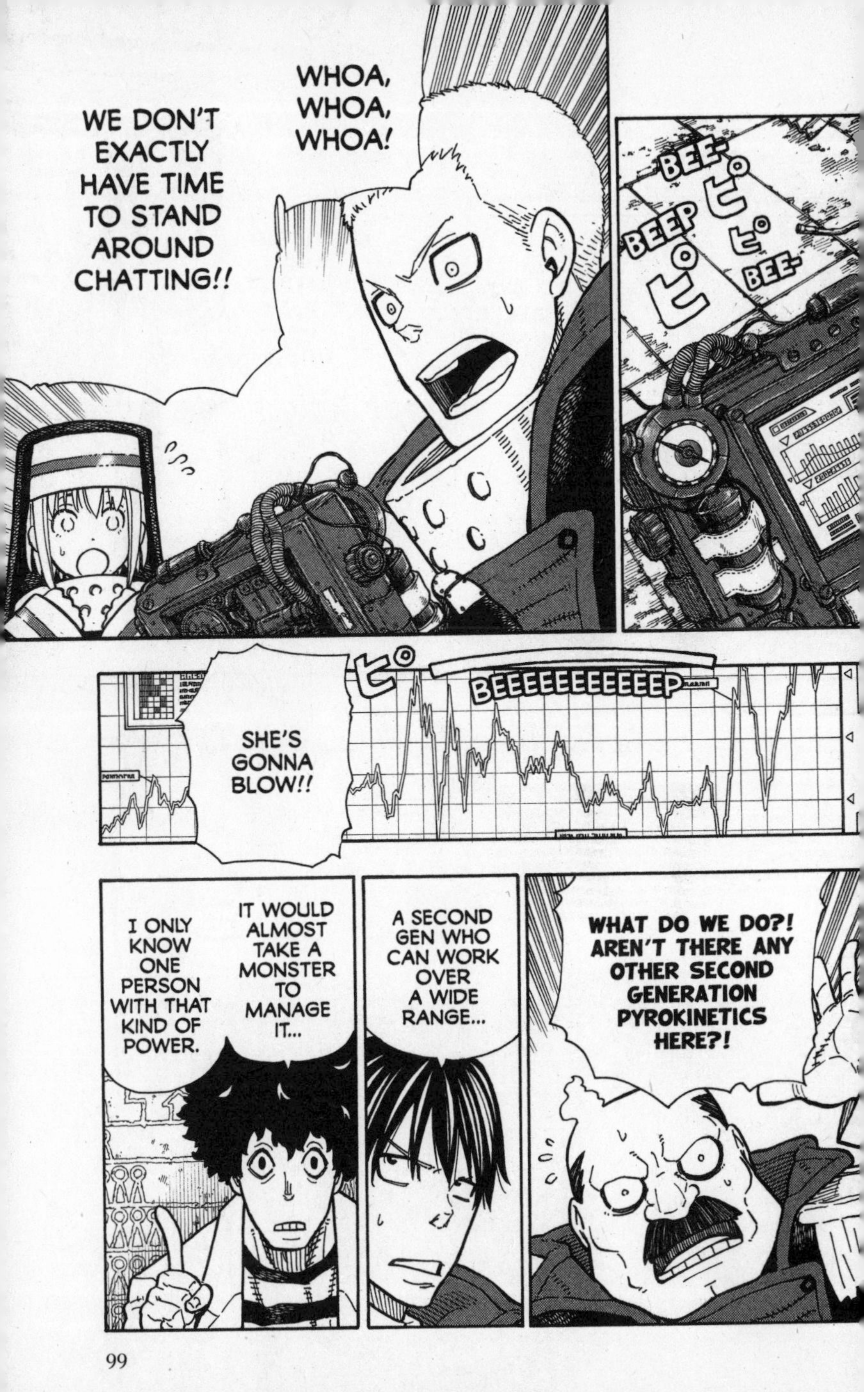
BEE-
BEEP
BEE-
WHOA, WHOA, WHOA!
WE DON'T EXACTLY HAVE TIME TO STAND AROUND CHATTING!!
BEEEEEEEEEEEP
SHE'S GONNA BLOW!!
WHAT DO WE DO?! AREN'T THERE ANY OTHER SECOND GENERATION PYROKINETICS HERE?!
A SECOND GEN WHO CAN WORK OVER A WIDE RANGE...
IT WOULD ALMOST TAKE A MONSTER TO MANAGE IT...
I ONLY KNOW ONE PERSON WITH THAT KIND OF POWER.

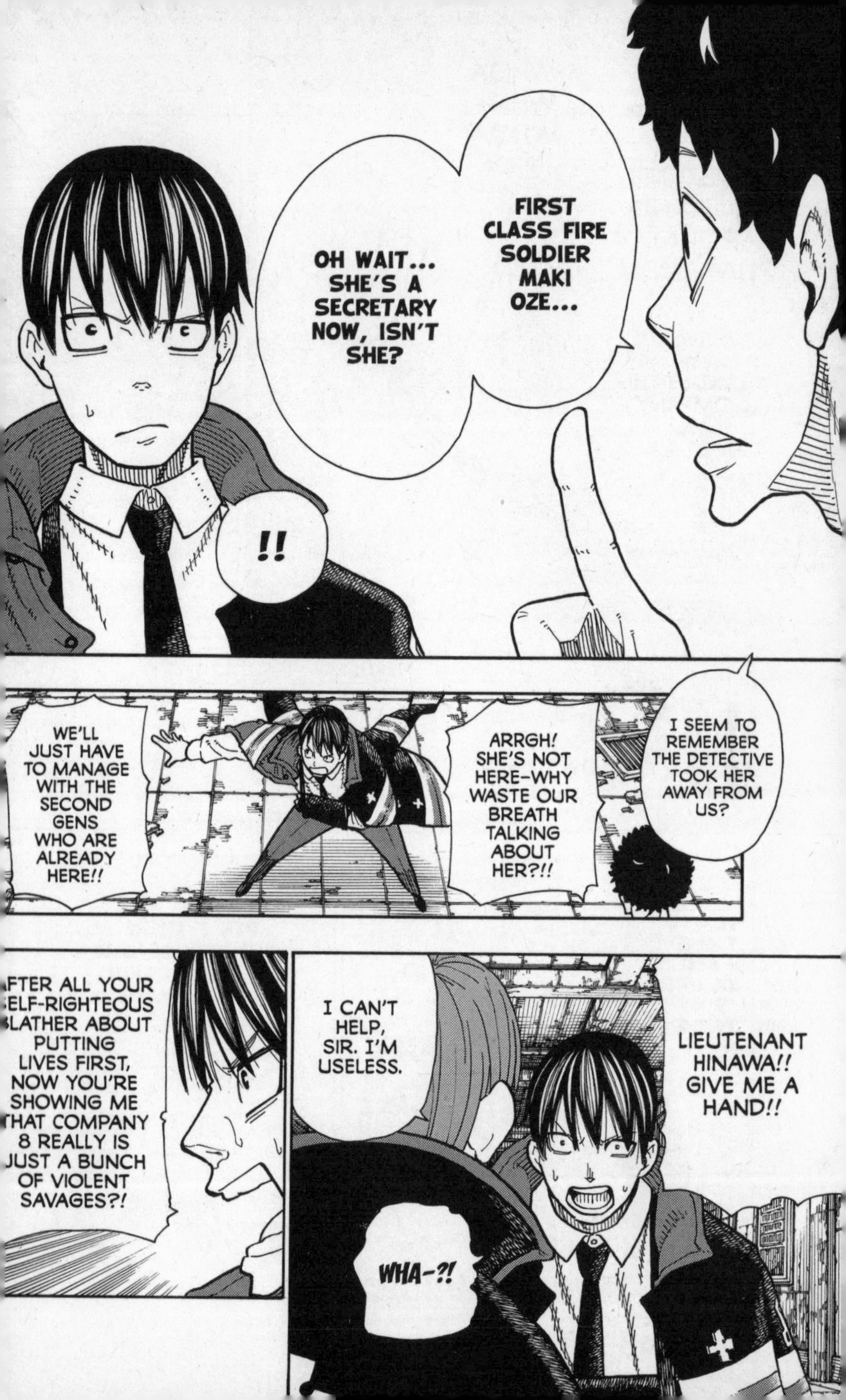
FIRST CLASS FIRE SOLDIER MAKI OZE...
OH WAIT... SHE'S A SECRETARY NOW, ISN'T SHE?
!!
I SEEM TO REMEMBER THE DETECTIVE TOOK HER AWAY FROM US?
ARRGH! SHE'S NOT HERE–WHY WASTE OUR BREATH TALKING ABOUT HER?!!
WE'LL JUST HAVE TO MANAGE WITH THE SECOND GENS WHO ARE ALREADY HERE!!
LIEUTENANT HINAWA!! GIVE ME A HAND!!
I CAN'T HELP, SIR. I'M USELESS.
WHA-?!
FTER ALL YOUR ELF-RIGHTEOUS LATHER ABOUT PUTTING LIVES FIRST, NOW YOU'RE SHOWING ME HAT COMPANY 8 REALLY IS UST A BUNCH OF VIOLENT SAVAGES?!

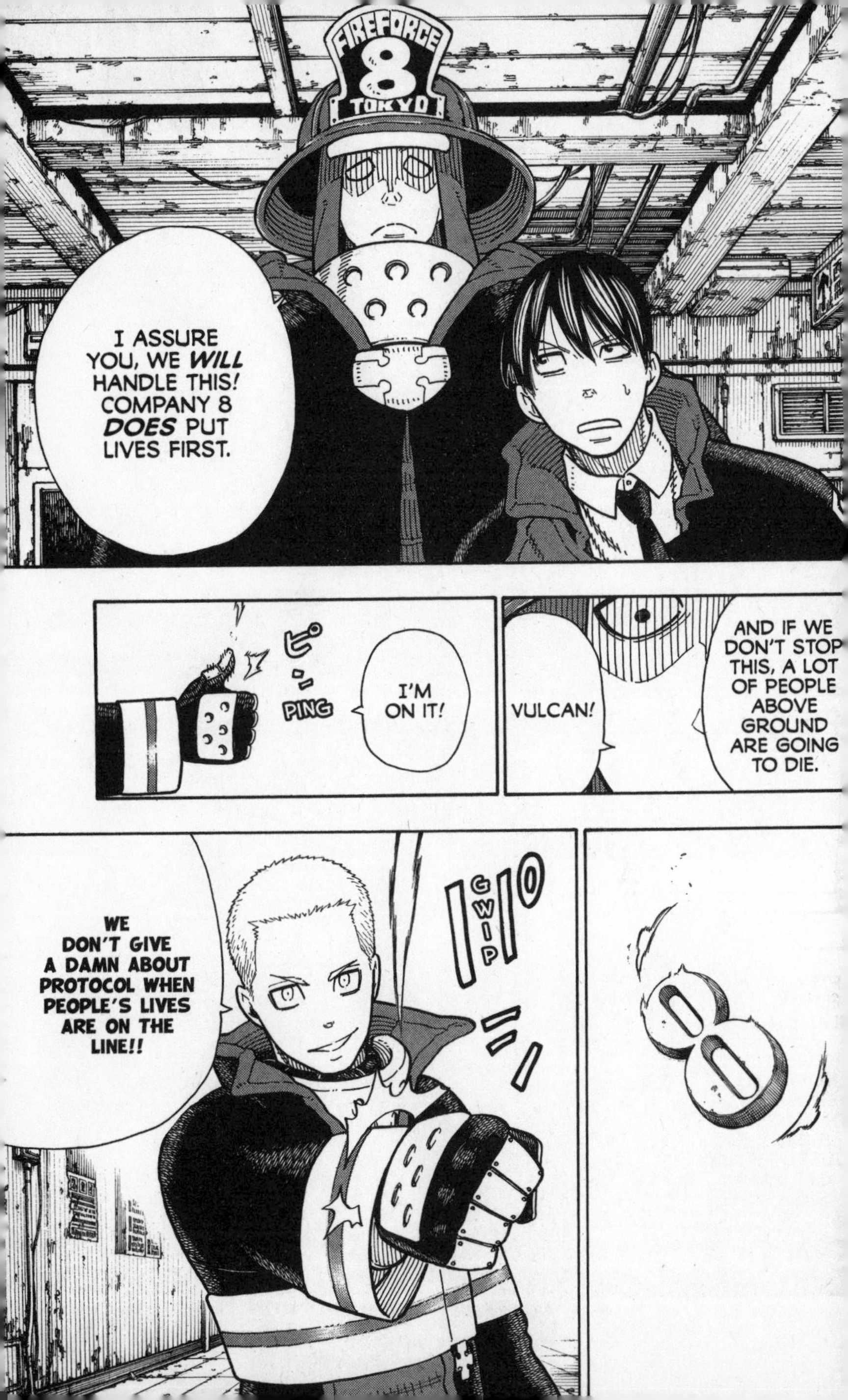
FIREFORCE
8
TOKYO
I ASSURE YOU, WE *WILL* HANDLE THIS! COMPANY 8 *DOES* PUT LIVES FIRST.
AND IF WE DON'T STOP THIS, A LOT OF PEOPLE ABOVE GROUND ARE GOING TO DIE.
VULCAN!
I'M ON IT!
ピ
PING
WE DON'T GIVE A DAMN ABOUT PROTOCOL WHEN PEOPLE'S LIVES ARE ON THE LINE!!
GWIP

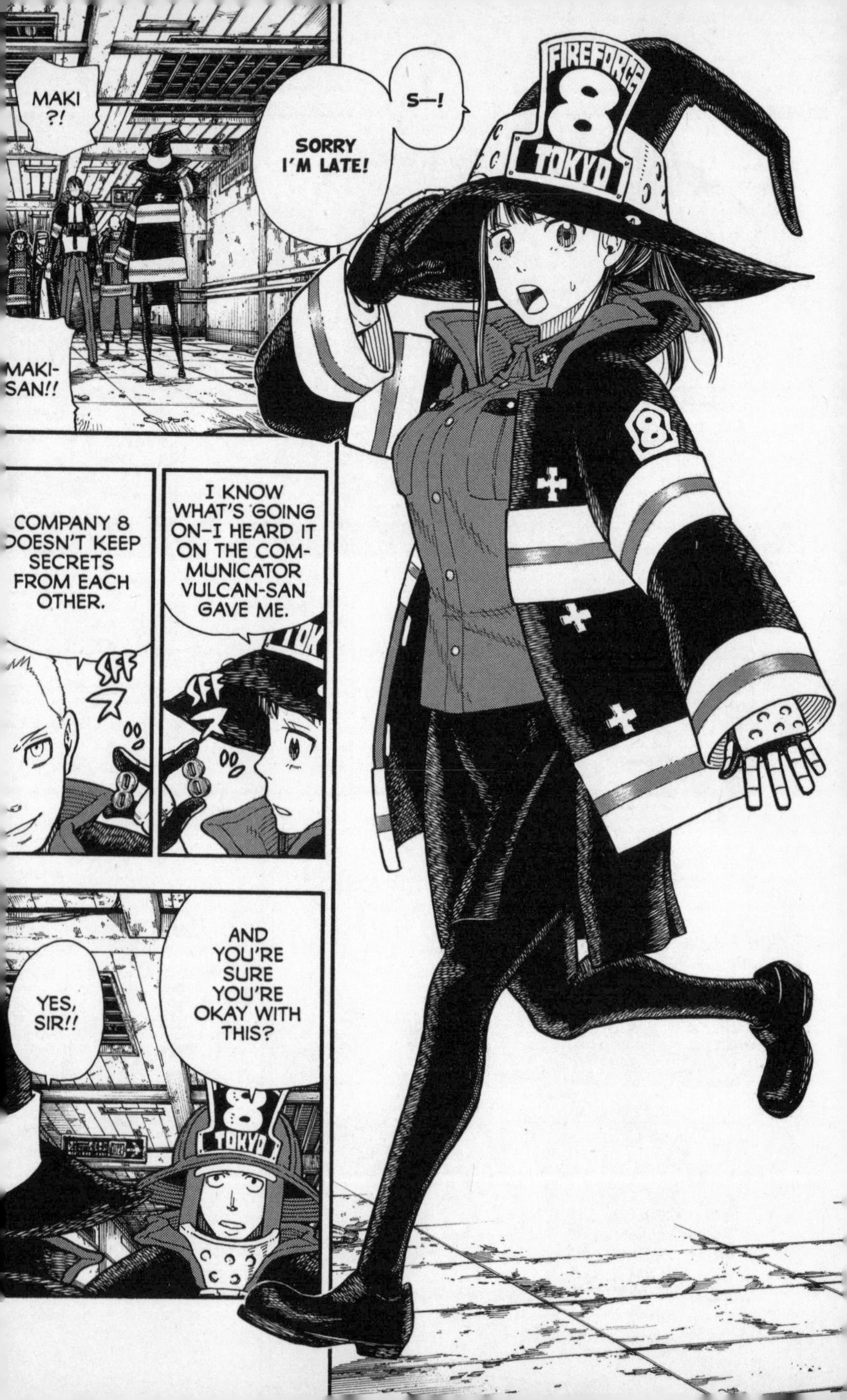
FIREFORCE 8 TOKYO
S—!
SORRY I'M LATE!
MAKI ?!
MAKI-SAN!!
I KNOW WHAT'S GOING ON—I HEARD IT ON THE COMMUNICATOR VULCAN-SAN GAVE ME.
SFF
COMPANY 8 DOESN'T KEEP SECRETS FROM EACH OTHER.
SFF
AND YOU'RE SURE YOU'RE OKAY WITH THIS?
YES, SIR!!
8 TOKYO

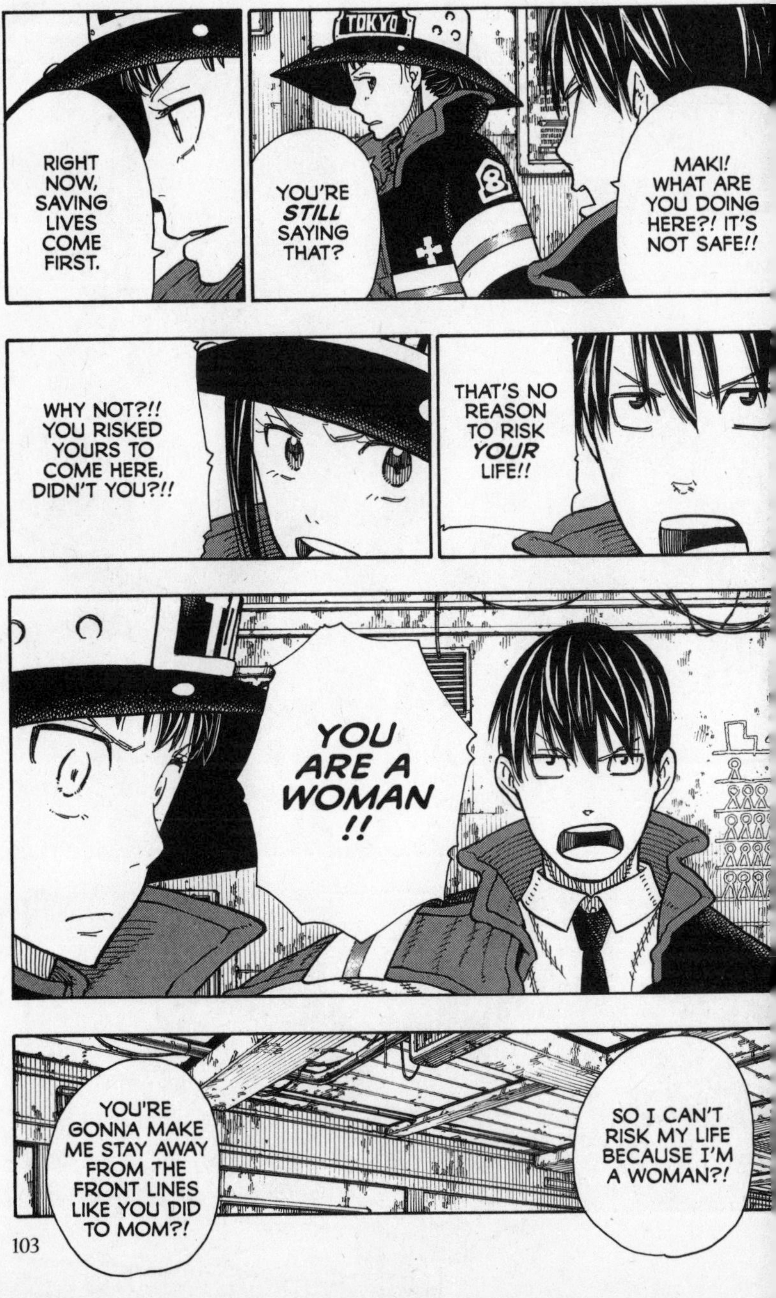

MAKI! WHAT ARE YOU DOING HERE?! IT'S NOT SAFE!!
YOU'RE *STILL* SAYING THAT?
RIGHT NOW, SAVING LIVES COME FIRST.
THAT'S NO REASON TO RISK *YOUR* LIFE!!
WHY NOT?!! YOU RISKED YOURS TO COME HERE, DIDN'T YOU?!!
TOKYO
YOU ARE A WOMAN!!
SO I CAN'T RISK MY LIFE BECAUSE I'M A WOMAN?!
YOU'RE GONNA MAKE ME STAY AWAY FROM THE FRONT LINES LIKE YOU DID TO MOM?!

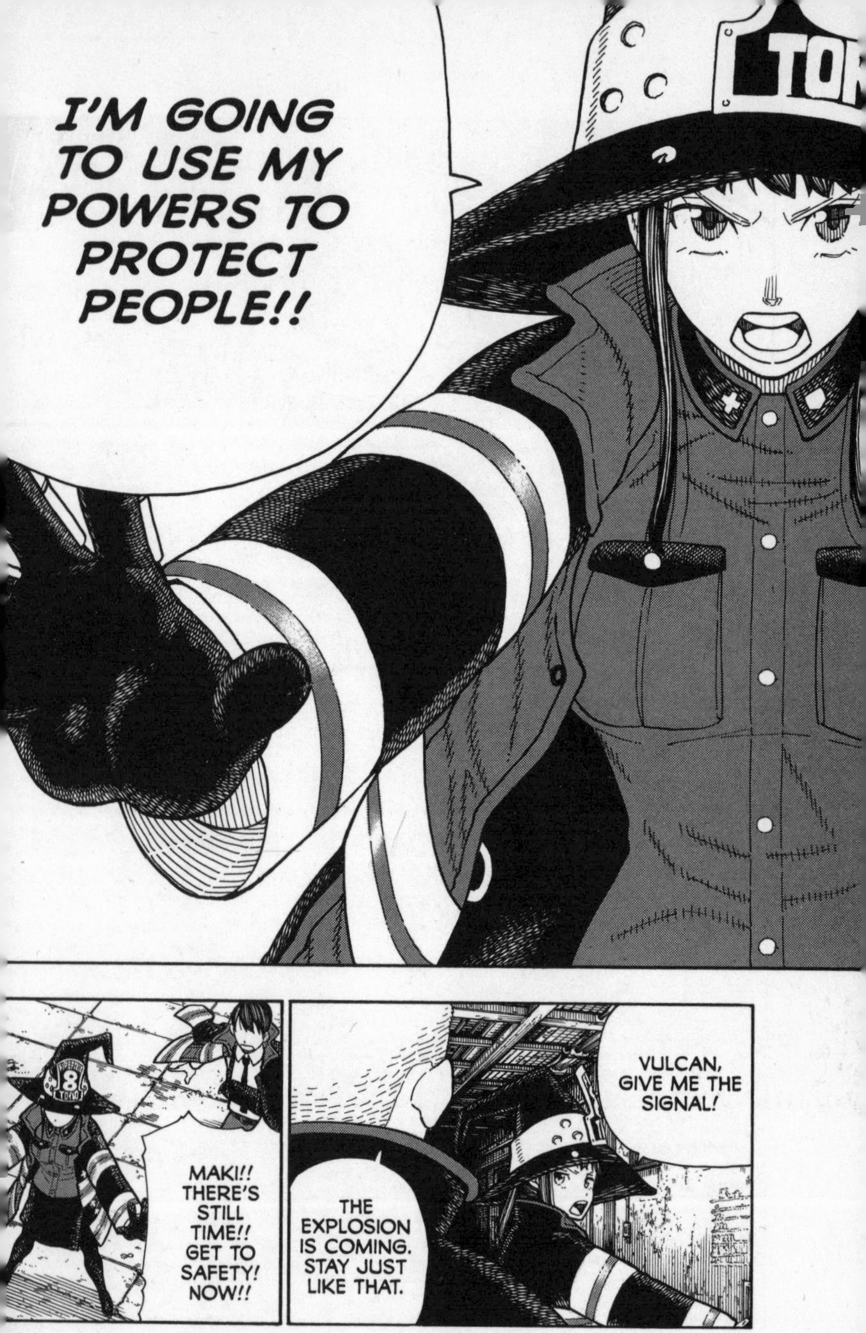
I'M GOING TO USE MY POWERS TO PROTECT PEOPLE!!
VULCAN, GIVE ME THE SIGNAL!
THE EXPLOSION IS COMING. STAY JUST LIKE THAT.
MAKI!! THERE'S STILL TIME!! GET TO SAFETY! NOW!!

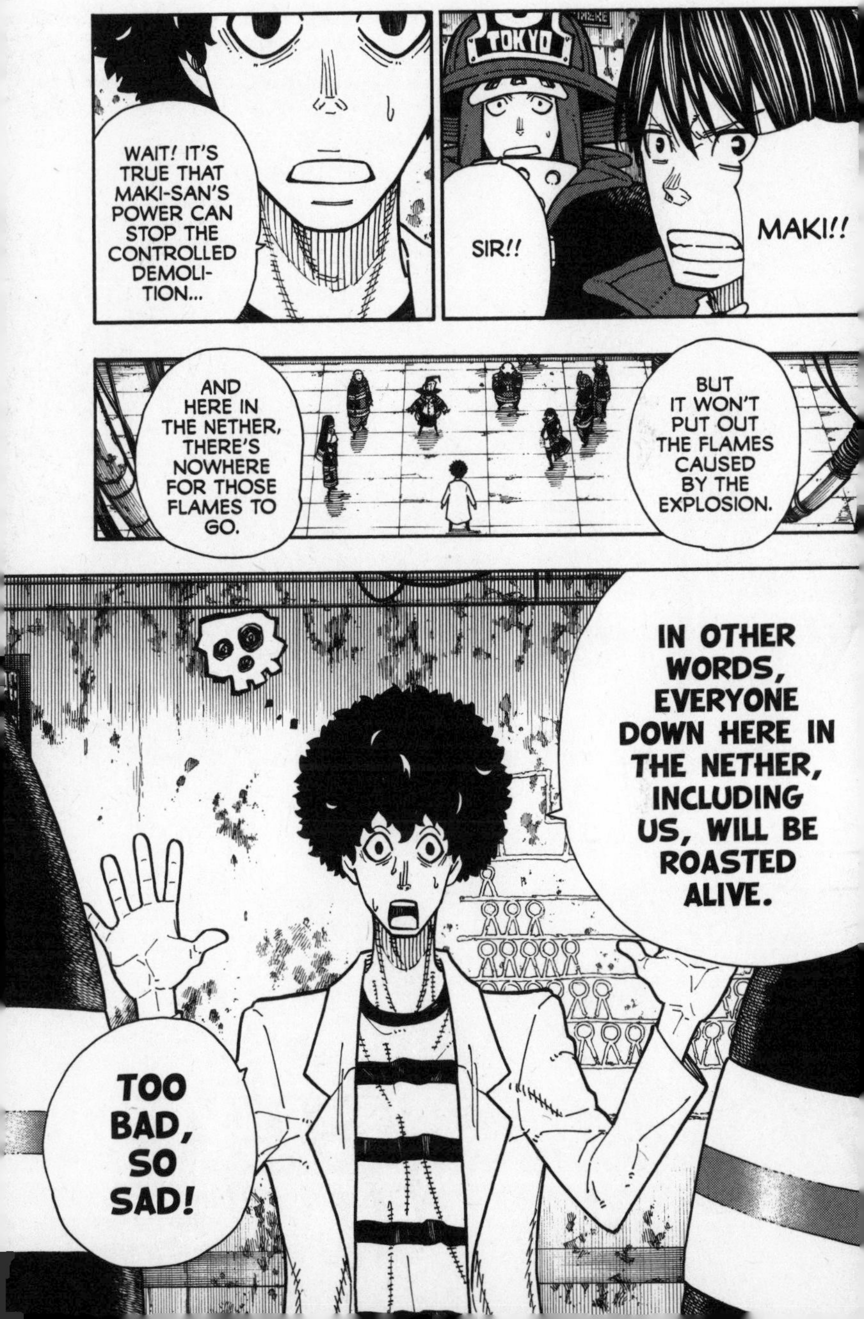
MAKI!!
SIR!!
WAIT! IT'S TRUE THAT MAKI-SAN'S POWER CAN STOP THE CONTROLLED DEMOLITION...
BUT IT WON'T PUT OUT THE FLAMES CAUSED BY THE EXPLOSION.
AND HERE IN THE NETHER, THERE'S NOWHERE FOR THOSE FLAMES TO GO.
IN OTHER WORDS, EVERYONE DOWN HERE IN THE NETHER, INCLUDING US, WILL BE ROASTED ALIVE.
TOO BAD, SO SAD!

FIRE FORCE

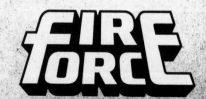

CHAPTER CLXV: LAST-WITCH ATTEMPT

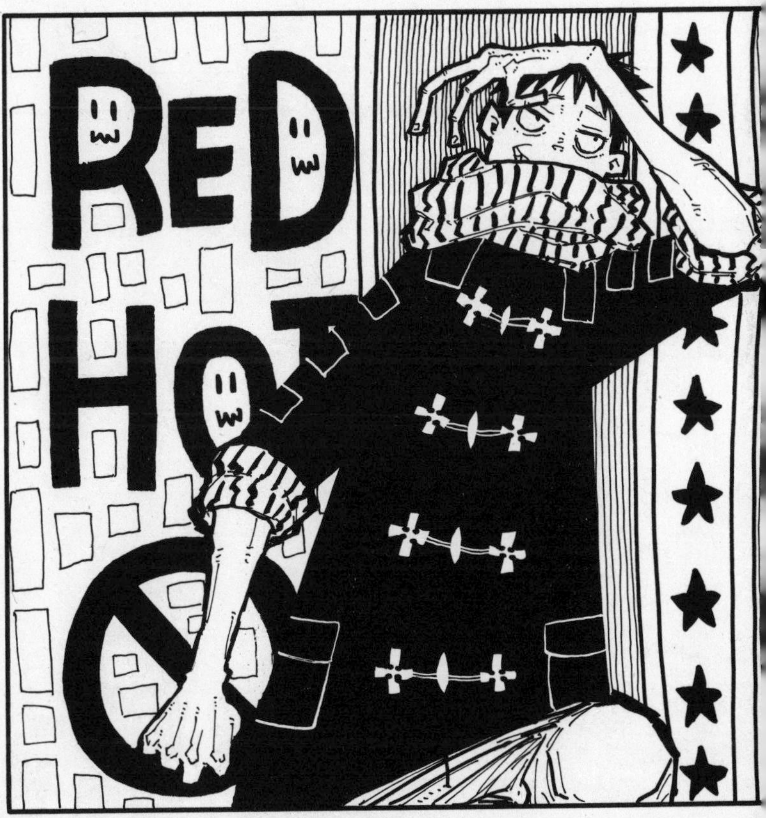

RED HOT

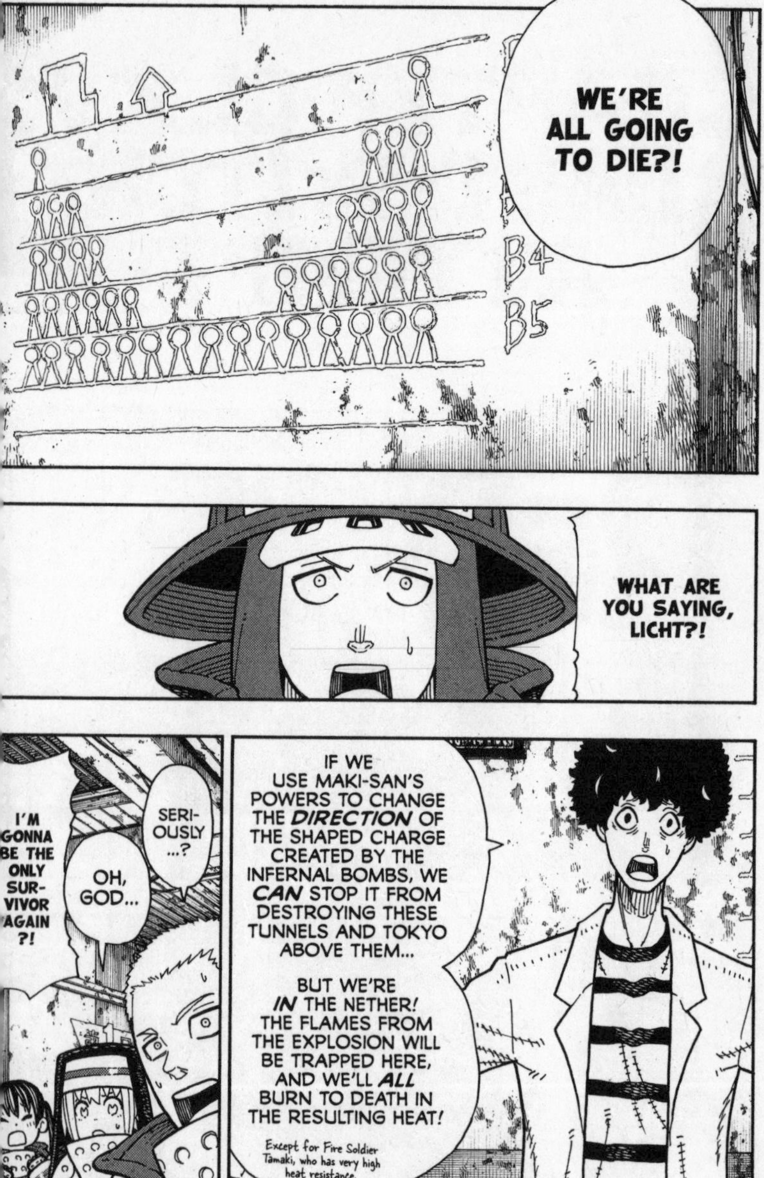
B4
B5
WE'RE ALL GOING TO DIE?!
WHAT ARE YOU SAYING, LICHT?!
IF WE USE MAKI-SAN'S POWERS TO CHANGE THE *DIRECTION* OF THE SHAPED CHARGE CREATED BY THE INFERNAL BOMBS, WE *CAN* STOP IT FROM DESTROYING THESE TUNNELS AND TOKYO ABOVE THEM...
BUT WE'RE *IN* THE NETHER! THE FLAMES FROM THE EXPLOSION WILL BE TRAPPED HERE, AND WE'LL *ALL* BURN TO DEATH IN THE RESULTING HEAT!
Except for Fire Soldier Tamaki, who has very high heat resistance.
SERIOUSLY...?
OH, GOD...
I'M GONNA BE THE ONLY SURVIVOR AGAIN?!

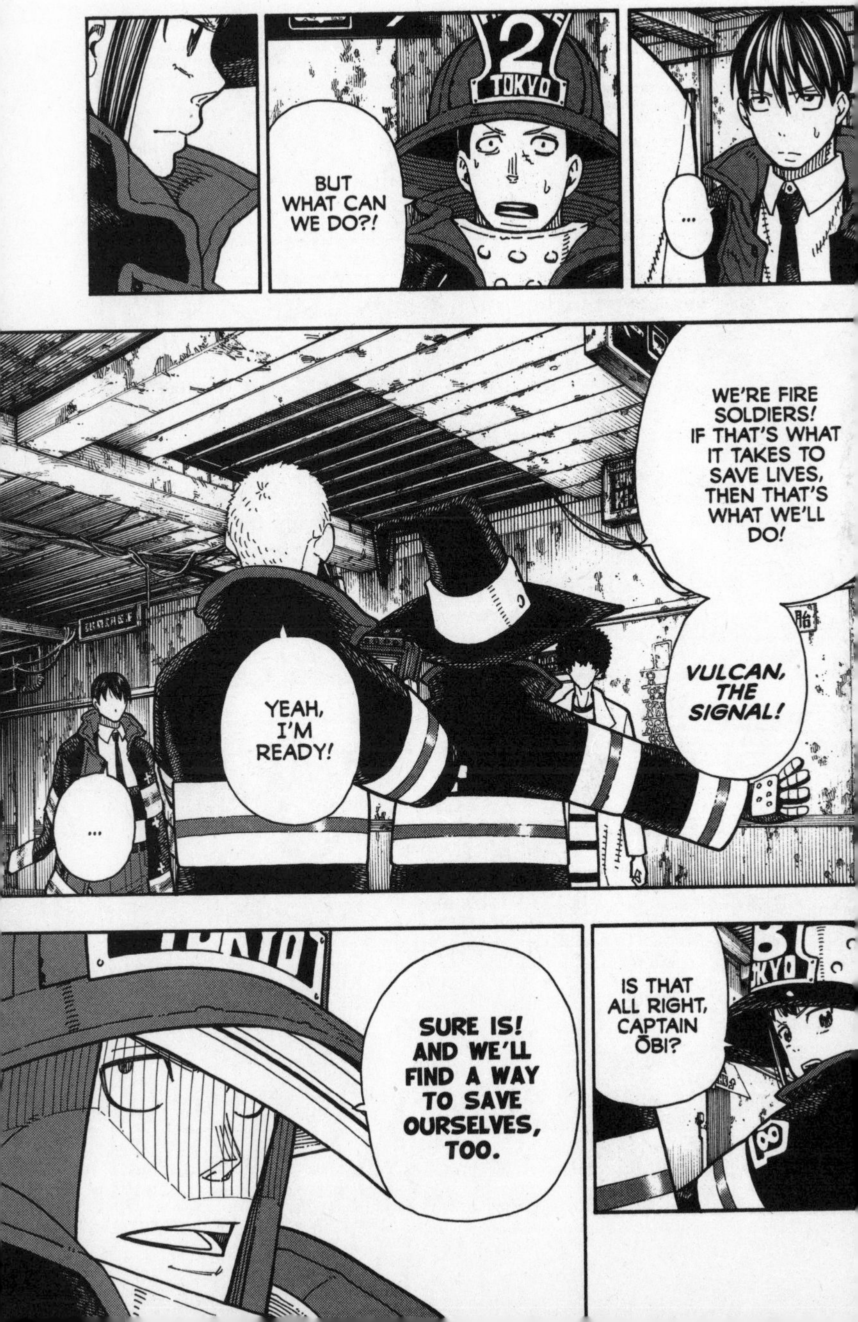
...
BUT WHAT CAN WE DO?!
WE'RE FIRE SOLDIERS! IF THAT'S WHAT IT TAKES TO SAVE LIVES, THEN THAT'S WHAT WE'LL DO!
VULCAN, THE SIGNAL!
YEAH, I'M READY!
...
IS THAT ALL RIGHT, CAPTAIN ŌBI?
SURE IS! AND WE'LL FIND A WAY TO SAVE OURSELVES, TOO.

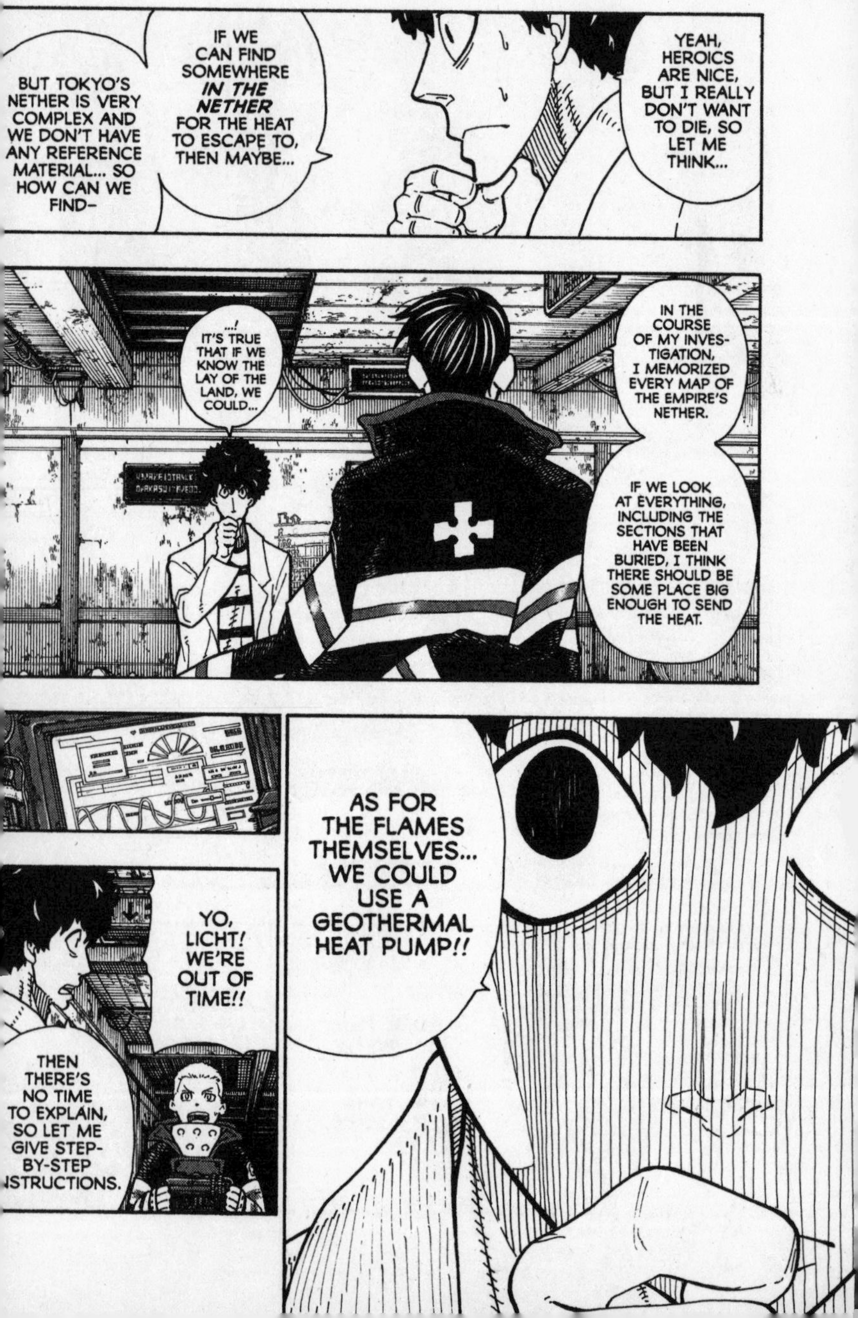
YEAH, HEROICS ARE NICE, BUT I REALLY DON'T WANT TO DIE, SO LET ME THINK...
IF WE CAN FIND SOMEWHERE *IN THE NETHER* FOR THE HEAT TO ESCAPE TO, THEN MAYBE...
BUT TOKYO'S NETHER IS VERY COMPLEX AND WE DON'T HAVE ANY REFERENCE MATERIAL... SO HOW CAN WE FIND–
IN THE COURSE OF MY INVES-TIGATION, I MEMORIZED EVERY MAP OF THE EMPIRE'S NETHER.
IF WE LOOK AT EVERYTHING, INCLUDING THE SECTIONS THAT HAVE BEEN BURIED, I THINK THERE SHOULD BE SOME PLACE BIG ENOUGH TO SEND THE HEAT.
...! IT'S TRUE THAT IF WE KNOW THE LAY OF THE LAND, WE COULD...
AS FOR THE FLAMES THEMSELVES... WE COULD USE A GEOTHERMAL HEAT PUMP!!
YO, LICHT! WE'RE OUT OF TIME!!
THEN THERE'S NO TIME TO EXPLAIN, SO LET ME GIVE STEP-BY-STEP ISTRUCTIONS.

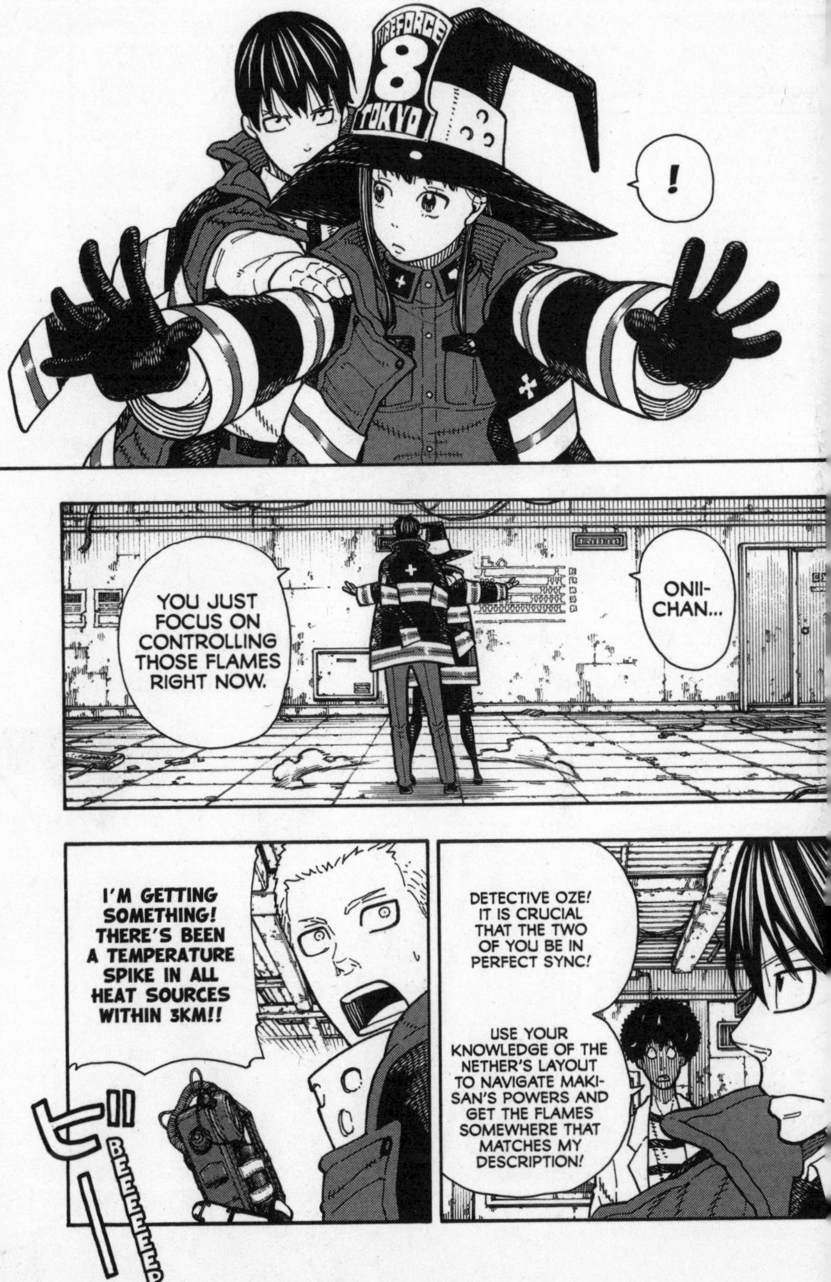
!
ONII-CHAN...
YOU JUST FOCUS ON CONTROLLING THOSE FLAMES RIGHT NOW.
DETECTIVE OZE! IT IS CRUCIAL THAT THE TWO OF YOU BE IN PERFECT SYNC!
USE YOUR KNOWLEDGE OF THE NETHER'S LAYOUT TO NAVIGATE MAKI-SAN'S POWERS AND GET THE FLAMES SOMEWHERE THAT MATCHES MY DESCRIPTION!
I'M GETTING SOMETHING! THERE'S BEEN A TEMPERATURE SPIKE IN ALL HEAT SOURCES WITHIN 3KM!!
BEEEEEEP

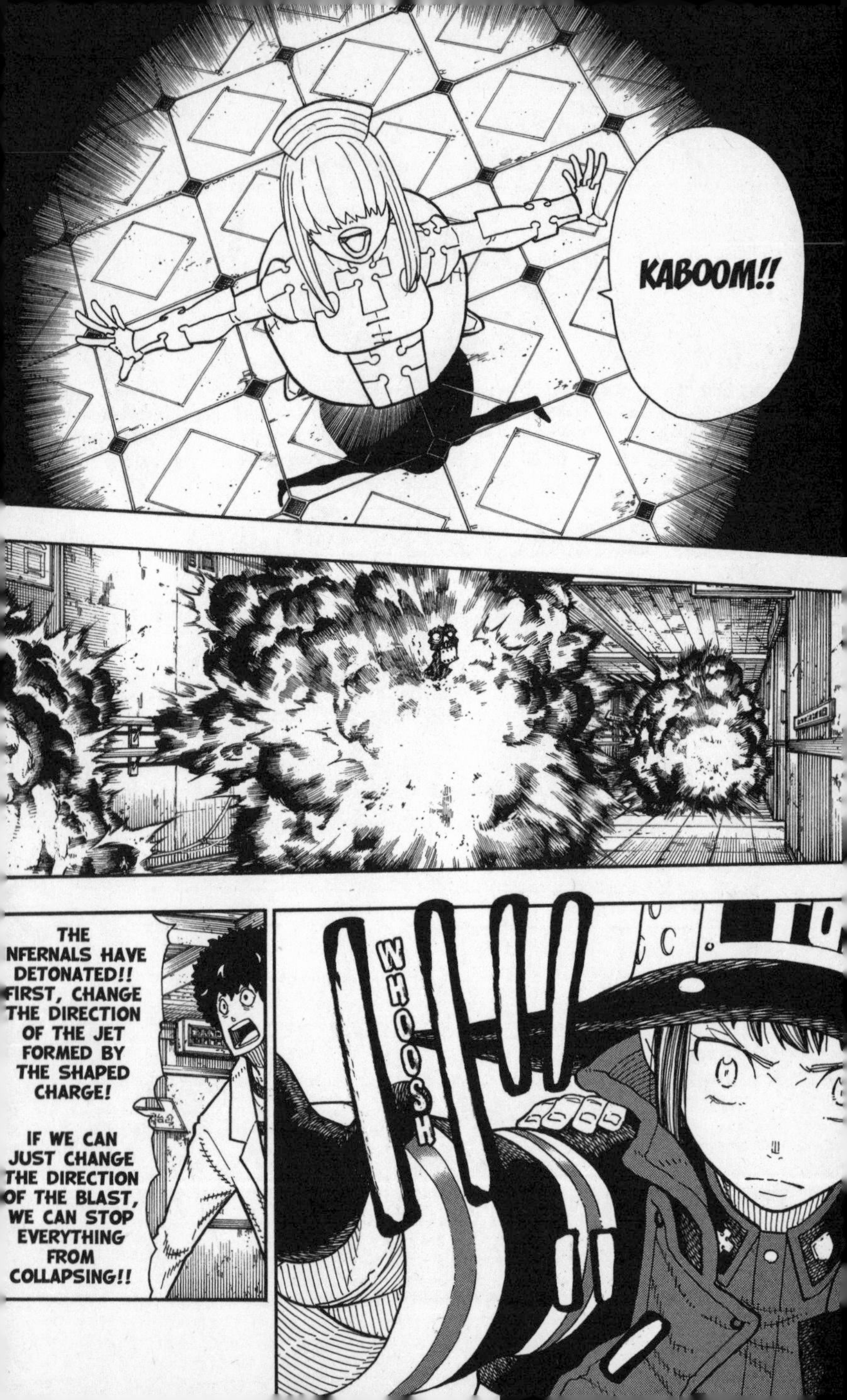
KABOOM!!
WHOOSH
THE NFERNALS HAVE DETONATED!! FIRST, CHANGE THE DIRECTION OF THE JET FORMED BY THE SHAPED CHARGE!
IF WE CAN JUST CHANGE THE DIRECTION OF THE BLAST, WE CAN STOP EVERYTHING FROM COLLAPSING!!

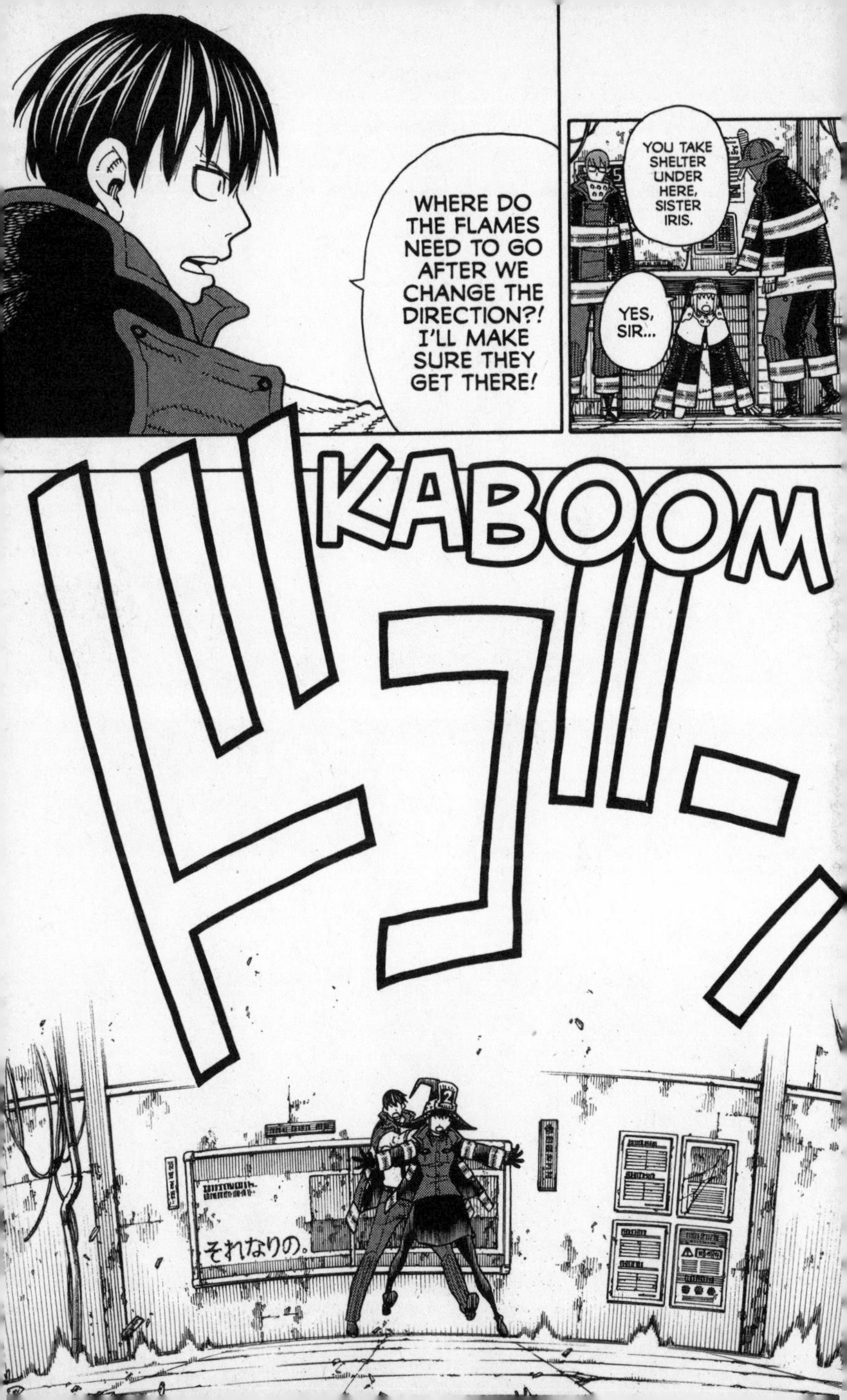
YOU TAKE SHELTER UNDER HERE, SISTER IRIS.
YES, SIR...
WHERE DO THE FLAMES NEED TO GO AFTER WE CHANGE THE DIRECTION?! I'LL MAKE SURE THEY GET THERE!
KABOOM
それなりの。

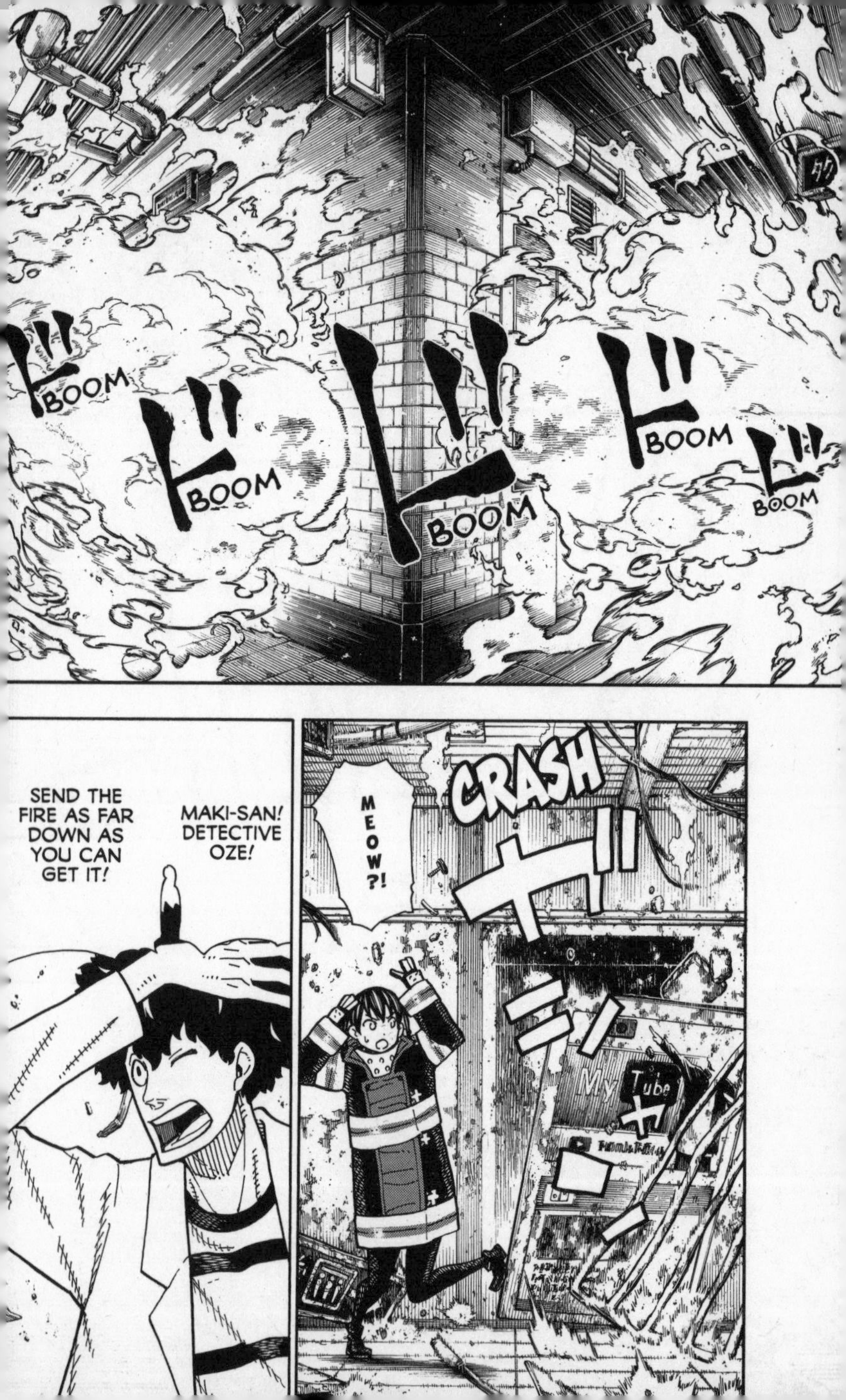
BOOM
BOOM
BOOM
BOOM
BOOM
CRASH
MEOW?!
My Tube
MAKI-SAN! DETECTIVE OZE!
SEND THE FIRE AS FAR DOWN AS YOU CAN GET IT!

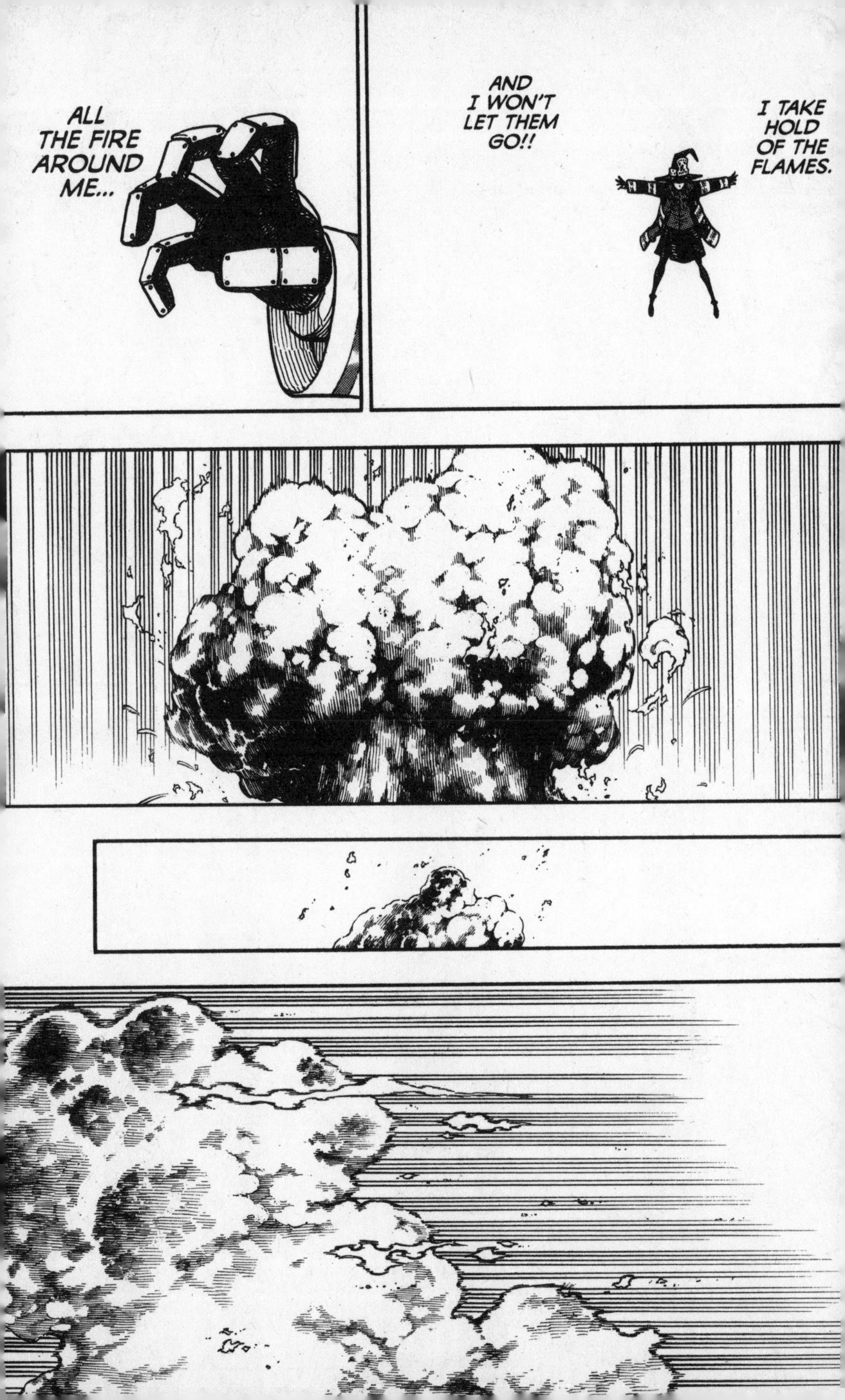
I TAKE HOLD OF THE FLAMES.
AND I WON'T LET THEM GO!!
ALL THE FIRE AROUND ME...

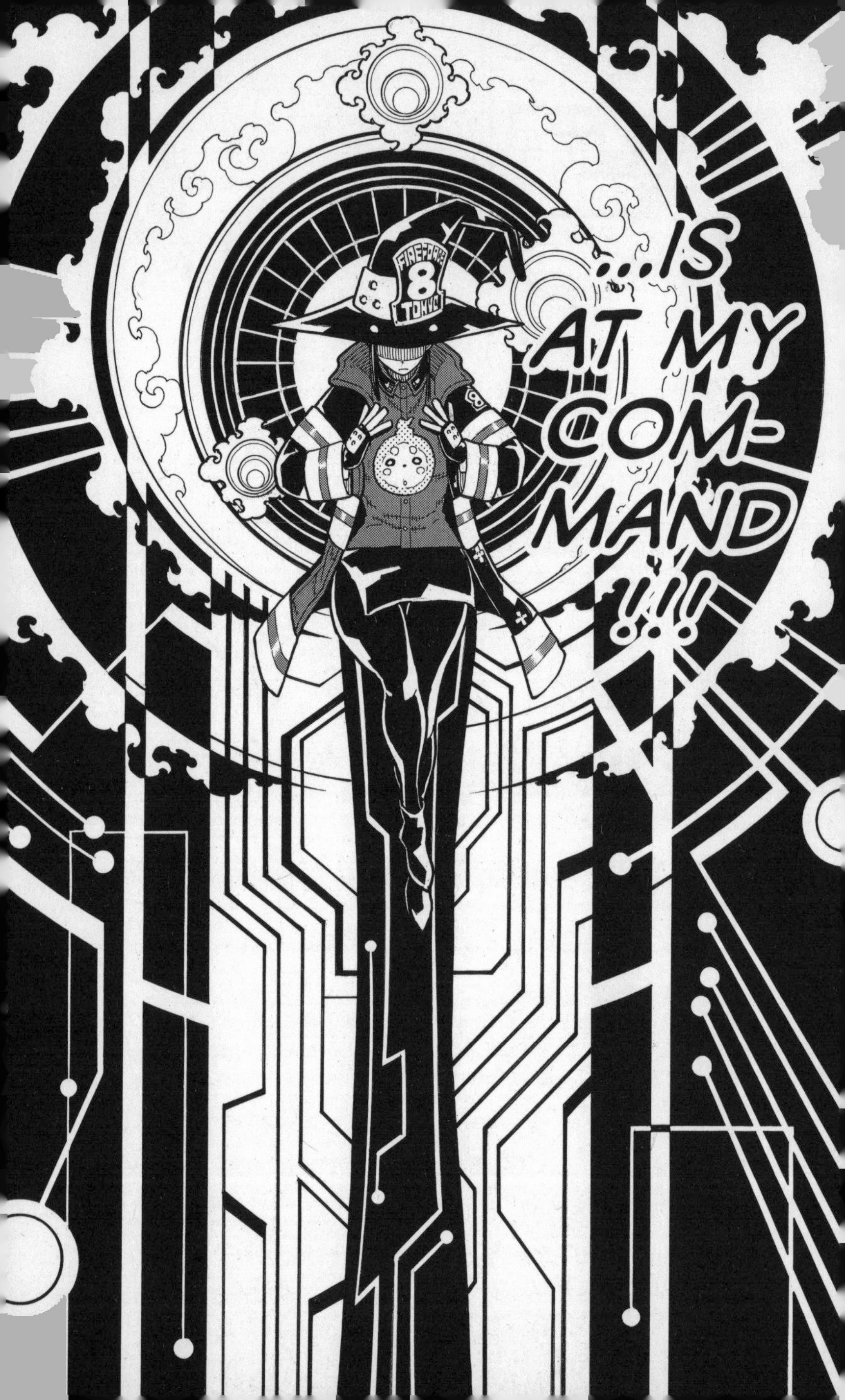
...IS AT MY COM-MAND !!!
FIRE FORCE 8 TOKYO

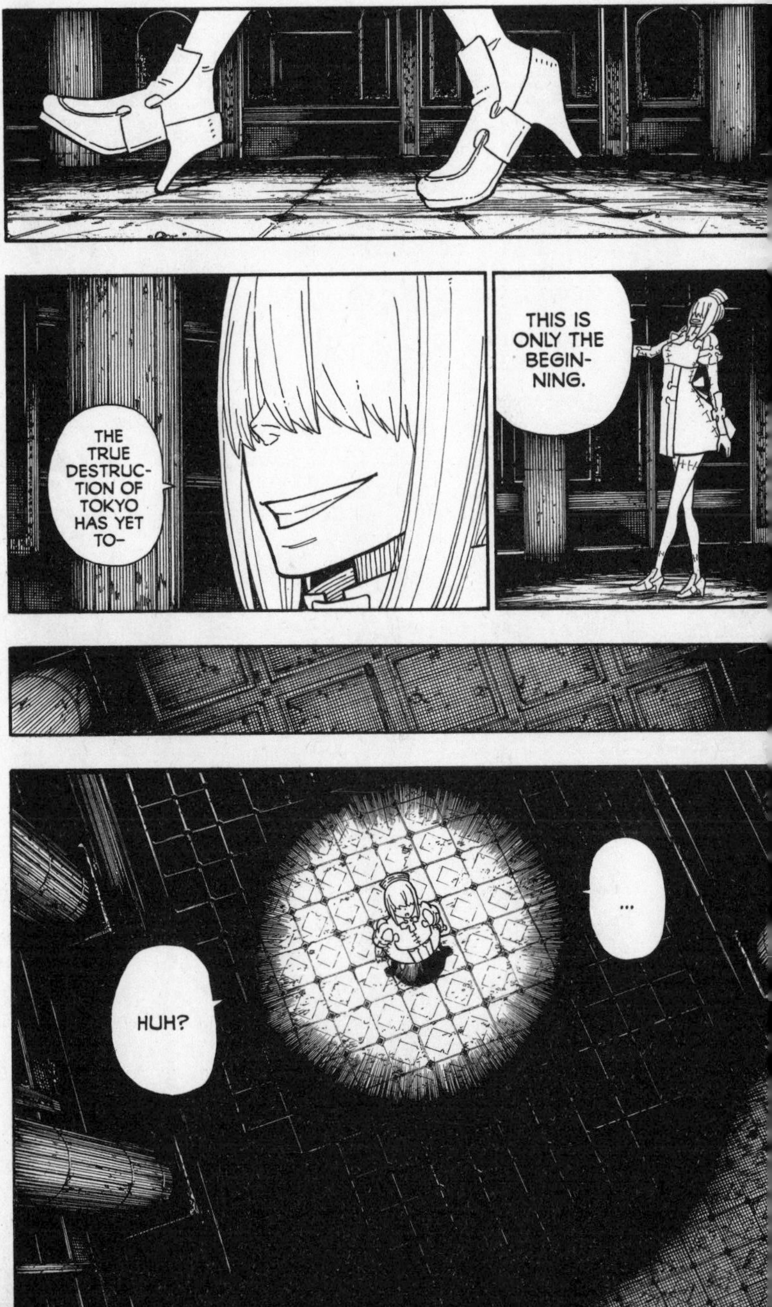
THIS IS ONLY THE BEGINNING.
THE TRUE DESTRUCTION OF TOKYO HAS YET TO–
...
HUH?

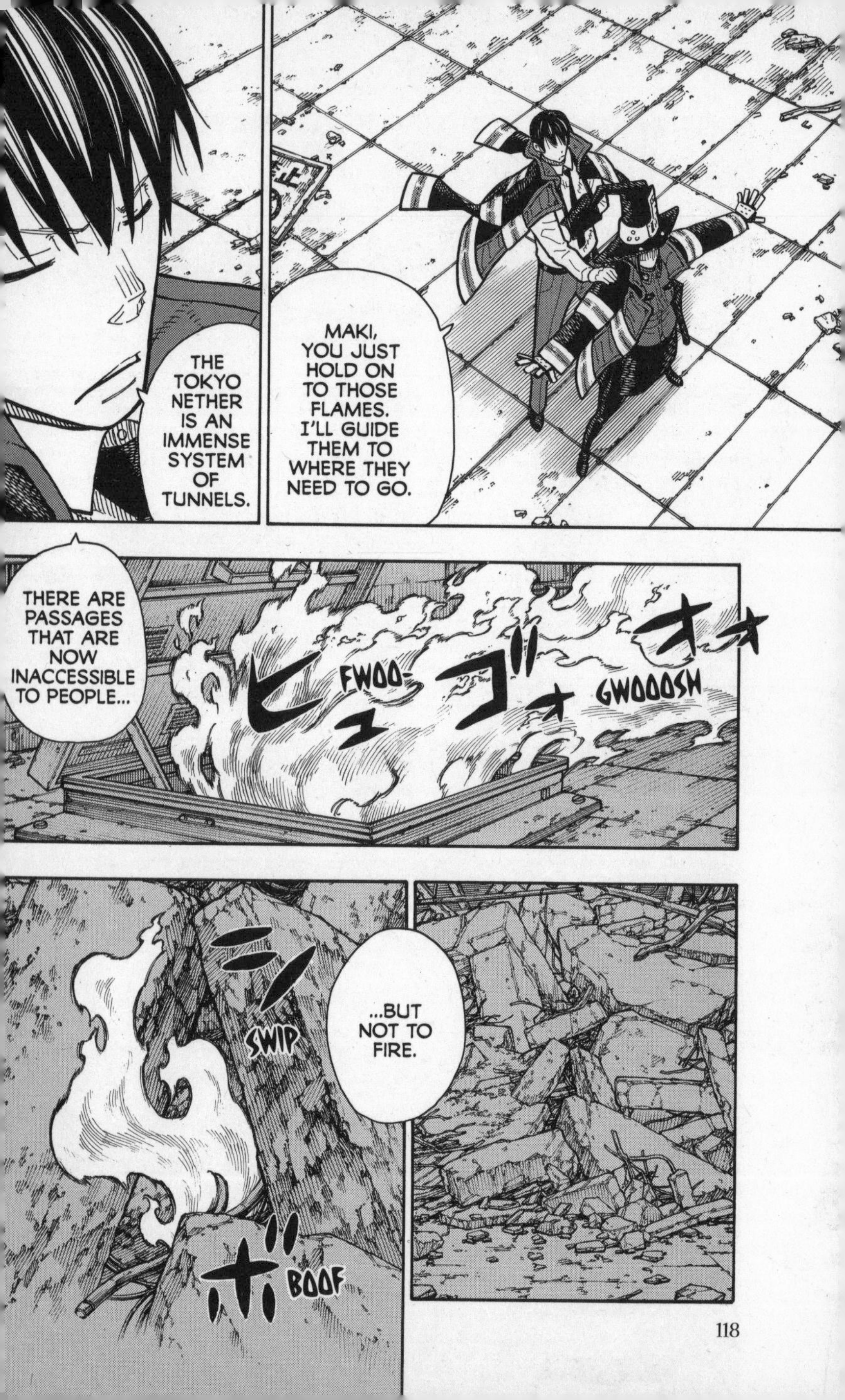
MAKI, YOU JUST HOLD ON TO THOSE FLAMES. I'LL GUIDE THEM TO WHERE THEY NEED TO GO.
THE TOKYO NETHER IS AN IMMENSE SYSTEM OF TUNNELS.
THERE ARE PASSAGES THAT ARE NOW INACCESSIBLE TO PEOPLE...
GWOOOSH
FWOO-
...BUT NOT TO FIRE.
SWIP
BOOF

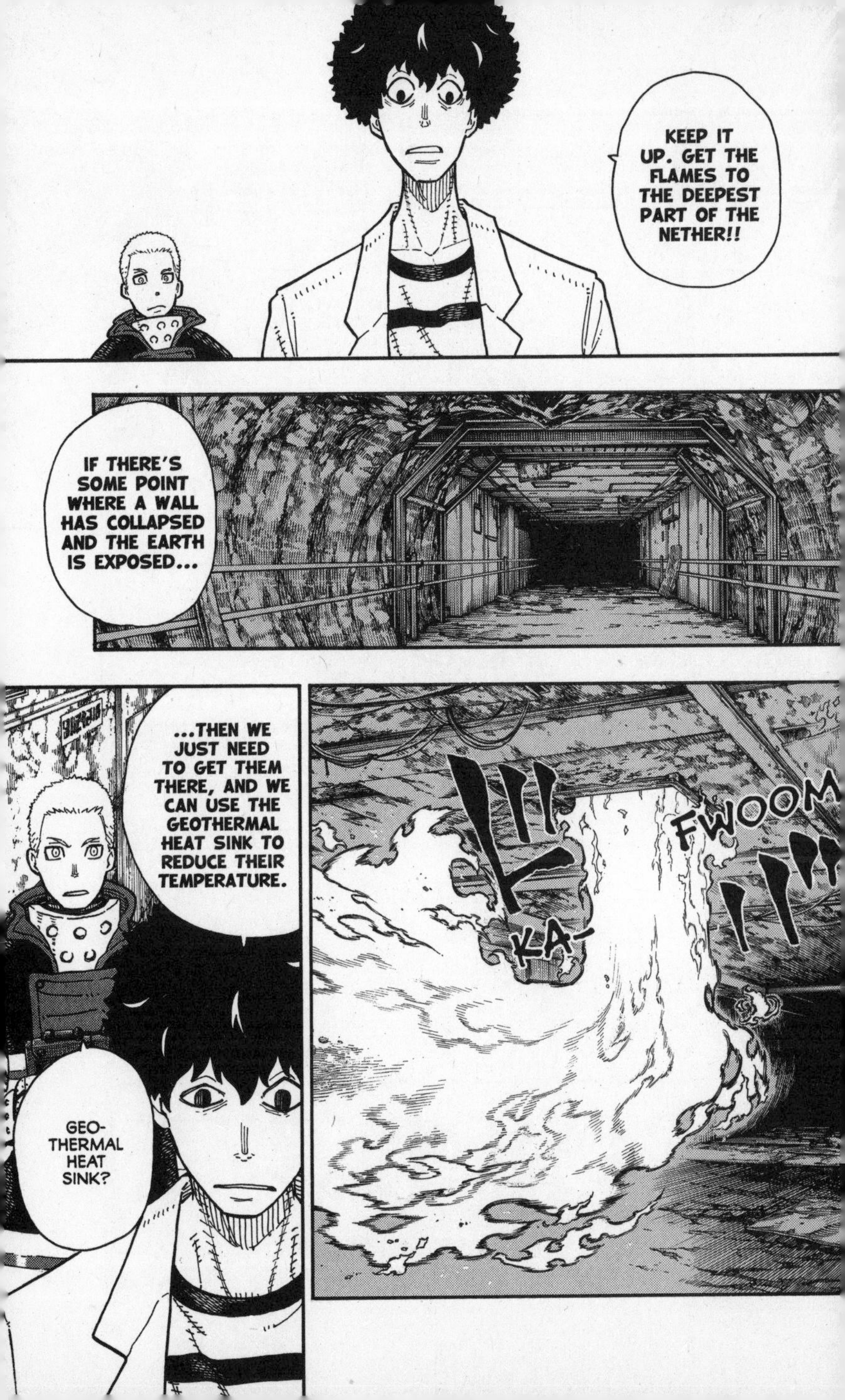
KEEP IT UP. GET THE FLAMES TO THE DEEPEST PART OF THE NETHER!!
IF THERE'S SOME POINT WHERE A WALL HAS COLLAPSED AND THE EARTH IS EXPOSED...
FWOOM
KA-
...THEN WE JUST NEED TO GET THEM THERE, AND WE CAN USE THE GEOTHERMAL HEAT SINK TO REDUCE THEIR TEMPERATURE.
GEO-THERMAL HEAT SINK?

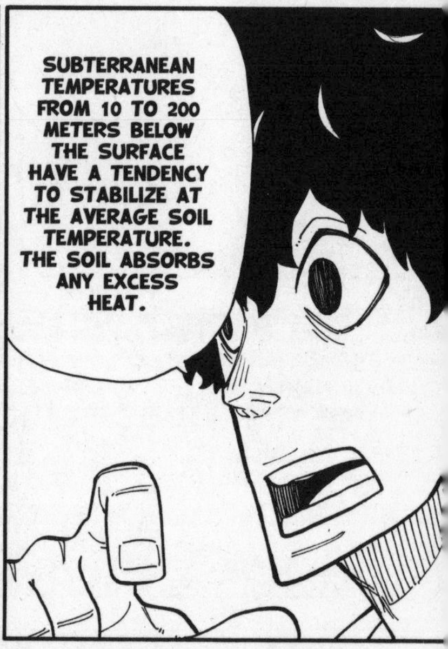
SUBTERRANEAN TEMPERATURES FROM 10 TO 200 METERS BELOW THE SURFACE HAVE A TENDENCY TO STABILIZE AT THE AVERAGE SOIL TEMPERATURE. THE SOIL ABSORBS ANY EXCESS HEAT.

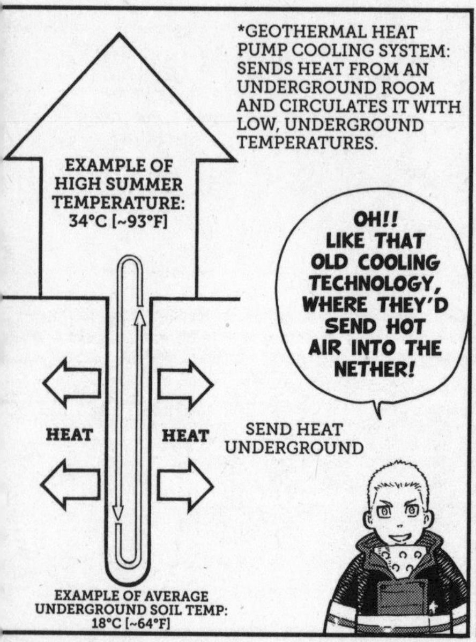
*GEOTHERMAL HEAT PUMP COOLING SYSTEM: SENDS HEAT FROM AN UNDERGROUND ROOM AND CIRCULATES IT WITH LOW, UNDERGROUND TEMPERATURES.
OH!! LIKE THAT OLD COOLING TECHNOLOGY, WHERE THEY'D SEND HOT AIR INTO THE NETHER!
EXAMPLE OF HIGH SUMMER TEMPERATURE: 34°C [~93°F]
HEAT
HEAT
SEND HEAT UNDERGROUND
EXAMPLE OF AVERAGE UNDERGROUND SOIL TEMP: 18°C [~64°F]

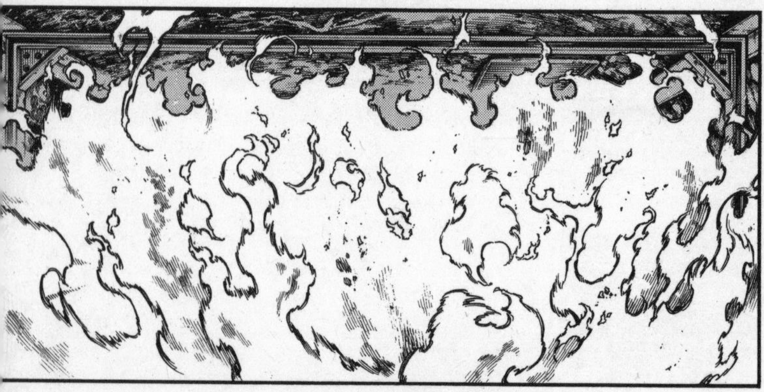

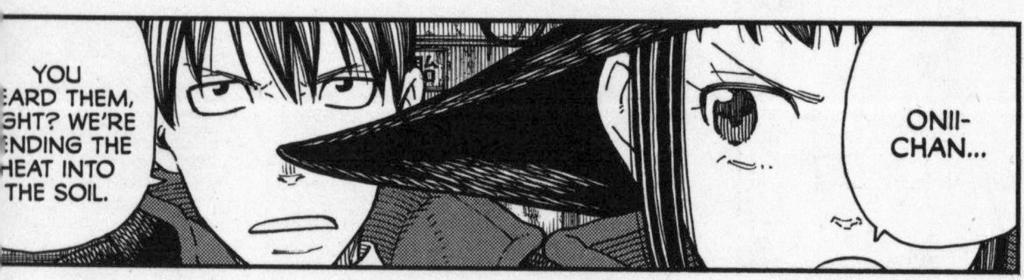
ONII-CHAN...
YOU EARD THEM, GHT? WE'RE ENDING THE HEAT INTO THE SOIL.

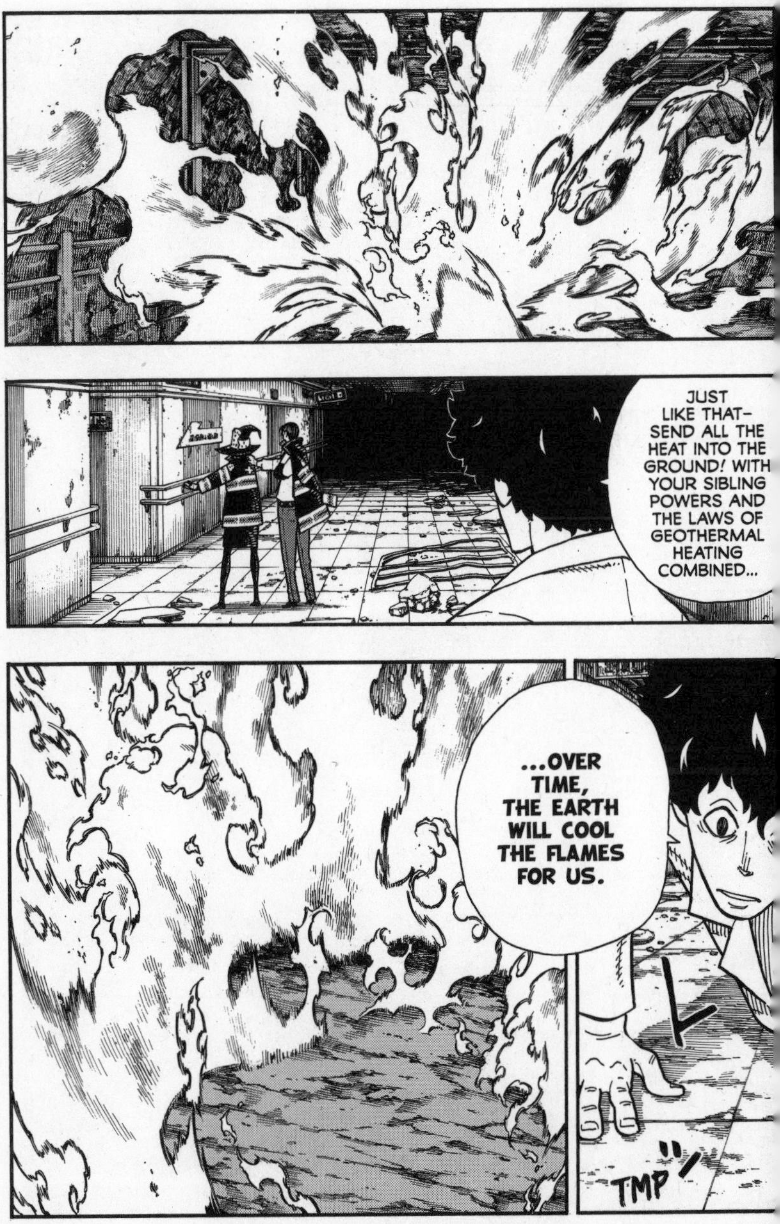
JUST LIKE THAT–SEND ALL THE HEAT INTO THE GROUND! WITH YOUR SIBLING POWERS AND THE LAWS OF GEOTHERMAL HEATING COMBINED...
...OVER TIME, THE EARTH WILL COOL THE FLAMES FOR US.
TMP

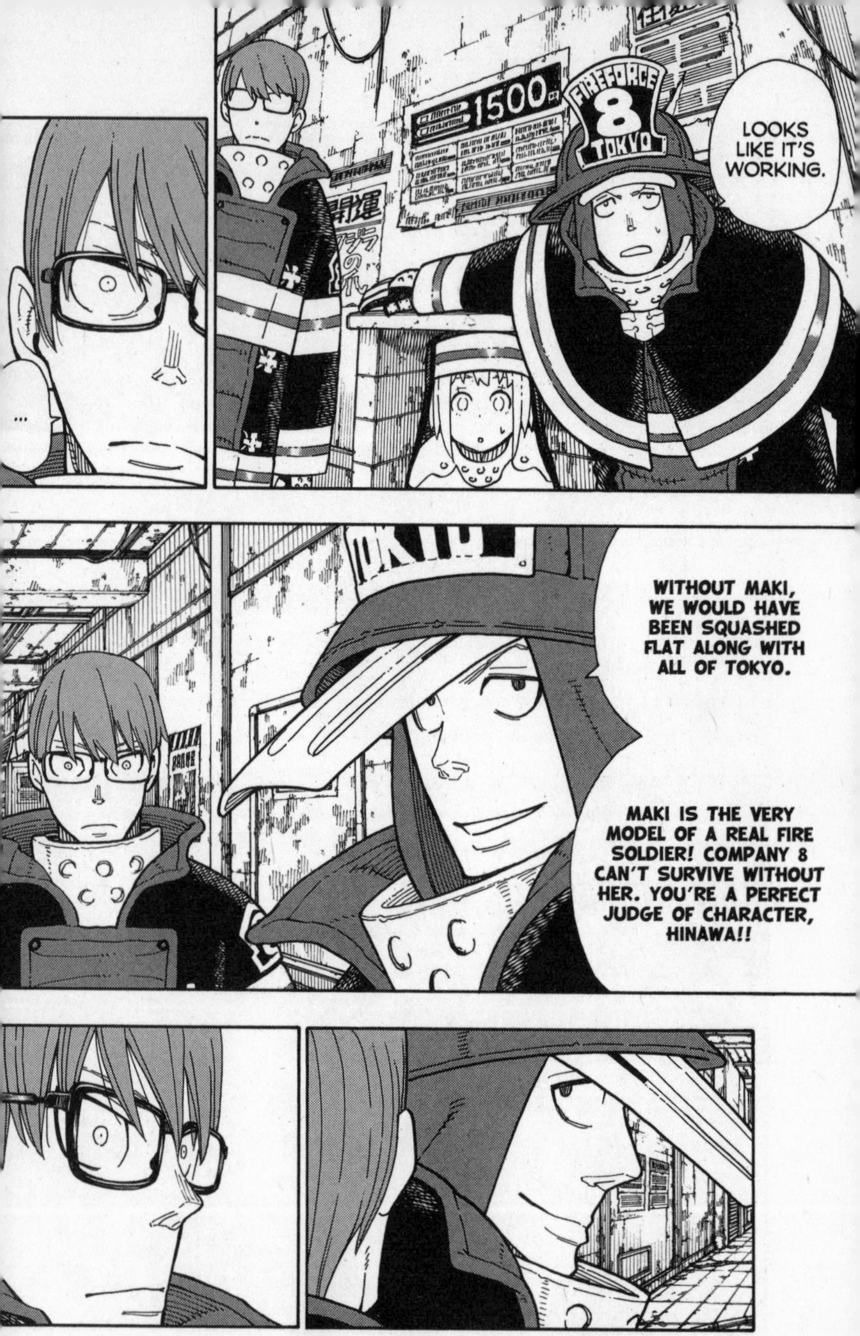
FIREFORCE 8 TOKYO
1500
LOOKS LIKE IT'S WORKING.
...
WITHOUT MAKI, WE WOULD HAVE BEEN SQUASHED FLAT ALONG WITH ALL OF TOKYO.
MAKI IS THE VERY MODEL OF A REAL FIRE SOLDIER! COMPANY 8 CAN'T SURVIVE WITHOUT HER. YOU'RE A PERFECT JUDGE OF CHARACTER, HINAWA!!

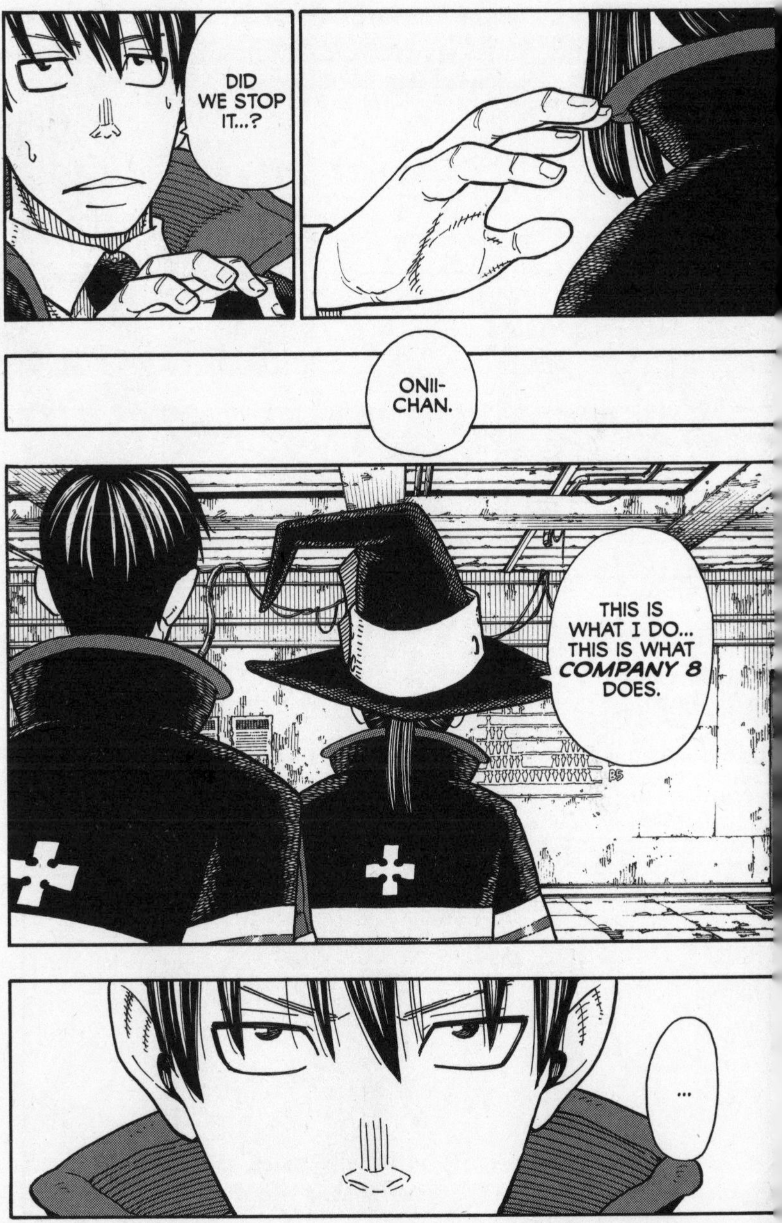
DID WE STOP IT...?
ONII-CHAN.
THIS IS WHAT I DO... THIS IS WHAT COMPANY 8 DOES.
B5
...

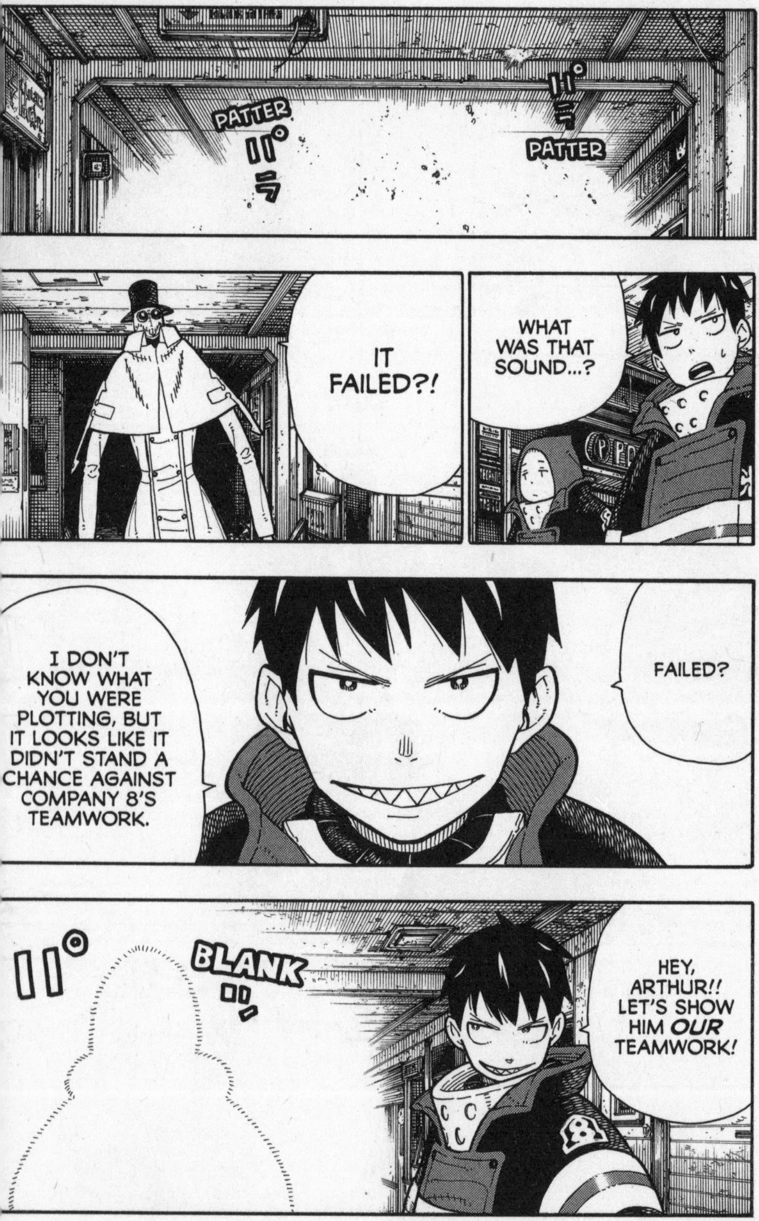
パラ
PATTER
PATTER
パラ
WHAT WAS THAT SOUND...?
IT FAILED?!
FAILED?
I DON'T KNOW WHAT YOU WERE PLOTTING, BUT IT LOOKS LIKE IT DIDN'T STAND A CHANCE AGAINST COMPANY 8'S TEAMWORK.
HEY, ARTHUR!! LET'S SHOW HIM *OUR* TEAMWORK!
BLANK

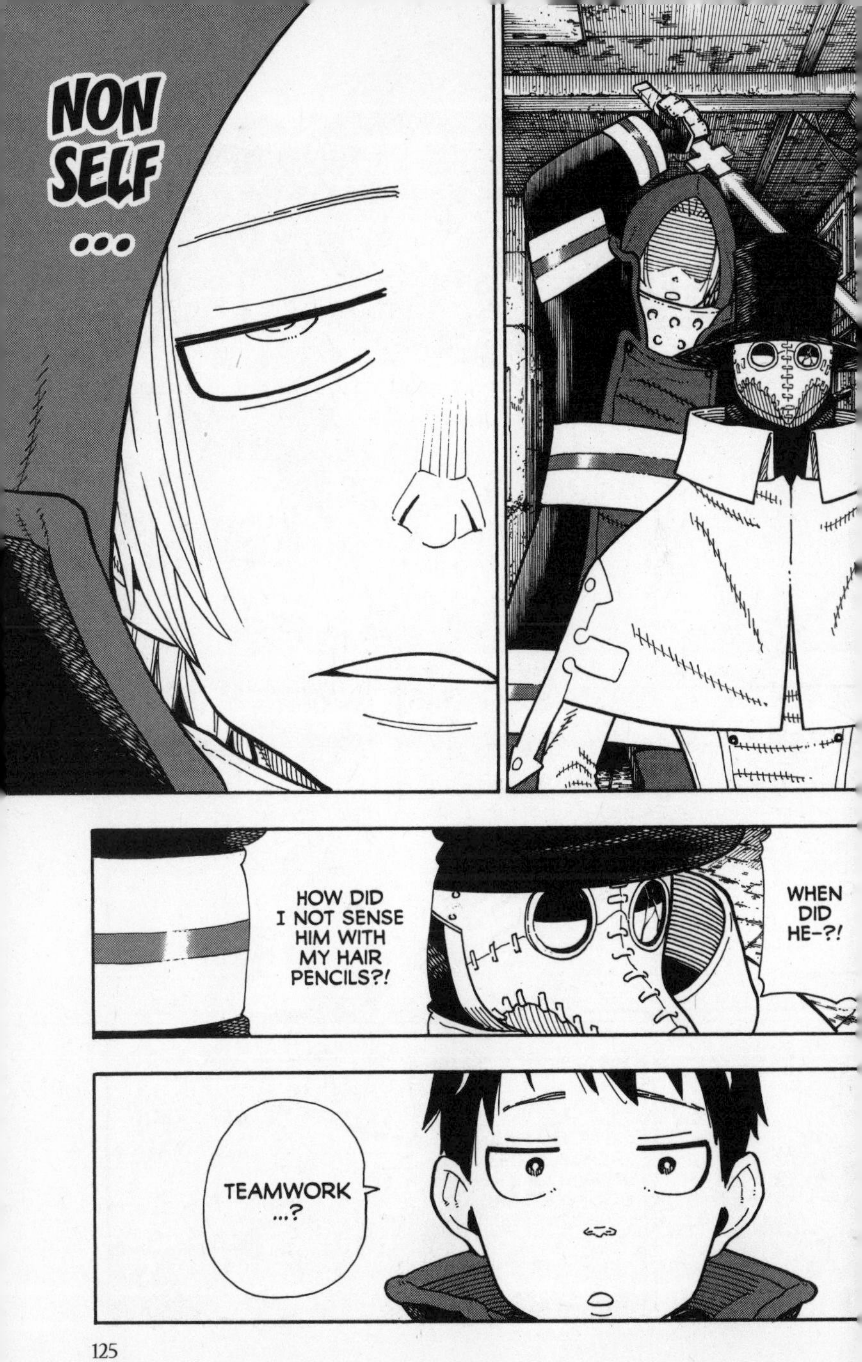
NON SELF ...
WHEN DID HE-?!
HOW DID I NOT SENSE HIM WITH MY HAIR PENCILS?!
TEAMWORK ...?

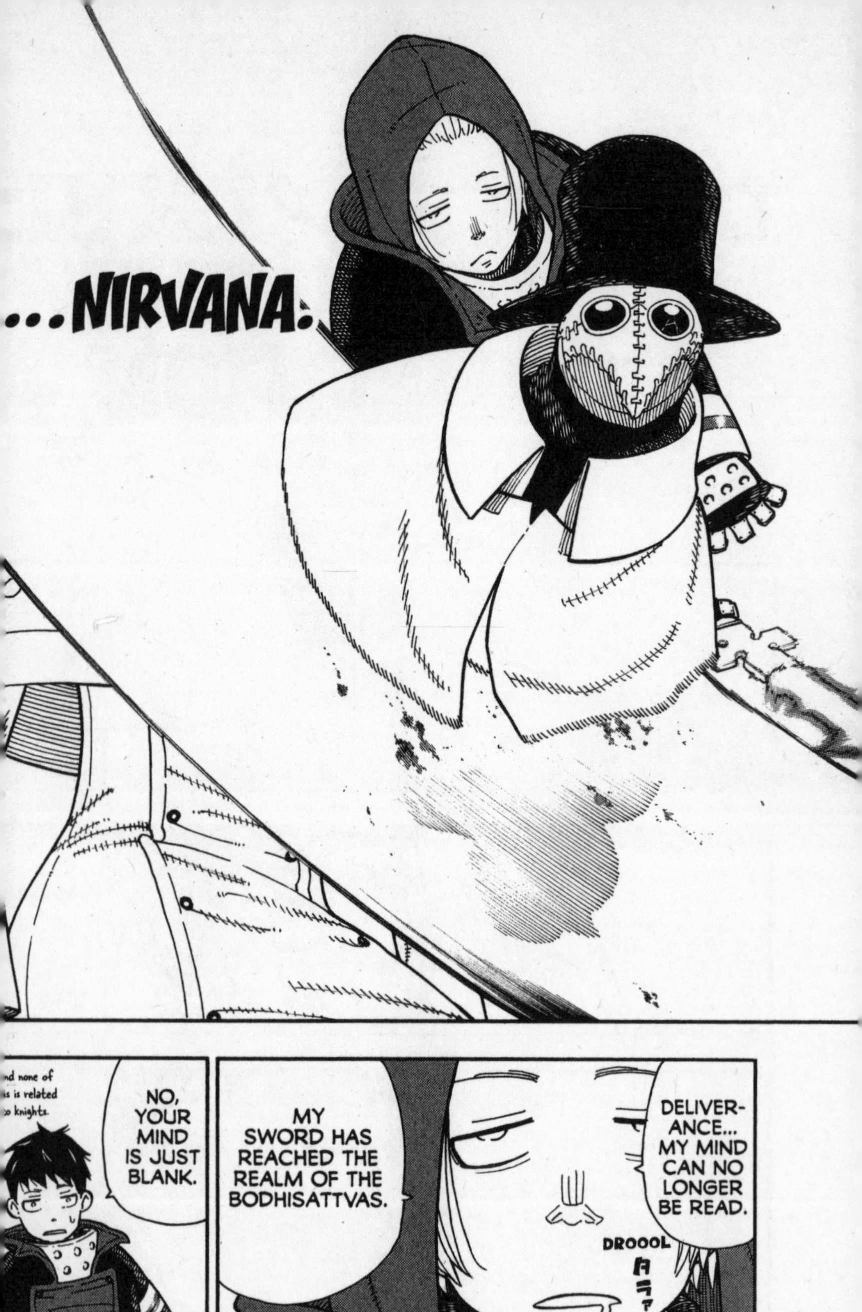
...NIRVANA.
DELIVERANCE... MY MIND CAN NO LONGER BE READ.
MY SWORD HAS REACHED THE REALM OF THE BODHISATTVAS.
DROOOL
NO, YOUR MIND IS JUST BLANK.
nd none of is is related o knights.

CHAPTER CLXVI: TRACING THE CONNECTION

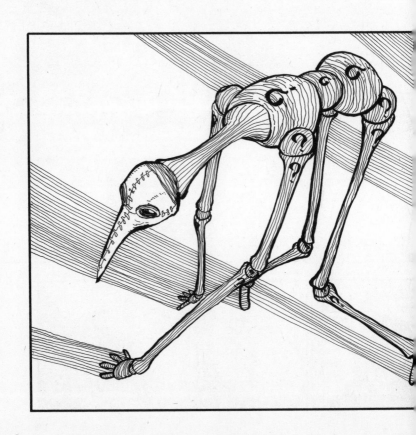

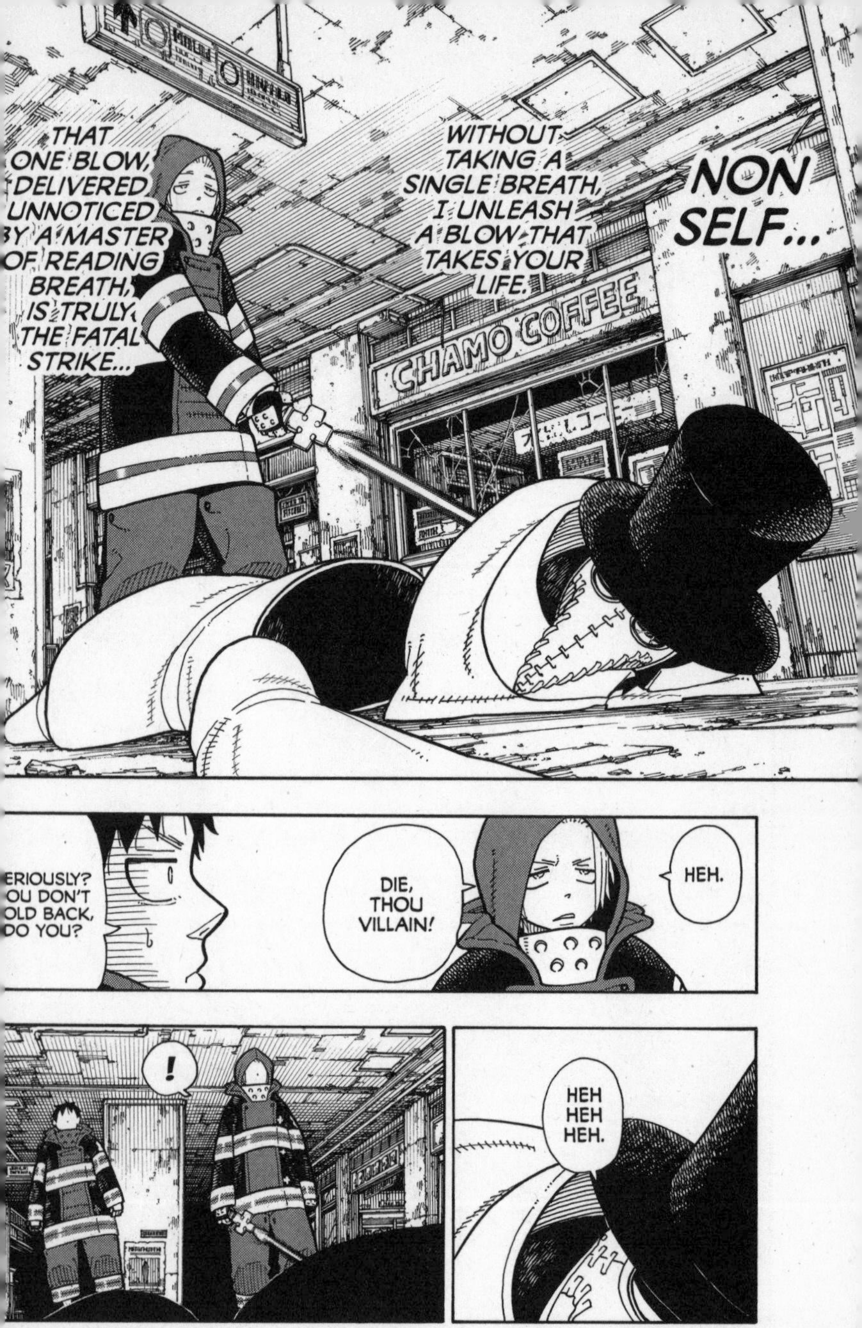
NON SELF...
WITHOUT TAKING A SINGLE BREATH, I UNLEASH A BLOW THAT TAKES YOUR LIFE.
THAT ONE BLOW, DELIVERED UNNOTICED BY A MASTER OF READING BREATH, IS TRULY THE FATAL STRIKE...
CHAMO COFFEE
HEH.
DIE, THOU VILLAIN!
ERIOUSLY? OU DON'T OLD BACK, DO YOU?
HEH HEH HEH.
!

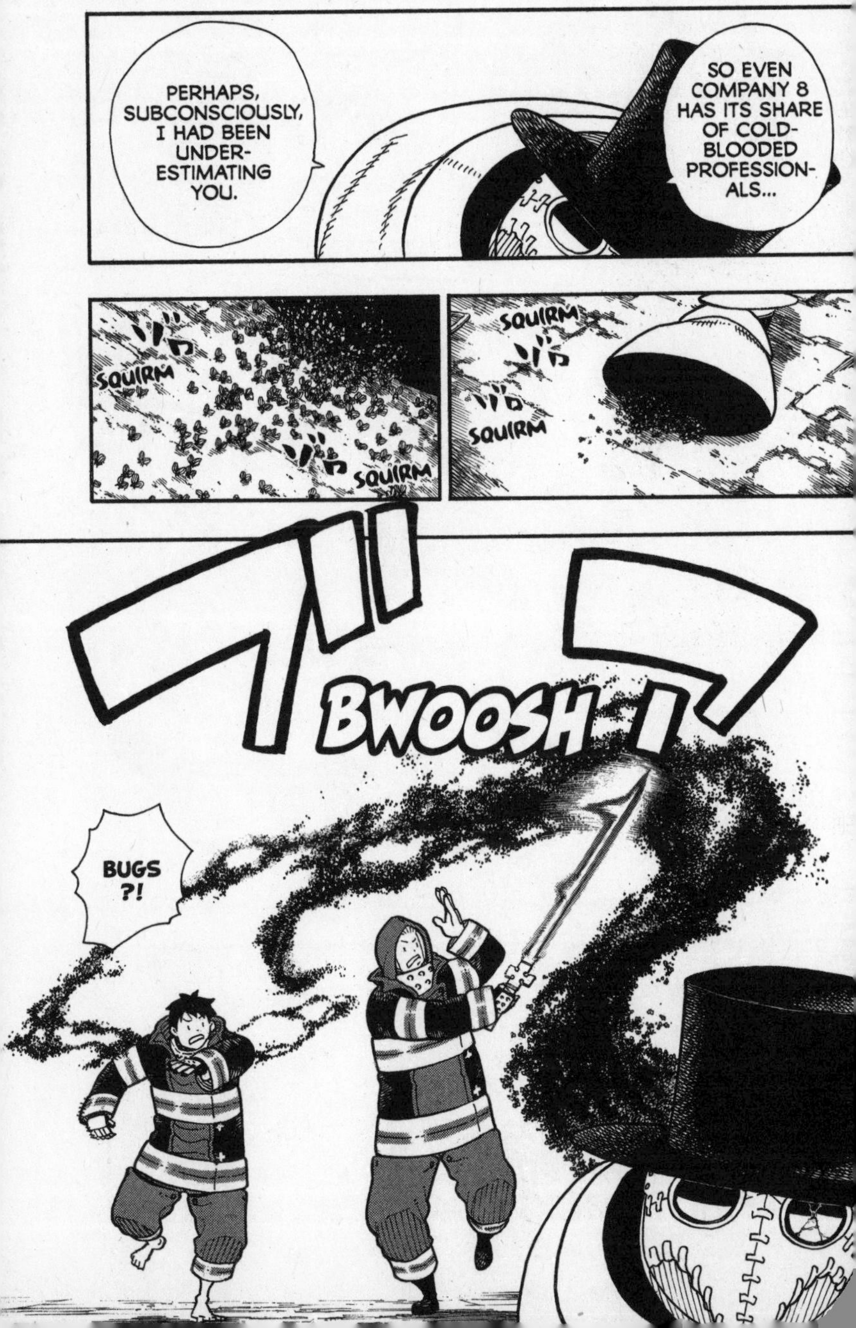
SO EVEN COMPANY 8 HAS ITS SHARE OF COLD-BLOODED PROFESSION-ALS...
PERHAPS, SUBCONSCIOUSLY, I HAD BEEN UNDER-ESTIMATING YOU.
SQUIRM
SQUIRM
SQUIRM
SQUIRM
BWOOSH
BUGS ?!

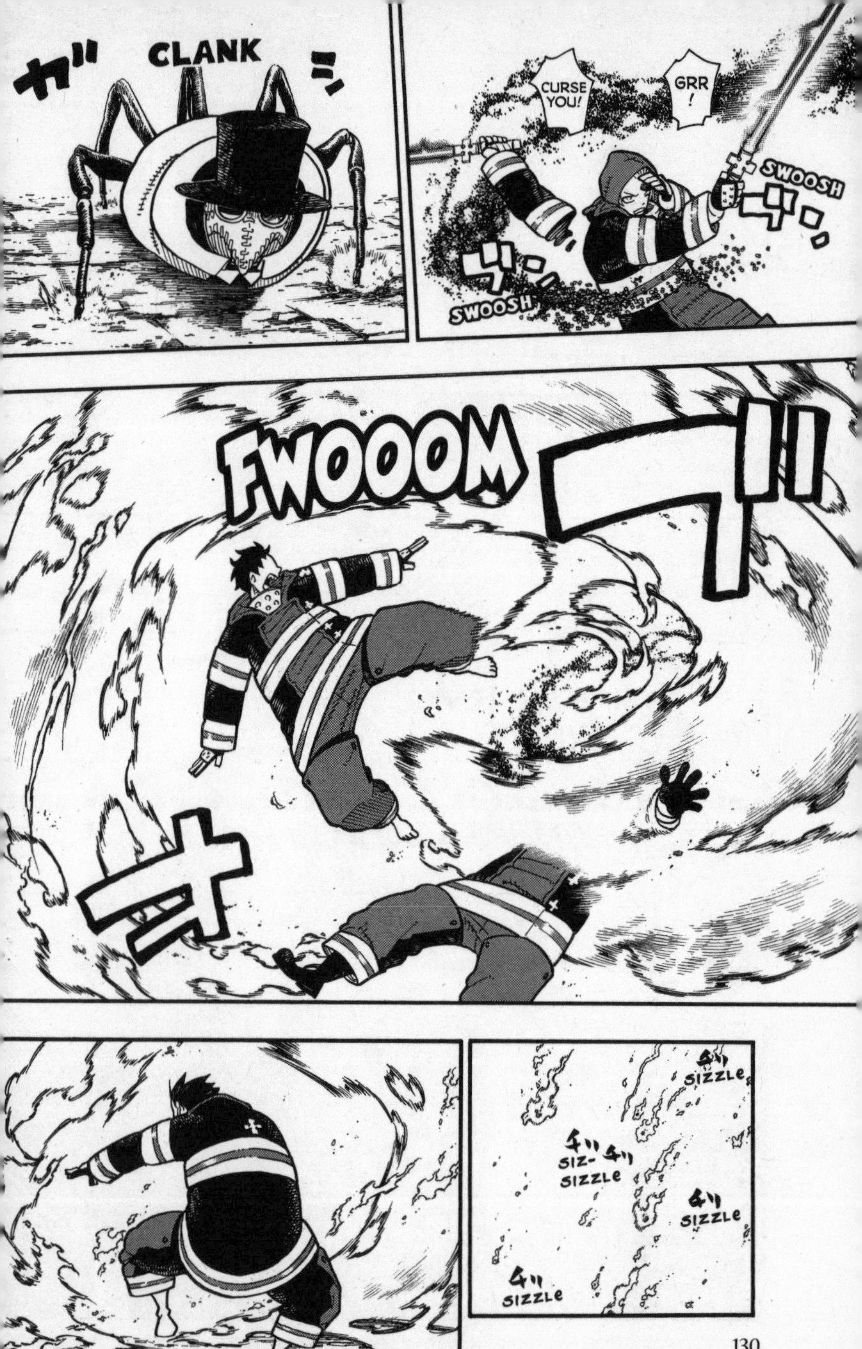
GRR!
CURSE YOU!
SWOOSH
SWOOSH
CLANK
FWOOOM
SIZZLE
SIZ- SIZZLE
SIZZLE
SIZZLE

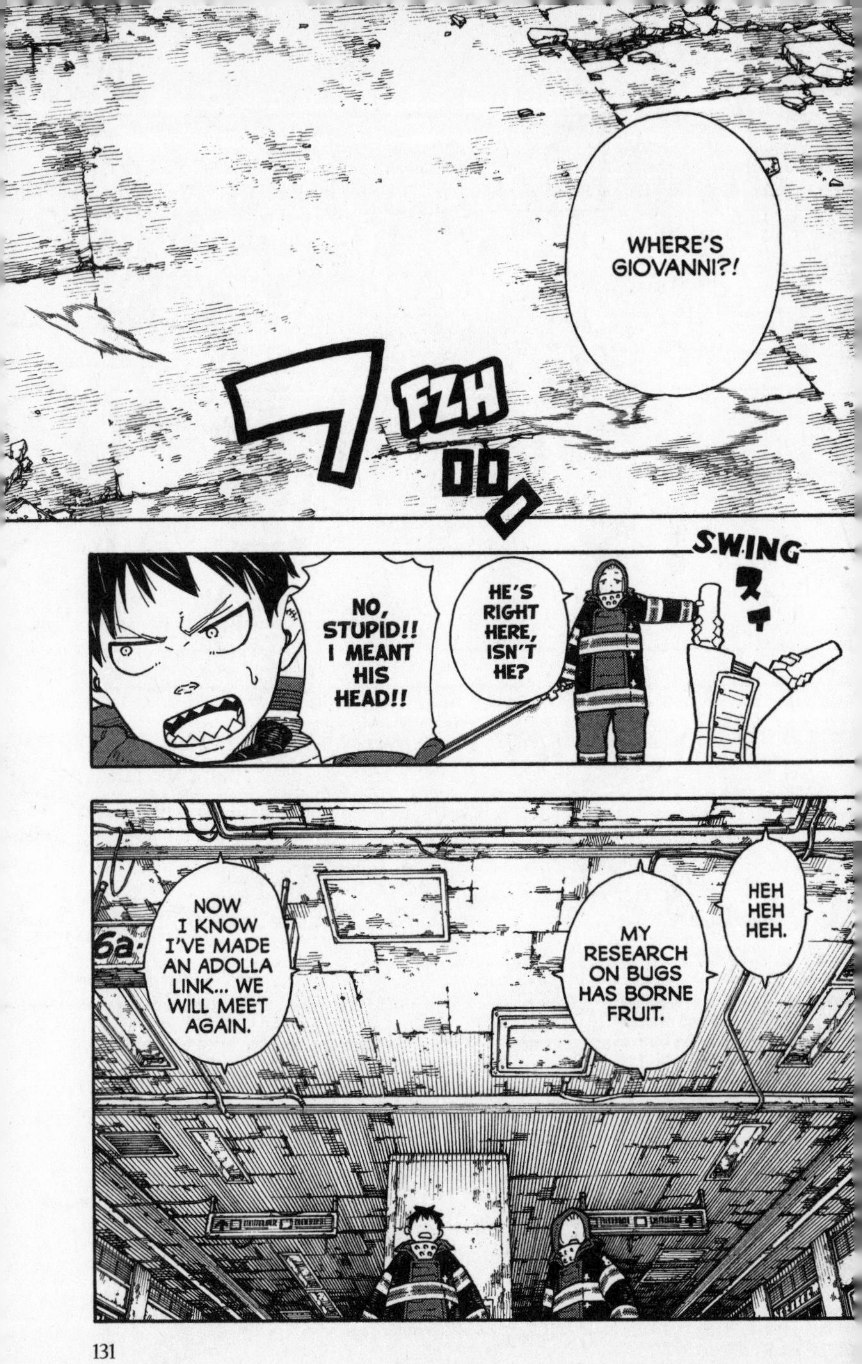
WHERE'S GIOVANNI?!
FZH
S.W.ING
HE'S RIGHT HERE, ISN'T HE?
NO, STUPID!! I MEANT HIS HEAD!!
HEH HEH HEH.
MY RESEARCH ON BUGS HAS BORNE FRUIT.
NOW I KNOW I'VE MADE AN ADOLLA LINK... WE WILL MEET AGAIN.

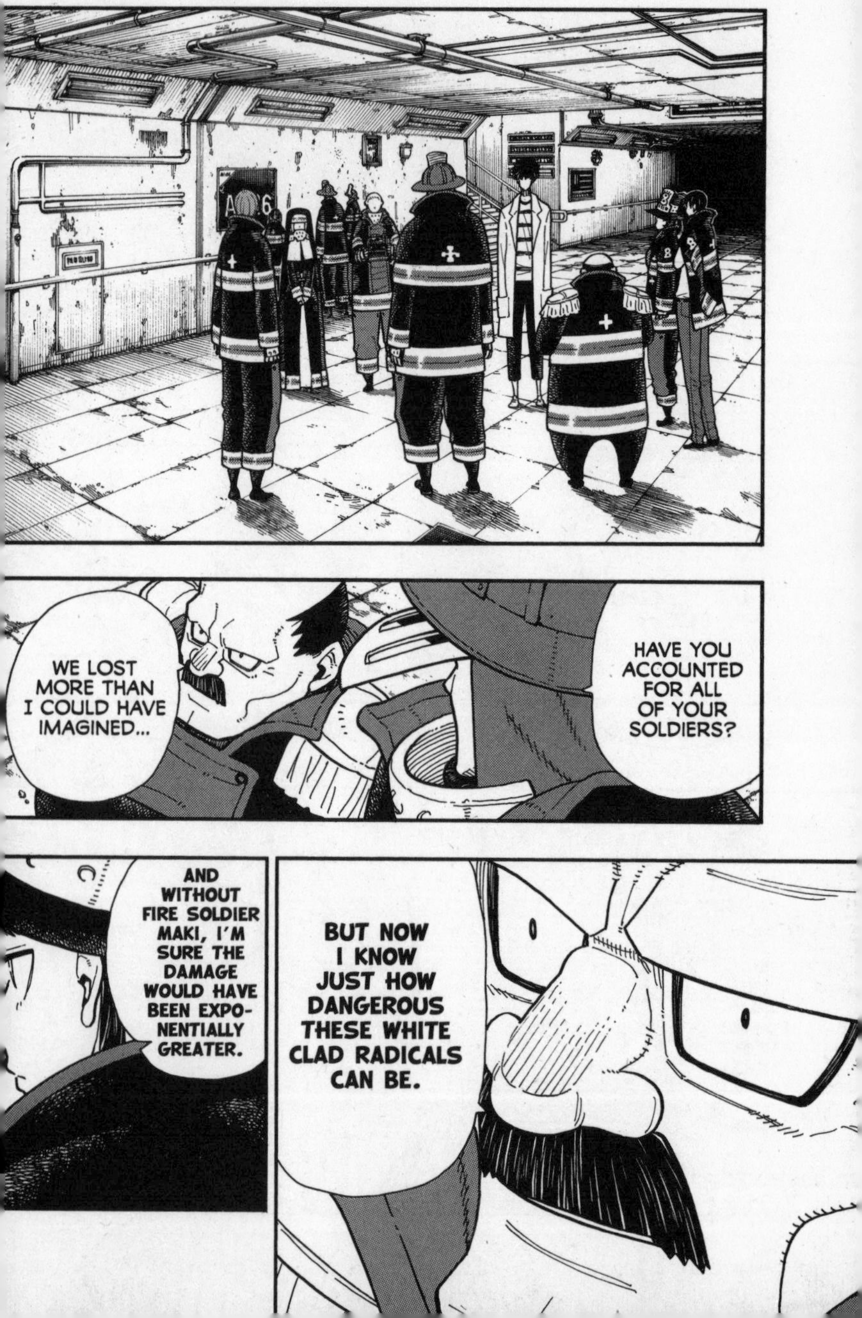
HAVE YOU ACCOUNTED FOR ALL OF YOUR SOLDIERS?
WE LOST MORE THAN I COULD HAVE IMAGINED...
BUT NOW I KNOW JUST HOW DANGEROUS THESE WHITE CLAD RADICALS CAN BE.
AND WITHOUT FIRE SOLDIER MAKI, I'M SURE THE DAMAGE WOULD HAVE BEEN EXPONENTIALLY GREATER.

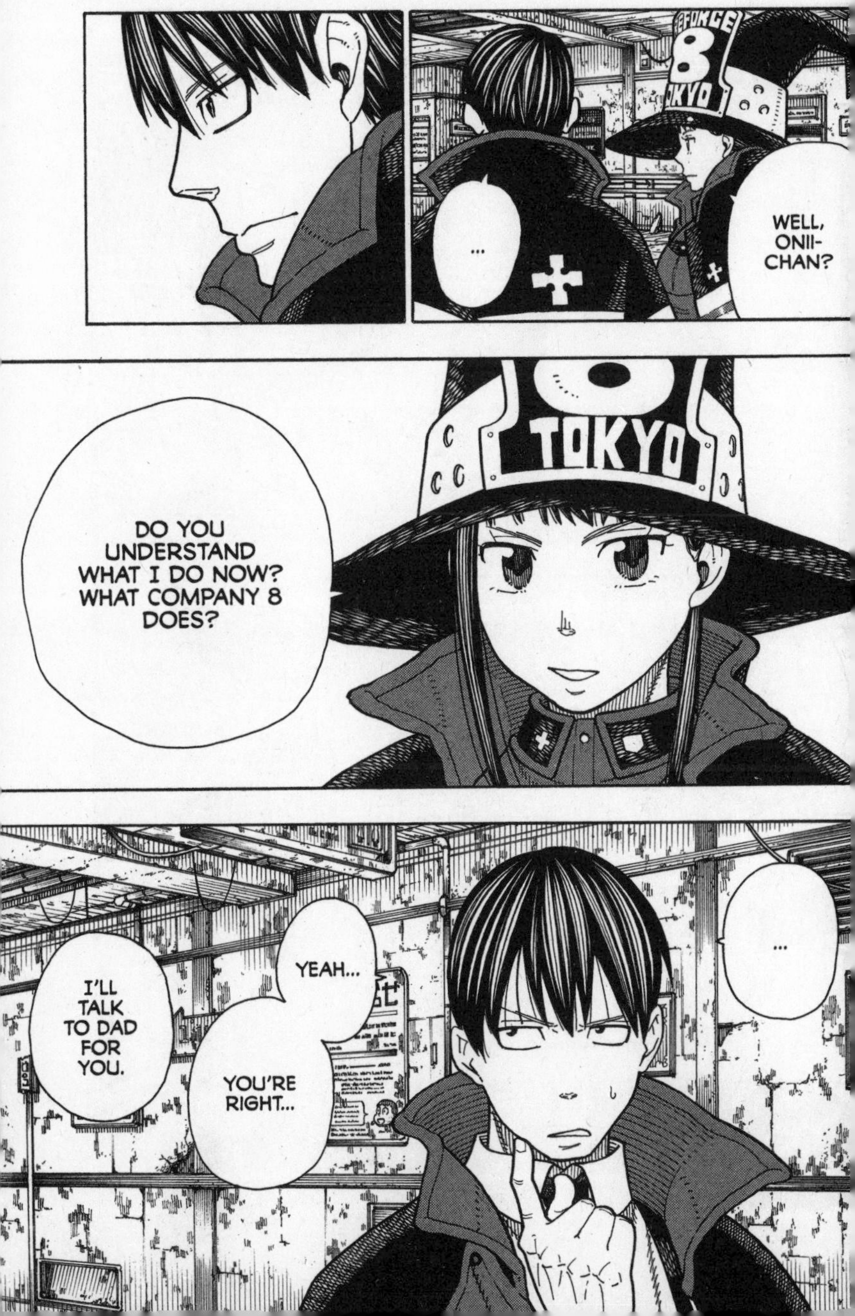
WELL, ONII-CHAN?
...
TOKYO
DO YOU UNDERSTAND WHAT I DO NOW? WHAT COMPANY 8 DOES?
...
YEAH...
YOU'RE RIGHT...
I'LL TALK TO DAD FOR YOU.

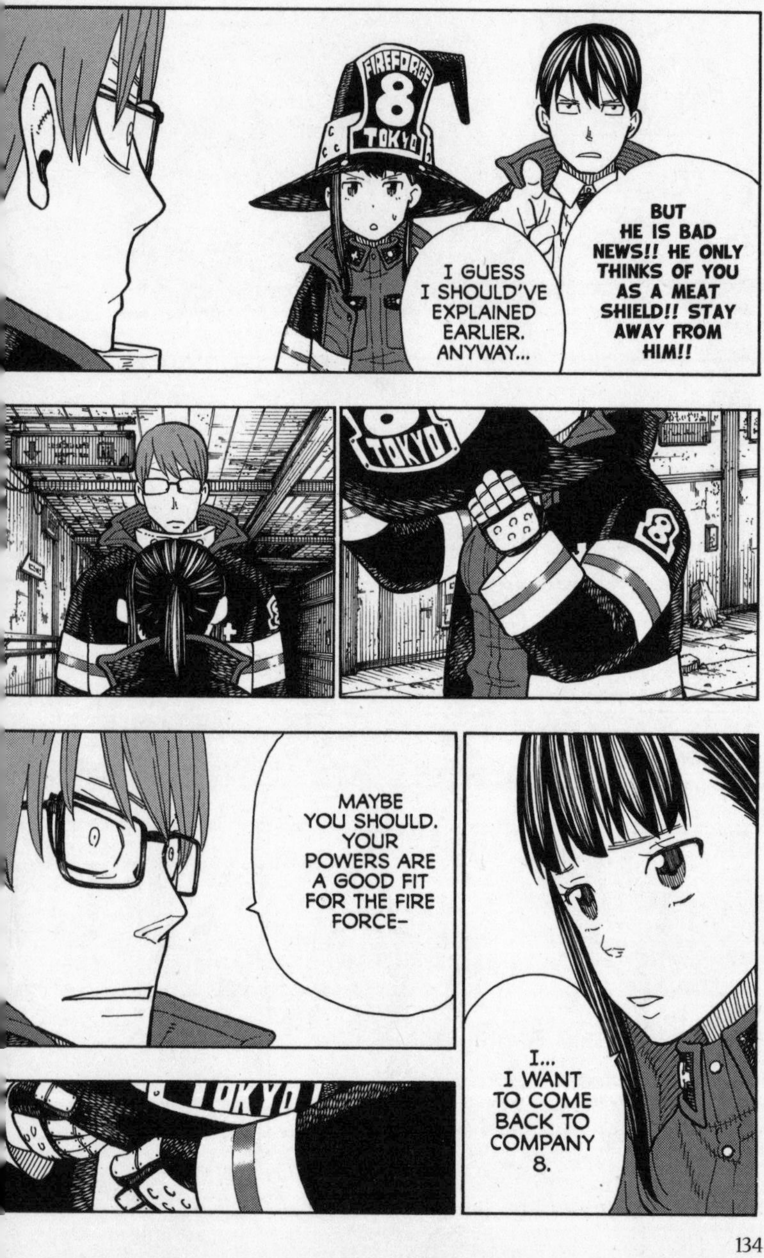
BUT HE IS BAD NEWS!! HE ONLY THINKS OF YOU AS A MEAT SHIELD!! STAY AWAY FROM HIM!!
I GUESS I SHOULD'VE EXPLAINED EARLIER. ANYWAY...
I... I WANT TO COME BACK TO COMPANY 8.
MAYBE YOU SHOULD. YOUR POWERS ARE A GOOD FIT FOR THE FIRE FORCE-

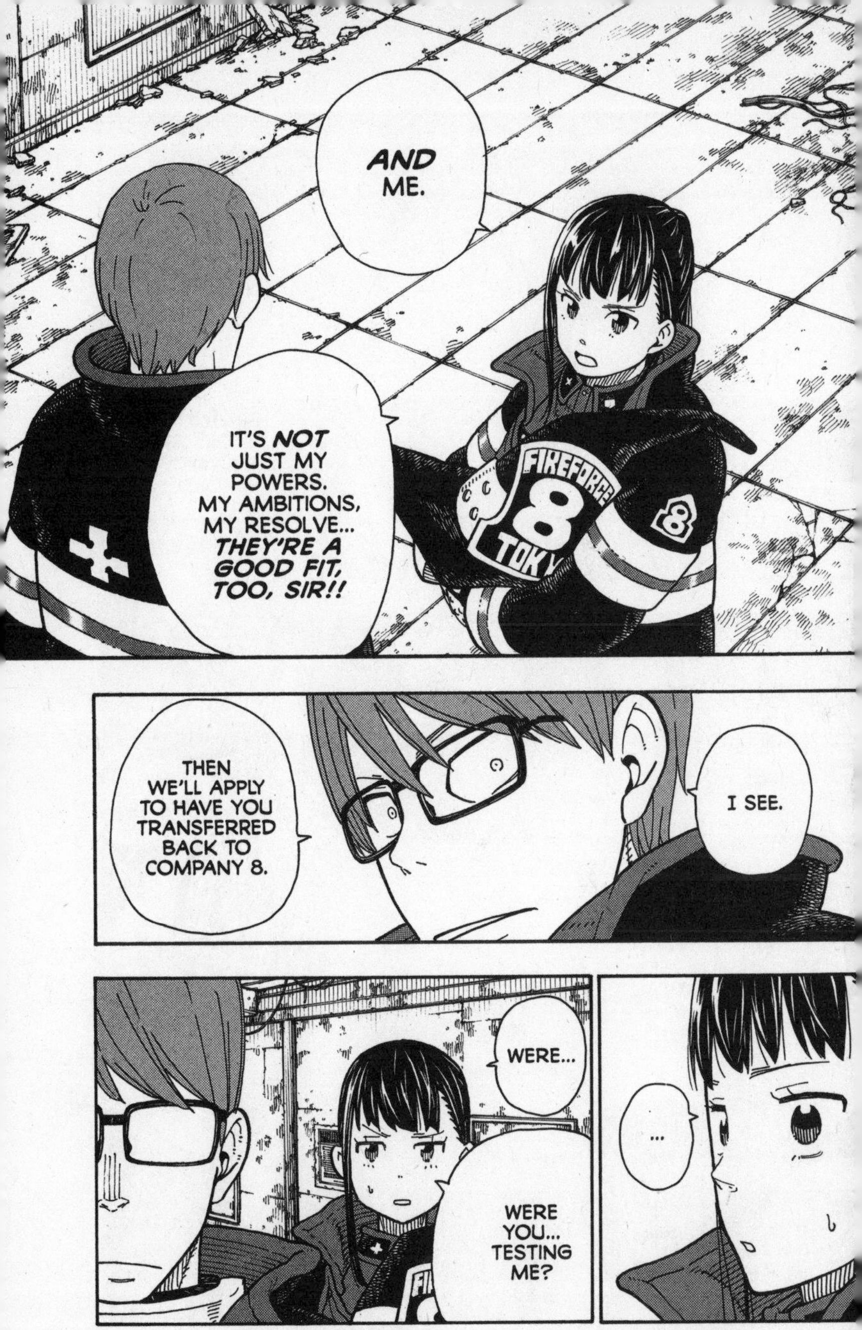
AND ME.
IT'S NOT JUST MY POWERS. MY AMBITIONS, MY RESOLVE... THEY'RE A GOOD FIT, TOO, SIR!!
FIREFORCE 8 TOKY
I SEE.
THEN WE'LL APPLY TO HAVE YOU TRANSFERRED BACK TO COMPANY 8.
...
WERE...
WERE YOU... TESTING ME?

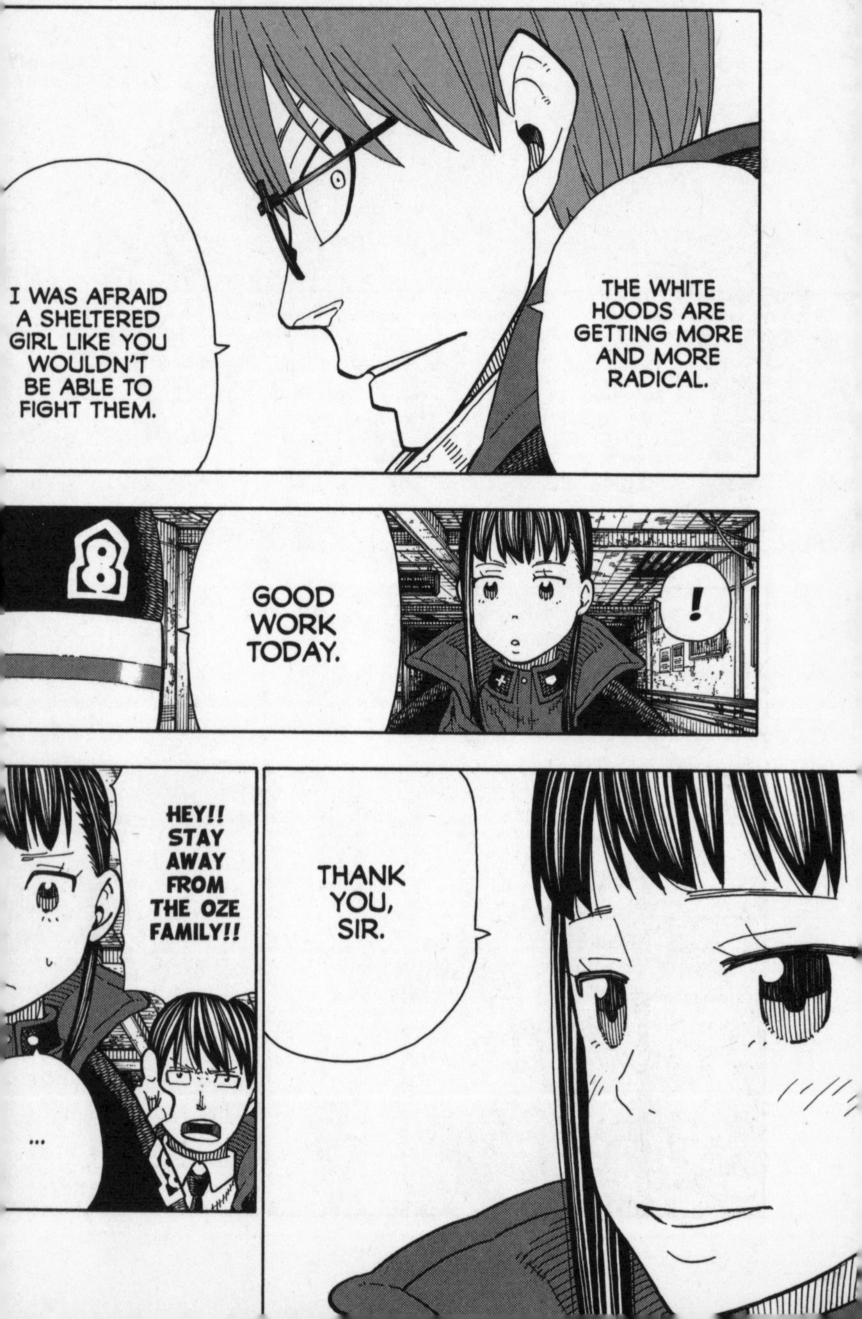
THE WHITE HOODS ARE GETTING MORE AND MORE RADICAL.
I WAS AFRAID A SHELTERED GIRL LIKE YOU WOULDN'T BE ABLE TO FIGHT THEM.
!
GOOD WORK TODAY.
THANK YOU, SIR.
HEY!! STAY AWAY FROM THE OZE FAMILY!!
...

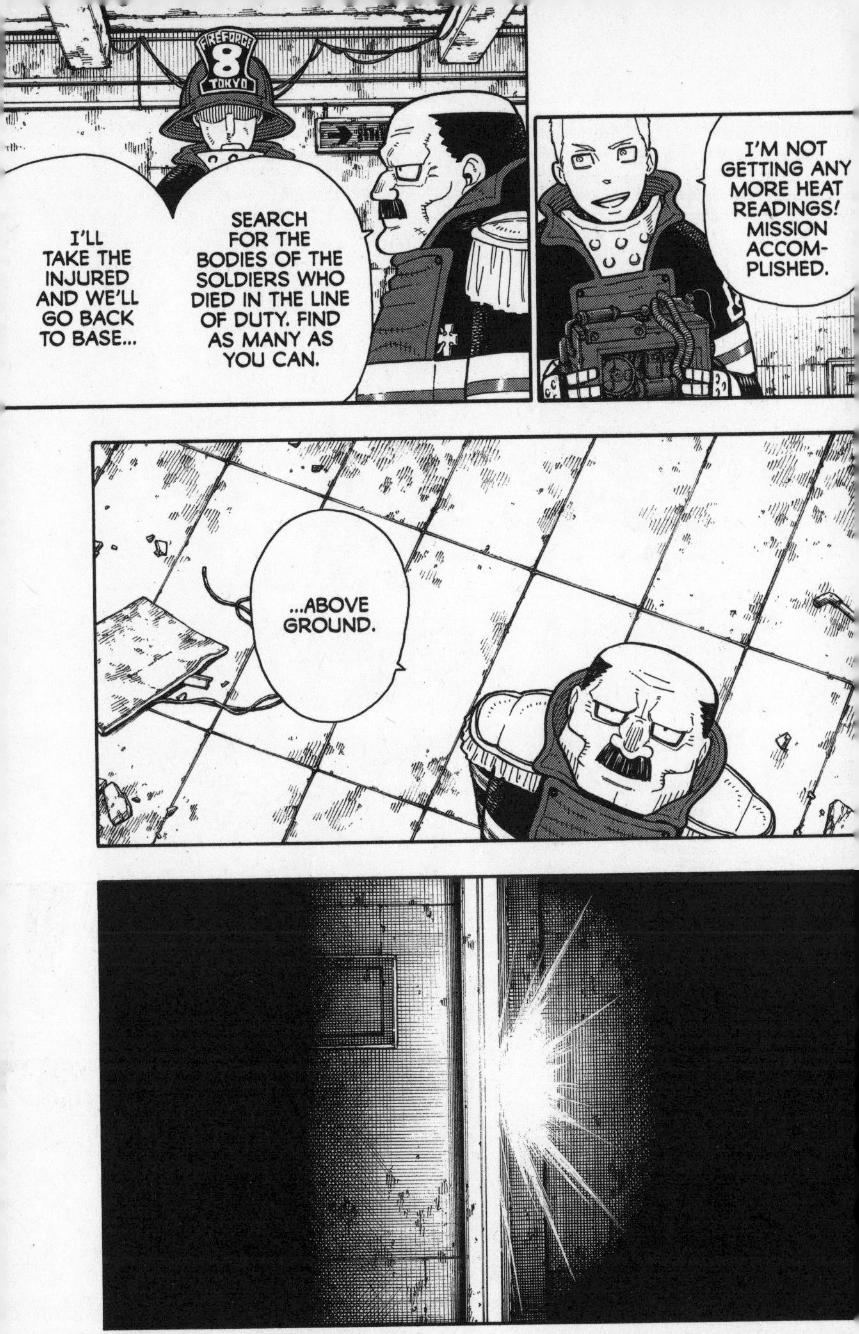

I'M NOT GETTING ANY MORE HEAT READINGS! MISSION ACCOM-PLISHED.
SEARCH FOR THE BODIES OF THE SOLDIERS WHO DIED IN THE LINE OF DUTY. FIND AS MANY AS YOU CAN.
I'LL TAKE THE INJURED AND WE'LL GO BACK TO BASE...
...ABOVE GROUND.

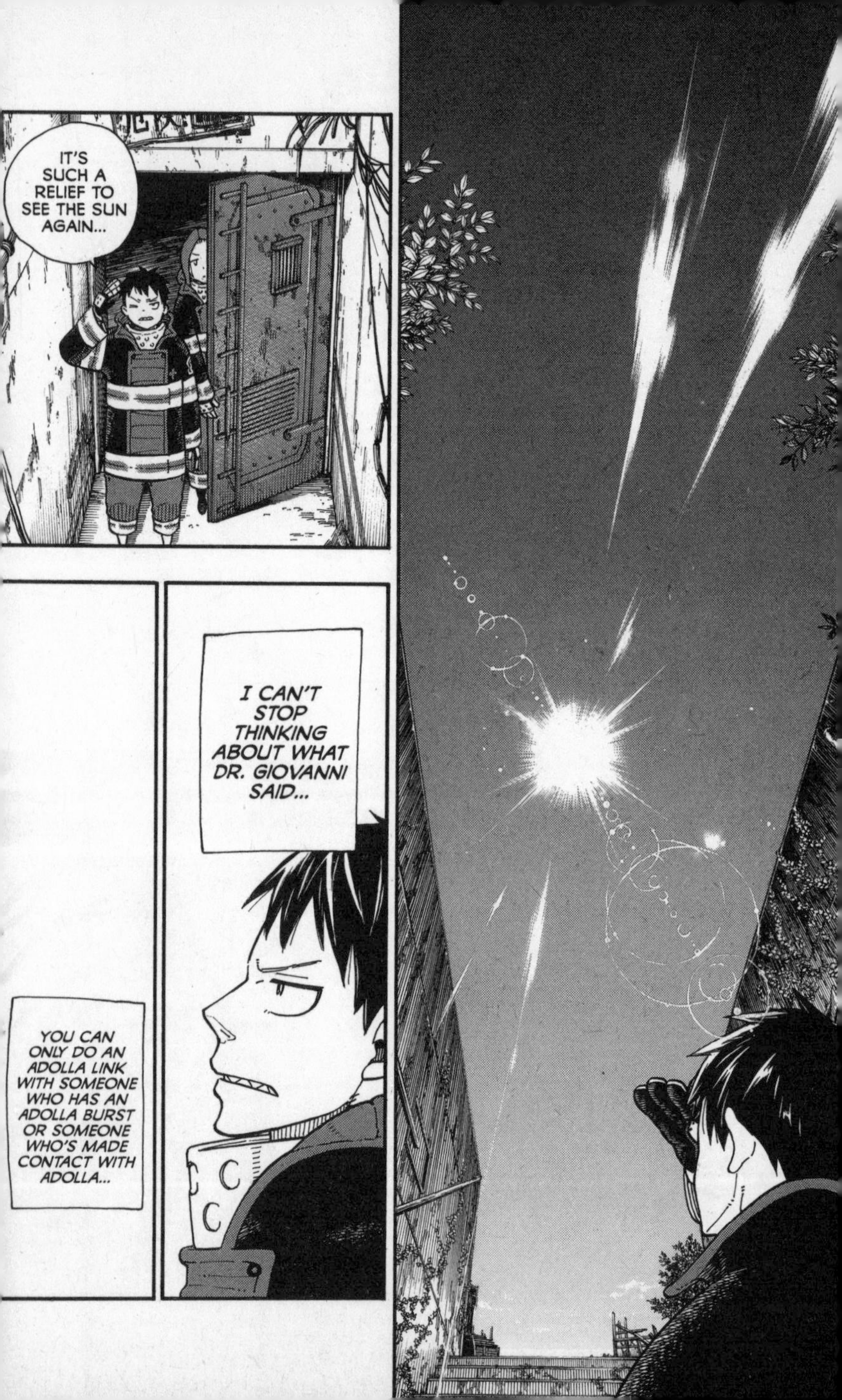
IT'S SUCH A RELIEF TO SEE THE SUN AGAIN...
I CAN'T STOP THINKING ABOUT WHAT DR. GIOVANNI SAID...
YOU CAN ONLY DO AN ADOLLA LINK WITH SOMEONE WHO HAS AN ADOLLA BURST OR SOMEONE WHO'S MADE CONTACT WITH ADOLLA...

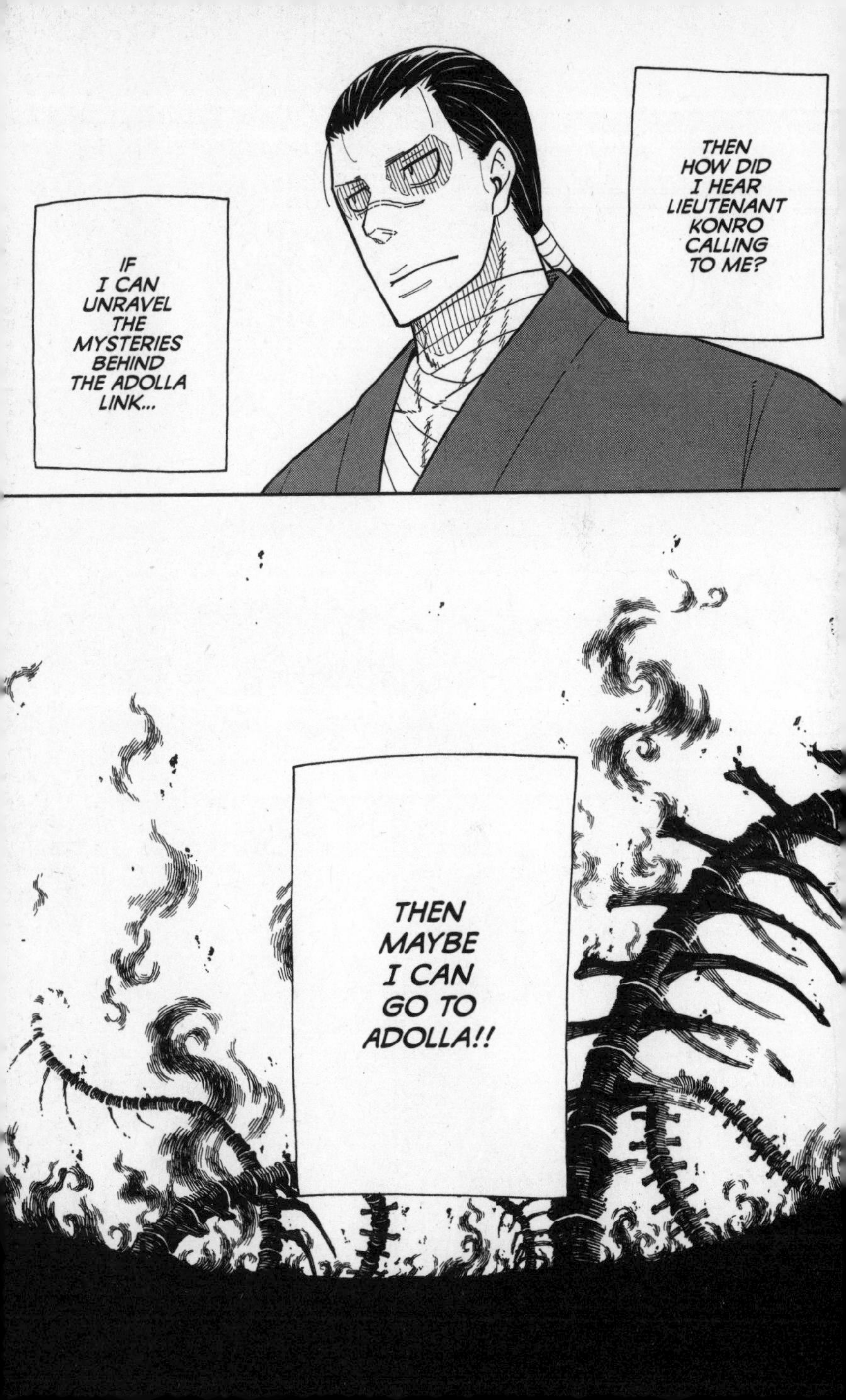
THEN HOW DID I HEAR LIEUTENANT KONRO CALLING TO ME?
IF I CAN UNRAVEL THE MYSTERIES BEHIND THE ADOLLA LINK...
THEN MAYBE I CAN GO TO ADOLLA!!

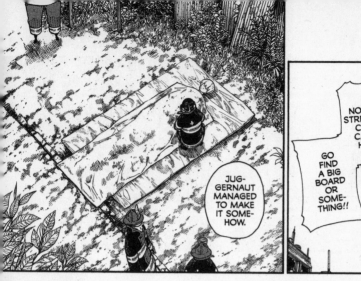

A NORMAL STRETCHER CAN'T CARRY HIM!!

GO FIND A BIG BOARD OR SOMETHING!!

JUGGERNAUT MANAGED TO MAKE IT SOMEHOW.

HE LOST HIS RIGHT HAND AND LEFT LEG, AND THERE ARE CUTS AND BURNS ALL OVER HIM... BUT HE'S STILL ALIVE. HE'S GOT THE VITALITY OF A POTATO.

JUGGERNAUT. YOU HUNG IN THERE UNTIL WE DUG YOU UP. GOOD JOB.

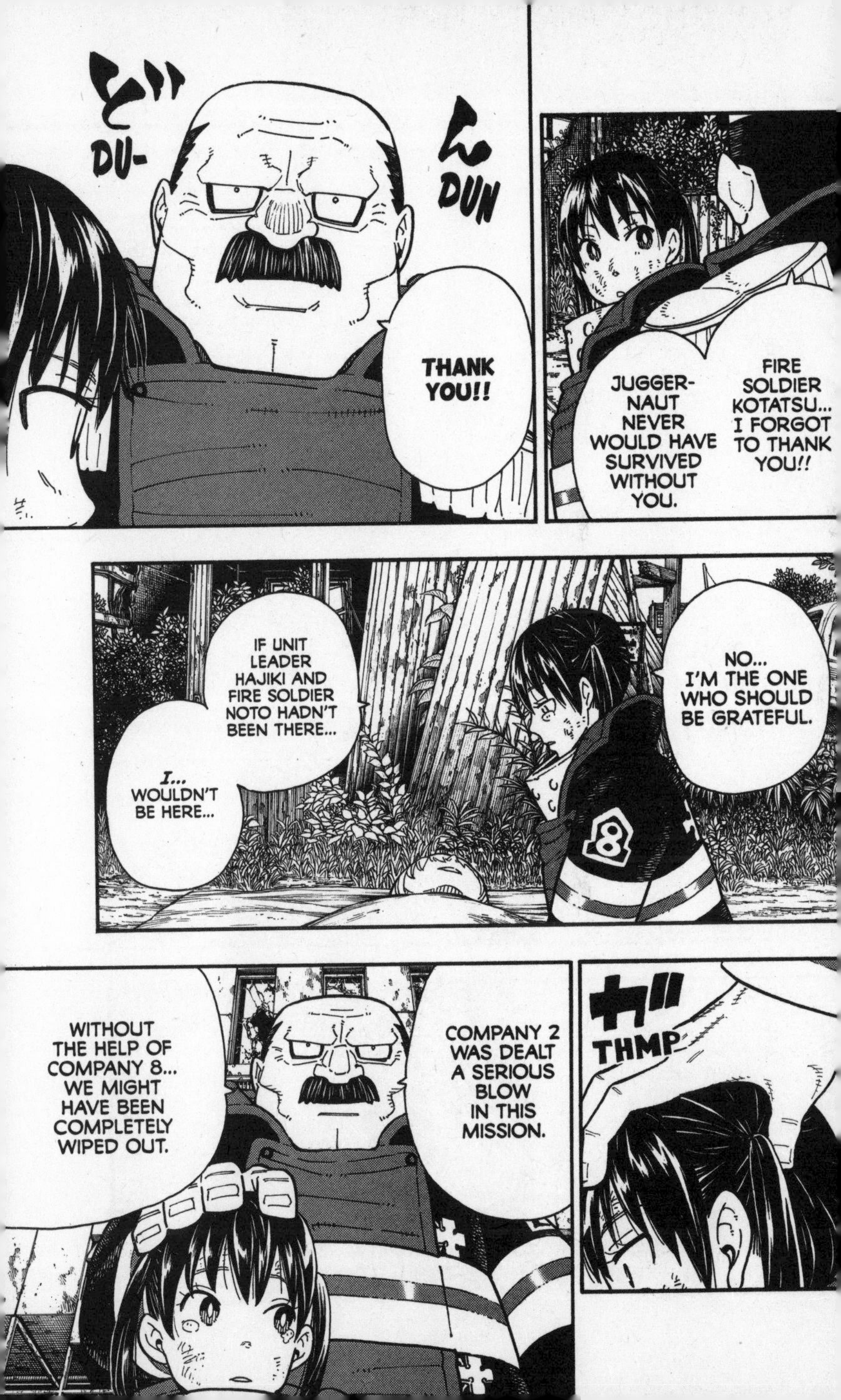
FIRE SOLDIER KOTATSU... I FORGOT TO THANK YOU!!
JUGGER-NAUT NEVER WOULD HAVE SURVIVED WITHOUT YOU.
ど
DU-
ん
DUN
THANK YOU!!
NO... I'M THE ONE WHO SHOULD BE GRATEFUL.
IF UNIT LEADER HAJIKI AND FIRE SOLDIER NOTO HADN'T BEEN THERE...
I... WOULDN'T BE HERE...
ガ
THMP
COMPANY 2 WAS DEALT A SERIOUS BLOW IN THIS MISSION.
WITHOUT THE HELP OF COMPANY 8... WE MIGHT HAVE BEEN COMPLETELY WIPED OUT.

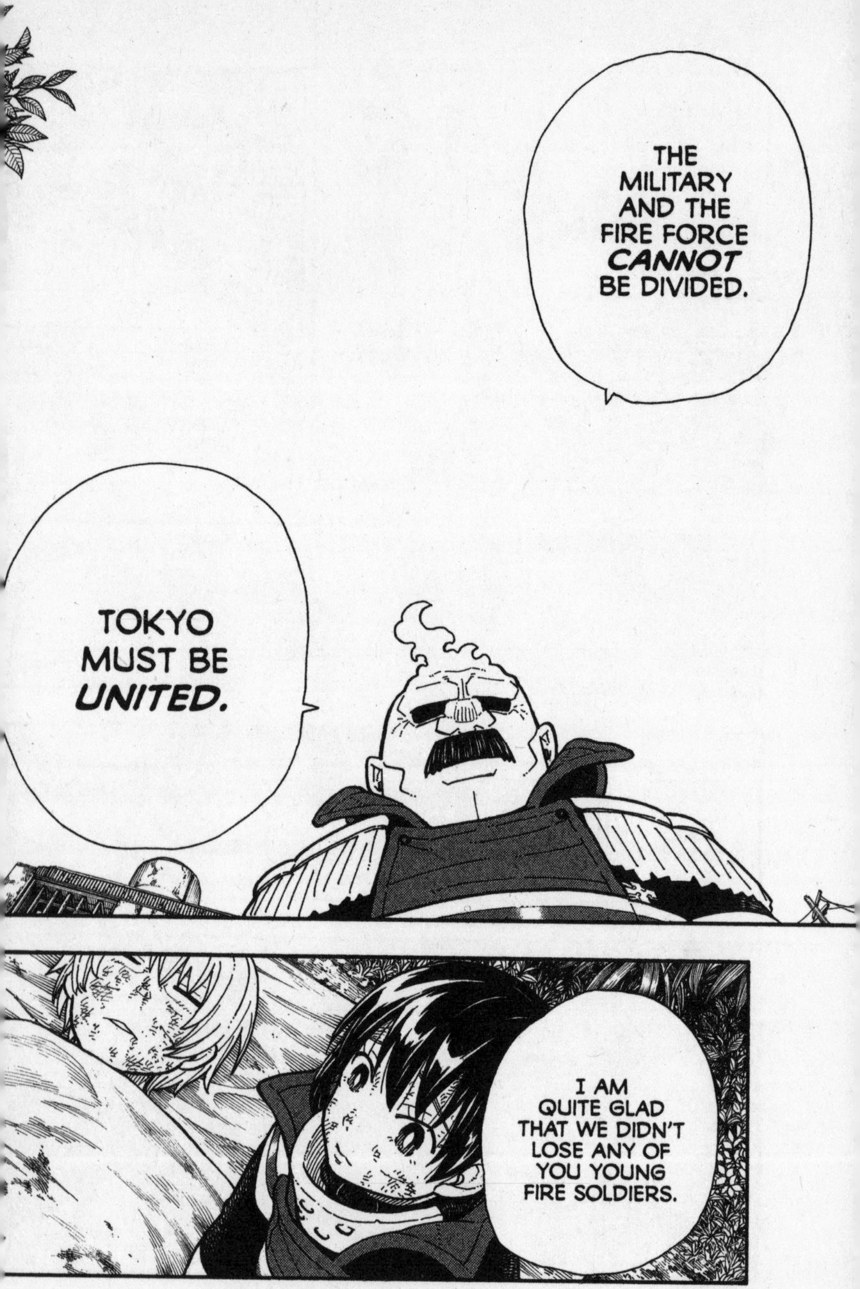
THE MILITARY AND THE FIRE FORCE *CANNOT* BE DIVIDED.
TOKYO MUST BE ***UNITED.***
I AM QUITE GLAD THAT WE DIDN'T LOSE ANY OF YOU YOUNG FIRE SOLDIERS.

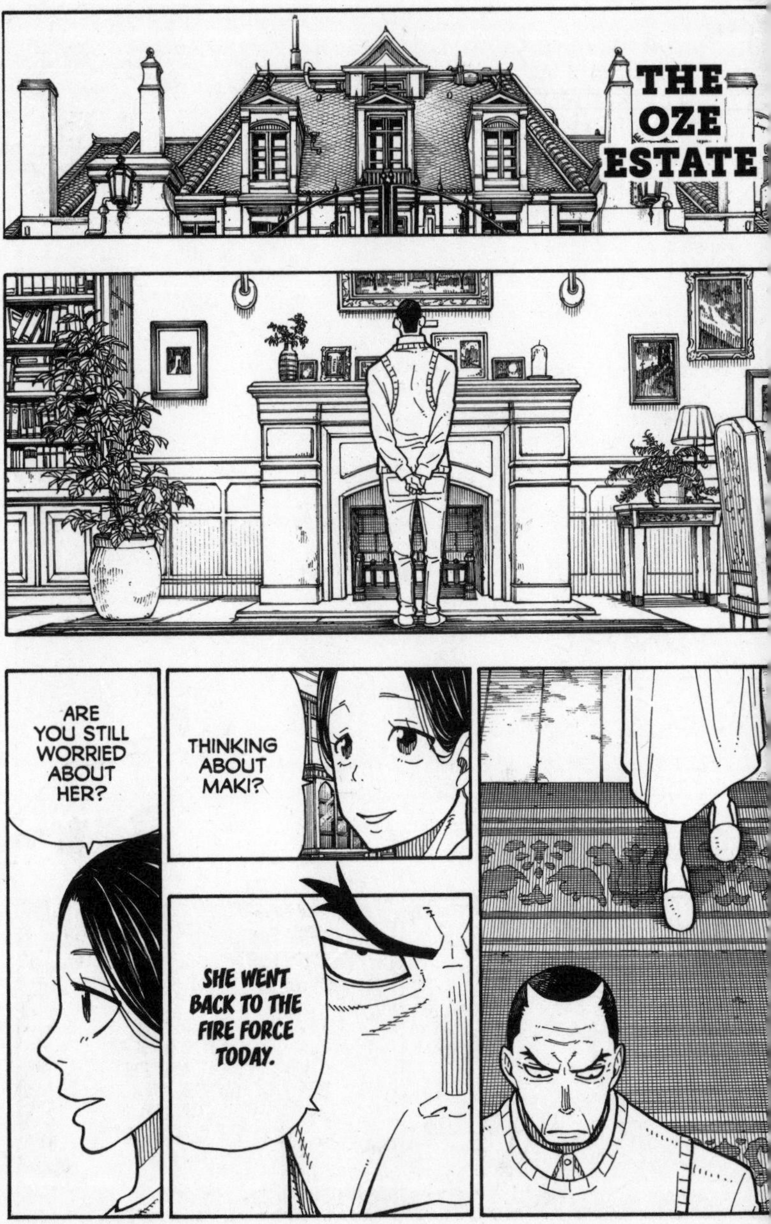
THE OZE ESTATE
THINKING ABOUT MAKI?
SHE WENT BACK TO THE FIRE FORCE TODAY.
ARE YOU STILL WORRIED ABOUT HER?

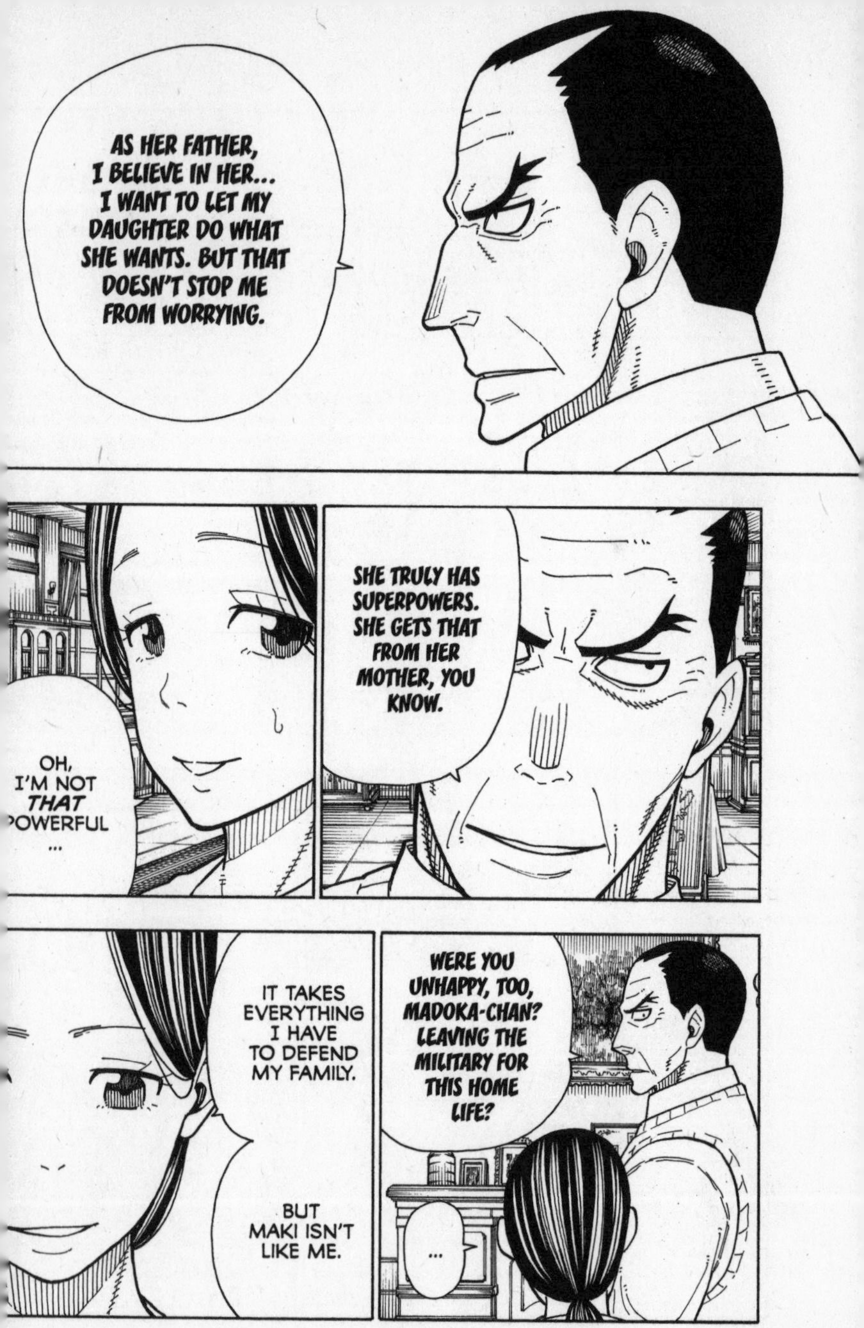
AS HER FATHER, I BELIEVE IN HER... I WANT TO LET MY DAUGHTER DO WHAT SHE WANTS. BUT THAT DOESN'T STOP ME FROM WORRYING.
SHE TRULY HAS SUPERPOWERS. SHE GETS THAT FROM HER MOTHER, YOU KNOW.
OH, I'M NOT *THAT* POWERFUL ...
WERE YOU UNHAPPY, TOO, MADOKA-CHAN? LEAVING THE MILITARY FOR THIS HOME LIFE?
...
IT TAKES EVERYTHING I HAVE TO DEFEND MY FAMILY.
BUT MAKI ISN'T LIKE ME.

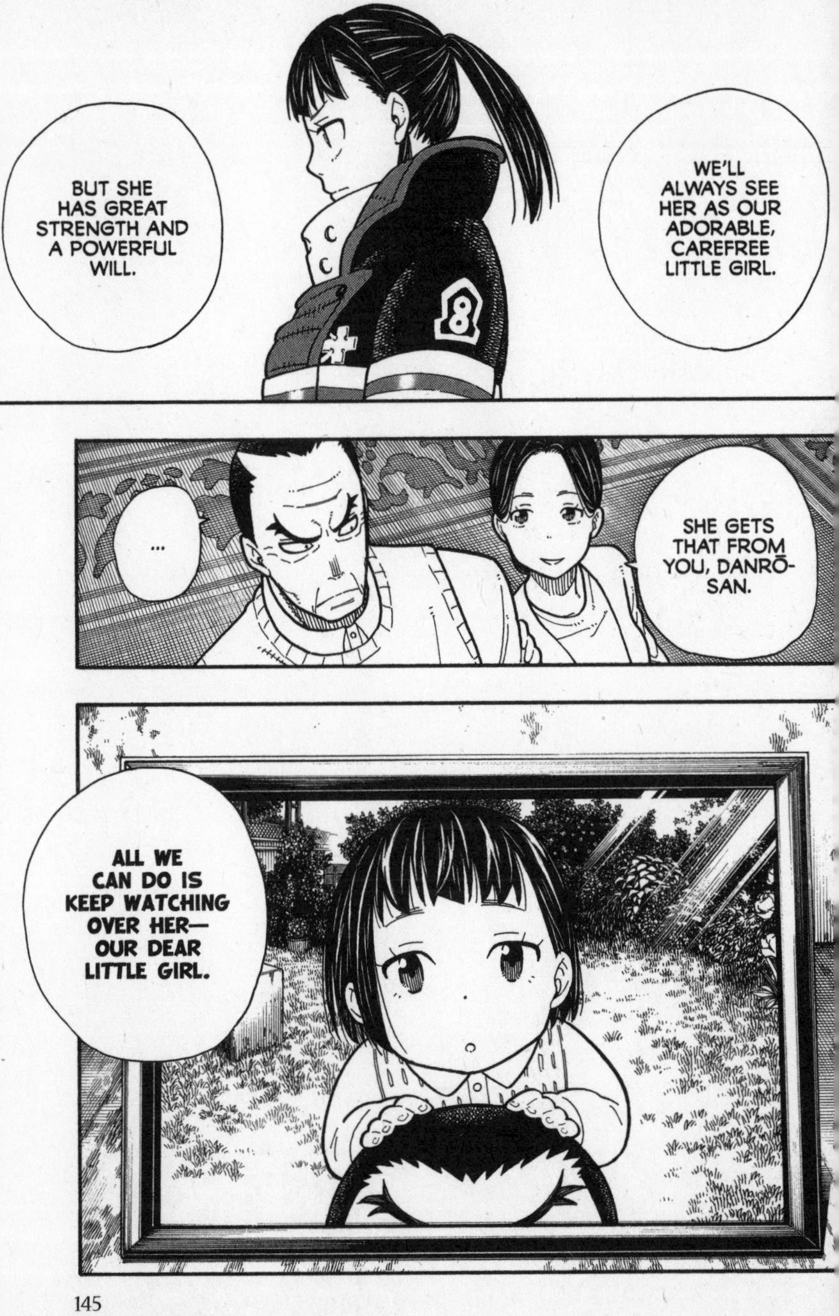
WE'LL ALWAYS SEE HER AS OUR ADORABLE, CAREFREE LITTLE GIRL.
BUT SHE HAS GREAT STRENGTH AND A POWERFUL WILL.
SHE GETS THAT FROM YOU, DANRŌ-SAN.
...
ALL WE CAN DO IS KEEP WATCHING OVER HER—OUR DEAR LITTLE GIRL.

FIRE FORCE

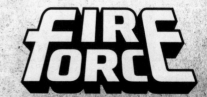

CHAPTER CLXVII: A MAN OF HONOR

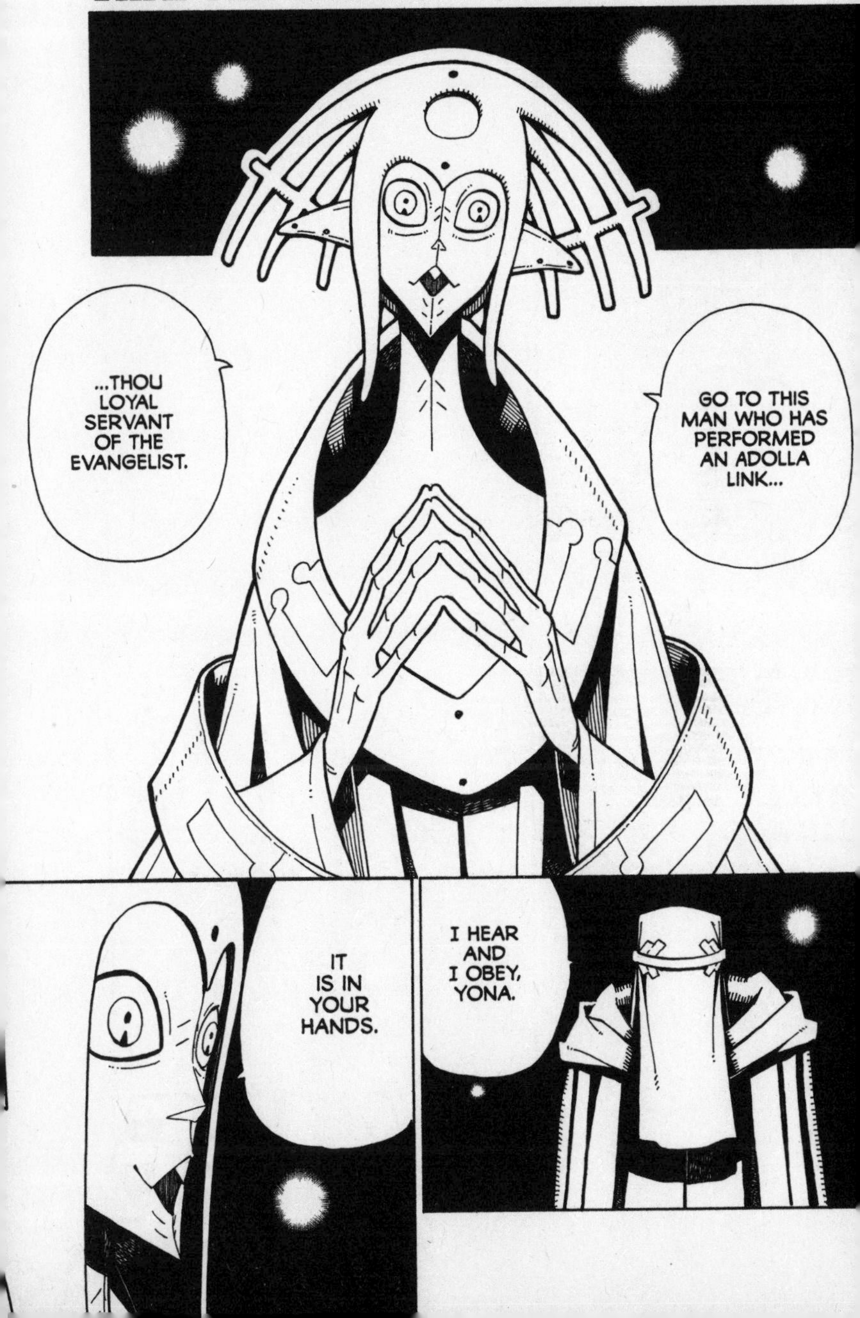
GO TO THIS MAN WHO HAS PERFORMED AN ADOLLA LINK...
...THOU LOYAL SERVANT OF THE EVANGELIST.
I HEAR AND I OBEY, YONA.
IT IS IN YOUR HANDS.

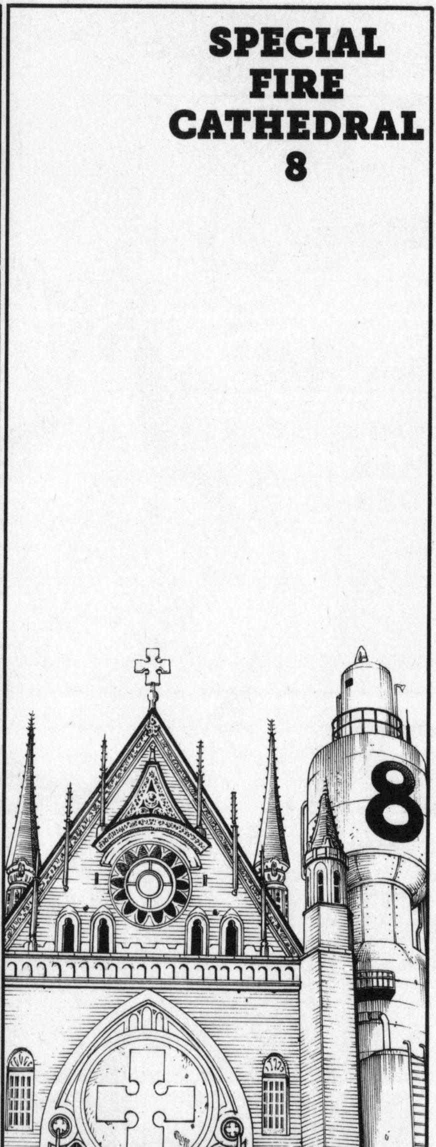
SPECIAL FIRE CATHEDRAL 8
8

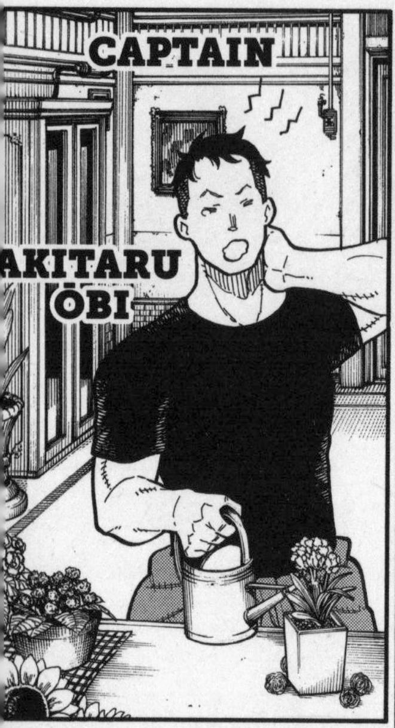
CAPTAIN
AKITARU ŌBI

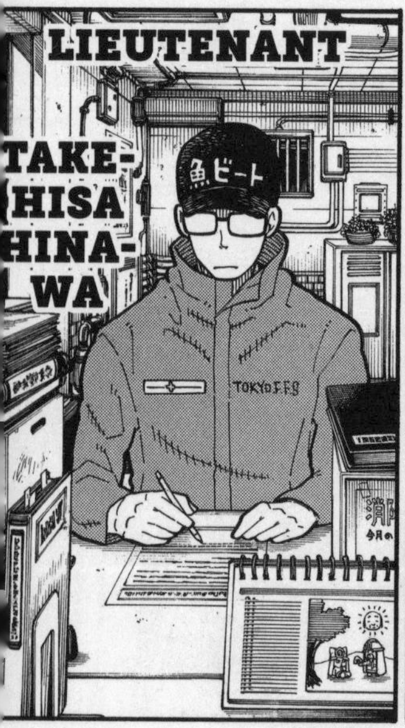
LIEUTENANT
TAKE-HISA HINA-WA
魚ビート
TOKYO F.F.S

Hat: Fish Beat

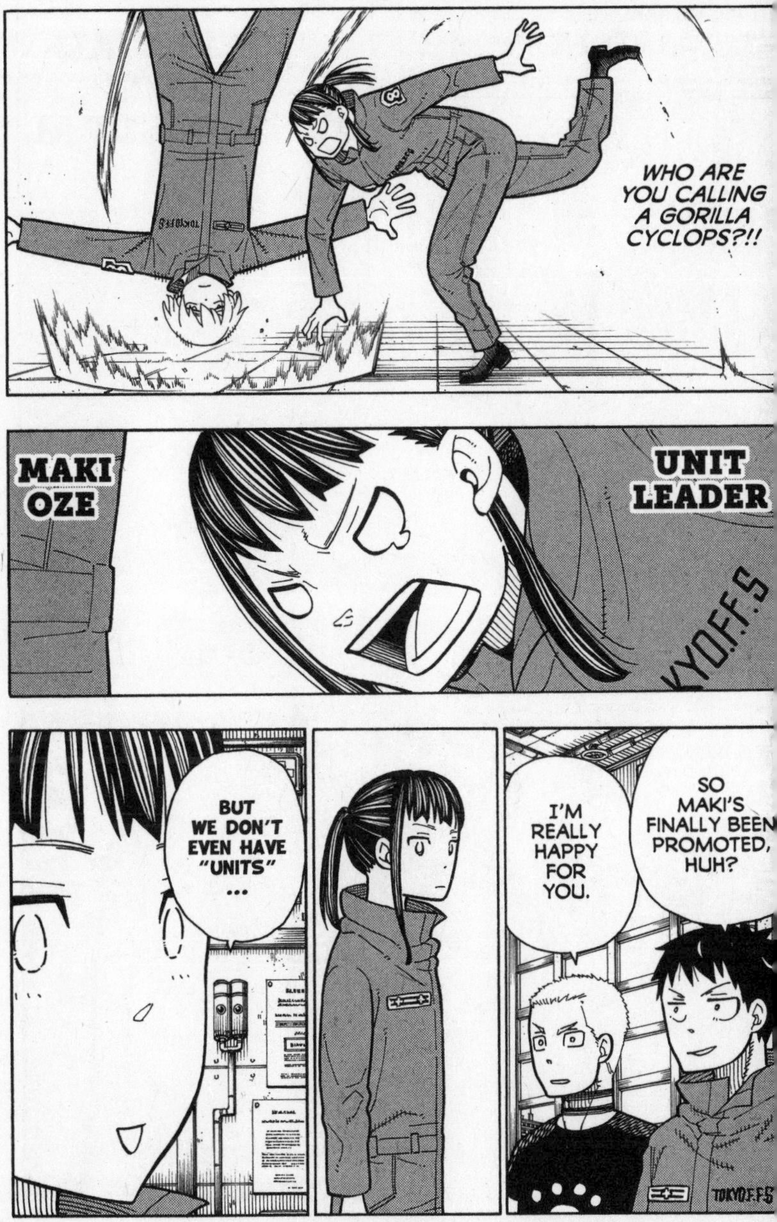
WHO ARE YOU CALLING A GORILLA CYCLOPS?!!
UNIT LEADER
MAKI OZE
SO MAKI'S FINALLY BEEN PROMOTED, HUH?
I'M REALLY HAPPY FOR YOU.
BUT WE DON'T EVEN HAVE "UNITS" ...

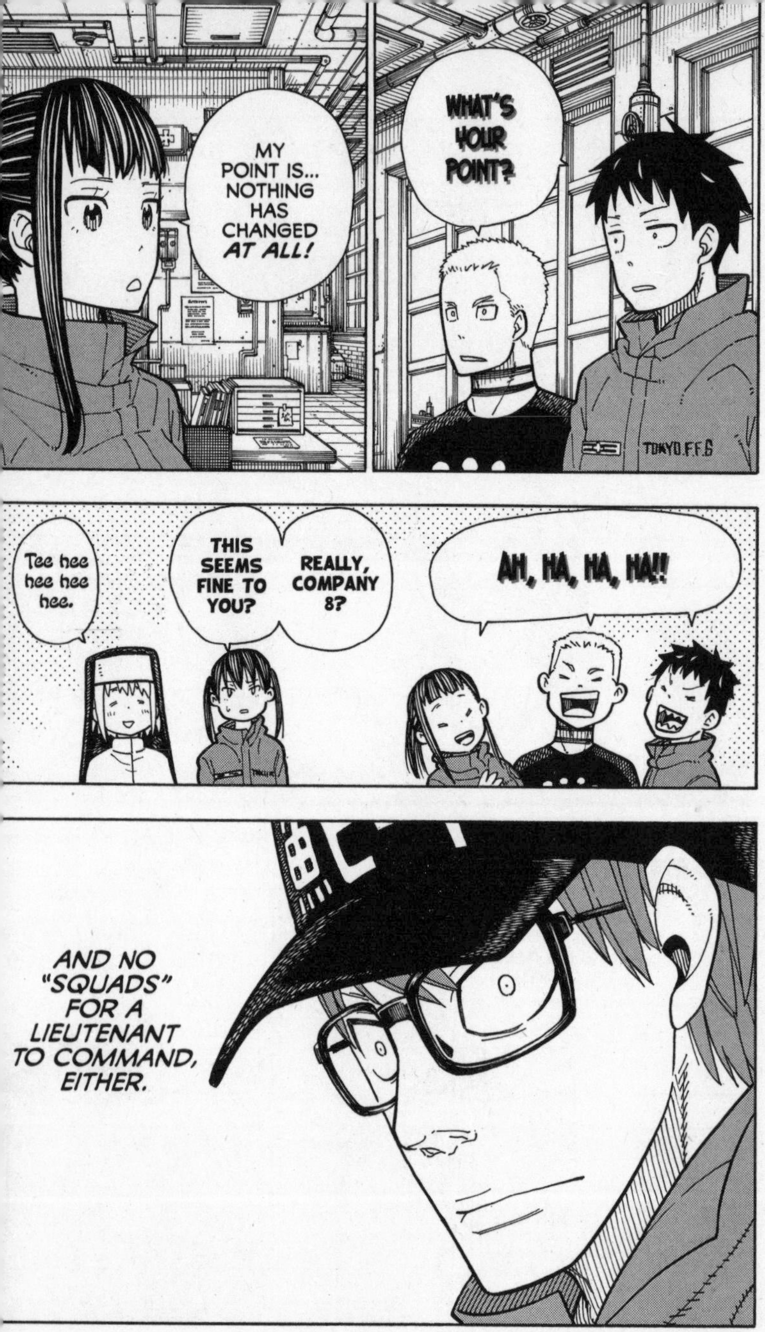
WHAT'S YOUR POINT?
TOKYO F.F.6
MY POINT IS... NOTHING HAS CHANGED *AT ALL!*
AH, HA, HA, HA!!
REALLY, COMPANY 8?
THIS SEEMS FINE TO YOU?
Tee hee hee hee hee.
AND NO "SQUADS" FOR A LIEUTENANT TO COMMAND, EITHER.

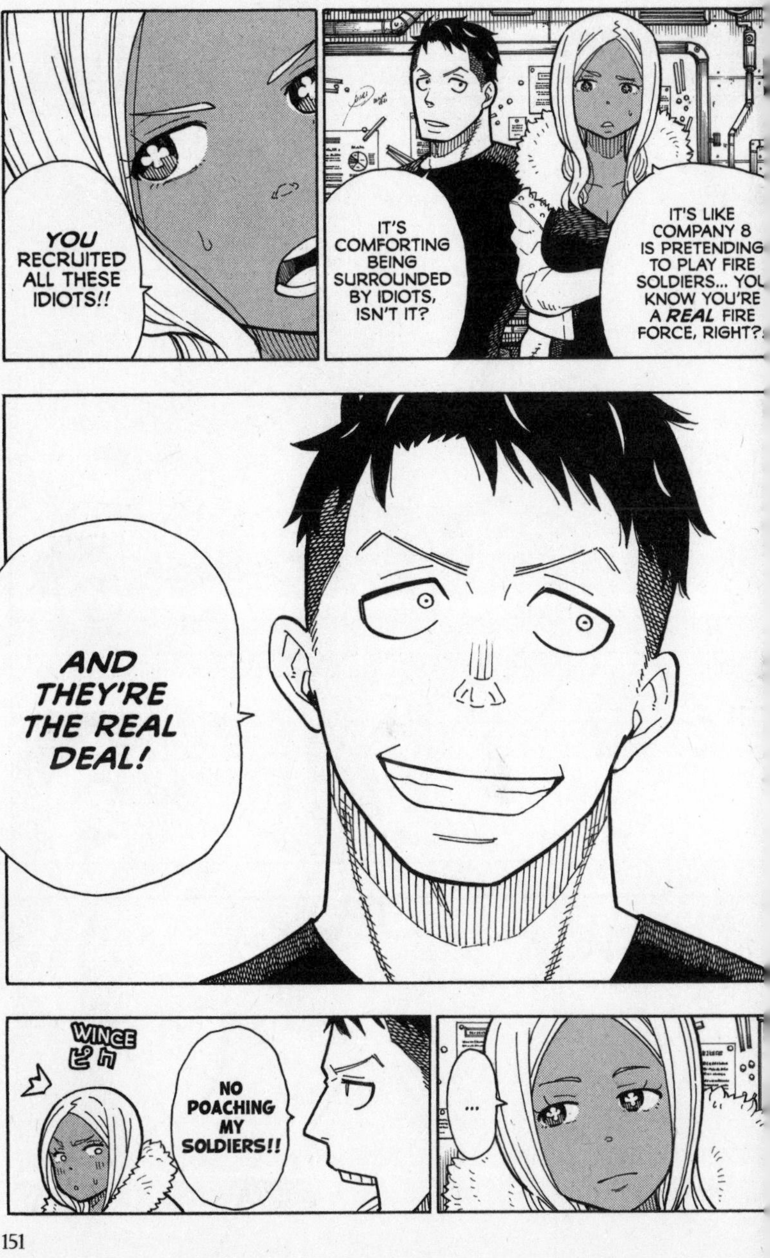
IT'S LIKE COMPANY 8 IS PRETENDING TO PLAY FIRE SOLDIERS... YOU KNOW YOU'RE A *REAL* FIRE FORCE, RIGHT?
IT'S COMFORTING BEING SURROUNDED BY IDIOTS, ISN'T IT?
YOU RECRUITED ALL THESE IDIOTS!!
AND THEY'RE THE REAL DEAL!
...
NO POACHING MY SOLDIERS!!
WINCE
ピク

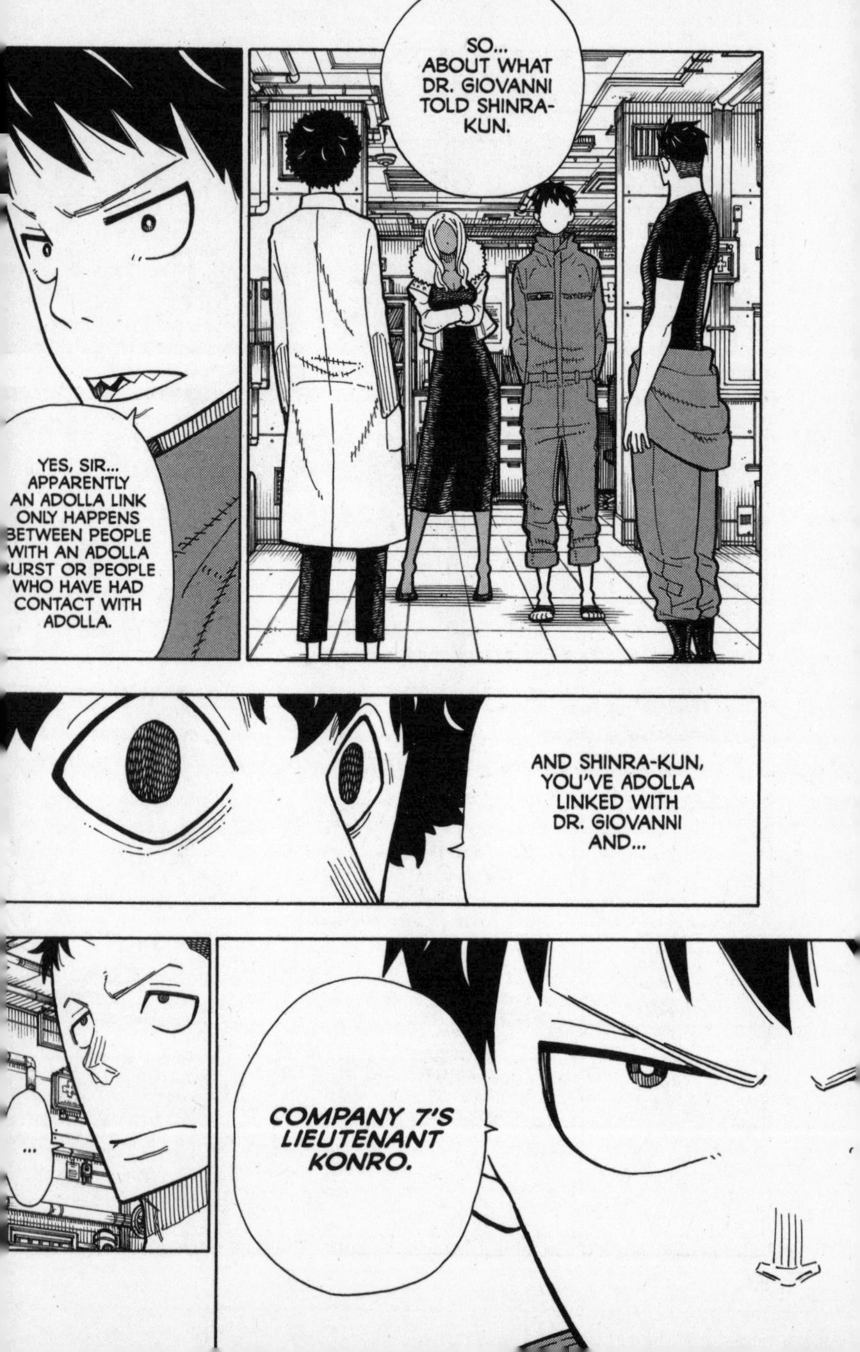
SO... ABOUT WHAT DR. GIOVANNI TOLD SHINRA-KUN.
YES, SIR... APPARENTLY AN ADOLLA LINK ONLY HAPPENS BETWEEN PEOPLE WITH AN ADOLLA URST OR PEOPLE WHO HAVE HAD CONTACT WITH ADOLLA.
AND SHINRA-KUN, YOU'VE ADOLLA LINKED WITH DR. GIOVANNI AND...
COMPANY 7'S LIEUTENANT KONRO.
...

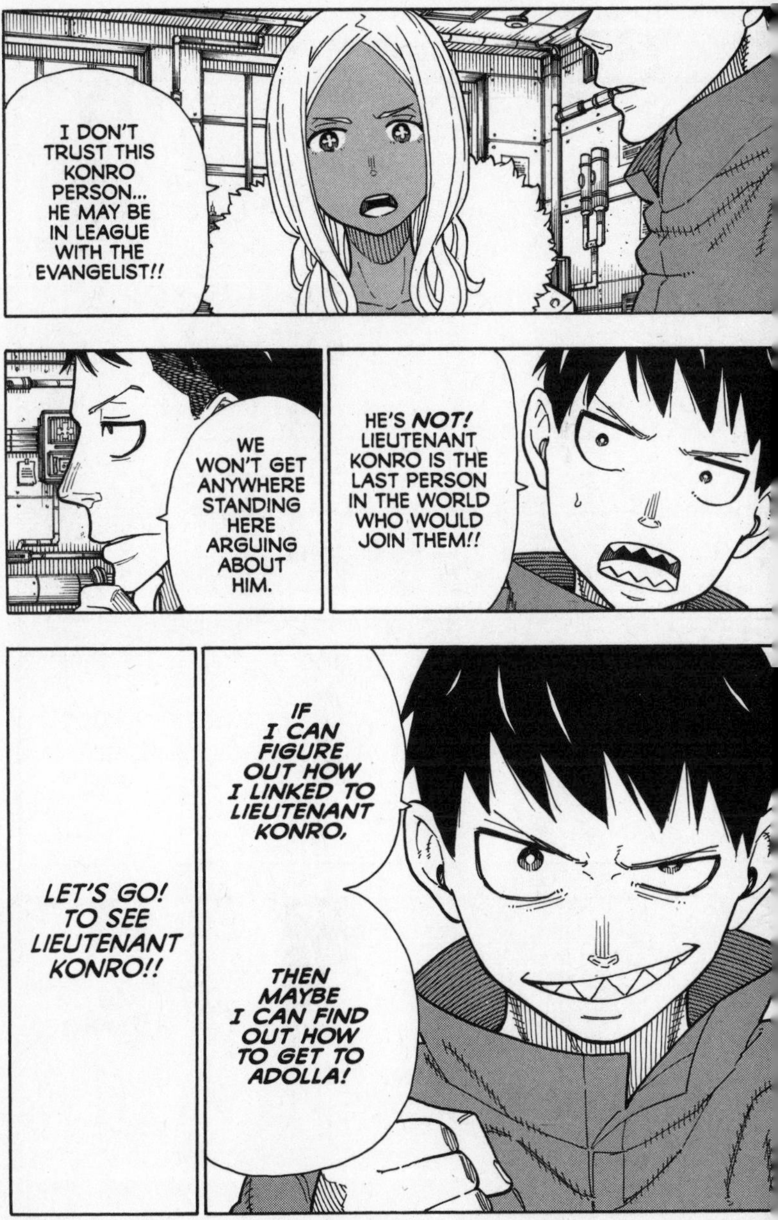
I DON'T TRUST THIS KONRO PERSON... HE MAY BE IN LEAGUE WITH THE EVANGELIST!!
HE'S **NOT!** LIEUTENANT KONRO IS THE LAST PERSON IN THE WORLD WHO WOULD JOIN THEM!!
WE WON'T GET ANYWHERE STANDING HERE ARGUING ABOUT HIM.
IF I CAN FIGURE OUT HOW I LINKED TO LIEUTENANT KONRO,
THEN MAYBE I CAN FIND OUT HOW TO GET TO ADOLLA!
LET'S GO! TO SEE LIEUTENANT KONRO!!

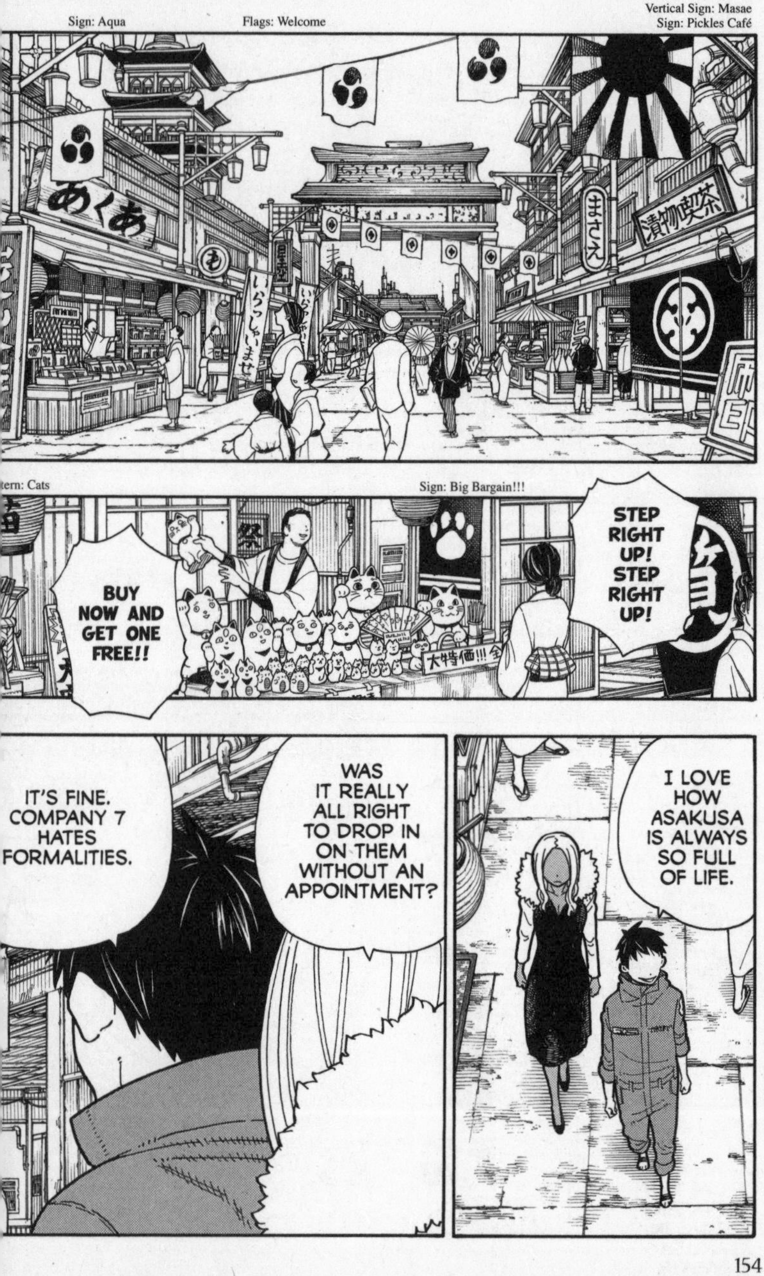
Vertical Sign: Masae
Sign: Pickles Café
Flags: Welcome
Sign: Aqua
STEP RIGHT UP! STEP RIGHT UP!
Sign: Big Bargain!!!
BUY NOW AND GET ONE FREE!!
tern: Cats
I LOVE HOW ASAKUSA IS ALWAYS SO FULL OF LIFE.
WAS IT REALLY ALL RIGHT TO DROP IN ON THEM WITHOUT AN APPOINTMENT?
IT'S FINE. COMPANY 7 HATES FORMALITIES.

Sign: Beware of Fires

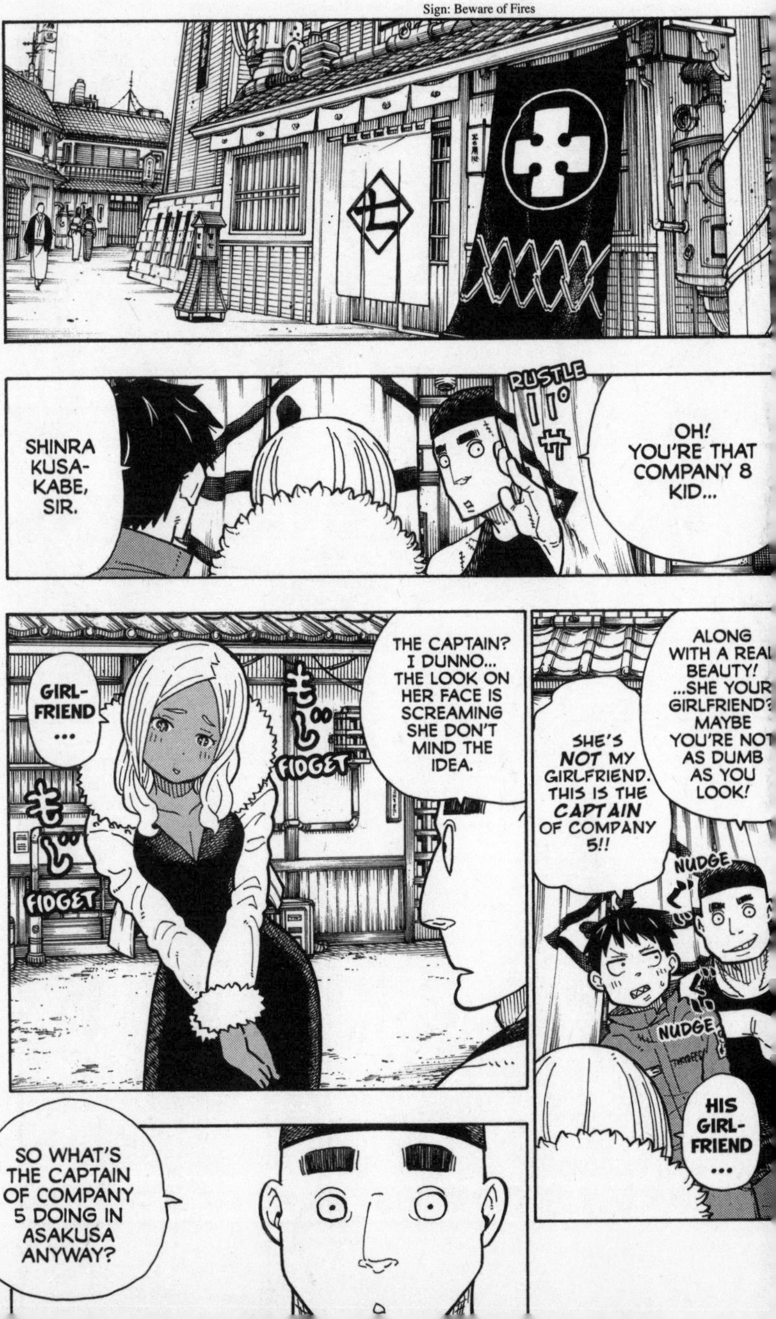
RUSTLE
OH! YOU'RE THAT COMPANY 8 KID...
SHINRA KUSA-KABE, SIR.
ALONG WITH A REAL BEAUTY! ...SHE YOUR GIRLFRIEND? MAYBE YOU'RE NOT AS DUMB AS YOU LOOK!
SHE'S *NOT* MY GIRLFRIEND. THIS IS THE *CAPTAIN* OF COMPANY 5!!
NUDGE
NUDGE
HIS GIRL-FRIEND...
THE CAPTAIN? I DUNNO... THE LOOK ON HER FACE IS SCREAMING SHE DON'T MIND THE IDEA.
FIDGET
GIRL-FRIEND...
FIDGET
SO WHAT'S THE CAPTAIN OF COMPANY 5 DOING IN ASAKUSA ANYWAY?

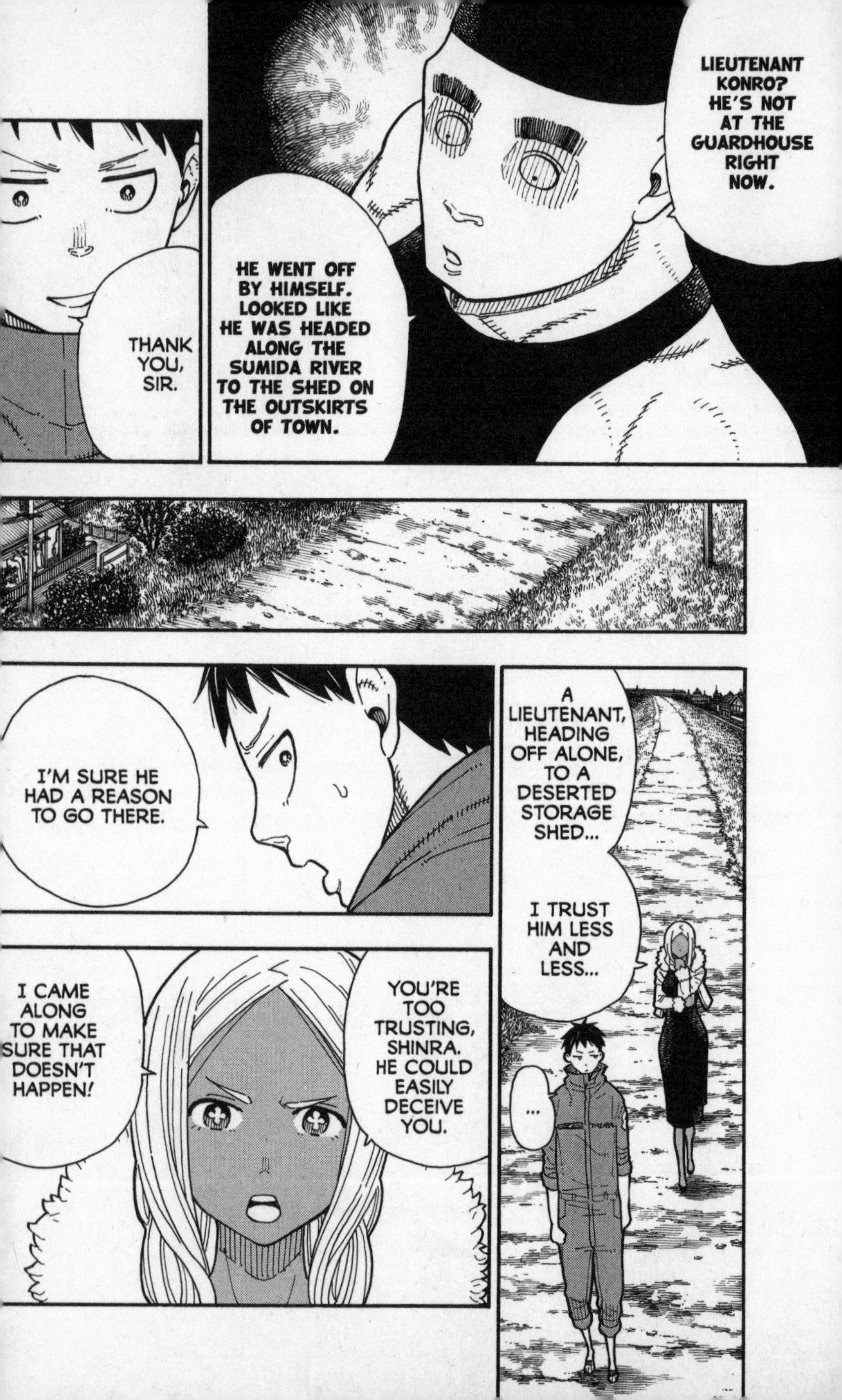
LIEUTENANT KONRO? HE'S NOT AT THE GUARDHOUSE RIGHT NOW.
HE WENT OFF BY HIMSELF. LOOKED LIKE HE WAS HEADED ALONG THE SUMIDA RIVER TO THE SHED ON THE OUTSKIRTS OF TOWN.
THANK YOU, SIR.
A LIEUTENANT, HEADING OFF ALONE, TO A DESERTED STORAGE SHED...
I TRUST HIM LESS AND LESS...
...
I'M SURE HE HAD A REASON TO GO THERE.
YOU'RE TOO TRUSTING, SHINRA. HE COULD EASILY DECEIVE YOU.
I CAME ALONG TO MAKE SURE THAT DOESN'T HAPPEN!

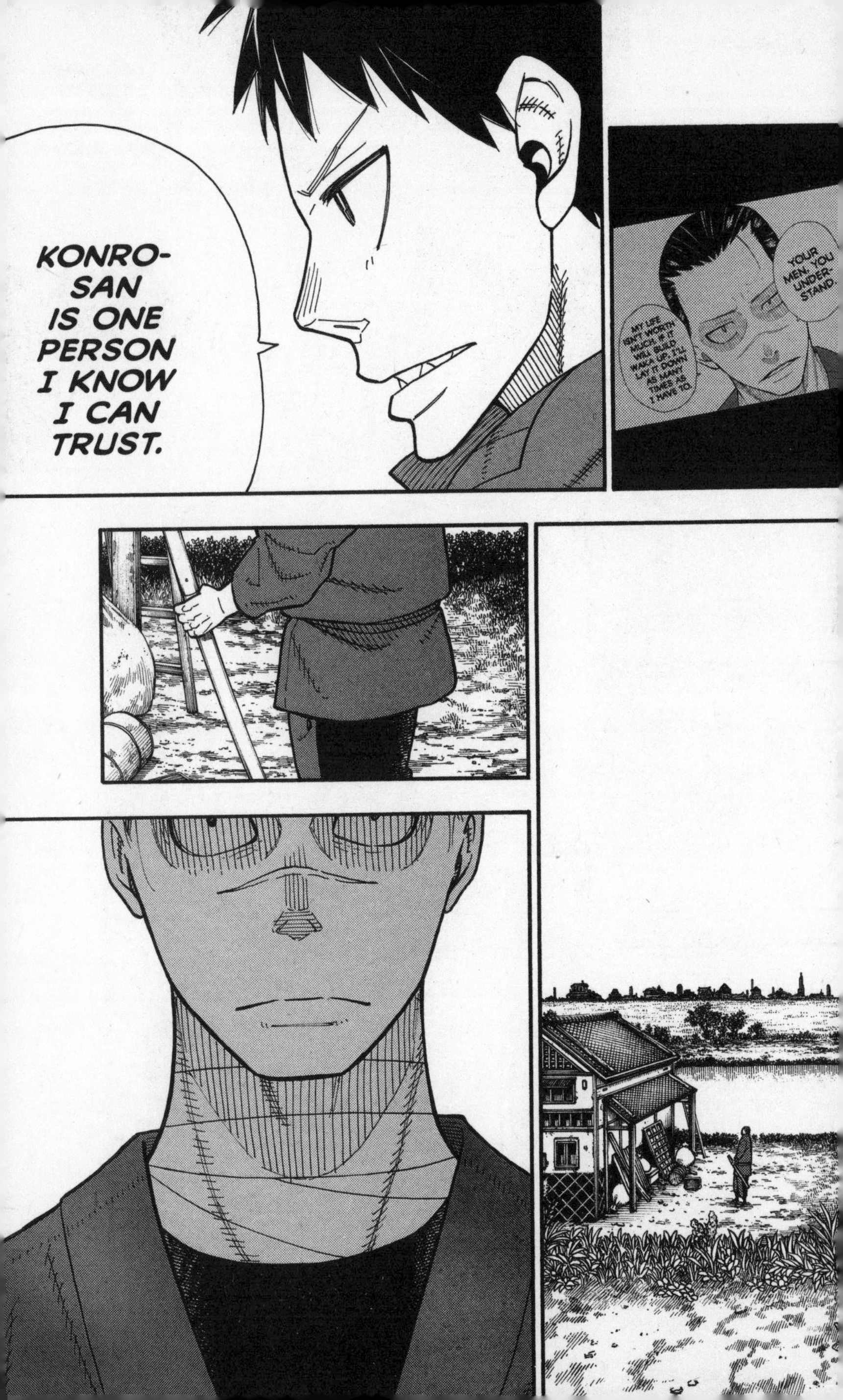
YOUR MEN. YOU UNDERSTAND.
MY LIFE ISN'T WORTH MUCH IF IT WILL BUILD WAKA UP, I'LL LAY IT DOWN AS MANY TIMES AS I HAVE TO.
KONRO-SAN IS ONE PERSON I KNOW I CAN TRUST.

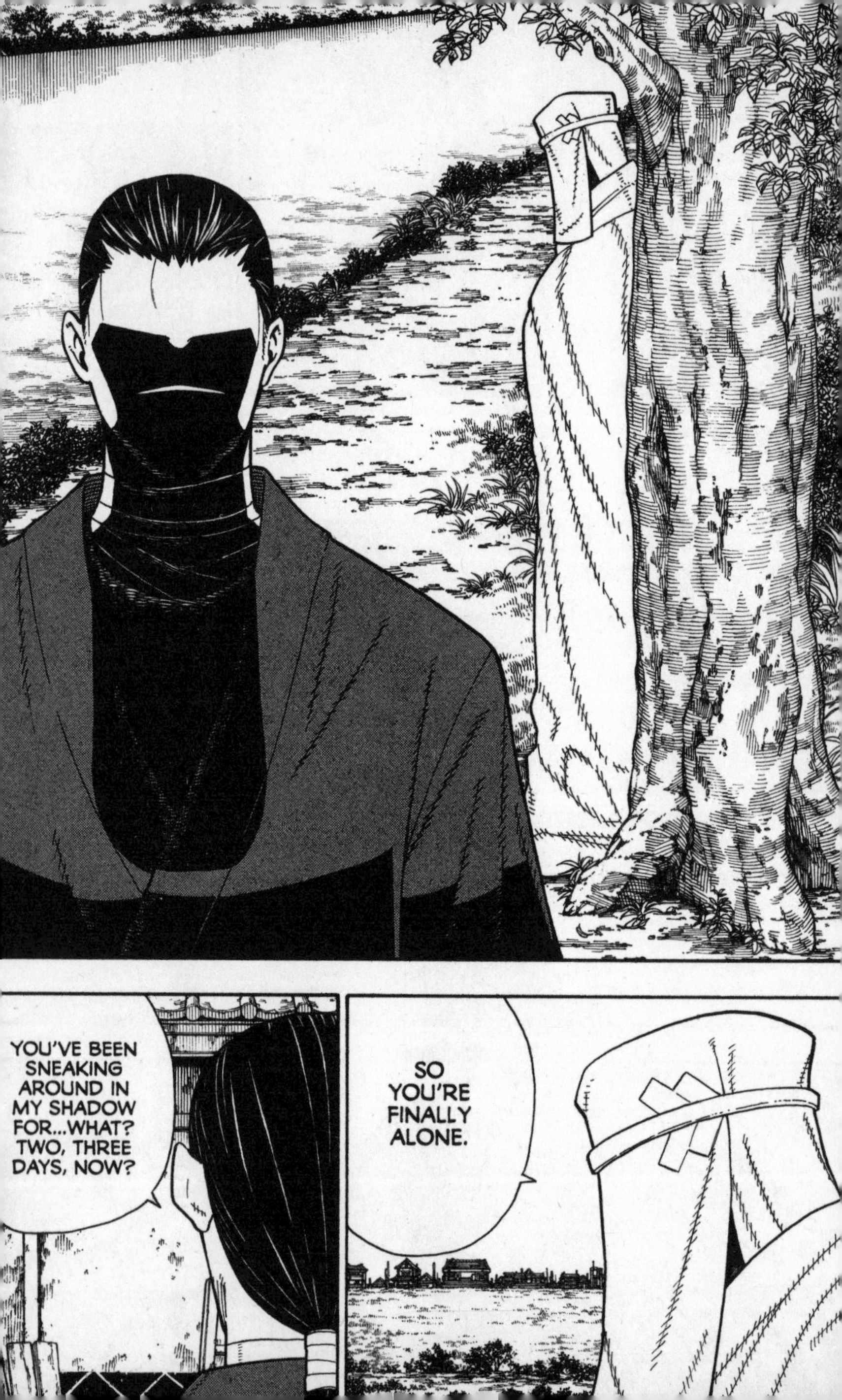
SO YOU'RE FINALLY ALONE.
YOU'VE BEEN SNEAKING AROUND IN MY SHADOW FOR...WHAT? TWO, THREE DAYS, NOW?

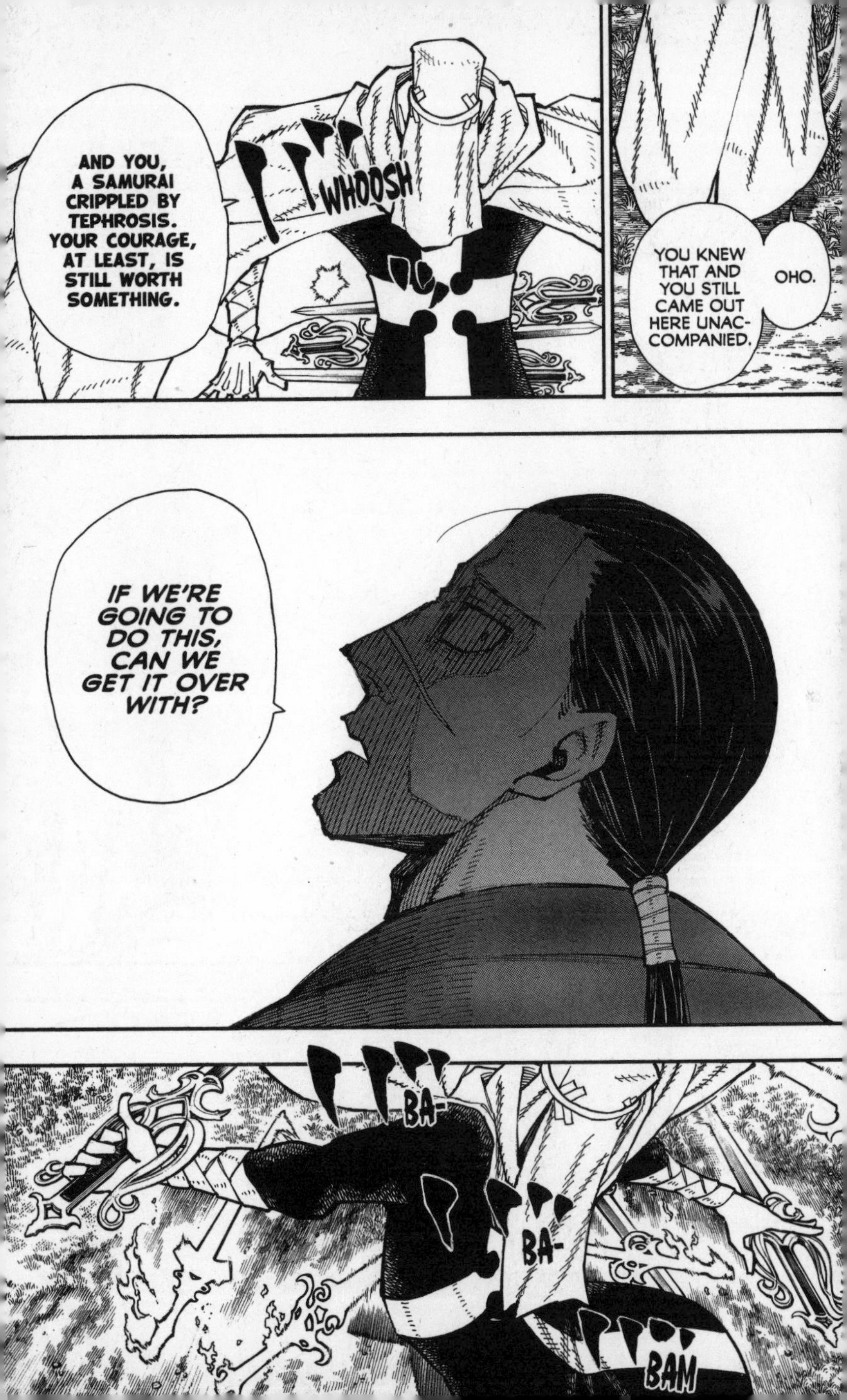
OHO.
YOU KNEW THAT AND YOU STILL CAME OUT HERE UNACCOMPANIED.
WHOOSH
AND YOU, A SAMURAI CRIPPLED BY TEPHROSIS. YOUR COURAGE, AT LEAST, IS STILL WORTH SOMETHING.
IF WE'RE GOING TO DO THIS, CAN WE GET IT OVER WITH?
BA-
BA-
BAM

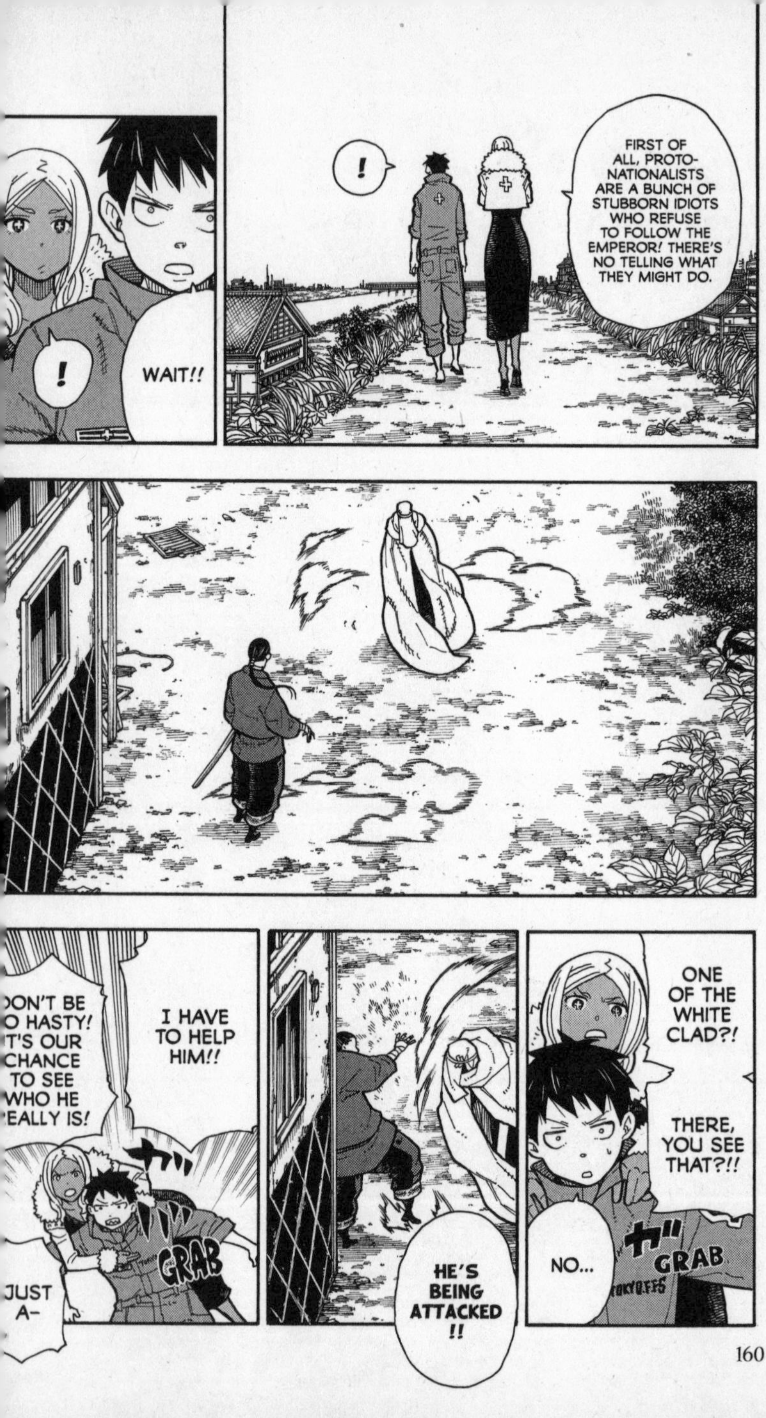
FIRST OF ALL, PROTO-NATIONALISTS ARE A BUNCH OF STUBBORN IDIOTS WHO REFUSE TO FOLLOW THE EMPEROR! THERE'S NO TELLING WHAT THEY MIGHT DO.
!
!
WAIT!!
ONE OF THE WHITE CLAD?!
THERE, YOU SEE THAT?!!
NO...
GRAB
HE'S BEING ATTACKED!!
I HAVE TO HELP HIM!!
ON'T BE O HASTY! T'S OUR CHANCE TO SEE WHO HE EALLY IS!
GRAB
JUST A-

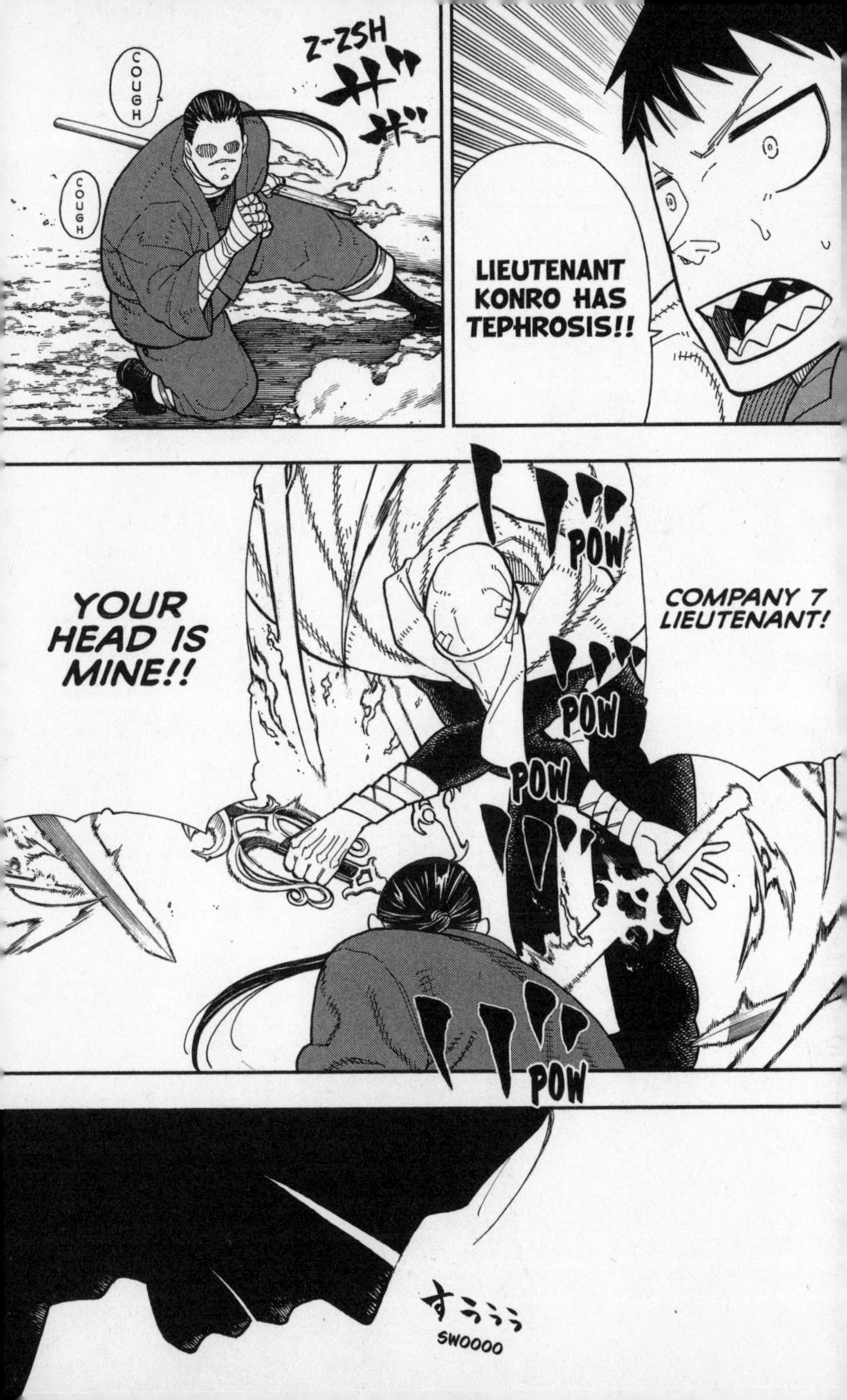
LIEUTENANT KONRO HAS TEPHROSIS!!
Z-ZSH
COUGH
COUGH
COMPANY 7 LIEUTENANT!
POW
POW
POW
YOUR HEAD IS MINE!!
POW
SWOOOO

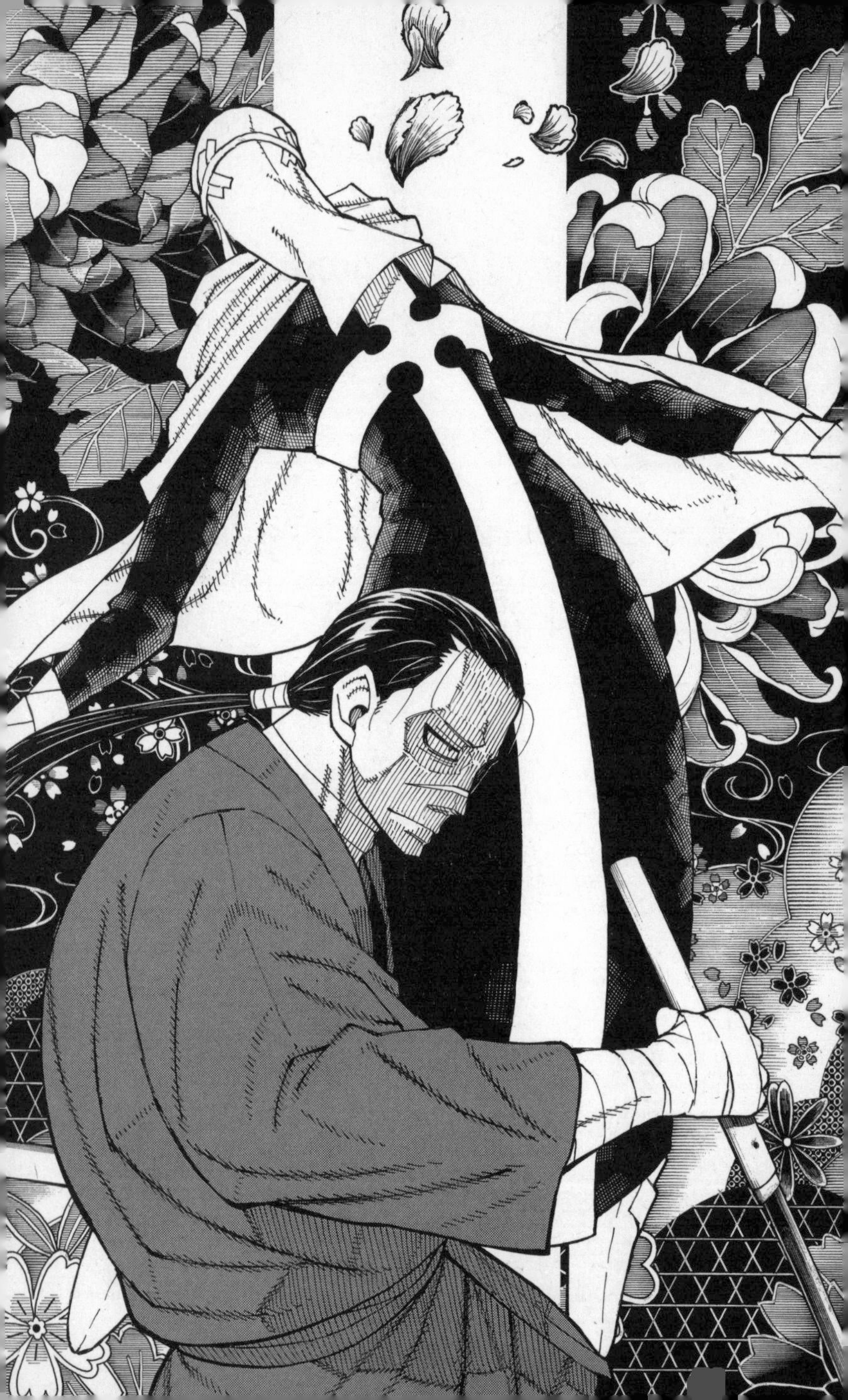

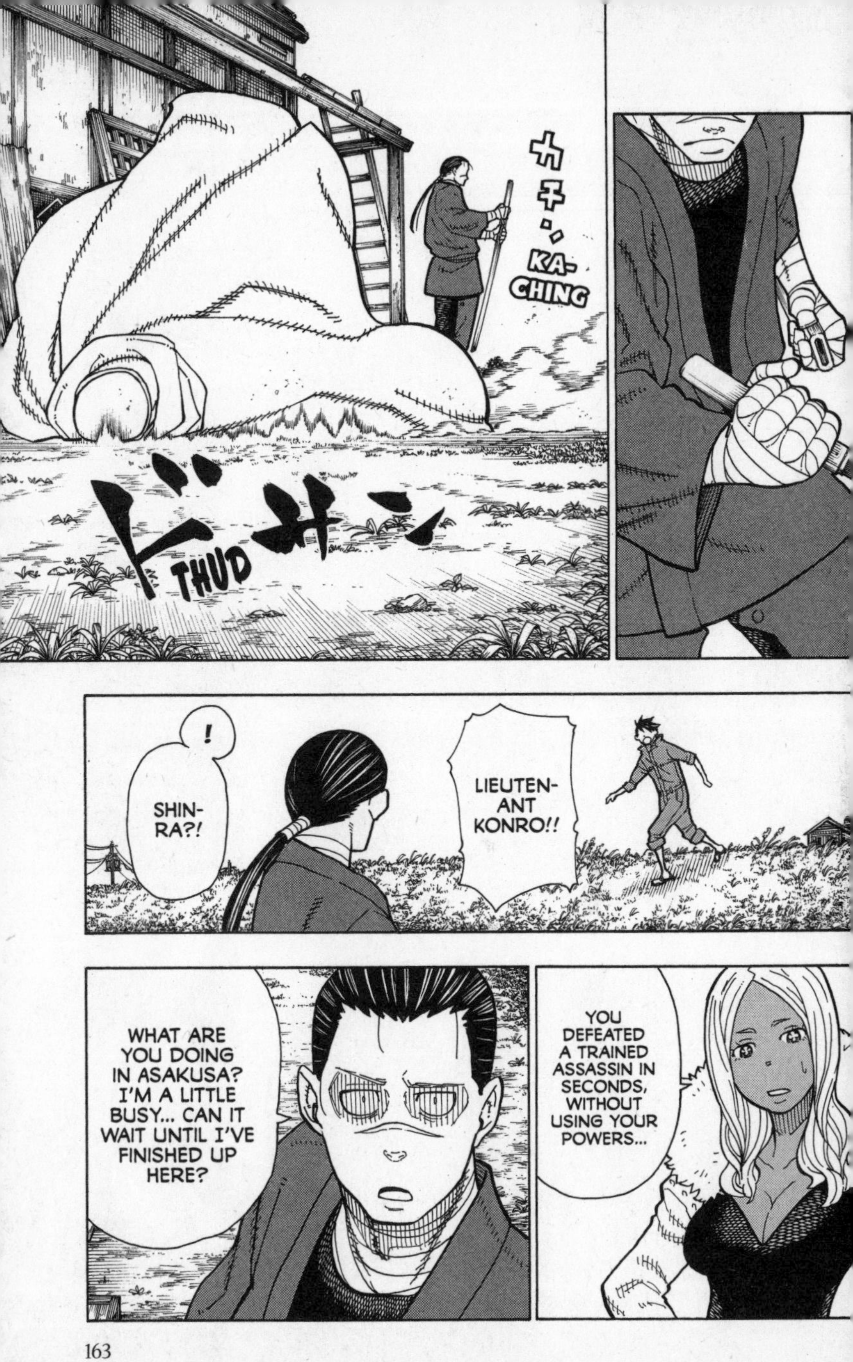

カチ
KA-CHING
ドサッ
THUD
LIEUTEN-ANT KONRO!!
!
SHIN-RA?!
YOU DEFEATED A TRAINED ASSASSIN IN SECONDS, WITHOUT USING YOUR POWERS...
WHAT ARE YOU DOING IN ASAKUSA? I'M A LITTLE BUSY... CAN IT WAIT UNTIL I'VE FINISHED UP HERE?

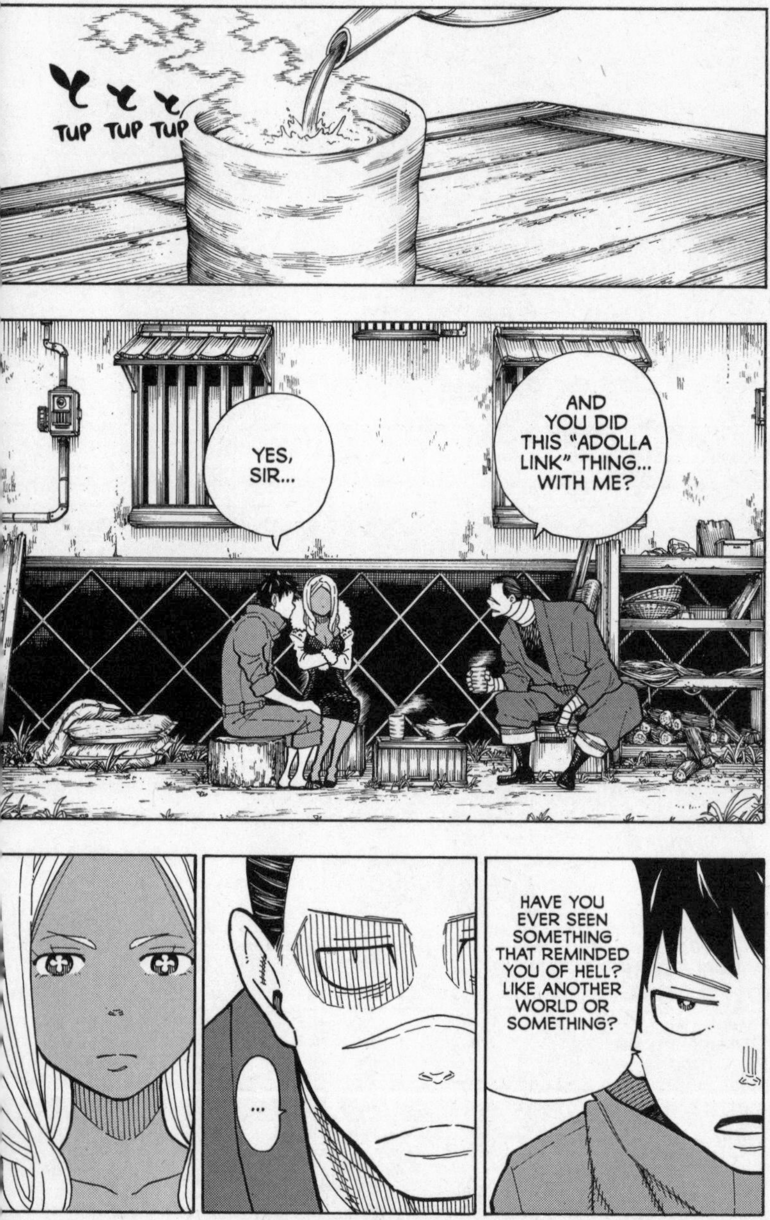
TUP TUP TUP
AND YOU DID THIS "ADOLLA LINK" THING... WITH ME?
YES, SIR...
HAVE YOU EVER SEEN SOMETHING THAT REMINDED YOU OF HELL? LIKE ANOTHER WORLD OR SOMETHING?
...

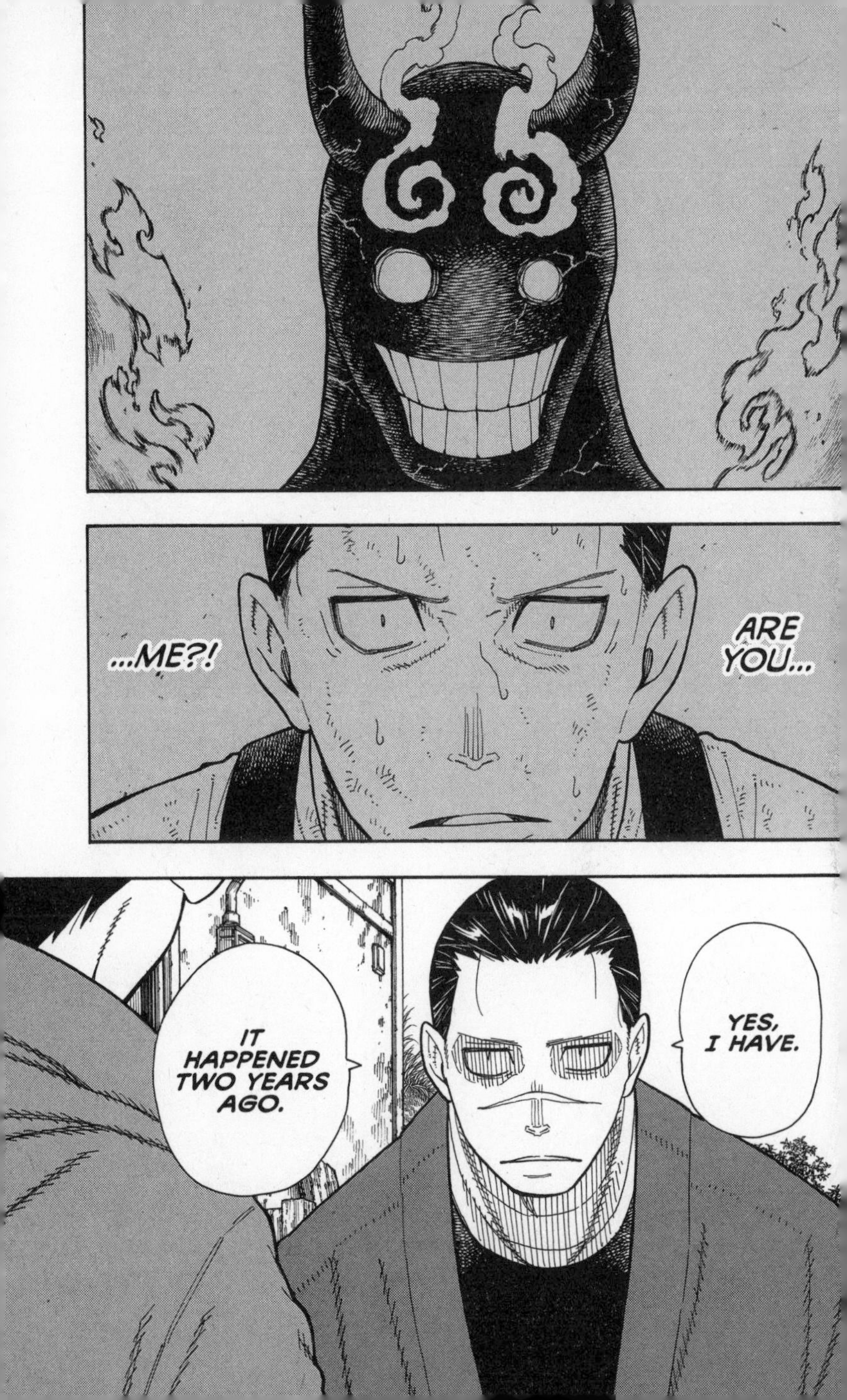
ARE YOU...
...ME?!
YES, I HAVE.
IT HAPPENED TWO YEARS AGO.

FIRE FORCE

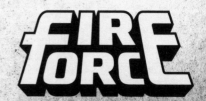

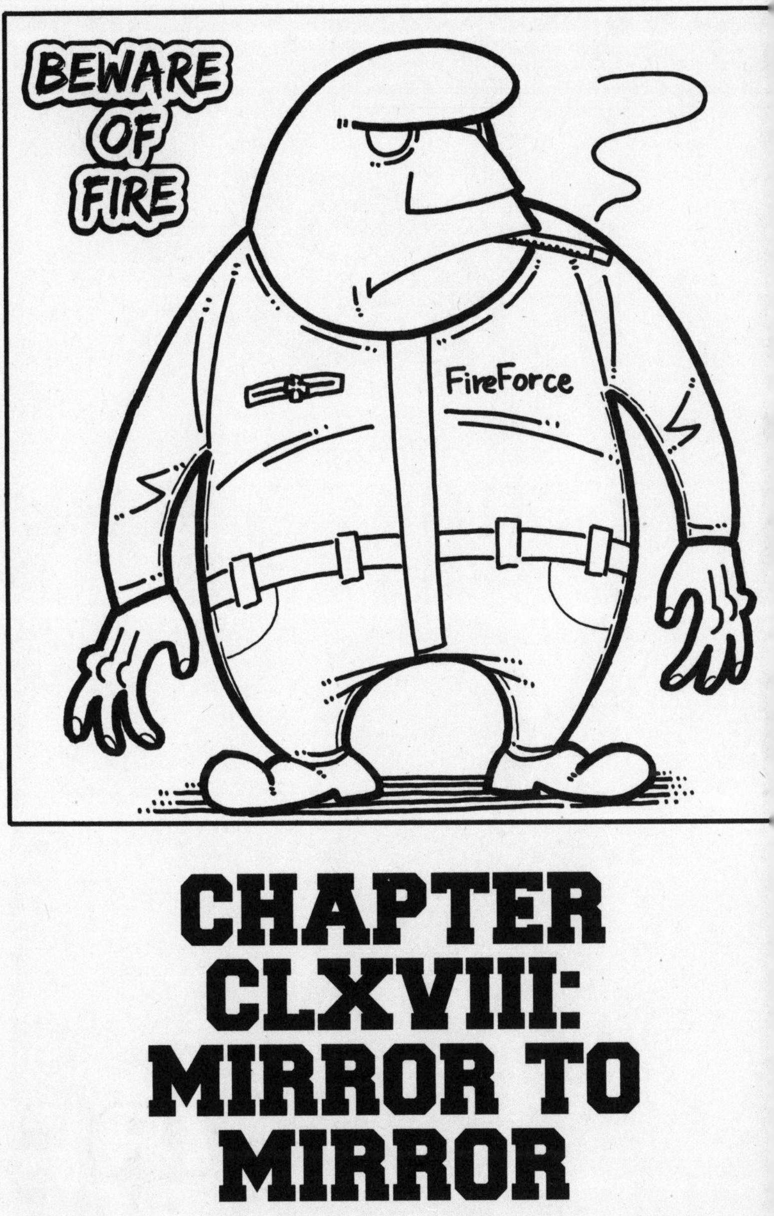
BEWARE OF FIRE
FireForce

CHAPTER CLXVIII: MIRROR TO MIRROR

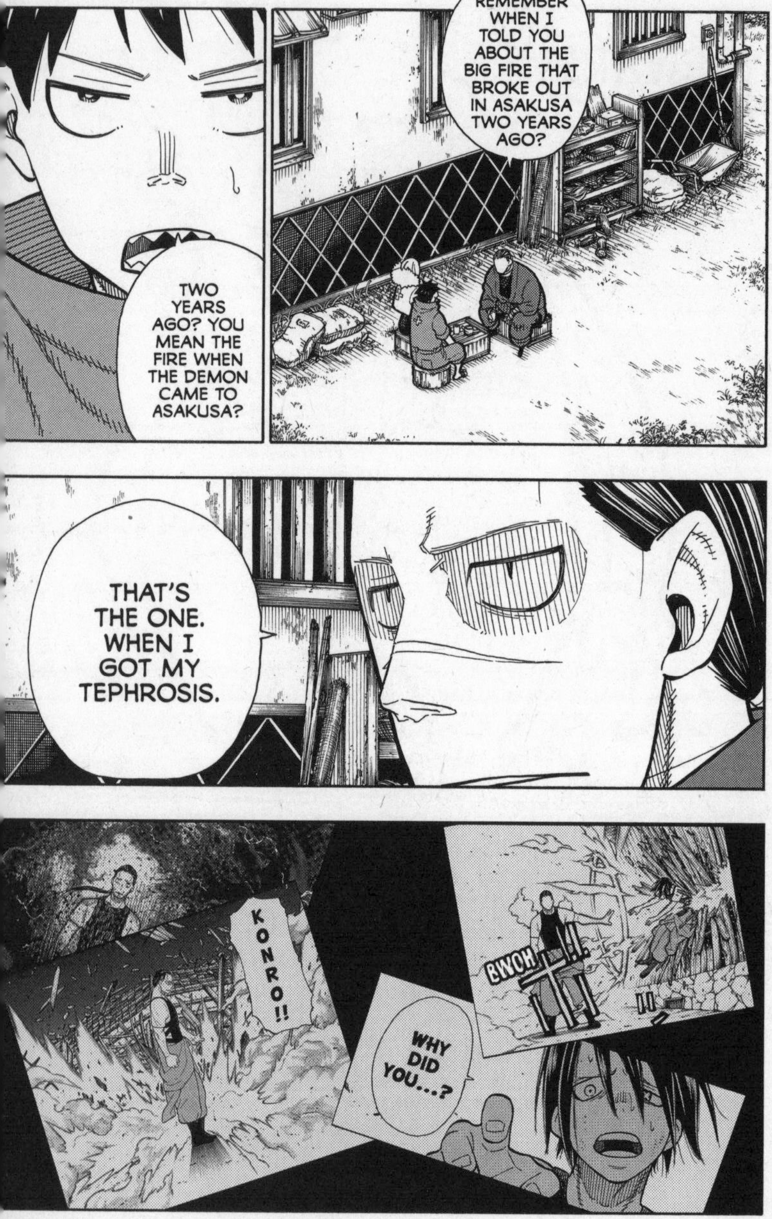
REMEMBER WHEN I TOLD YOU ABOUT THE BIG FIRE THAT BROKE OUT IN ASAKUSA TWO YEARS AGO?
TWO YEARS AGO? YOU MEAN THE FIRE WHEN THE DEMON CAME TO ASAKUSA?
THAT'S THE ONE. WHEN I GOT MY TEPHROSIS.
BWOH
WHY DID YOU...?
KONRO!!

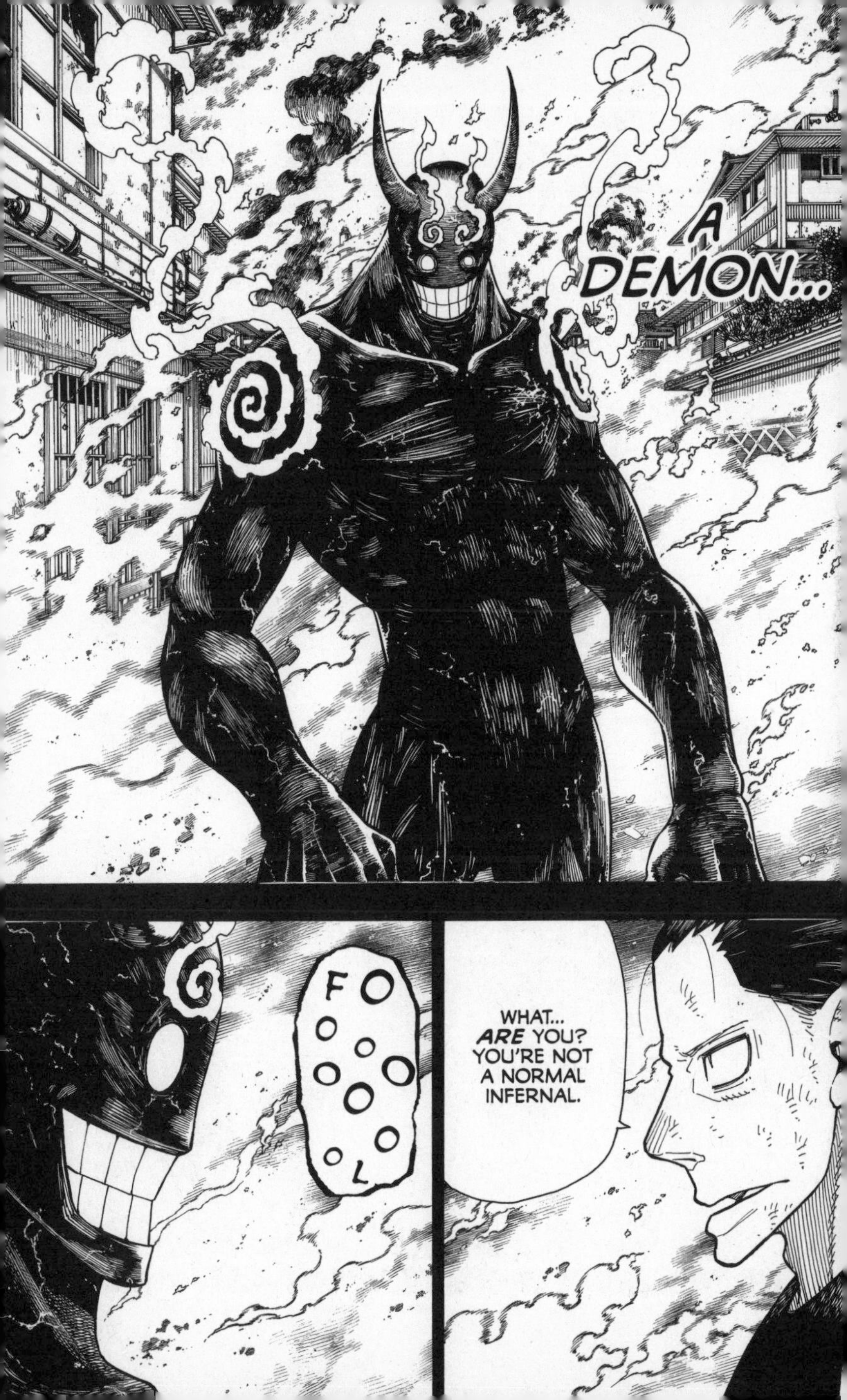
A DEMON...
WHAT... *ARE* YOU? YOU'RE NOT A NORMAL INFERNAL.
FOOOOOOOOOOL

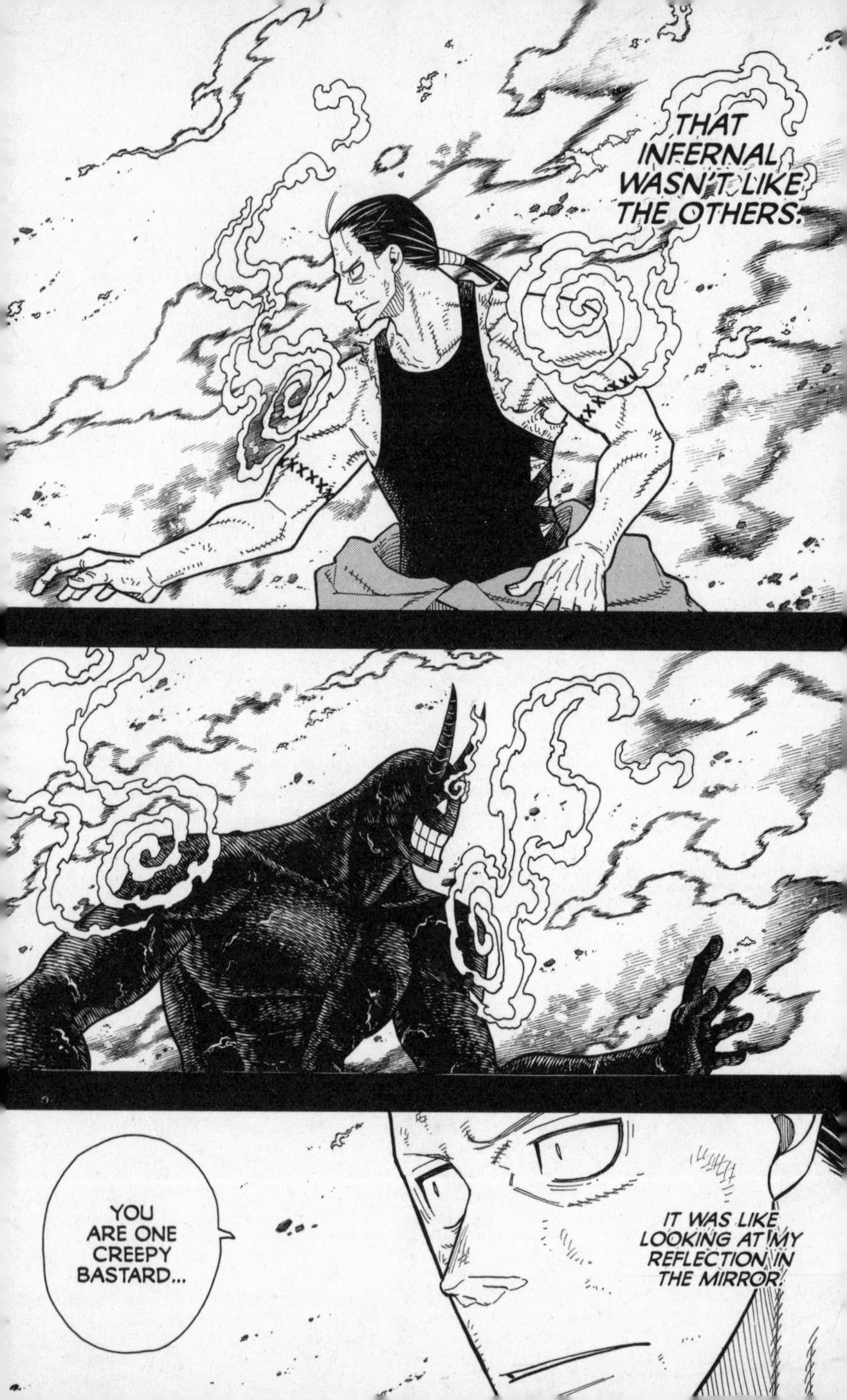
THAT INFERNAL WASN'T LIKE THE OTHERS.
IT WAS LIKE LOOKING AT MY REFLECTION IN THE MIRROR.
YOU ARE ONE CREEPY BASTARD...

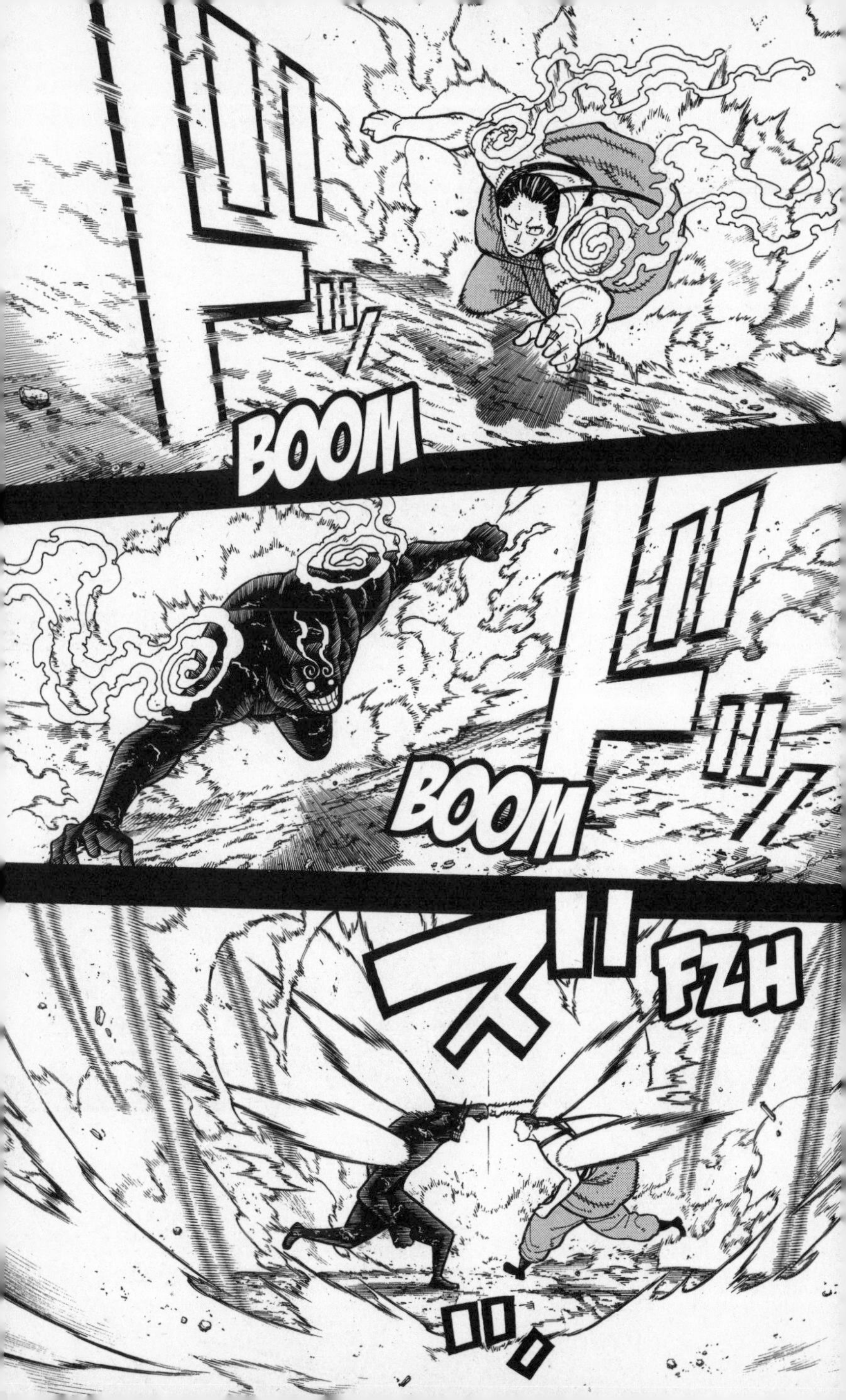
BOOM
BOOM
FZH

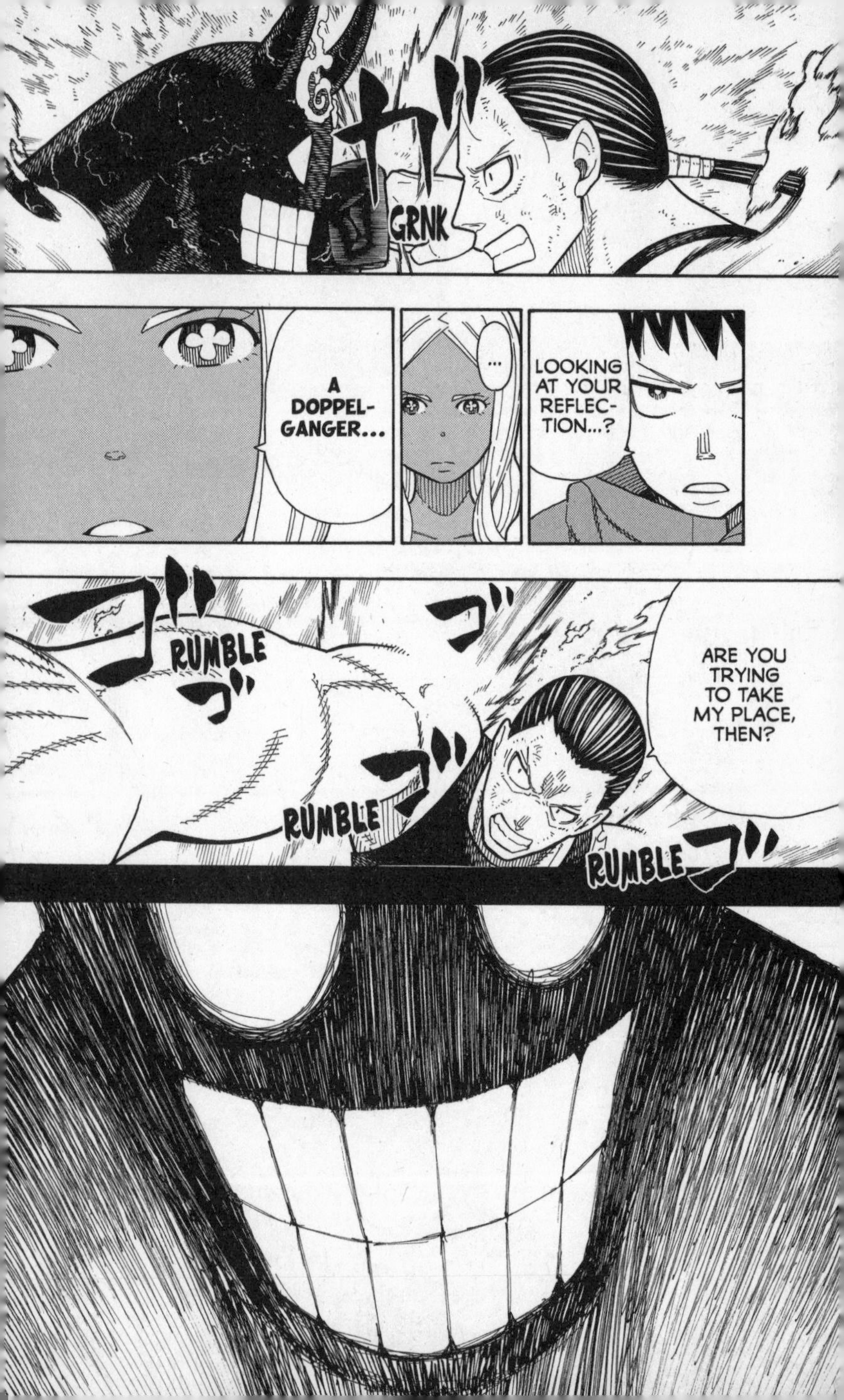
GRNK
LOOKING AT YOUR REFLEC-TION...?
...
A DOPPEL-GANGER...
ARE YOU TRYING TO TAKE MY PLACE, THEN?
RUMBLE
RUMBLE
RUMBLE

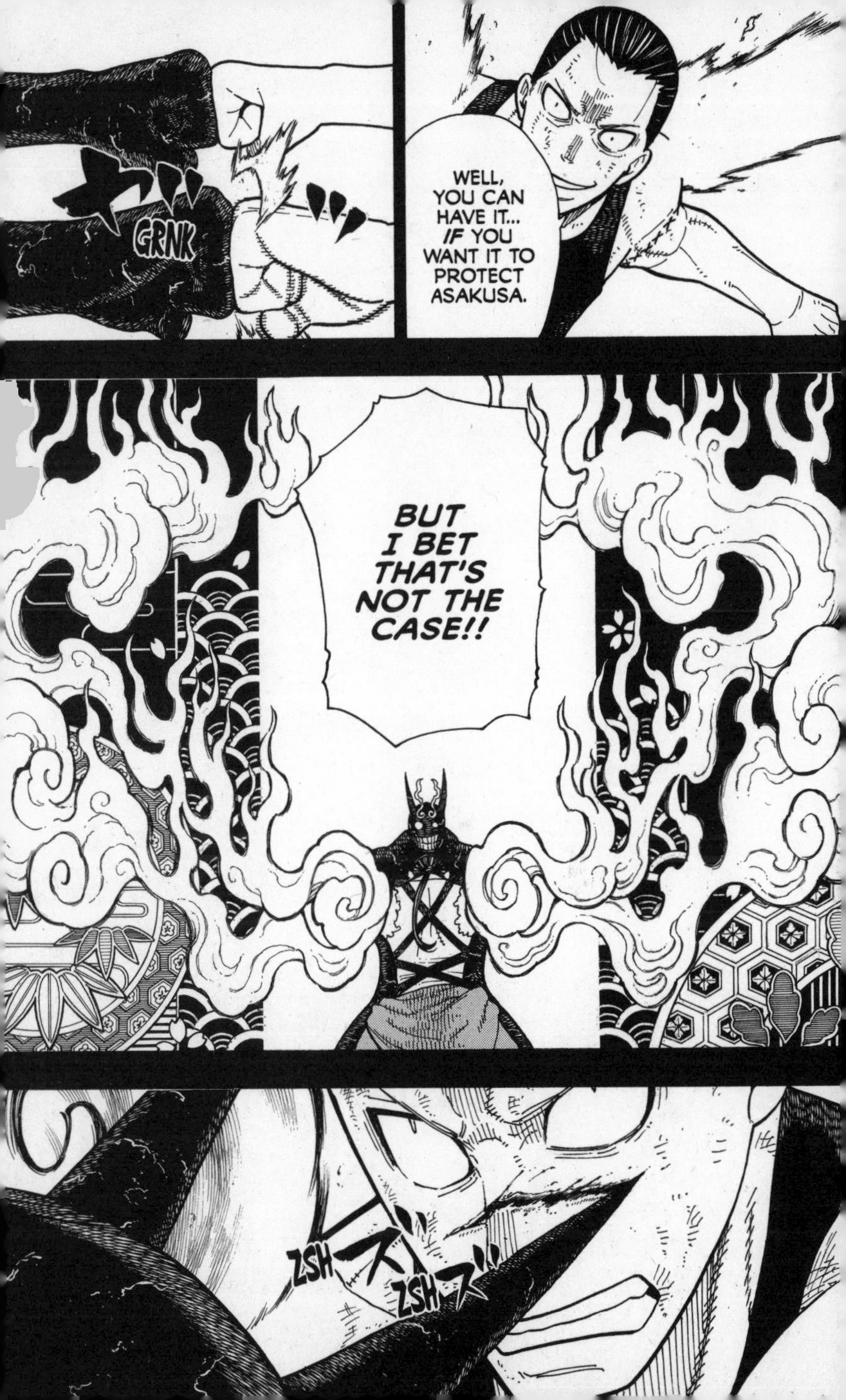
WELL, YOU CAN HAVE IT... *IF* YOU WANT IT TO PROTECT ASAKUSA.
GRNK
BUT I BET THAT'S NOT THE CASE!!
ZSH
ZSH

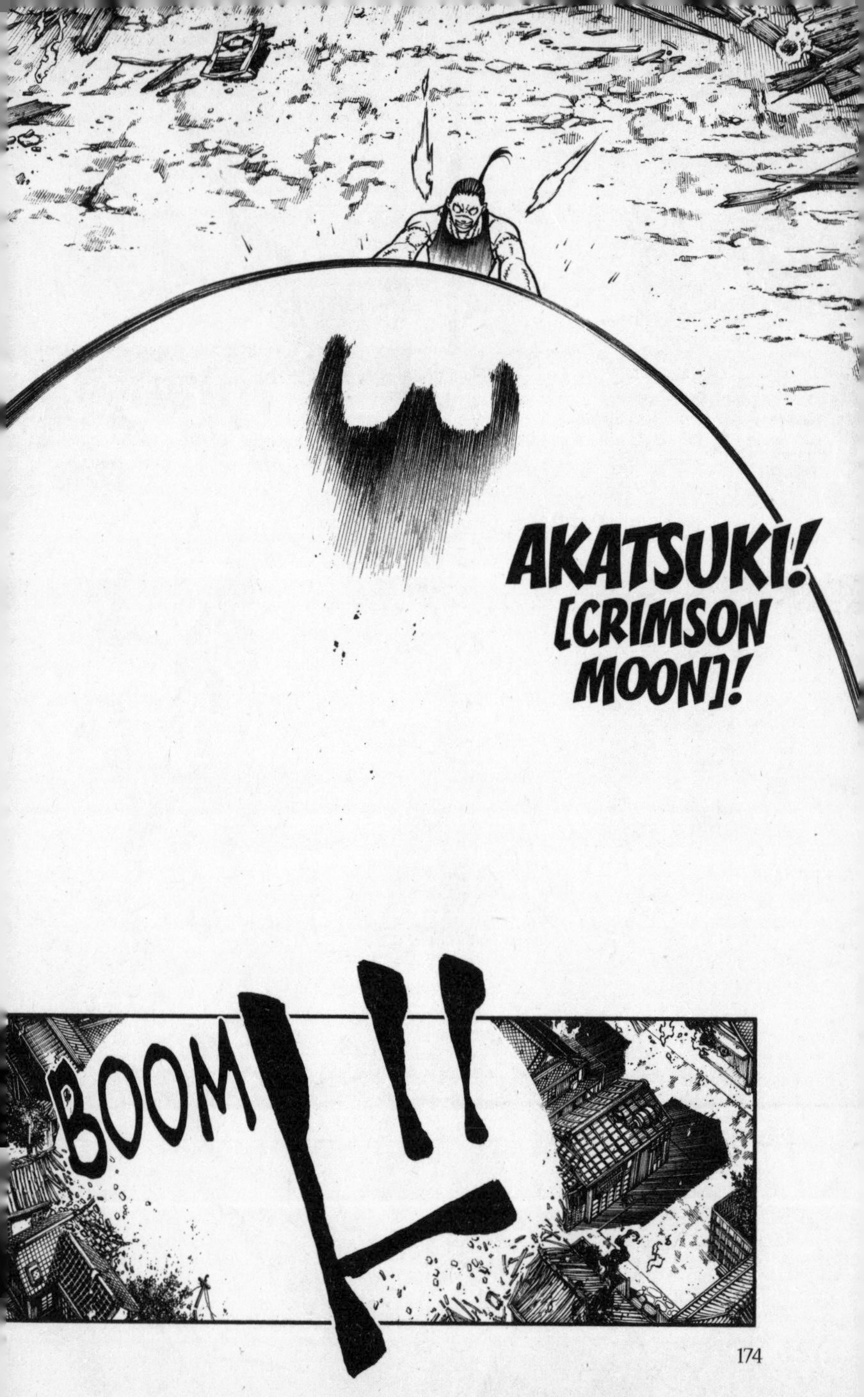
AKATSUKI! [CRIMSON MOON]!
BOOM!!!

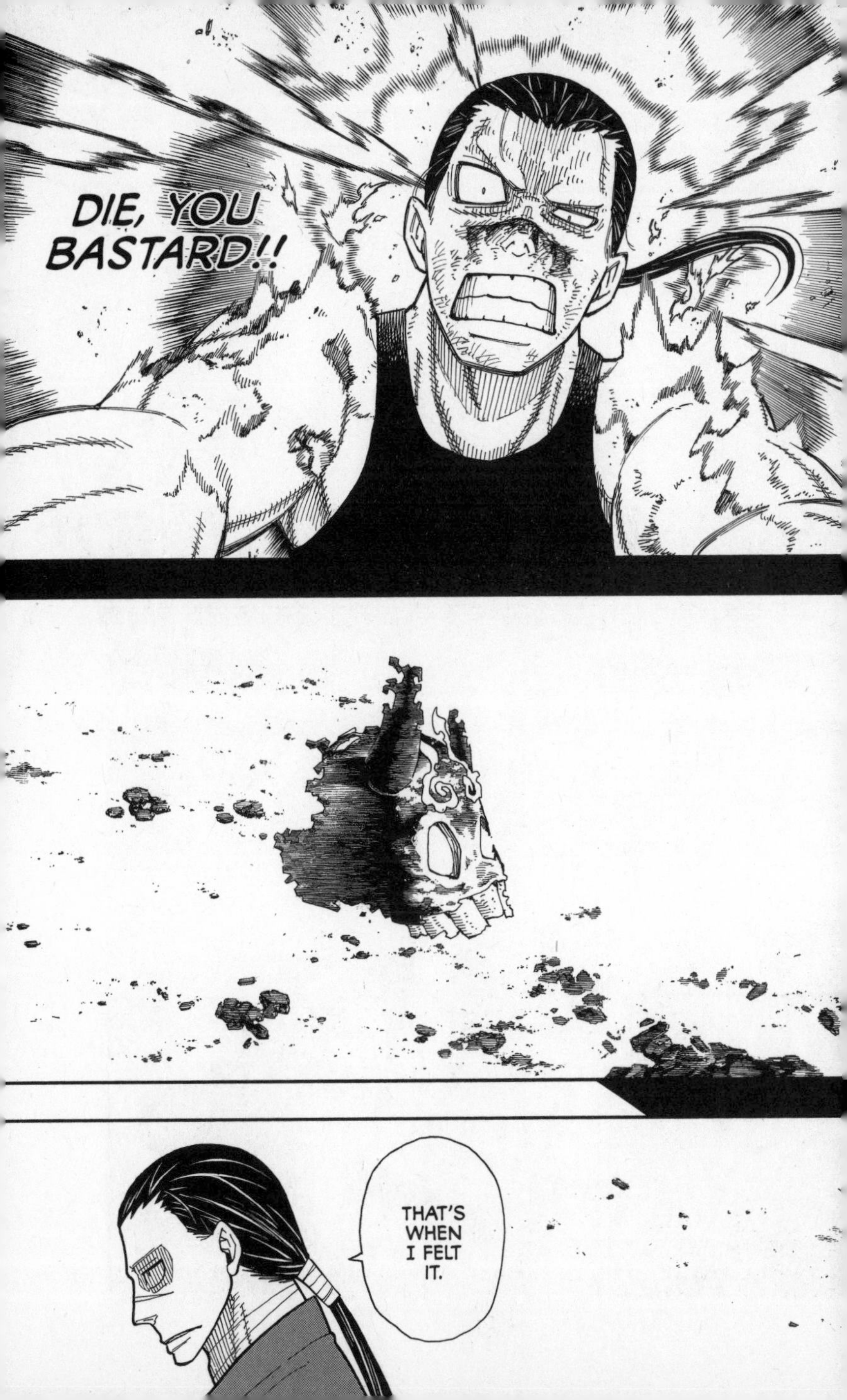
DIE, YOU BASTARD!!
THAT'S WHEN I FELT IT.

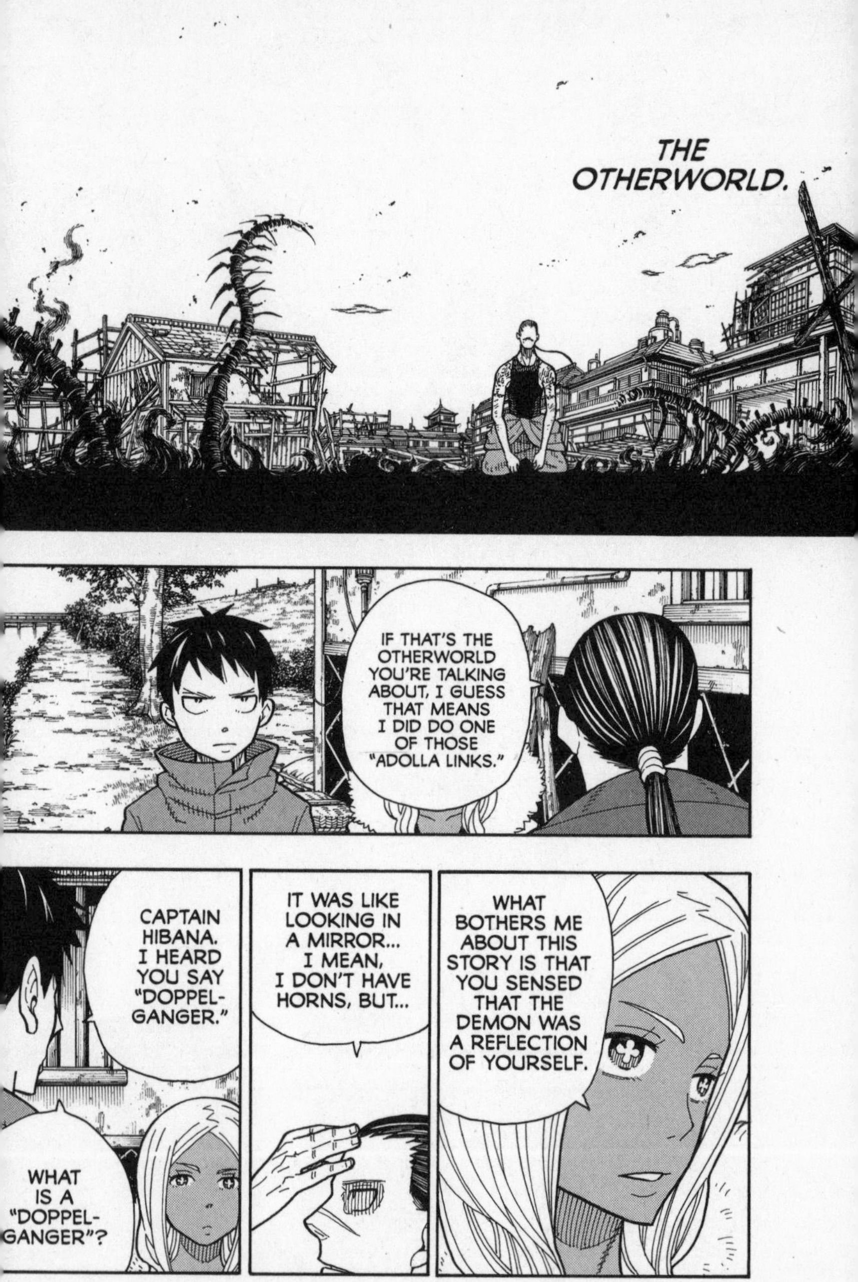
THE OTHERWORLD.
IF THAT'S THE OTHERWORLD YOU'RE TALKING ABOUT, I GUESS THAT MEANS I DID DO ONE OF THOSE "ADOLLA LINKS."
WHAT BOTHERS ME ABOUT THIS STORY IS THAT YOU SENSED THAT THE DEMON WAS A REFLECTION OF YOURSELF.
IT WAS LIKE LOOKING IN A MIRROR... I MEAN, I DON'T HAVE HORNS, BUT...
CAPTAIN HIBANA. I HEARD YOU SAY "DOPPEL-GANGER."
WHAT IS A "DOPPEL-GANGER"?

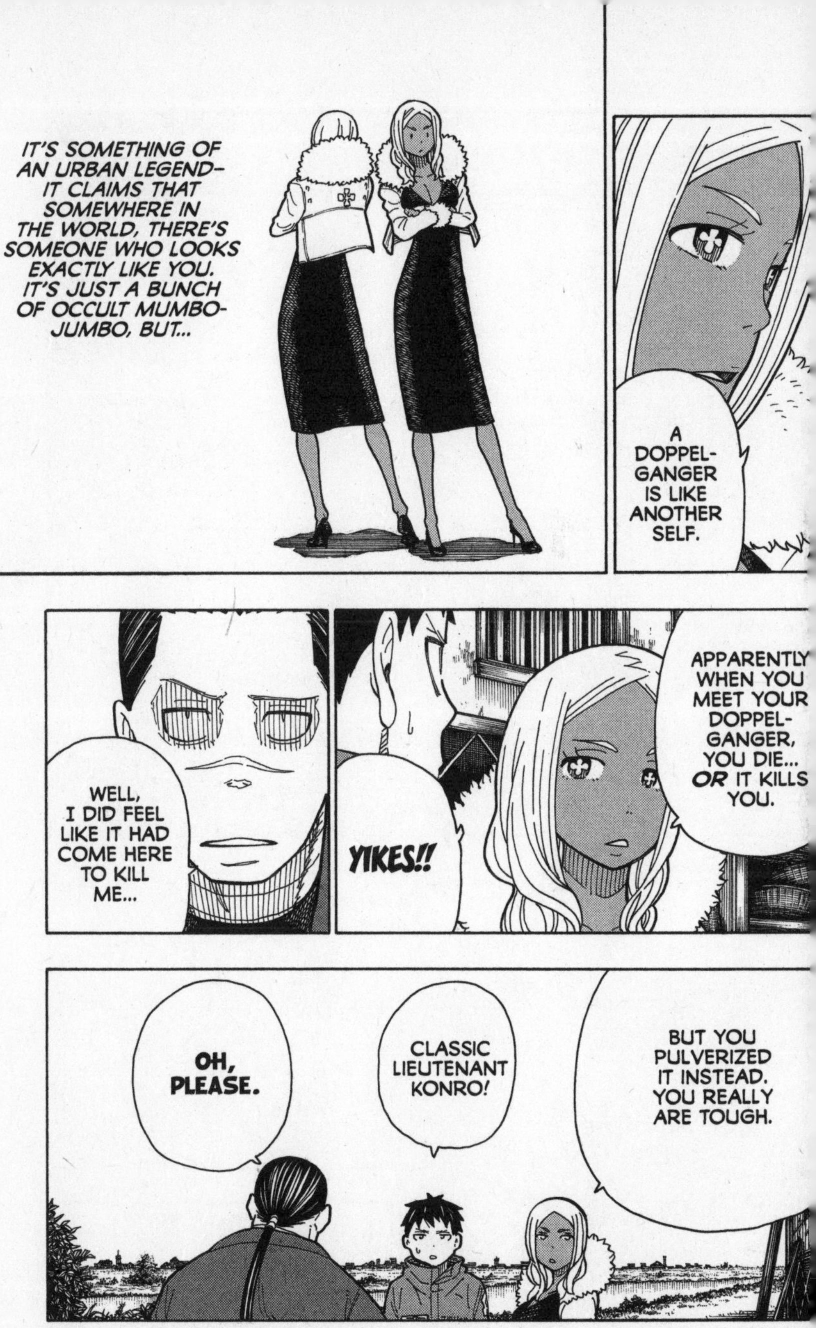
A DOPPEL-GANGER IS LIKE ANOTHER SELF.
IT'S SOMETHING OF AN URBAN LEGEND– IT CLAIMS THAT SOMEWHERE IN THE WORLD, THERE'S SOMEONE WHO LOOKS EXACTLY LIKE YOU. IT'S JUST A BUNCH OF OCCULT MUMBO-JUMBO, BUT...
APPARENTLY WHEN YOU MEET YOUR DOPPEL-GANGER, YOU DIE... OR IT KILLS YOU.
YIKES!!
WELL, I DID FEEL LIKE IT HAD COME HERE TO KILL ME...
BUT YOU PULVERIZED IT INSTEAD. YOU REALLY ARE TOUGH.
CLASSIC LIEUTENANT KONRO!
OH, PLEASE.

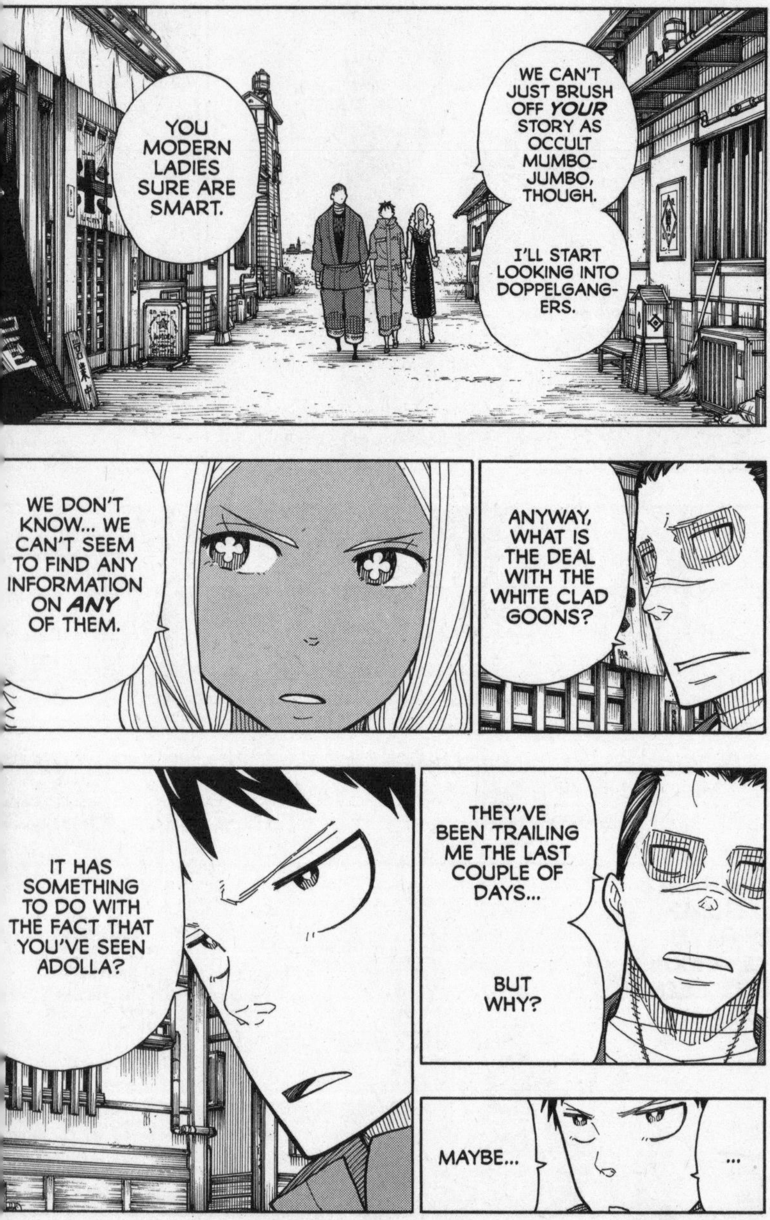
WE CAN'T JUST BRUSH OFF *YOUR* STORY AS OCCULT MUMBO-JUMBO, THOUGH.
I'LL START LOOKING INTO DOPPELGANGERS.
YOU MODERN LADIES SURE ARE SMART.
ANYWAY, WHAT IS THE DEAL WITH THE WHITE CLAD GOONS?
WE DON'T KNOW... WE CAN'T SEEM TO FIND ANY INFORMATION ON *ANY* OF THEM.
THEY'VE BEEN TRAILING ME THE LAST COUPLE OF DAYS...
BUT WHY?
MAYBE...
...
IT HAS SOMETHING TO DO WITH THE FACT THAT YOU'VE SEEN ADOLLA?

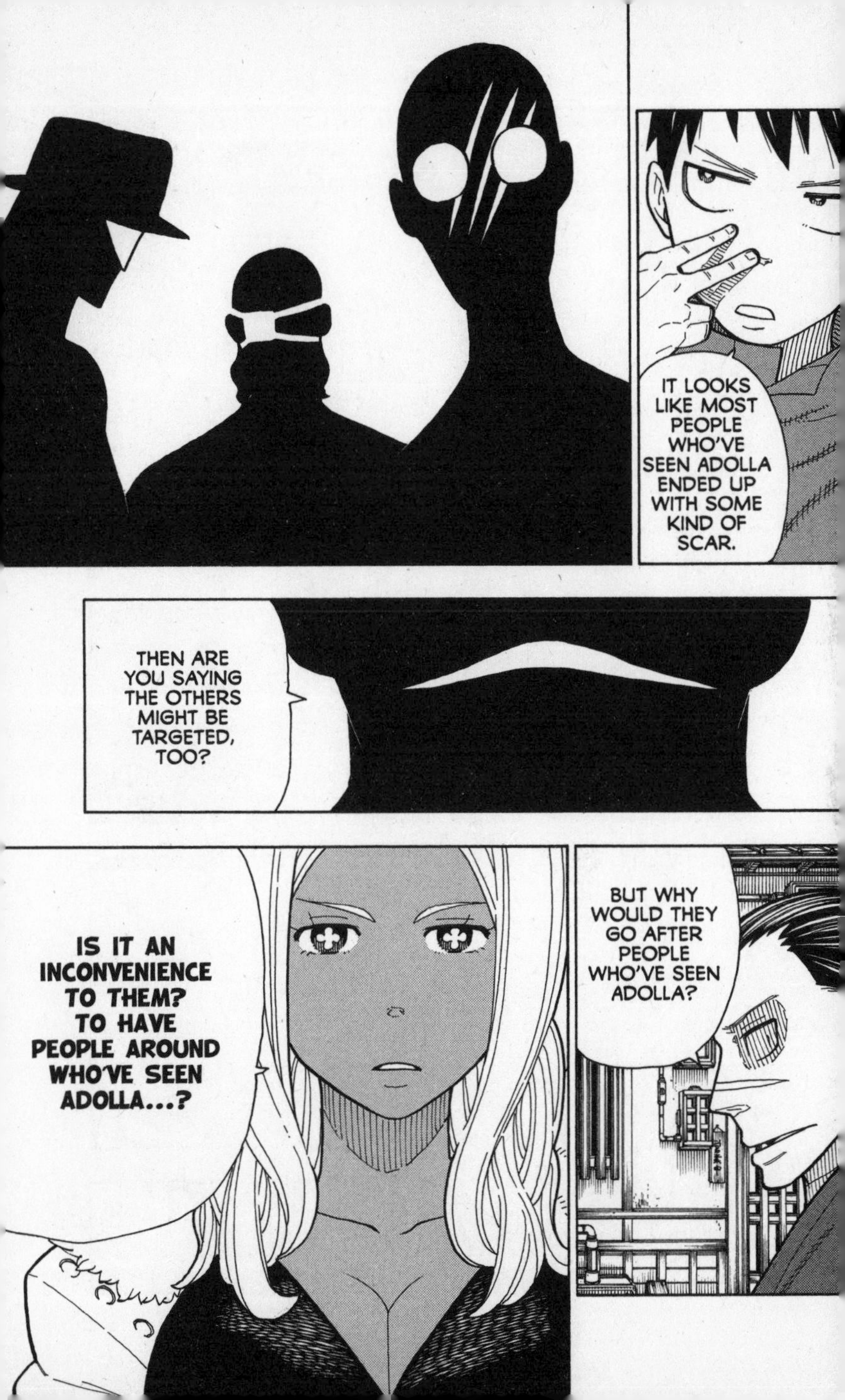
IT LOOKS LIKE MOST PEOPLE WHO'VE SEEN ADOLLA ENDED UP WITH SOME KIND OF SCAR.
THEN ARE YOU SAYING THE OTHERS MIGHT BE TARGETED, TOO?
BUT WHY WOULD THEY GO AFTER PEOPLE WHO'VE SEEN ADOLLA?
IS IT AN INCONVENIENCE TO THEM? TO HAVE PEOPLE AROUND WHO'VE SEEN ADOLLA...?

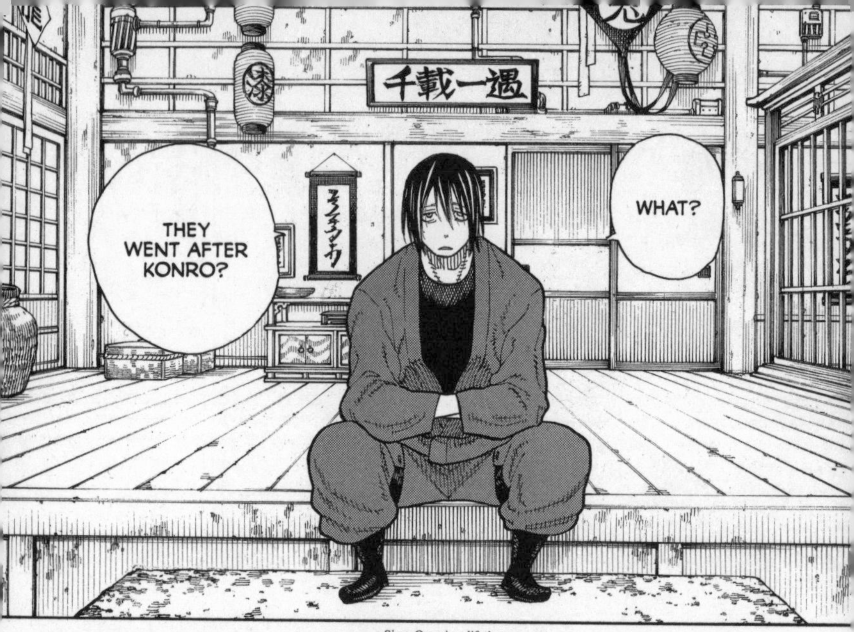
千載一遇
WHAT?
THEY WENT AFTER KONRO?

Sign: Once in a lifetime

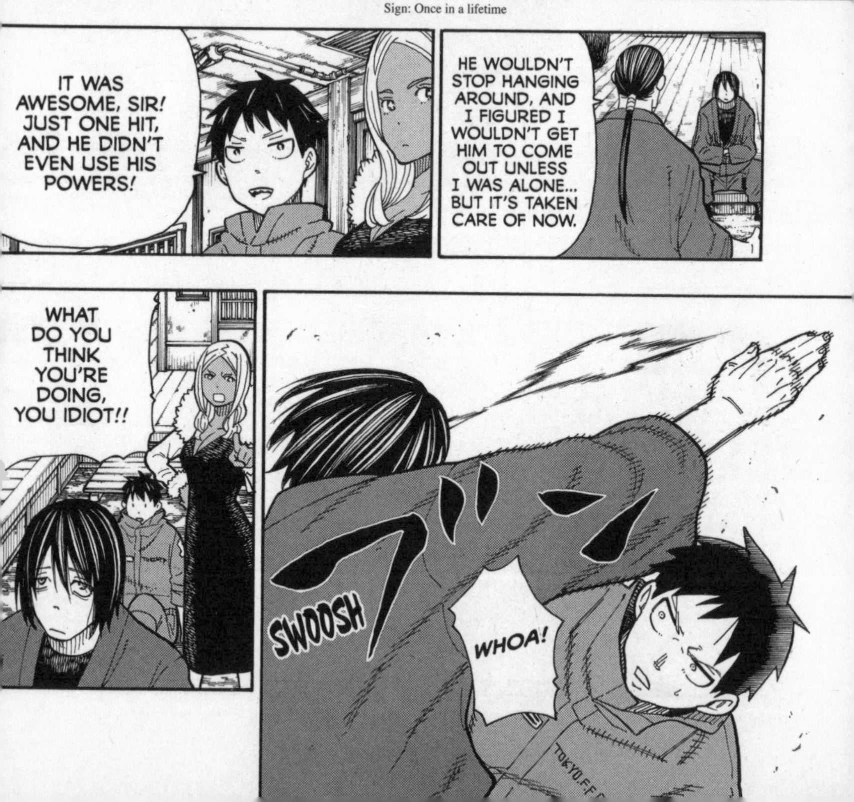
HE WOULDN'T STOP HANGING AROUND, AND I FIGURED I WOULDN'T GET HIM TO COME OUT UNLESS I WAS ALONE... BUT IT'S TAKEN CARE OF NOW.
IT WAS AWESOME, SIR! JUST ONE HIT, AND HE DIDN'T EVEN USE HIS POWERS!
SWOOSH
WHOA!
WHAT DO YOU THINK YOU'RE DOING, YOU IDIOT!!

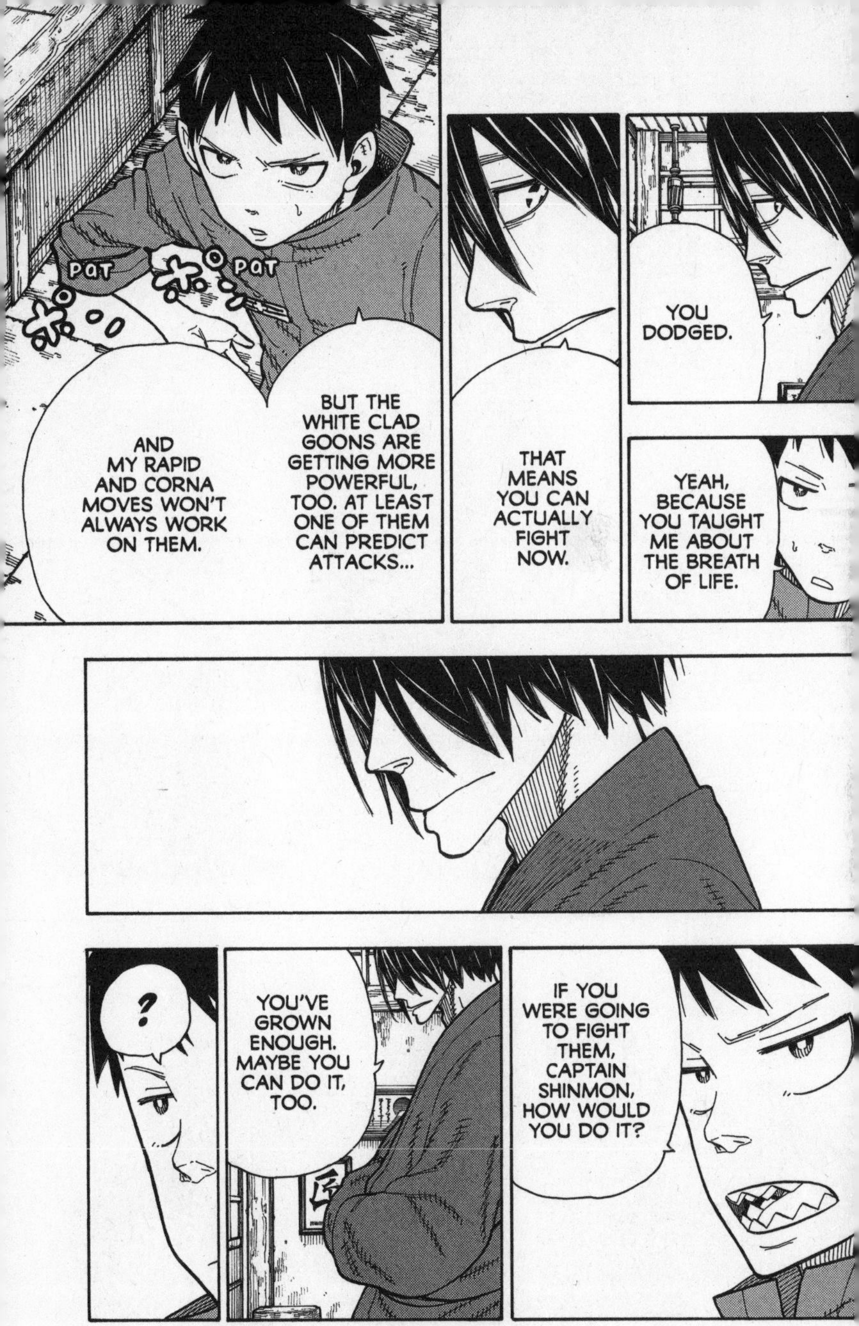
YOU DODGED.
YEAH, BECAUSE YOU TAUGHT ME ABOUT THE BREATH OF LIFE.
THAT MEANS YOU CAN ACTUALLY FIGHT NOW.
PAT
PAT
BUT THE WHITE CLAD GOONS ARE GETTING MORE POWERFUL, TOO. AT LEAST ONE OF THEM CAN PREDICT ATTACKS...
AND MY RAPID AND CORNA MOVES WON'T ALWAYS WORK ON THEM.
IF YOU WERE GOING TO FIGHT THEM, CAPTAIN SHINMON, HOW WOULD YOU DO IT?
YOU'VE GROWN ENOUGH. MAYBE YOU CAN DO IT, TOO.
?

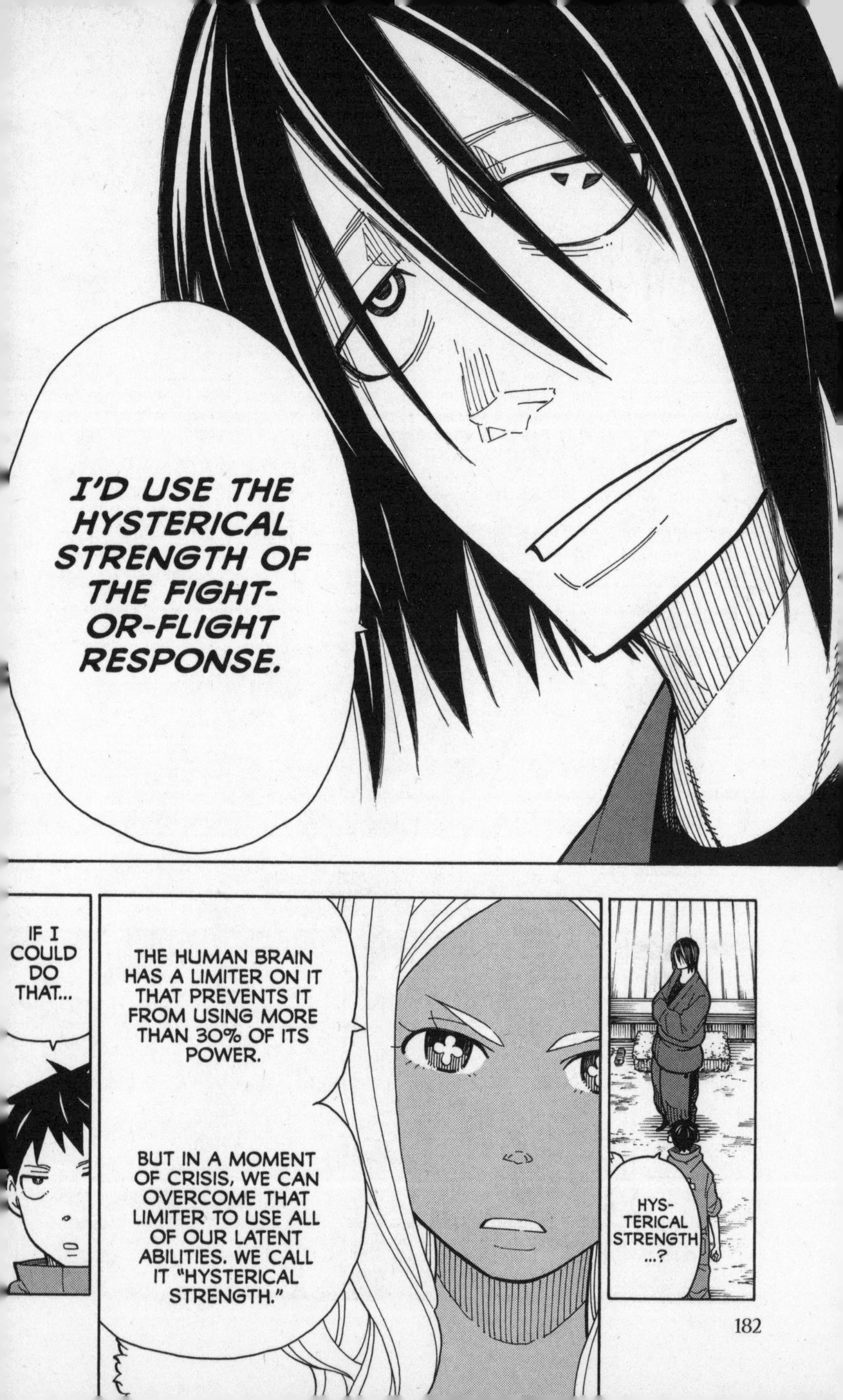
I'D USE THE HYSTERICAL STRENGTH OF THE FIGHT-OR-FLIGHT RESPONSE.
HYS-TERICAL STRENGTH ...?
THE HUMAN BRAIN HAS A LIMITER ON IT THAT PREVENTS IT FROM USING MORE THAN 30% OF ITS POWER.
BUT IN A MOMENT OF CRISIS, WE CAN OVERCOME THAT LIMITER TO USE ALL OF OUR LATENT ABILITIES. WE CALL IT "HYSTERICAL STRENGTH."
IF I COULD DO THAT...

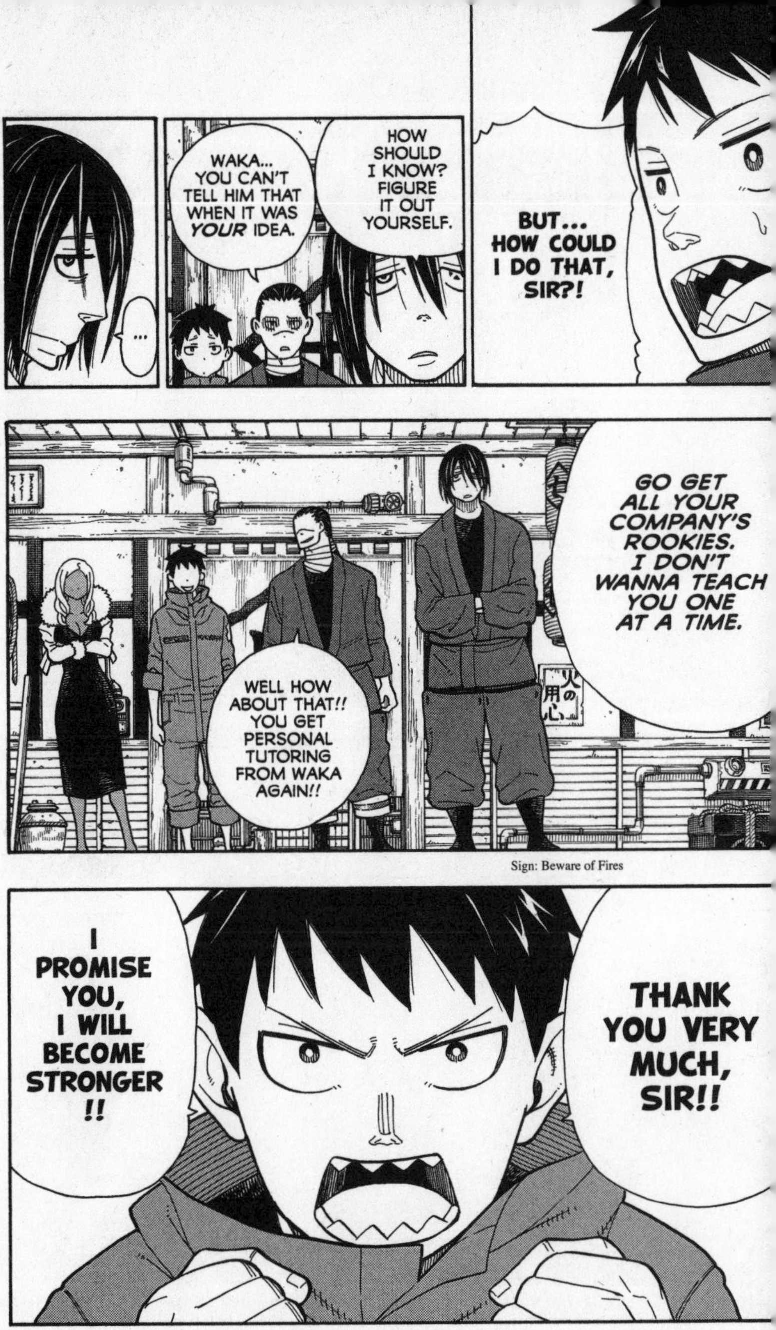
BUT... HOW COULD I DO THAT, SIR?!
HOW SHOULD I KNOW? FIGURE IT OUT YOURSELF.
WAKA... YOU CAN'T TELL HIM THAT WHEN IT WAS *YOUR* IDEA.
...
GO GET ALL YOUR COMPANY'S ROOKIES. I DON'T WANNA TEACH YOU ONE AT A TIME.
火の用心
WELL HOW ABOUT THAT!! YOU GET PERSONAL TUTORING FROM WAKA AGAIN!!
THANK YOU VERY MUCH, SIR!!
I PROMISE YOU, I WILL BECOME STRONGER!!

Sign: Beware of Fires

Sign: Tobacco

Sign: Tempura Restaurant

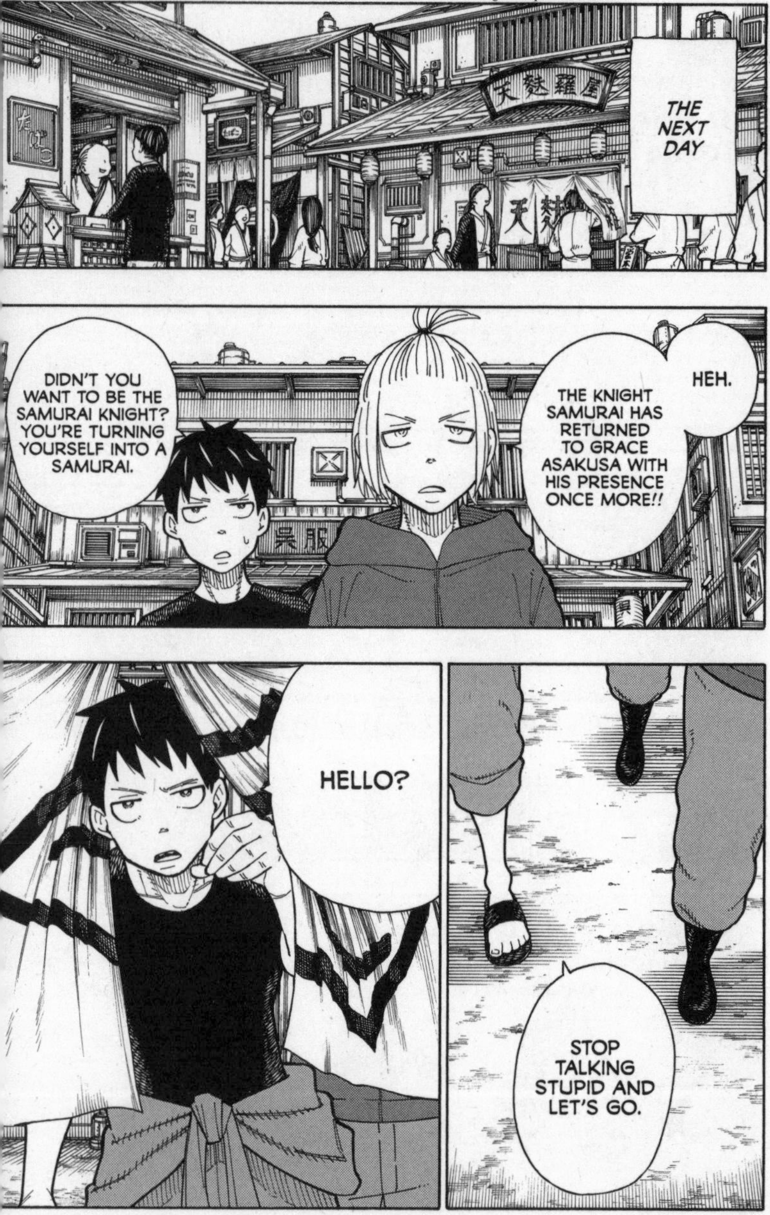
THE NEXT DAY
HEH.
THE KNIGHT SAMURAI HAS RETURNED TO GRACE ASAKUSA WITH HIS PRESENCE ONCE MORE!!
DIDN'T YOU WANT TO BE THE SAMURAI KNIGHT? YOU'RE TURNING YOURSELF INTO A SAMURAI.
STOP TALKING STUPID AND LET'S GO.
HELLO?

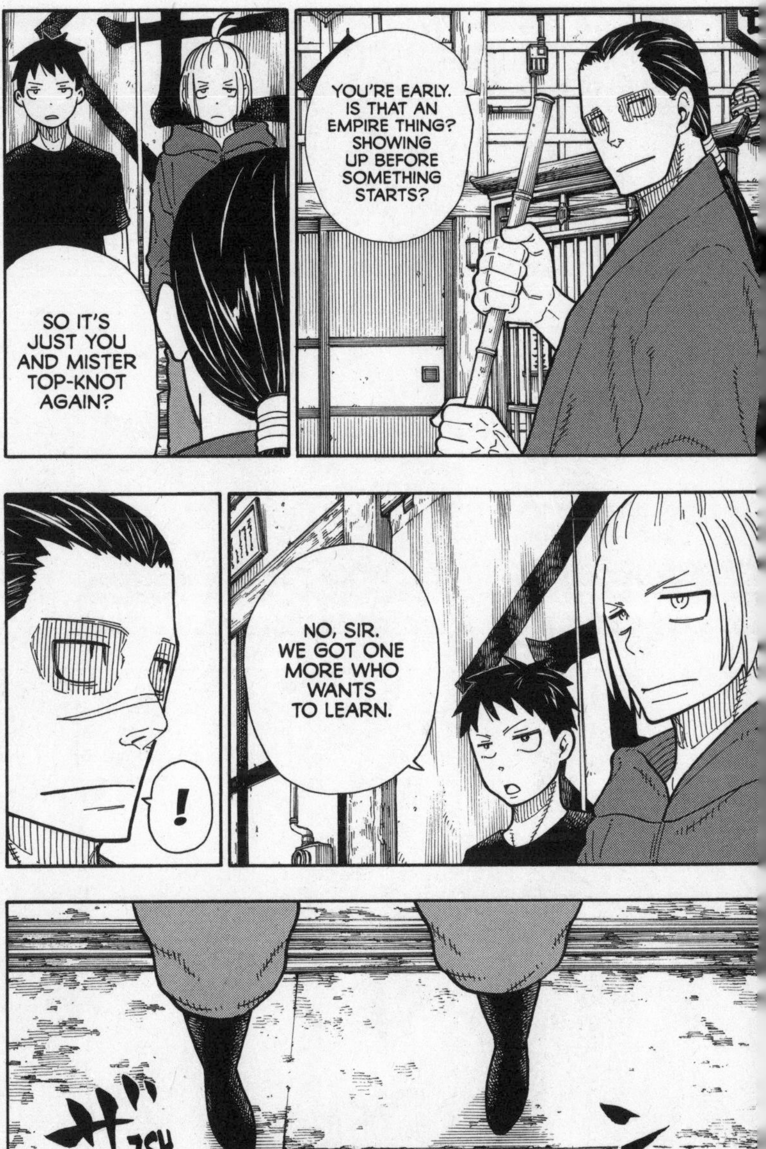
YOU'RE EARLY. IS THAT AN EMPIRE THING? SHOWING UP BEFORE SOMETHING STARTS?
SO IT'S JUST YOU AND MISTER TOP-KNOT AGAIN?
NO, SIR. WE GOT ONE MORE WHO WANTS TO LEARN.
!
ZSH

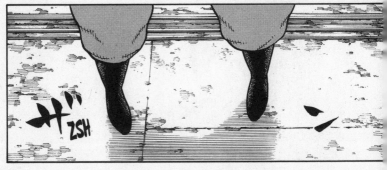

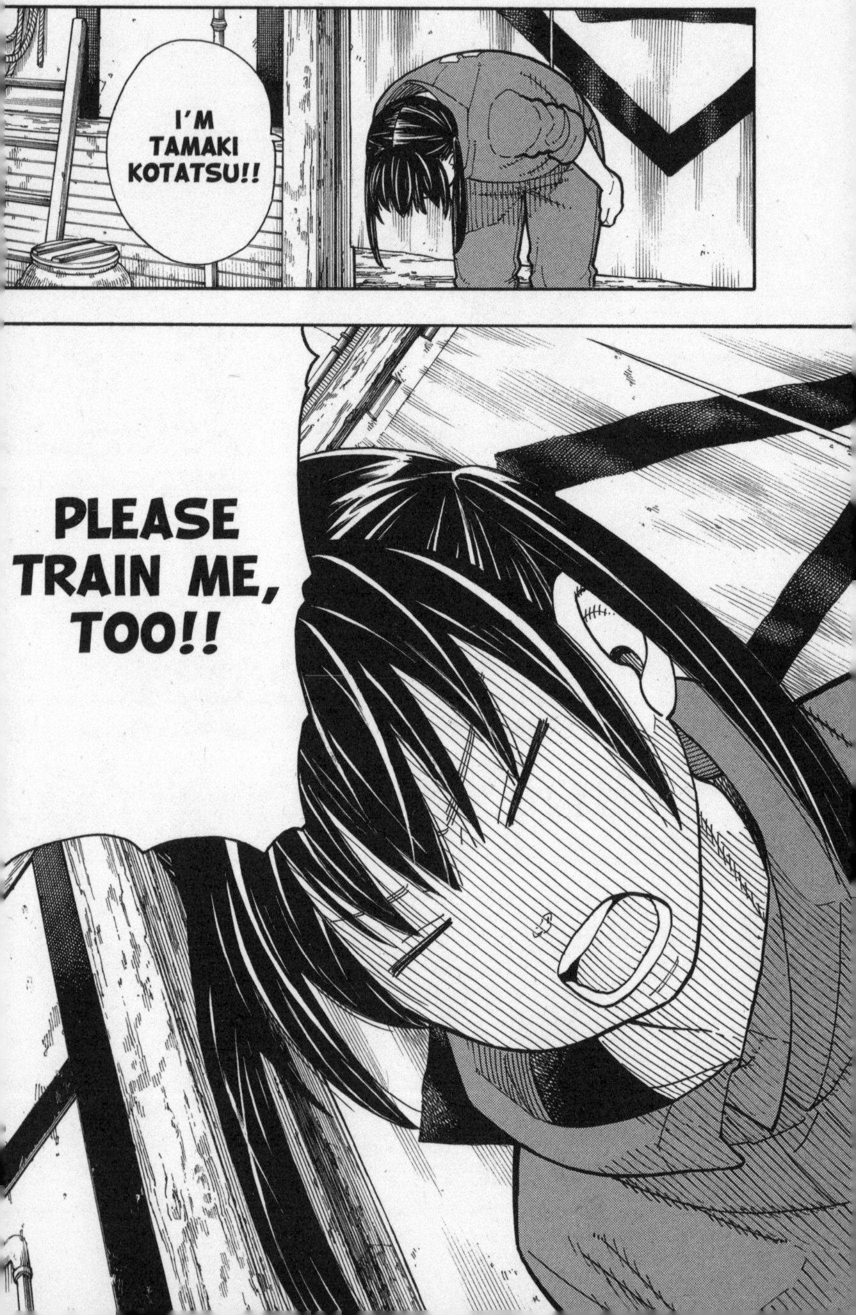
I'M TAMAKI KOTATSU!!
PLEASE TRAIN ME, TOO!!

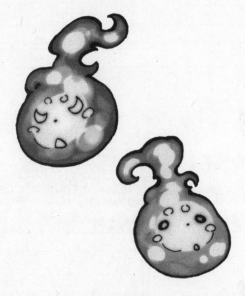

TO BE CONTINUED IN VOLUME 20!!

AFTERWORD MANGA: ATSUSHIYA

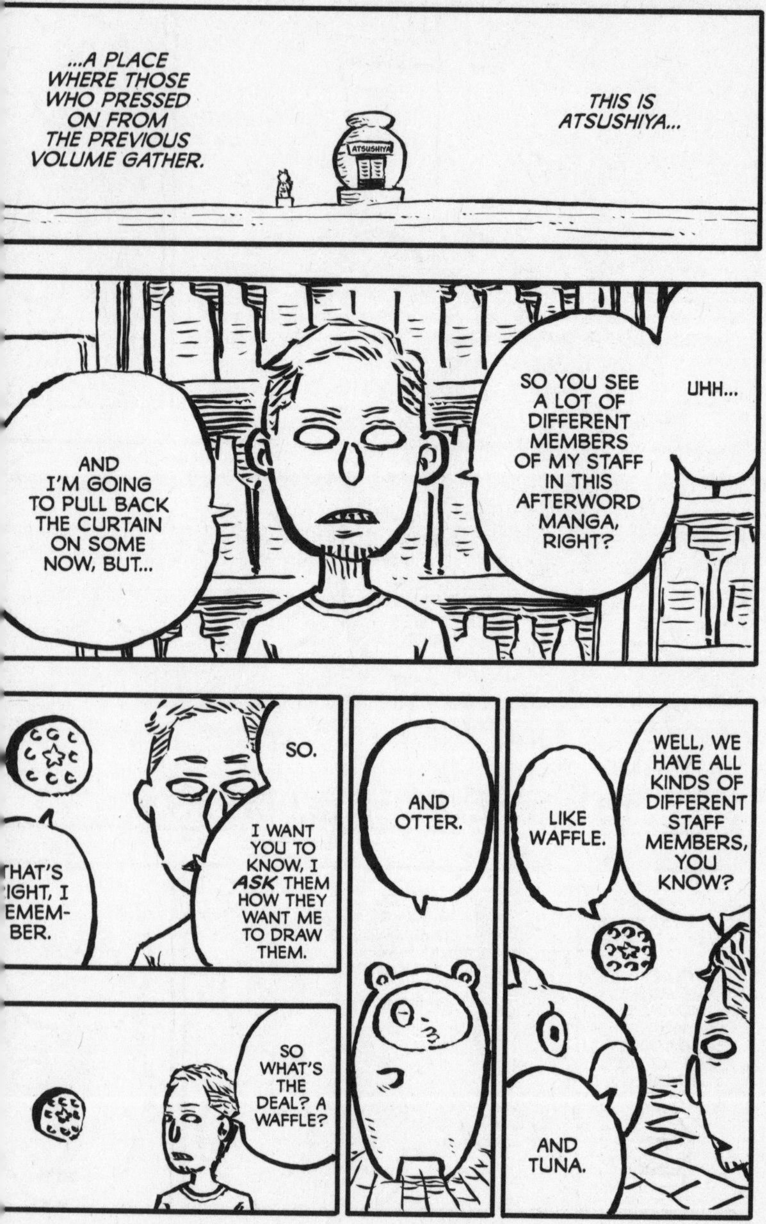
THIS IS ATSUSHIYA...
ATSUSHIYA
...A PLACE WHERE THOSE WHO PRESSED ON FROM THE PREVIOUS VOLUME GATHER.
UHH...
SO YOU SEE A LOT OF DIFFERENT MEMBERS OF MY STAFF IN THIS AFTERWORD MANGA, RIGHT?
AND I'M GOING TO PULL BACK THE CURTAIN ON SOME NOW, BUT...
WELL, WE HAVE ALL KINDS OF DIFFERENT STAFF MEMBERS, YOU KNOW?
LIKE WAFFLE.
AND TUNA.
AND OTTER.
SO.
I WANT YOU TO KNOW, I *ASK* THEM HOW THEY WANT ME TO DRAW THEM.
THAT'S IGHT, I EMEM- BER.
SO WHAT'S THE DEAL? A WAFFLE?

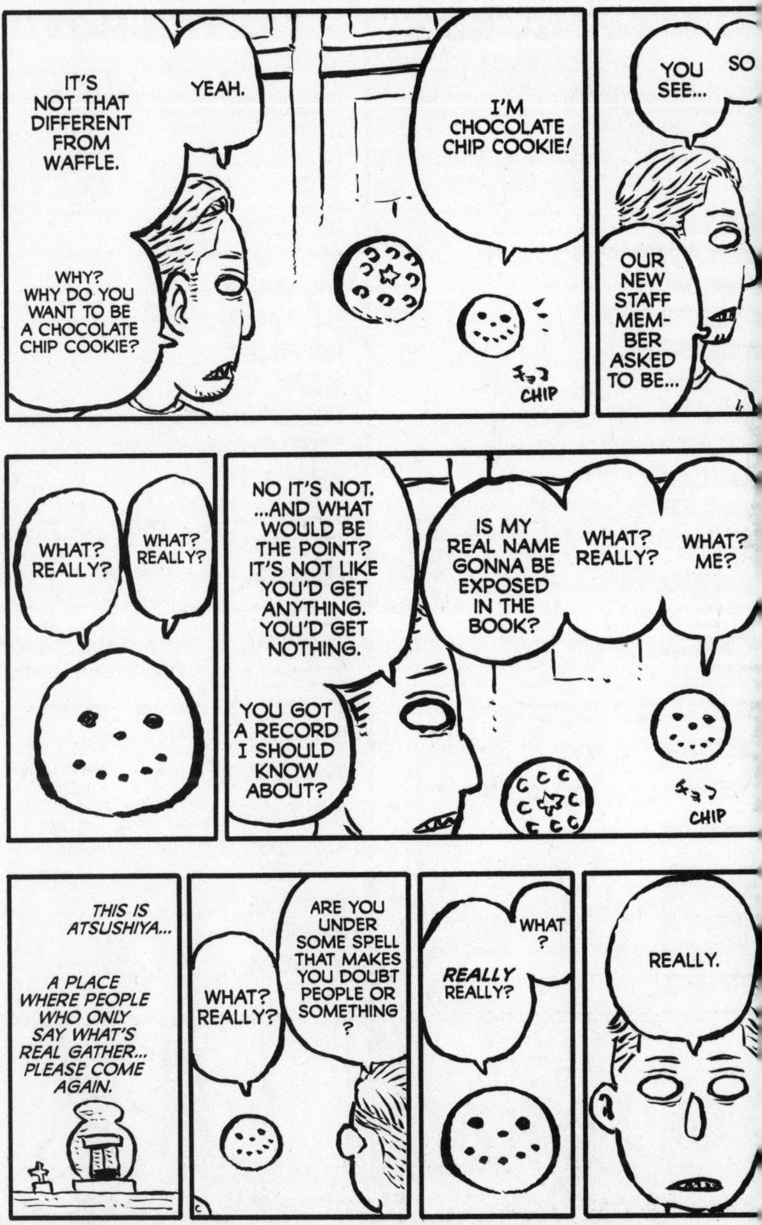
SO YOU SEE...
OUR NEW STAFF MEMBER ASKED TO BE...
I'M CHOCOLATE CHIP COOKIE!
チョコ CHIP
YEAH.
IT'S NOT THAT DIFFERENT FROM WAFFLE.
WHY? WHY DO YOU WANT TO BE A CHOCOLATE CHIP COOKIE?
WHAT? ME?
WHAT? REALLY?
IS MY REAL NAME GONNA BE EXPOSED IN THE BOOK?
チョコ CHIP
NO IT'S NOT. ...AND WHAT WOULD BE THE POINT? IT'S NOT LIKE YOU'D GET ANYTHING. YOU'D GET NOTHING.
YOU GOT A RECORD I SHOULD KNOW ABOUT?
WHAT? REALLY?
WHAT? REALLY?
REALLY.
WHAT?
REALLY REALLY?
ARE YOU UNDER SOME SPELL THAT MAKES YOU DOUBT PEOPLE OR SOMETHING?
WHAT? REALLY?
THIS IS ATSUSHIYA...
A PLACE WHERE PEOPLE WHO ONLY SAY WHAT'S REAL GATHER... PLEASE COME AGAIN.

GUSTAV HONDA

AFFILIATION: **SPECIAL FIRE FORCE COMPANY 2**
RANK: **CAPTAIN**
ABILITY: **THIRD GENERATION PYROKINETIC**

Can produce high-powered flames from the top of his head

Height	165cm [5'5"]
Weight	110kg [242.5lbs.]
Age	46
Birthday	November 3
Sign	Scorpio
Bloodtype	O
Nickname	The Empire's Pachycephalo
Self-Proclaimed	A hard-working captain
Favorite Foods	Hotpot, milk tea
Least Favorite Food	Blind hotpot. It's blasphemy against hotpot!
Favorite Music	The Imperial Anthem, and that fight song that the kids are singing these days. Sorry, I don't know the name.
Favorite Animal	I feel an affinity toward bovines.
Favorite Color	Green
Favorite Type	I have to say my wife.
Who He Respects	General Oze, my parents
Who He Hates	Ne'er-do-wells who fight against the Empire, people who take over at a hotpot meal
Who He's Afraid Of	I have to say my wife. Please keep this profile confidential.
Hobbies	Lately, I most look forward to hearing my subordinates discuss their love lives.
Daily Routine	Making my wife and daughter happy; it's an uphill battle.
Dream	To work hard to make a better nation
Shoe Size	27cm [10]
Eyesight	1.5 [20/12.5], but they're getting worse with age
Favorite Subject	I was good at language arts and social studies.
Least Favorite Subject	None

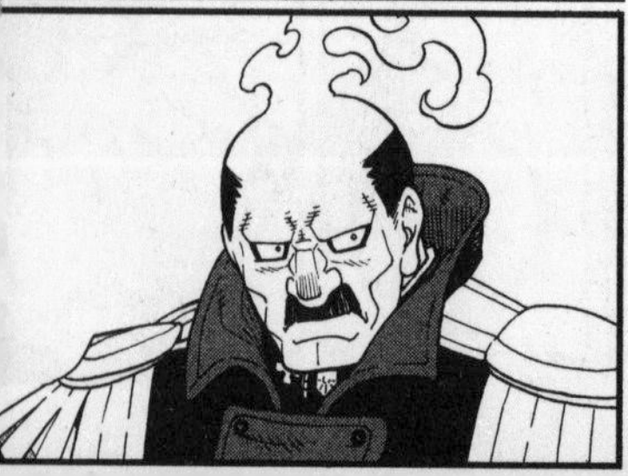

TAKERU NOTO

AFFILIATION: **SPECIAL FIRE FORCE COMPANY 2**
RANK: **SECOND CLASS FIRE SOLDIER**
ABILITY: **THIRD GENERATION PYROKINETIC**

Can transform flames into missiles and other such weapons to attack

Height	Height: 203cm [6'8"]
Weight	85kg [187.4lbs.]
Age	18
Birthday	May 30
Sign	Gemini
Bloodtype	B
Nickname	Juggernaut
Self-Proclaimed	The yellow-bellied chicken farmer
Favorite Foods	Potato dishes
Least Favorite Food	None...is what I'd like to say, but truth be told, I ain't so keen on raw tomatoes.
Favorite Music	"One More Good Harvest, Once Again Good Harvest"
Favorite Animal	We run a lil' milk-dairy farm, so I like our critters.
Favorite Color	Potato color
Favorite Type	Purdy girls. Like Ta...T-Ta...Tamaki...Kotatsu-san...
Who He Respects	All the fire soldiers who can fight without being a-scared of the flames
Who He Hates	Them pesky varmints that raid our crops.
Who He's Afraid Of	It ain't a person, but I'm afeared of fire.
Hobbies	Raisin' and researchin' potatoes, servin' potato dishes
Daily Routine	Oh, back in Xinqing Dao, I sure liked lookin' at the tater field, but Tokyo's downright scary, yup.
Dream	To get married to a purdy wife and take over the potato farm.
Shoe Size	32cm [16]
Eyesight	2.0 [20/10] I reckon it might be a heap better than that.
Favorite Subject	Cooking
Least Favorite Subject	P.E. I'm so big, everyone expects me to be good at it, but I can't do nothing

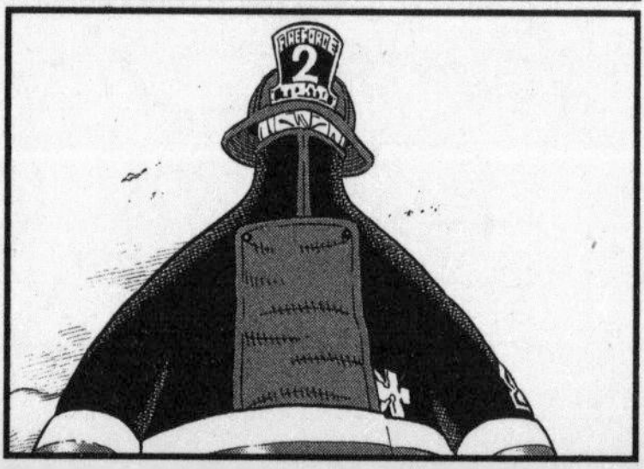
FIRE FORCE
2

Translation Notes:

Hard as rock, page 31

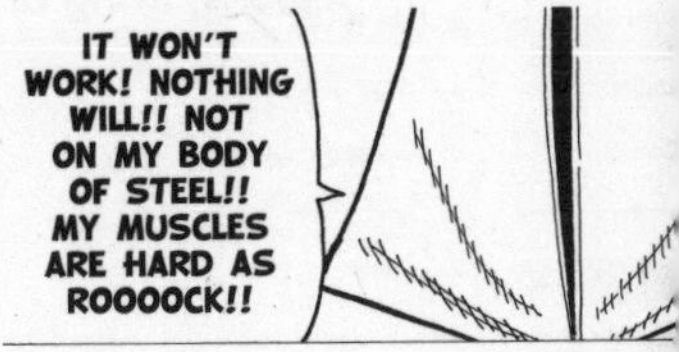
IT WON'T WORK! NOTHING WILL!! NOT ON MY BODY OF STEEL!! MY MUSCLES ARE HARD AS ROOOOCK!!

Specifically, Iron describes his muscles as *katchi-kachi*, which is a rather emphatic (especially with the extra T in the first *katchi*) sound effect to indicate that something is hard. The concept of *katchi-kachi* muscles was popularized by Ayumu Katō, member of comedy duo Xabungle, who would try to show off his intimidatingly hard muscles in a comedy sketch.

Non Self, etc., page 125

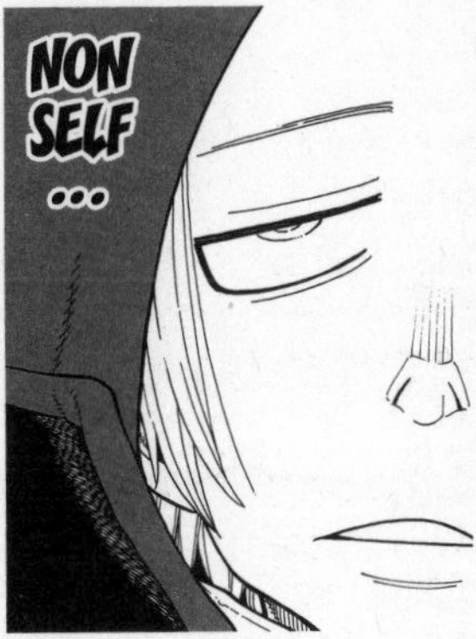
NON SELF ...

The concept of non-self, or *anatta*, is one of the three Right Understandings of Buddhism. This doctrine states that there is no permanent, underlying soul in living beings, including human beings. The ability to accept that there is no "self" is a step to enlightenment. When one attains enlightenment, one may find release or deliverance from the pains of this world, and go to Nirvana. A bodhisattva is someone, similar to gods, who have gained enlightenment but, instead of going to Nirvana, has chosen to rema on Earth to guide others. They may be considere on the same level as the gods.

Hysterical strength, page 182

In Japanese, the common description of this type of strength is *kajiba no bakajikara*, which literally translates to "insane strength at the scene of a fire."

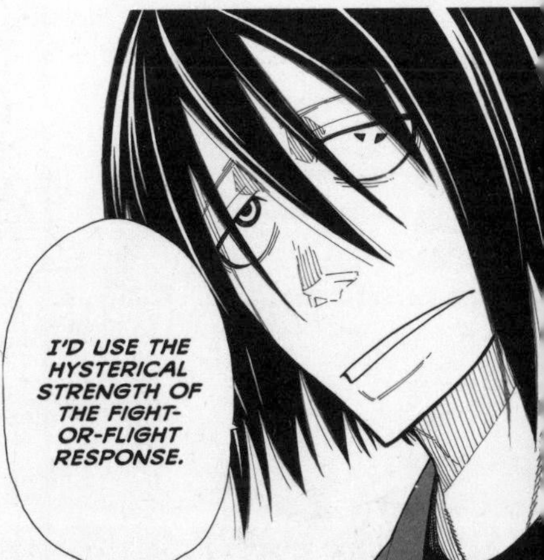
I'D USE THE HYSTERICAL STRENGTH OF THE FIGHT-OR-FLIGHT RESPONSE.

YA

Fire Force 19
08/19/2020

A Kodansha Comics Trade Paperback Original
Fire Force 19 copyright © 2019 Atsushi Ohkubo
English translation copyright © 2020 Atsushi Ohkubo

Published in the United States by Kodansha Comics, an imprint of
Kodansha USA Publishing, LLC, New York.

Publication rights for this English edition arranged through
Kodansha Ltd., Tokyo.

First published in Japan in 2019 by Kodansha Ltd., Tokyo.

ISBN 978-1-63236-908-6

Printed in the United States of America.

www.kodanshacomics.com

9 8 7 6 5 4 3 2 1
Translation: Alethea Nibley & Athena Nibley
Lettering: AndWorld Design
Editing: Haruko Hashimoto
Kodansha Comics edition cover design by Phil Balsman

Publisher: Kiichiro Sugawara

Director of publishing services: Ben Applegate
Associate director of operations: Stephen Pakula
Publishing services managing editor: Noelle Webster
Assistant production manager: Emi Lotto, Angela Zurlo